An
Analytical Commentary
on Wittgenstein's
Philosophical Investigations

W9-DIN-511

An

Analytical Commentary

on Wittgenstein's

Philosophical Investigations

———

G. P. Baker & P. M. S. Hacker

Volume 1

The University of Chicago Press

The University of Chicago Press, Chicago 60637
Basil Blackwell Publisher Limited, Oxford

94 93 92 91 90 89 88 87 86 85   5 4 3 2 1

Library of Congress Cataloging-in-Publication Data

Baker, Gordon P.
  An analytical commentary on Wittgenstein's
Philosophical investigations.

  "Volume 1."
  Reprint. Originally published: Wittgenstein, under-
standing and meaning. Chicago: University of Chicago
Press, 1980. (An analytical commentary on the
Philosophical investigations; v. 1) Now reissued in
2 v. under titles: Wittgenstein, meaning and under-
standing, and An analytical commentary on
Wittgenstein's Philosophical investigations.
  Includes bibliographical references and index.
  1. Wittgenstein, Ludwig, 1889–1951. Philosophische
Untersuchungen.   2. Philosophy.   3. Languages—
Philosophy.   4. Semantics (Philosophy)   I. Hacker,
P. M. S. (Peter Michael Stephan)   II. Baker, Gordon P.
Wittgenstein, understanding and meaning.   III. Title.
B3376.W563P53233   1985   192   85-20837
ISBN 0-226-03539-5 (paper)

For Anne and Sylvia

Contents

Preface to the Paperback edition

In 1980 we published a 692 page volume entitled *Wittgenstein – Understanding and Meaning, an analytical commentary on the* PHILOSOPHICAL INVESTIGATIONS. This consisted of detailed analysis of Wittgenstein's argument in the first 184 remarks of the *Investigations*. In the exegesis of Wittgenstein's text we analysed each remark, examined its role in his argumentative strategy, and, where it was illuminating to do so, traced its ancestry to Wittgenstein's voluminous *Nachlass*. Where necessary, we contrasted his arguments with those of the *Tractatus*, and where possible we identified his targets in the works of Frege and Russell. Interspersed at the appropriate places in the exegesis were seventeen essays surveying the central themes of this part of his book. Here we not only tried to give a synoptic view of his philosophical ideas, and to compare and contrast them with those of Frege, Russell and the *Tractatus*, but also to make clear their bearing on contemporary philosophical endeavours, in particular in philosophical logic and philosophy of language.

For the paperback edition we have split our original book into two, this volume consisting of the original exegesis and a companion volume of the essays entitled *Wittgenstein – Meaning and Understanding*. Each can be read and used independently of the other, although they are, of course, complementary.

Apart from structural alterations essential for the bifurcation of the original volume, the changes we have introduced are minimal.

First, internal cross-references within the original text have now been replaced by cross-references to the companion volume. In this volume references in the exegesis to themes developed at length in the philosophical essays of the companion volume *Wittgenstein – Meaning and Understanding* are signified (as in the original) by a quoted essay title. The page reference accompanying it gives its location in the companion paperback edition. We have also indicated the locus in the exegesis of the essays now printed separately, and identified the contents of each essay by printing its title and section headings in a frame.

Secondly, we have adapted the original Introduction to match it to each of the two volumes.

Thirdly, we have taken the opportunity to correct minor errors and typographical mistakes in the hard cover edition.

In the original edition we introduced our first substantial remarks on Frege with the following observation: 'Philosophers commonly assume that one of Frege's philosophical projects is to construct a general theory of meaning for a natural language. There are many reasons to doubt this assumption, but we shall not challenge it here. Rather, the picture of Frege's philosophy of language we shall present will conform to the standard average modern interpretation of his theories.' In the intervening years since we wrote this, we have come to realize, as we did not then, how deep the gulf is between the historical Frege and the 'standard average modern interpretation' of his mature theory. Had our book been on the *Tractatus*, which feeds so extensively on Frege's work (largely by way of critical reaction and far reaching modification), we would undoubtedly have had to rewrite it. As it is, we have now spelt out our conception of Frege's enterprise in *Frege: Logical Excavations*, and our original Galtonian picture of Frege as viewed by the moderns may stand. As long as it is appreciated what exactly it is, we still think it neither unfair not without substantial point. For Frege's impact upon late twentieth century philosophical logic has been largely via the standard average modern interpretation.

Two final points: first, through oversight we employed the abbreviation 'LA' for page references to Wittgenstein's *Lectures and Conversations on Aesthetics, Psychology and Religion*, and also for page references to Russell's 'The Philosophy of Logical Atomism'. Since the contexts in which the two books are referred to do not overlap, and since in each context it is clear to which writer and text we are referring, we have not rectified this regrettable ambiguity. Secondly, since we wrote the book various primary and derivative primary source materials have been published. In particular, there is now available Wittgenstein's *Remarks on the Philosophy of Psychology* in two volumes, and his *Vermischte Bemerkungen (Culture and Value)*. This material was available to us in the form of the original manuscripts and typescripts, and was referred to, where necessary, by TS or MS number and page. We have not changed this. However, Desmond Lee's *Wittgenstein's Lectures, Cambridge 1930–32* and Alice Ambrose's *Wittgenstein's Lectures, Cambridge 1932–35* were not available to us. They contain much that is of interest and importance, and ideally we should have liked to incorporate references to remarks in these volumes that bear on the subjects we discuss. However, nothing in either book has led us to revise our judgment, and much in both volumes merely gives further confirmation to our interpretations. Consequently we have, with some slight regret, refrained from the luxury of dismantling set pages to insert references to these lecture notes.

G.P.B. & P.M.S.H.
Oxford, 1981

Acknowledgements

While composing this book we have been much assisted by institutions, friends and colleagues.

We are grateful to the British Academy for a generous grant for our research. Our publishers, Basil Blackwell Publisher Ltd., in particular Mr J. K. D. Feather and Mr D. Martin, have been most helpful in steering a difficult publishing project through all its stages. To our college, St John's, we are indebted for many facilities which eased and expedited our work. To Cornell University Library, and to the Bodleian Library, in particular Mr D. G. Vaisey and his staff, we are thankful for the services and space provided for us. To Mr C. Morgenstern we are most grateful for advice about lay-out and typography.

Mr J. M. Baker, Mr M. A. E. Dummett, Dr W. Künne, Mr B. F. McGuinness, Professor J. Meiland, Mr B. Rundle and Dr C. Wright all gave us generous help, advice, and criticism in reading and commenting on various parts of early drafts, raising numerous questions, answering queries and in general stimulating us into rethinking our position on many issues. Mr T. J. Reed put at our disposal his extensive knowledge of German literature and also aided us in translating difficult passages. Dr A. J. P. Kenny and Dr J. Raz read and commented on substantial portions of the text and gave us the benefit of much advice and constructive criticism. Above all we are indebted to Dr Joachim Schulte, who not only read the whole typescript and gave us extensive and penetrating criticisms of earlier versions, but also checked all our German transcriptions and translations. His help has been invaluable, his kindness memorable.

Finally, we are grateful to the Wittgenstein executors for permission to quote from the unpublished *Nachlass*. In particular we are indebted to Professor G. H. von Wright for his generosity in sending us the results of his extensive bibliographical research into the *Nachlass*, and for his kindness in answering numerous questions.

G.P.B. & P.M.S.H.
St John's College, Oxford
1978

Thoughts reduced to paper are generally nothing
more than the footprints of a man walking in
the sand. It is true that we see the path he
has taken; but to know what he saw on the way,
we must use our own eyes.

Schopenhauer

Introduction

The *Philosophical Investigations* was published a quarter of a century ago. It was hailed by some as the masterpiece of the 'first philosopher of the age'. Others have viewed it as a haphazard collection of perhaps profound, but at any rate exceedingly obscure, aperçus. Russell, at the other extreme, could see no merit in it whatsoever.

It is evident that the philosophical community is far from clear what it has received. Despite a veritable flood of secondary writings, there is little consensus on the main contour lines of the book, let alone upon details of interpretation. Although it is written in a lucid, non-technical style, and although individual remarks appear superficially clear (and often innocuous), the *Philosophical Investigations* is an exceedingly difficult book to understand. The welter of conflicting interpretations and contradictory evaluations bear witness to the fact that philosophers have found it baffling and opaque.

At the grand-strategic level some have argued that the *Investigations* is a further development of the philosophy propounded in the *Tractatus*, adding to and modifying, but by no means demolishing, the core of that work. Others have seen it as a wholly new departure, built upon the ashes of a magnificent failure. So its relation to its august predecessor, though crucial to its correct interpretation, is unclear. All agree that its structure is often non-sequential, but some claim that it is wholly lacking in order and that this indeed reflects Wittgenstein's repudiation of any systematicity in philosophizing. Others have discerned behind the apparently unruly organization a highly systematic philosophy, e.g., a generalization to philosophy of language of the principles of an intuitionist philosophy of mathematics. So it is unclear whether Wittgenstein propounds any integrated coherent philosophy—in method, in conception of the nature of the problems, or in their resolution. Many of Wittgenstein's remarks have a pronounced negative tinge. Some commentators hold that the *Investigations* is, as it were, a prolegomenon to any future philosophy—a prolegomenon which is followed by deafening silence. If the *Tractatus* was the swan-song of metaphysics, this seems the death-knell of philosophy. This is belied by the indisputable fertility of the book, most obviously in the philosophy of mind, which had changed

but little since the eighteenth century. Is the *Investigations* intended as the
final negation of all philosophy?

Similar polarization of views has occurred at the strategic level.
Wittgenstein frequently appeals to our ordinary use of words (in contrast
with philosophers' misuse). He has, by some, been classified (and abused)
as an 'ordinary language philosopher' (and grouped with J. L. Austin).
But for an 'ordinary language philosopher' he appeals remarkably
infrequently to subtleties of idiom and usage beloved by Austinians.
Again, he often raises questions of how language is learnt, how a child is
taught to use a given expression. Is this not armchair learning theory?
Would it not be preferable to substitute empirical data from psycholin-
guists? And how are considerations of learning and teaching furthered by
constructing imaginary systems of communication and imaginary pro-
cedures for instructing imaginary half-wits to operate them? In his
reflections upon meaning, he hints at numerous apparent equations:
meaning is use, sense is given by assertion-conditions, how a sentence is
verified will reveal what it means, etc. These are not obviously consistent, let alone equivalent. On top of this he denies the legitimacy in
philosophy of *any* theories—but are *these* pronouncements not theories?
Is not inconsistency here piled upon inconsistency?

The tactical level is no less baffling. Wittgenstein begins the book with
a sketch of Augustine's remarks on how he conceived himself to have
learnt language. What is the point of *that*? It was not part of Augustine's
philosophy but of his autobiography, and it is not evidently a view any
philosopher has adhered to. He criticizes ostensive definition at length,
yet also argues that ostensive definition is as legitimate a form of
definition as the most rigorous *Merkmal*-definition (even of numerals!).
He embarks upon a long discussion of vagueness, in an apparent criticism
of Frege. But what is his point? To add a smudge-operator to a
neo-Fregean semantics? To insist that ordinary language is everywhere
vague, and *then* to say that that is just as it should be? Between §§156 and
178 he interpolates a detailed discussion of reading. But what is the point
of his showing that reading, deriving, being guided, etc., are family
resemblance concepts? To many his philosophy of mind seems a form of
behaviourism—neither original nor reputable.

At the level of interpretation of particular passages and lines, no less
confusion reigns. Are his remarks on Frege's assertion-sign an agreement
or disagreement with Frege? Can a supporter of phrastics and neustics
invoke the footnote about sentence-radicals in favour of his theses or not?
Is the single sentence about the standard metre being neither a metre long
nor not a metre long a piece of wilful obscurantism (does he *really* mean
to say that the metre bar has no length)?

These interminable controversies provided part of our motive in
undertaking the task of trying to explain in detail, as well as delineate in

general, the argument of the *Philosophical Investigations*. This perhaps betokens lack of adequate humility—rushing in (with the rest of the crowd) where the wise (if not the angels) wait. It has been suggested to us that it is too soon to embark on such a project. We were, however, emboldened by three considerations. First, the increased accessibility of the Wittgenstein *Nachlass* made some of our aims reasonably realistic. The *Nachlass* throws invaluable light not only upon particular passages of the *Investigations*, but also upon the development of Wittgenstein's thought after 1929. Secondly, if this kind of project were delayed for another half-century or more, the intellectual milieu and philosophical atmosphere of Wittgenstein's work (in particular Frege, Russell, the Vienna Circle), already increasingly remote for our generation, will be irremediably alien (cf. the fate of Kant's *Critique*). The risks of distortion and misunderstanding that we have had to run through lack of a longer perspective, though serious, must be balanced against the dangers of losing through the passage of time valuable information about, and sensitivity to, the problem-setting context of Wittgenstein's work. Finally, it is not unknown (here again Kant springs to mind) for great philosophical insights to be lost through misunderstanding, dogmatic misinterpretation, tides of fashion, and a naïve belief in progress. Although almost all Wittgenstein's philosophy bears directly upon central issues of current philosophical debate, usually negatively, much of it is ignored, to the detriment of the resultant 'theories'. Take, e.g., so-called 'philosophical semantics', thought by many to constitute the centre of the philosophical universe. If this activity is to be profitable, the semanticist must clarify (or at least consider!) what counts as 'giving the meaning' of an expression, how this is related to ordinary explanations and how those are related to meaning, since he aims to produce a theory of *meaning*. The concept of explanation cannot be allowed to take care of itself while the semanticist takes care of possible worlds, builds Chinese boxes of speakers' intentions, and 'postulates' abstract entities. Similarly, since such 'theories of meaning' purport to be systems of *rules*, we must first grasp the nature of rules, their role and application. It is foolish to concentrate exclusively on the precise formulation of meaning-rules and to ignore the issue of how grasping a meaning-rule is internally related to linguistic behaviour. Through misunderstanding or neglect, numerous controversies take place in blithe ignorance or disregard of powerful arguments in Wittgenstein's writings which, wholly or partly, undermine their presuppositions, methods, or putative resolutions. One of our hopes is that this study will go some way to remedy what seems to us a deplorable state of affairs. Whether Wittgenstein's arguments are correct or not, they should be confronted. They pose the questions to shake up the fashionable solutions to many of the problems of philosophy.

It has been characteristic of much Wittgensteinian commentary to take

the apparently disjointed structure of the *Investigations* as a licence to quote
and analyse sections or even lines out of context. This has led to frequent
distortion and incoherence. Debates rage over Wittgenstein's remarks on,
e.g., the standard metre, sentence-radicals, meaning and use,
philosophy's 'leaving everything as it is', in total disregard of the
argumentative context of quoted passages. But what his views were
(whether correct or not) can only be discovered by careful examination of
the context of his remarks. Close scrutiny reveals much more *argument*
than is commonly thought. For this reason we do not recommend using
this volume of exegesis as a kind of concordance or 'instant commentary'
from which the full significance of each remark can be gathered from the
corresponding exegesis irrespective of its antecedents and sequel. Wittgenstein's painstaking arrangement of his remarks, though often disjointed, involves an intricate weaving together of multiple strands of
argument. In accord with the articulation of its subject-matter we have
divided the *Investigations* into chapters. Each of our corresponding
chapters is preceded by an introduction which surveys briefly the salient
points of Wittgenstein's discussion in the relevant *Bemerkungen* (numbered
remarks which we refer to as 'sections'), explains the argumentative
structure of the chapter (illustrated by tree diagrams[1]), and gives tables of
correlation with the 1937 version of the *Investigations* (i.e. TS. 220, which
we call 'Proto-Philosophical Investigations' ('PPI')) and R. Rhees's 1939
translation of it (i.e. TS. 226, designated 'PPI (R)'). PPI is the immediate
source of most of the material in the *Invesitgations* §§1–189, hence especially valuable for those who are not going to comb the many thousands of
pages of material in the *Nachlass*. PPI (R), though an incomplete translation of PPI, has special interest in respect of Wittgenstein's corrections to
Rhees's translation. Our exegesis should ideally be read chapter by chapter, for only thus will the role of each of Wittgenstein's individual
Bemerkungen in the over-all argument become clear.

The method of exegesis for each section can be quickly explained.
Different paragraphs in a section are referred to by lower-case letters. Five
different kinds of comments are marked out by marginal numerals 1,1.1,
2,2.1,3. 1 consists of commentary and argument on the section as a whole.
1.1 consists of comments on specific lines, phrases or words in the section,
as well as important modifications of the English translation. 2 cites and
discusses parallel remarks from Wittgenstein's other published works or

---

[1] It would have been possible to indicate forms of logical dependence and degrees of
subordination between sections by means of a numbering system akin to that used in the
Tractatus. However, the two-dimensionality of tree diagrams makes them more readily
surveyable. Connecting lines between numbers indicate logical dependence in the development of the argument. Numbers printed on the same line signify that the remarks are
coordinate in their importance relative to their superordinate section. A number printed at
the side and joined to another number in the main tree by a broken line shows a more or less
explicit back-reference.

Nachlass. We have limited ourselves here to passages which are philosophically illuminating, either by way of further elaboration or by way of contrast highlighting change and development. Our system of abbreviated references to other works is explained below (pp. xxi–xxv). 2.1 consists of parallel lines or phrases in Wittgenstein's other writings which amplify or clarify matters of detail. 3 is reserved for 'any other business'. Small roman numerals are used when an enumeration of argumentative points is necessary. (Enumeration within enumeration has forced us occasionally to have recourse to arabic numerals or lower-case letters.) Since these notational conventions were chosen for their perspicuity, we have readily violated them where, for some reason, they stood in the way of clarity.

Whenever a passage is quoted from the *Nachlass* it is followed in parentheses by our translation. In these quotations we have copied two of Wittgenstein's notational devices. An expression enclosed by obliques '/' or '//' signifies alternative phrasings between which he had not decided. A broken line underneath a word signifies some qualification about the choice of word (cf. WWK 166). For typographical convenience we have not reproduced words written above other words, but where it seemed worthwhile we have employed obliques instead.

Two self-imposed limitations should be noted. First, we have not attempted a concordance of passages, nor tried to give all the sources in which a given passage occurs. This for three reasons: (i) it would be philosophically pointless: only where the context of a source is philosophically illuminating is it worth pointing out; (ii) given the volume of the *Nachlass* and human frailty, it would be impossible to do this authoritatively; (iii) some future project of computerizing and publishing the total *Nachlass* should incorporate a retrieval system designed to fulfil just this task. Secondly, we have assiduously avoided discussing secondary source material. Important points and controversies have been dealt with in a perfectly general way.

In our original book the articulation of the argumentative structure of the *Investigations* was emphasized not only by our division of the exegetical commentary into chapters, and by the structural analysis of the argument in terms of tree diagrams and accompanying explanation in the introduction to each chapter, but also by the major essay which followed each introduction as well as by the other essays interspersed in the exegesis at appropriate places. This, of course, is not to be found in this paperback edition, but in the companion paperback entitled *Wittgenstein – Meaning and Understanding.* This volume of analytical exegesis delineates the strategy and tactics of Wittgenstein's argument. The grand strategy, as it were, is more evident from the comprehensive essays which attempt to give a synoptic view of his philosophical thought on the relevant themes, to subject it to critical scrutiny and to highlight its bearing on contemporary philosophical reflection. As noted in the Preface, the original locus of the essays, as well as their contents, are indicated in the text of this paperback edition.

This volume of exegesis goes only as far as §184. Considerations of space apart, many reasons justify this decision. This dividing line corresponds most closely to the 1937 version (PPI), which ends at PI §189, and to that extent forms a unitary fragment. Consequently, the vast majority of the sources antedate 1938. The sequel raises a host of fresh problems needing detailed treatment. First, one must consider the various plans for the continuation of PPI, in particular Wittgenstein's work in philosophy of mathematics. Why was this originally conceived to belong here, and why did Wittgenstein change his mind? Secondly, one must consider the further attempts to complete the book (i.e. the 1943 and 1945 versions), as well as the compilation of *Bemerkungen I* (TS. 228) and its cannibalization for the final version of the *Investigations*. Thirdly, the source material for the sequel, especially §§198–427, dates largely (though not exclusively) from 1938–45, in particular 1944–5, hence presents a new set of 'archaeological' problems. These three reasons concern the structure and history of the book.

Nevertheless, since §§143–242 surely form the heart of the argument of the *Investigations*, should we not then have continued until §243? Historical reasons apart, two further considerations militated against this. Although §§143–242 form an integral unity, the sequel to §242, i.e. the private language argument, is a crucially important and immediate application of the conclusions drawn from the rich argument of those hundred sections. So it would be no more justifiable to stop at §243 than at §184. Secondly, the sheer number of central philosophical topics so densely packed in §§185–242 (e.g. necessity and possibility, rules and their application, identity, agreement in judgements and definitions) require such detailed consideration and necessitate drawing so heavily from sources in Wittgenstein's philosophy of mathematics, as to make it quite impracticable to try to encompass all this in the scope of one volume.

If we are right in considering §§143–242 as the core of the book, and liken it to a mountain range that must be crossed before Wittgenstein's philosophy can be understood (and, among other things, the famous private language argument seen aright), then this volume can be seen as taking us to the top of the mountain passes. We conclude it (in Chapter 6) with an examination of the 'subjective' aspect of rule-following—what it is to be guided by a rule, follow a rule, derive something from a rule. A subsequent volume, to be entitled *Wittgenstein – Meaning and Mind* (occasionally referred to in the text as 'Volume 2'), will complement this by examining (§§185–242) the philosophical complexities surrounding the objective aspects of rule-following—what it is for something to follow from, be derived from or necessitated by, a rule. And it will then go on to apply these insights not only to obtain a better grasp of meaning and understanding but also to cast fresh light on philosophy of mind, and other topics discussed by Wittgenstein in the sequel.

Three final points: use, grammar and criteria. Neither in this volume, nor in the companion volume of essays is there any general sustained discussion of any of these three crucial notions. The explanation is straightforward. Although it is true that the term 'use' in *vacuo* is too nebulous to give much guidance, Wittgenstein's employment of it is by no means nebulous: in each context his point is clear. Relative to each context we have, in the exegesis, tried to explain in detail what he meant. In the essay entitled 'Uses of sentences' we have elaborated his views on that subject and delineated his objections to distinguishing in each sentence its force, as signified by a mood-operator, from its sense, conceived as a truth-value bearing description of a possible state of affairs. As for the rest, it should be clear enough that the whole of this book and its companion volume of essays (not to mention the projected Volume 2) is concerned, either directly or obliquely, with exploring the significance and ramifications of Wittgenstein's revolutionary association of the meanings of linguistic expressions with their uses in the actions and transactions of human beings. Secondly, Wittgenstein's use of the term 'grammar' is unusual and idiosyncratic. It will be scrutinized in detail in Volume 2. In the meantime we have followed his use. Thirdly, the controversial term 'criterion' is frequently invoked in the following pages. Our employment of it is not intended to be arcane or theory-laden, and in these respects is intended to match Wittgenstein's own use. By it we mean something that is *a priori*, defeasible evidence for something else. Doubtless much seems problematic here, and to the extent that this is so we have in fact drawn a blank cheque upon Volume 2, in which the topic will be thoroughly discussed. We would have liked to consider everything at once. But because of 'merely medical limitations', we have had to content ourselves with a linear exposition. Clarifying the concept of a criterion cannot be done successfully prior to (independently of) a correct conception of meaning, and, conversely, this conception turns on the notion of criteria of understanding. Wittgenstein's philosophy is like a stone arch; each stone supports all the others—or, at least, nothing stands up until everything is in place. What we have tried to do in this volume is to prepare the place for each stone, although of course not everything is yet in place.

Abbreviations

1. Published works

The following abbreviations are used to refer to Wittgenstein's published works, listed in chronological order (where possible; some works straddle many years). The list includes derivative primary sources, i.e. Waismann's books,[1] and lecture notes taken by others.

NB   *Notebooks 1914–16*, ed. G. H. von Wright and G. E. M. Anscombe, tr. G. E. M. Anscombe (Blackwell, Oxford, 1961).

PT   *Prototractatus—An Early Version of Tractatus Logico-Philosophicus*, ed. B. F. McGuinness, T. Nyberg, G. H. von Wright, tr. D. F. Pears and B. F. McGuinness (Routledge and Kegan Paul, London, 1971).

TLP   *Tractatus Logico-Philosophicus*, tr. D. F. Pears and B. F. McGuinness (Routledge and Kegan Paul, London, 1961).

LF   'Some Remarks on Logical Form', *Proceedings of the Aristotelian Society*, supp. vol. ix (1929), pp. 162–71.

WWK   *Ludwig Wittgenstein und der Wiener Kreis*, shorthand notes recorded by F. Waismann, ed. B. F. McGuinness (Blackwell, Oxford, 1967).

PR   *Philosophical Remarks*, ed. R. Rhees, tr. R. Hargreaves and R. White (Blackwell, Oxford, 1975).

LE   'A Lecture on Ethics', *Philosophical Review* 74 (1965), pp. 3–12.

M   'Wittgenstein's Lectures in 1930–33', in G. E. Moore, *Philosophical Papers* (Allen and Unwin, London, 1959).

PG   *Philosophical Grammar*, ed. R. Rhees, tr. A. J. P. Kenny (Blackwell, Oxford, 1974).

GB   'Remarks on Frazer's "Golden Bough"', tr. A. C. Miles and R. Rhees, *The Human World* no. 3 (May 1971), pp. 28–41.

BB   *The Blue and Brown Books* (Blackwell, Oxford, 1958). Occasionally 'Bl.B.' and 'Br.B.' are used for special reference.

---

[1] For the history of the composition of these books and their importance for the study of Wittgenstein's philosophy, see G. P. Baker, '*Verehrung und Verkehrung*: Waismann and Wittgenstein' in *Wittgenstein: Sources and Perspectives*, ed. G. Luckhardt (Cornell University Press, Ithaca, 1979).

LPE   'Wittgenstein's Notes for Lectures on "Private Experience" and
        "Sense Data"', ed. R. Rhees, *Philosophical Review* 77 (1968),
        pp. 275–320.

EPB   *Eine Philosophische Betrachtung*, ed. R. Rhees, in *Ludwig Wittgen-
        stein: Schriften 5* (Suhrkamp, Frankfurt, 1970).

RFM   *Remarks on the Foundations of Mathematics*, ed. G. H. von Wright,
        R. Rhees, G. E. M. Anscombe, tr. G. E. M. Anscombe, revised
        edition (Blackwell, Oxford, 1978).

LA   *Lectures and Conversation on Aesthetics, Psychology and Religious
        Beliefs*, ed. C. Barrett (Blackwell, Oxford, 1970).

LFM   *Wittgenstein's Lectures on the Foundations of Mathematics, Cambridge
        1939*, ed. C. Diamond (Harvester Press, Sussex, 1976).

PI   *Philosophical Investigations*, ed. G. E. M. Anscombe and R. Rhees,
        tr. G. E. M. Anscombe, 2nd edition (Blackwell, Oxford,
        1958).

Z   *Zettel*, ed. G. E. M. Anscombe and G. H. von Wright, tr. G. E. M.
        Anscombe (Blackwell, Oxford, 1967).

C   *On Certainty*, ed. G. E. M. Anscombe and G. H. von Wright, tr.
        D. Paul and G. E. M. Anscombe (Blackwell, Oxford, 1969).

RC   *Remarks on Colour*, ed. G. E. M. Anscombe, tr. L. L. McAlister and
        M. Schättle (Blackwell, Oxford, [1977]).

EMD   *Einführung in das mathematische Denken*, F. Waismann (Gerold,
        Vienna, 1936).

IMT   *Introduction to Mathematical Thinking*, F. Waismann, tr. T. J. Benac
        (Hafner, London, 1951).

PLP   *The Principles of Linguistic Philosopy*, F. Waismann, ed. R. Harré
        (Macmillan and St Martin's Press, London and New York,
        1965).

LSP   *Logik, Sprache, Philosophie*, F. Waismann mit einer Vorrede von
        M. Schlick, herausgegeben von G. P. Baker und B. McGuinness
        unter Mitwirkung von J. Schulte (Reclam, Stuttgart, 1976).

Reference style: all references to *Philosophical Investigations* Part I are to
sections (e.g. PI §1), except those to notes below the line on various pages.
References to Part II are to pages (e.g. PI p. 202). References to other
printed works are either to numbered remarks (TLP, PT) or to sections
(Z) signified '§'; in all other cases references are to pages (e.g. LFM 21 =
LFM page 21).

2. Nachlass

All references to unpublished material cited in the von Wright catalogue
(*Philosophical Review* 78 (1969), pp. 483–503) are by MS. or TS. number

followed by page number. Wherever possible, we make use of the pagination or foliation entered in the original document (although these numerations follow no uniform pattern). For memorability, we have introduced the following special abbreviations.

Manuscripts

Vol. I   refer to the eighteen large manuscript volumes (= MSS. 105–22)
Vol. II written between 2 February 1929 and 1944. The reference style
etc.   Vol. VI, 241 is to Volume VI, page 241. References to Vol. X, Um.
         refer to W.'s pagination of the *Umarbeitung* of the 'Big Type-
         script'. The *Umarbeitung* begins on folio 31^b of Vol. X and is
         consecutively paginated 1–228.
C1   refer to eight notebooks (= MSS. 145–52) written between 1933
to   and 1936. The reference style C3, 42 is to C3, page 42.
C8

Typescripts

EBT   'Early Big Typescript' (TS. 211): a typescript composed from
       Vols. VI–X, 1932, 771 pp. All references are to page numbers.
BT   The 'Big Typescript' (TS. 213): a rearrangement, with modifica-
       tions, written additions and deletions, of EBT, 1933, vi pp. table of
       contents, 768 pp. All references are to page numbers. Where the
       numeral is followed by 'v.', this indicates a handwritten addition
       on the reverse side of the TS. page.
PPI   'Proto-Philosophical Investigations'[1] (TS. 220): a typescript of the
       first half of the pre-war version of the *Philosophical Investigations*
       (up to §189 of the final version, but with many differences); 1937
       or 1938, 137 pp. All references are to sections (§).
PPI(R) R. Rhees's pre-war translation of PPI (TS. 226): this goes up to PPI
       §95 (= PI §107), and is extensively corrected in Wittgenstein's
       hand; 1939, 72 pp. All references are to sections (§).
PPI(A) a fragmentary carbon copy of PPI consisting of part of a re-
       arrangement of PPI §§96–116 with renumberings, corrections and
       additions in Wittgenstein's hand. It is not cited in the catalogue. All
       references are to sections.
PPI(B) a 137-page typescript (not cited in the catalogue) consisting of the
       four-page 1945 preface and a carbon copy of PPI with renumber-
       ings, corrections and additions in Wittgenstein's hand. PPI(B)
       §§109–48 consists of a rearrangement of PPI §§93–116, which
       correspond to PPI(A). PPI(A) and (B) were compiled sometime
       between 1939 and 1945. The fragments of PPI(A) are nearly identi-

---

[1] Our title.

cal with the corresponding parts of (B). The corrections throughout PPI(B) are generally closely followed in TS. 227 (the final
typescript). (Where the fragmentary PPI(A) differs from (B) it is
(B) that is followed in TS. 227.) All references are to sections.

PPI(I)   The so-called 'Intermediate Version', reconstructed by von
         Wright; it consists of 300 numbered remarks; 1945, 195 pp. All
         references are to sections (§).

B i   *Bemerkungen I* (TS. 228), 1945–6, 185 pp. All references are to
         sections (§).

3. Abbreviations for works by Frege

BG   *Begriffsschrift, eine der arithmetischen nachgebildete Formelsprache des
         reinen Denkens* (Halle a/S., 1879).

FA   *The Foundations of Arithmetic*, tr. J. L. Austin, 2nd edition (Black-
         well, Oxford, 1959).

FC   'Function and Concept' ⎫ in *Translations from the Philosophical
CO   'On Concept and Object' ⎪ Writings of Gottlob Frege,*
SR   'On Sense and Reference' ⎬ ed. Peter Geach and
N   'Negation'   ⎭ Max Black (Blackwell, Oxford, 1960).

GAi,ii   *Grundgesetze der Arithmetik, begriffsschriftlich abgeleitet*, Band I,
         1893, Band II, 1903 (Hermann Pohle, Jena).

FG   *On the Foundations of Geometry and Formal Theories of Arithmetic*, ed.
         and tr. E.-H. W. Kluge (Yale University Press, New Haven, 1971).

T   'The Thought', repr. in *Philosophical Logic*, ed. P. F. Strawson
         (Oxford University Press, London, 1967).

NS   *Nachgelassene Schriften*, ed. H. Hermes, F. Kambartel, F. Kaulbach
         (Felix Meiner Verlag, Hamburg, 1969).

4. Abbreviations for works by Russell

PrM   *The Principles of Mathematics*, 2nd edition (revised) (Allen and
         Unwin, London, 1937).

PM i   *Principia Mathematica*, Vol. i (with A. N. Whitehead), 2nd edition
         (Cambridge University Press, Cambridge, 1927).

PP   *The Problems of Philosophy* (Home University Library, London,
         1912).

OK   *Our Knowledge of the External World as a Field for Scientific Method in
         Philosophy*, revised edition (Allen and Unwin, London, 1926).

LA   'The Philosophy of Logical Atomism', in *Logic and Knowledge,
         Essays 1901–1950*, ed. R. C. Marsh, pp. 175–281 (Allen and
         Unwin, London, 1956).

ML   *Mysticism and Logic* (Longmans, Green, London, 1918).
IMP   *Introduction to Mathematical Philosophy* (Allen and Unwin, London, 1919).
AM   *Analysis of Mind* (Allen and Unwin, London, 1921).

Analytical
Commentary

THE TITLE

W. used the title 'Philosophische Untersuchungen, Versuch einer Umarbeitung' as the heading of his 1936 revision of Br. B. in Vol. XI, 118–292 (published as EPB). According to von Wright, he also used the name 'Philosophische Untersuchungen' for the manuscript of PPI (the now missing MS. 142). PPI and PPI(B) both employ this title. However, when W. approached the Syndics of the Cambridge University Press in 1938 with the suggestion of publishing PPI in both German and English, the work was referred to (in the Syndics' minutes) as 'Philosophical Remarks'. But when he again contacted the Press in September 1943 with the idea of publishing his work in one volume with TLP, it was referred to in the minutes under the title 'Philosophical Investigations'. The carbon copy of the final typescript of PI (TS. 227) has this title at the top of the first page above the motto from Hertz (later replaced by the quotation from Nestroy).

The folder containing TS. 227 bears the words 'Die Philosophie der Psychologie' in W.'s handwriting. It is noteworthy that in MS. 169, 37 (1949?) W. wrote: 'Ich will die Betrachtungen über Mathematik die meinen Philosophischen Untersuchungen angehören "Anfänge der Mathematik" nennen.' ('I want to call the enquiries into mathematics that belong to my Philosophical Investigations "Beginnings of Mathematics".') If the title on the folder of TS. 227 belongs with its contents, then perhaps 'Philosophy of Psychology' was a parallel subtitle of the first part of the planned book.

THE MOTTO

1   The quotation from Nestroy comes from *Der Schützling* (*The Protégé*), Act IV, scene 10. In its original context it expresses such negative views on progress as would harmonize with W.'s own repudiation of this aspect, and this ideal, of European culture (cf. Foreword to PR and its earlier drafts, Vol. V, 204 ff.).

Es gibt so viele Ausrottungs- und Vertilgungs-mittel, und doch ist noch so wenig Übles ausgerottet, so wenig Böses vertilgt auf dieser Welt, dass man deutlich sieht, sie erfinden eine Menge, aber doch's Rechte nicht. Und wir leben doch in der Zeit des Fortschrittes. Der Fortschritt ist halt wie ein neuentdecktes Land; ein blühendes Kolonialsystem an der Küste, das Innere noch Wildnis, Steppe, Prärie. Überhaupt hat der Fortschritt das an sich, dass er viel grösser ausschaut, als er wirklich ist.

(There are so many means of extirpating and eradicating, and nevertheless so little evil has yet been extirpated, so little wickedness eradicated from this world, that one clearly sees that people invent a lot of things, but not the right one. And yet we live in the era of progress, don't we? I s'pose progress is like a newly discovered land; a flourishing colonial system on the coast, the interior still wilderness, steppe, prairie. It is in the nature of all progress that it looks much greater than it really is.)

It remains, however, unclear what Nestroy's remark is intended to convey as a motto for PI. It might be suggested that it intimates that the advance made in PI over the philosophy of TLP is less substantial than it appears. This is unlikely. More probable is the hypothesis that the intention behind the motto echoes the end of the Preface to TLP: 'the value of this work . . . is that it shows how little is achieved when these problems are solved'.

2   W. toyed with various mottoes for 'the book' between 1930 and 1947.

(i) The quotation from Nestroy was written into the final typescript of PI sometime after 25 April 1947,[1] replacing an earlier motto from Hertz's introduction to his *Principles of Mechanics*: 'Sind diese schmerzenden Widersprüche entfernt, so ist nicht die Frage nach dem Wesen beantwortet, aber der nicht mehr gequälte Geist hört auf, die für ihn unberechtigte Frage zu stellen.'[2] ('When these painful contradictions are removed, the question as to the nature [of force] will not have been answered; but our minds, no longer vexed, will cease to ask illegitimate questions.') W.

---

[1] The quotation, under the heading 'Motto', is entered in MS. 134 on 25 April 1947.
[2] H. Hertz, *Die Prinzipien der Mechanik*, Einleitung (Barth, Leipzig, 1910), p. 9.

long admired this essay, which he had read in his youth. He refers to it in
BB 26, 169, and also occasionally in his notebooks.

(ii) In 1946, while he was still evidently searching for a more resonant
motto than the quotation from Hertz, W. jotted down (apparently from
memory, since there is an error in transcription (MS. 130, 121)) a
quotation from Goethe's 1820 poem 'Allerdings': 'Natur hat weder Kern
noch Schale. Du frage Dich . . .' ('Nature has neither core nor husk. You
ask yourself . . .'). This poem is a polemical reply to Haller, whom
Goethe quotes: 'Ins Innre der Natur/Dringt kein erschaffner Geist' and
'Glückselig, wenn sie nur/Die äussre Schale weist' ('No created spirit
penetrates to the innermost heart of nature' and 'One is in bliss even
if it displays only the outer husk'). Goethe, who detested the idea
of a hidden reality beneath phenomena, to be inferred by a *theory*,
responds:

Das hör ich sechzig Jahre wiederholen
Und fluche drauf, aber verstohlen,
Sage mir tausendmale:
Alles gibt sie reichlich und gern,
Natur hat weder Kern
Noch Schale,
Alles ist sie mit einemmale
Dich prüfe du nur allermeist,
Ob du Kern oder Schale seist.

(I have heard this reiterated for sixty years—
And cursed at it, on the quiet.
I tell myself a thousand times:
Nature gives everything amply and gladly,
She has neither core
Nor husk,
She is everything at once.
You just ask yourself,
Whether you are core or husk.)

The aptness of these lines as a motto for PI consists in the parallels
between Goethe's conception of knowledge of nature and W.'s conception of philosophical understanding.

(iii) In MS. 162 (b), 54, W. noted as a possible motto, presumably for
PPI, 'Ein Schuft der mehr gibt als er hat' ('A rascal who gives more than
he has').

(iv) In Vol. XVI, 20 April 1938, W. wrote:

Longfellow: In the elder days of Art
        Builders wrought with greatest care,
        Each minute and unseen part,
        For the gods are everywhere.
(könnte mir als ein Motto dienen.)

It is unclear whether the sense of the parenthesis is that these verses could serve as a motto for the book, or as a motto for W. *himself*.

The stanza comes from Longfellow's poem 'The Builders'. (The last line should read 'For the gods see everywhere'.)

(v) At the stage of EBT (1931) W. considered another possible motto for his book: 'Seht ihr den Mond dort stehen? Er ist nur halb zu sehen, und ist doch rund und schön' (Vol. VI, 180). These are three lines from Matthias Claudius's poem 'Abendlied'. The stanza runs thus:

Seht ihr den Mond dort stehen?—
Er ist nur halb zu sehen
    Und ist doch rund und schön!
So sind wohl manche Sachen,
Die wir getrost belachen
    Weil unsre Augen sie nicht sehn.

(Do you see the moon there?
Only half of it is visible
    Yet it is round and beautiful!
Rather like that are many things,
At which we feel able to laugh
    For our eyes do not see them.)

(vi) M. O'C. Drury[3] relates that W. once thought of using as a motto a quotation from *King Lear*: 'I'll teach you differences'. This line occurs in Act I, scene iv, line 94.

(vii) G. Kreisel[4] reports that W. would have liked to use Bishop Butler's tag 'Everything is what it is, and not another thing' if not for the fact that Moore had used it as the motto for *Principia Ethica*.

It is striking how the Nestroy motto and (ii)–(v) display a kind of family resemblance. The image of husk and core, appearance and reality, the revealed and the concealed run through them, even though they alternate in evaluation.

[3] *Ludwig Wittgenstein: The Man and His Philosophy*, ed. K. T. Fann (Dell, New York, 1967), p. 69.
[4] G. Kreisel, 'The Motto of "Philosophical Investigations" and the Philosophy of Proofs and Rules', *Grazer Philosophische Studien* vol. 6 (1978) pp. 15 ff.

THE PREFACE

1   This Preface is to PI, Part I. There is no published evidence, nor any indication in the *Nachlass*, that Part II was conceived either as a continuation of Part I or as material to be worked into it (as suggested by the editors).

The dating of the Preface is deceptive in two respects. First, it suggests that the published version of PI was completed in January 1945. This is incorrect. W. amended the typescript of Part I extensively after 1945 (and the whole of Part II was written later). Secondly, the general outline of the Preface was written in 1938. This 1945 version was written as a preface to the intermediate version of PI. In the following discussions of the Preface, references to the *Philosophical Investigations* should be taken as limited to Part I. We shall comment on the Preface paragraph by paragraph ((a)–(j)).

(a) PI is the precipitate of sixteen years' work, i.e. from 1929 to 1945. The process of precipitation out of manuscripts and typescripts was complex.[1]

Of the subjects W. mentions here, it is noteworthy that the foundations of mathematics is *not* discussed in PI. However, the intermediate version of 1945 (as identified by von Wright) included a short section (PPI(I) pp. 135–43) taken from TS. 221, i.e. discussions in philosophy of mathematics. This explains the deceptive mention of this topic.

The different conceptions of a book of remarks alluded to can, with qualifications, be divided into three major variations. The first conception crystallizes around BT; the *Umarbeitung* (Vol. X), *Zweite Umarbeitung* (the *Grosses Format*—MS. 140) and the first part of Vol. XII are successive attempts to mould this material into a coherent whole. The second crystallizes around the Br.B. dictation; the brief (seven-page) German fragment (MS. 141) and EPB are further efforts to form this different material into an appropriate shape. The third major effort began in 1936 and ended with the published version of PI. It went through the following major stages. (i) PPI, written apparently at the end of 1936 (the MS. (142) is missing), consisting of 161 remarks and breaking off unfinished at the point that corresponds to PI §189(a). It contains much significant material omitted from PI. (It had a sequel, TS. 221, an early

---

[1] The task of tracing the remarks of PI back to their various MS. sources has been undertaken by Professor G. H. von Wright and Mr A. Maury, and a detailed account of the history of composition of PI has been written by Professor von Wright: 'The Origin and Composition of Wittgenstein's *Investigations*', in *Wittgenstein: Sources and Perspectives*, ed. G. Luckhardt. We are much indebted to this essay for many historical data.

version of RFM Part I.) (ii) PPI (A) and (B) are amended versions of PPI, perhaps being the versions considered for publication in 1943.[2] (iii) PPI (I), reconstructed by von Wright. It consists of 300 remarks, the last of which is identical with PI §421. These included PPI, fifty further pages whose MS. sources were written in 1944, and nine pages from TS. 221 (the mathematical sequel of PPI). It was for this volume that the published Preface was written. The fact that he rewrote the Preface suggests that he had publication in mind. (iv) The final typescript of PI, compiled in late 1945 or 1946. It is not however identical with the published version. W. continued to amend the TS., cutting out, amending, and adding material. PI, as published, is the *amended TS.*[3] which W. worked on until 1949 or 1950 (together with Part II).

It is noteworthy that the requirement that (a) imposes upon these attempts was a natural and unbroken order of thoughts.

(b) Here W. blames the nature of the investigation for his repeated failure to fulfil this requirement of a sequential ordering. (In 1937 he blamed himself rather than his material.) It is difficult to believe that it is impossible to represent the material in sequential exposition. Waismann's PLP, which attempted to do just that for W.'s work at the stage of BT, is not defective in the organization of the material (whatever defects it may have in Waismann's grasp of W.'s rapidly changing ideas at that time).

(c) The metaphor of an album of sketches is important. It signifies a confessed failing in the book, explicitly reaffirmed in the final paragraph of the Preface. The cutting down, rearranging, and rejecting of sketches is not merely figurative. W.'s method of composition involved writing down remarks in rough notebooks, transferring these, with alterations and some selection, to more polished MS. volumes from which remarks were selected for TSS. These TSS. were commonly cut up, sifted, rearranged, annotated, and amended. Sometimes further TSS. were then made, sometimes more radical revisions of TSS. involved reversions to MS. composition. It is possible that there was some work on loose sheets (now missing). PI is, as it were, a sketchbook of a master-artist who could not produce a finished canvas.

The number of 'rejects' was huge, and W. often expressed doubts about his judgement concerning his selection of remarks (e.g. Vol. XV, 65, 84). Numerous remarks only become fully intelligible when their

---

[2] W. first approached Cambridge University Press in 1938. On 30 September they had agreed to publish a book referred to in their minutes as 'Philosophical Remarks'. This was PPI together with its philosophy of mathematics sequel. W. asked R. Rhees to make a translation of the text, hence we have PPI (R) (going up to §116 (= PPI §95 = PI §107)). W. drew back from publication. He approached the Press again in September 1943. This too came to nothing.

[3] The top copy of the final TS., with W.'s handwritten corrections and attached *Randbemerkungen* (printed beneath a line at the foot of some pages), no longer exists. TS. 227 is a carbon copy with P. T. Geach's transcriptions of W.'s alterations to the original TS.

original surroundings are restored. Similarly, the 'cutting down' of individual remarks frequently achieves economy of expression at the cost of perspicuity. It is noteworthy that the sense of many remarks changes in the course of transcription through non-trivial alteration of a few words. Indeed, even verbatim repetitions may have different purposes and implications.

(d) It is unclear to which period 'up to a short time ago' refers. These words occur too in the 1938 drafts of a preface. Possibly therefore it alludes to W.'s abandonment of his revision of the BT material; alternatively, to abandonment of EPB.

The mention of mangled and watered-down results may allude to various items published by W.'s students or acquaintances.[4] Waismann had incurred W.'s wrath with 'Über den Begriff der Identität'[5] and other writings, and Alice Ambrose with 'Finitism in Mathematics'.[6] Braithwaite was publicly called to task in a letter in *Mind*.[7] Certainly Schlick's 'Meaning and Verification'[8] mangled the ideas from which it was derived.

(e) W. read TLP together with Nicholas Bachtin in 1943 (as reported by von Wright). The text wrongly suggests that this occurred in 1941. In 1944 drafts W. refers to the rereading as occurring two years earlier. The idea of publishing a version of PI in the same volume as TLP occurred in this context, and when W. reopened negotiations with Cambridge University Press in late 1943 the Syndics agreed to this condition. The idea of so publishing the two works is scrawled on the final page of MS. 128. Just how important it is to keep TLP in mind while reading PI will become clear in the sequel.

(f) Details of the discussions with Ramsey and Sraffa have yet to be published. The mention of discussions with Ramsey during the last *two* years of his life is *prima facie* erroneous. W. only came to Cambridge in January 1929, and Ramsey died on 19 January 1930.

(g) It is unclear what other reasons there are for points of contact apart from W.'s influence and teaching. Conceivably he is alluding to common sources of problems in Frege and Russell.

(h) W.'s anxieties about publication are marked throughout his later work and were written into all drafts of the Preface. His detestation of contemporary civilization, his deep cultural pessimism and sense of alienation (cf. Foreword to PR) inclined him to doubt whether his attempts to say what he had to say could possibly be understood (let

---

[4] For further details, see N. Malcolm, *Ludwig Wittgenstein, a Memoir* (Oxford University Press, London, 1966), pp. 56 ff.

[5] F. Waismann, 'Über den Begriff der Identität', *Erkenntnis* VI (1936), pp. 56–64.

[6] A. Ambrose, 'Finitism in Mathematics', *Mind* XLIV (1935), pp. 186–203, 317–40.

[7] 'Letter to the Editor', *Mind* XLII (1933), pp. 415 f.

[8] M. Schlick, 'Meaning and Verification', *Philosophical Review* XLV (1936), pp. 339–69.

alone the *Weltanschauung* that informs what he says, but is never overtly expressed). In 1930 (Vol. VI, 18) he remarked that his (projected) book is only for a small circle of people (who are not the élite of mankind, are not better or worse than others, but just different). They belong to his cultural circle, as it were his countrymen, in contrast to others, who are strangers. Drury reports his saying 'My type of thinking is not wanted in this present age, I have to swim so strongly against the tide. Perhaps in a hundred years people will really want what I am writing.'[9] In his 1939 lectures he lamented: 'The seed I'm most likely to sow is a certain jargon' (LFM 293). Still later (1947–8), he expressed his hesitations about publication, his fear that the work would fall into hands other than those he would wish, his hope that 'the philosophical journalists' would forget it quickly and that it would be preserved for a better kind of reader (MS. 136, 81: 'Zum Vorwort').

(i) In Vol. VIII, 226, W. remarked 'Ich soll nur der Spiegel sein, in welchem mein Leser sein eigenes Denken mit allen seinen Unförmigkeiten sieht und mit dieser Hilfe zurecht richten kann.' ('I should be merely the mirror in which my reader sees his own thought with all its distortions and with this help can set it aright.')

(j) W. was never satisfied with PI, despite the numerous redraftings.[10] By the standards to which he aspired, the book has defects.

2   The Preface went through uncountable drafts; uncountable, because W. sometimes redrafts a single sentence up to a dozen times in the context of a single attempt to write a preface. We shall list the various drafts chronologically and pick out their significant features.

(i) C8, 13: written in 1936, contains a two-paragraph preface, presumably to PPI.[11] It bears a remote resemblance to the final version. Paragraph (a) says that the book presents W.'s philosophical thought as it had developed over the previous eight years, and that, although he has done as well as he could, it is in many ways defective. He mentions here, and in (b), some of the defects, e.g. it is often too long, many of the examples could be better, and the structure is frequently poor. It has other defects too, W. concludes, but what he means *thereby* will only be seen by a reader who *really* understands something, and to him W. need not explain.

(ii) Vol. XIV, under 16 September 1937: to see this aright its context must be clarified. The broader context is a series of remarks on

[9] M. O'C. Drury, 'Some Notes on Conversations with Wittgenstein' in *Acta Philosophica Fennica* 28, *Essays in Honour of G. H. von Wright*, ed. J. Hintikka (North Holland, Amsterdam, 1976), p. 25.

[10] Cf. W.'s letters to Malcolm in 1945 (*Ludwig Wittgenstein, a Memoir*, pp. 42 f.).

[11] The context is the discussion of reading which is worked into PI §§156–78. It is probably derived from EPB (i.e. Vol. XI, 118 ff.), being a reworking for PPI; but it is only later in this MS. that we find draft material that occurs in PPI and *not* in EPB. So it is even *possible* that this is a draft preface for EPB, written before that work was abandoned.

philosophy of mathematics (one MS. source of TS. 221, the sequel of PPI). On 12 September 1937, W. expressed despair at his inability to continue writing a book. His remarks, he wrote, are satisfactory for teaching purposes, but not for composing a book. If he cannot but write in this way, drop by drop, without any direction, then it would be better not to write a book at all, but to restrict himself to writing remarks *tant bien que mal*, which might perhaps be published after his death.

Two days later W.'s spirits sank even lower:

Es ist grauenhaft, dass ich die Arbeitsfähigkeit, d.h. die philosophische Sehkraft, von einem Tag auf den andern verliere . . .

Ich hatte gestern Hoffnung, dass es mit dem Schreiben gehn wird. Heute aber ist meine Hoffnung wieder gesunken.

Und leider *brauche* ich die Arbeit, denn ich bin noch nicht resigniert, sie aufzugeben . . .

'Fang etwas Anderes an!' Aber ich will nicht! Wie soll ich die Kraft haben jetzt etwas anderes anzufangen? Es sei denn, dass ich gezwungen werde, wie durch einen Krieg.

(It is dreadful, that I lose the ability to work, i.e. the power of philosophical insight, from one day to the next . . .

I had hopes yesterday that the writing would go all right. Today my hope has sunk again.

And unfortunately I *need* the work, for I am not yet resigned to giving it up . . .

'Do something else!' But I do not want to! How should I find the strength to do something different now. Unless I were being forced, as in a war.)

On 15 September 1937 he remarked that when he thinks 'for himself', as it were, without having the composition of a book in mind, he circles around a topic ('so springe ich um das Thema herum').[12] This is his natural way of thinking; to be forced to think sequentially ('In einer Reihe gezwungen fortzudenken') is torture for him. Is it worth trying? He is wasting untold toil on an arrangement of his thoughts which, he writes, may be worthless.

It is plausible to think that his despair concerned his composition of the continuation of PPI. He was unable to graft on to PPI his reflections on mathematics, on rule-following, necessity, and possibility (the strains still show in PI §189 ff.), and hence despaired of completing a book.

The next day, 16 September 1937, he wrote a short 'Vorwort':

Dieses Buch besteht aus Bemerkungen die ich im Lauf von 8 Jahren über den Gegenstand der Philosophie geschrieben habe. Ich habe oft vergebens versucht sie in eine befriedigende Ordnung zu bringen oder am Faden *eines* Gedanken-

---

[12] He had remarked on this tendency in his thought earlier, in Vol. XIV, 149: 'I generally approach a question not like this: x ⟶ · but like this x⟍ . I shoot again and again past it, but always from a closer position' ('Ich schieße immer wieder an ihr vorbei, aber in immer näherem Abstand').

ganges aufzureihen. Das Ergebnis war künstlich und unbefriedigend, und meine Kraft erwies sich als viel zu gering es zu Ende zu führen. Die einzige Darstellung, deren ich noch fähig bin, ist die, diese Bemerkungen durch ein Netz von Zahlen so zu verbinden, dass ihr, äusserst komplizierter, Zusammenhang sichtbar wird.

Möge dies statt eines Besseren hingenommen werden,—was ich gerne geliefert hätte.

(This book consists of remarks on the subject of philosophy which I have written in the course of the last eight years. I have often tried, in vain, to put them into a satisfactory order or to thread them together in *one* string of thoughts. The result was artificial and unsatisfactory, and my strength turned out to be far too slight to pursue the matter to its conclusion. The only presentation of which I am still capable is to connect these remarks by a network of numbers which will make evident their extremely complicated connections.

May this be taken instead of something better which I should have liked to produce.)

This suggests that he had found what seemed to be a solution to his difficulty, namely to give up the idea of a sequential arrangement, opting instead for a numbering system which would display a network of connections rather than a linear development of thought. Since the breaking point seems to have been reached while attempting to compose the continuation of PPI, it is perhaps plausible to suggest that the network system would, in particular, connect the remarks in (roughly speaking) philosophy of mathematics with PPI. The manifold connections are evident: rule-following, logical and psychological compulsion, necessity and possibility, samples and paradigms, etc., are themes begun in PPI, and continued in the mathematical reflections of TS. 221.

(iii) MS. 159, 34–41: this pocket notebook contains what appears to be the first rough draft of the 1938 Preface. The manuscript does not contain a single date entry, but it is conjectured that it was written early in 1938. The draft Preface resembles the 'clean copy' drafts in Vol. XIII, and hence we will not discuss it separately.

(iv) Vol. XIII, 110–26 contains three drafts of a preface, the first dated '27.6.' and the last 'Cambridge im August 1938'. These, and MS. 159, differ from each other and from the final 1938 TS. Preface only marginally. The first and second drafts contain a dedication to his friends (who are not mentioned by name).

(v) TS. 225 is the typescript of the 1938 Preface. Comparing it with the final 1945 Preface reveals some interesting differences despite many similarities.

Paragraph (a) added to the list of the topics to be discussed Sense Data and the contrast between Idealism and Realism.

(b) differs in the following respects. (1) It begins 'Vor etwa 4 Jahren machte ich den ersten Versuch so einer Zusammenfassung. Das Ergebnis war ein unbefriedigendes, und ich machte weitere Versuche. Bis ich

endlich (einige Jahre später) zur Überzeugung gelangte, dass es vergebens sei; und ich alle solche Versuche aufzugeben hätte.' ('Some four
years ago I made the first attempt at such a collection. The result was
unsatisfactory, and I made further attempts. Until I finally (some years
later) was forced to the conclusion that it was in vain, and I had to give up
all such attempts.') (In the Vol. XIII drafts W. wrote not '(some years
later)', but 'after more than two years'; this he crossed out in the third
draft, altering it to the later variant.) (2) Instead of 'Und dies hing freilich
mit der Natur der Untersuchung' ('And this was, of course, connected
with the very nature of the investigation'), W. wrote: 'Dies hing
allerdings auch mit der Natur des Gegenstands' ('And this was, to be
sure, *also* connected with . . .'). (3) The penultimate sentence continues
'. . . durchreisen; dass die Gedanken in ihm in einem verwickelten Netz
von Beziehungen zueinander stehen' ('. . . direction; so that the thoughts
in it stand to each other in an intricate network of relationships'). This
metaphor prepares the way for the sequel.

(c) is quite different here.

Ich beginne diese Veröffentlichung mit dem Fragment meines letzten Ver-
suchs, meine philosophischen Gedanken in einer Reihe zu ordnen. Dies Fragment
hat vielleicht den Vorzug, verhältnismässig leicht einen Begriff von meiner
Methode vermitteln zu können. Diesem Fragment will ich eine Masse von
Bemerkungen in mehr oder weniger loser Anordnung folgen lassen. Die
Zusammenhänge der Bemerkungen aber, dort, wo ihre Anordnung sie nicht
erkennen lässt, will ich durch eine Numerierung erklären. Jede Bemerkung soll
eine laufende Nummer und ausserdem die Nummern solcher Bemerkungen
tragen, die zu ihr in wichtigen Beziehungen stehen.

(I start this book with the fragment of my latest attempt to arrange my
philosophical thoughts sequentially. This fragment has, perhaps, the virtue of
making it comparatively easy to obtain a grasp of my method. I want to continue
this fragment with a mass of more or less loosely ordered remarks. But the links
between these remarks, where the arrangement does not make them evident, I
shall clarify by means of a numbering system. Each remark will have a serial
number, and apart from that, the numbers of those remarks which are related to
it in important ways.)

What is the fragment alluded to? It is characterized as W.'s *latest attempt* to
arrange his thoughts sequentially. Furthermore, it must consist of
ordered remarks *itself*, since it is characterized as '. . . . Versuch, meine
. . . Gedanken in eine Reihe zu ordnen', and also because (a) introduced
the book with the words: 'In dem Folgenden will ich eine Auswahl der
philosophischen Bemerkungen veröffentlichen . . .' ('In the following I
wish to publish a collection of philosophical remarks . . .'). In the sequel
W. explains: 'Ich habe alle diese Gedanken ursprünglich als *Bemerkungen*,
kurze Absätze, niedergeschrieben' ('I originally wrote down all these
thoughts as remarks, short paragraphs'), and he goes on to confess his

inability to weld them together ('dass das Beste, was ich schreiben könnte, immer nur philosophische Bemerkungen bleiben würden' ('that the best that I could write would always be no more than philosophical remarks')). These two considerations rule out any part of the Br.B. trilogy (Br.B., MS. 141, EPB), since they were not composed as an ordering of remarks. Moreover, since giving up EPB, W. had worked intensively on PPI, *this was* his latest effort. It is plausible therefore to take PPI as this fragment. Against this conjecture speaks the fact that there exists no MS. or TS. of the continuation of PPI that contains any system of numbering such as is alluded to. Equally, PPI seems excessively long to be called a 'fragment'. Both objections can be countered. First, there is no oddity in referring to PPI as 'ein Fragment', since the German term 'Fragment' signifies an unfinished (fragmentary) work that breaks off before completion, whether large or small; thus, for example, Goethe's *Wilhelm Meisters Theatralische Sendung* is referred to as a 'Fragment'. Secondly, it is not obvious that the numbering system sketched in the 1938 Preface had already been carried out. The 'Vorwort' of 16 September 1937, as we have seen, contains a sketch of the same principle of numbering, and it is certain that *that* sketch was *prospective*, since it is a solution to W.'s painful doubts and hesitations about producing a sequential ordering expressed in the previous few days. It may well be that the identical numbering system described here is *still* a programme to be carried out. It would, after all, be quite natural to leave *that* until the writing was absolutely finished. Alternatively, it is possible that W. executed a planned numbering on separate sheets of paper[13] (since only the final numbering would be entered in the TS.) and that he later destroyed these, for once the idea lost its appeal, as it evidently did, such lists of interconnections would have little, if any, value.

(d) differs from the final Preface: 'Ich wollte, alle diese Bemerkungen wären besser, als sie sind.—Es fehlt ihnen—um es kurz zu sagen—an Kraft und an Präzision. Ich veröffentliche diejenigen hier, die mir nicht zu öde erscheinen.' ('I wish that all these remarks were better than they are. They are lacking—to put it briefly—in power and precision. I publish those here which do not seem to me too barren.')

(e)–(i) do not differ materially from the printed Preface but omit its final paragraph.

(vi) MS. 128, 40 ff., contains material for the Preface. It is clear that by this date (1943 or 1944) W. had given up the idea of the system of enumeration. He refers to the book as containing a 'conglomerate' ('Konglomerat') of remarks written over a sixteen-year period. In the end, he remarks, he had to order them in some way, no matter how loosely, and this conglomerate is what he proposes to publish. This

[13] Like his concordance (TS. 231) between B i and *Bemerkungen II*.

drafting gives way to various elaborations of the 'sketches of a landscape' metaphor.

MS. 128, 49 has the only draft of the final paragraph of the 1945 Preface: 'Dass dieses Buch nicht gut ist, weiss ich. Aber ich glaube dass die Zeit in der es von mir verbessert werden könnte vorüber ist, und diese Überzeugung hat mich zu seiner Veröffentlichung bewogen.' ('That this book is not good, I know. But I believe that the time is past in which I could improve it, and this conviction has moved me to publish it.') Typed into the Preface attached to PPI(B), this version was altered in pen in TS. 227.

(vii) MS. 129 contains numerous drafts written on special index sheets at the beginning of the volume. The first date in the MS. volume proper is 17 August 1944, but the drafts may well have been entered later. They are very close to the final version, but display strikingly how much care went into the composition. It is here that mention of Realism and Idealism, and of Sense Data, as topics to be discussed, is dropped. W. refers to his first attempt to weld his results together as occurring ten years before, i.e. 1934–5. Other variations in the redraftings are largely stylistic.

(viii) in MS. 180(a), 15 f. there is a further draft, not significantly different from those of MS. 129. Indeed, it may even precede those of MS. 129.

(ix) MS. 136, 81 contains a paragraph headed 'Zum Vorwort' (see p. 10).

CHAPTER 1

The Augustinian picture

(§§1–27(a))

INTRODUCTION

If we view §§1–27(a) as the opening chapter, we can find here an introduction to some of the main themes of the book. The central preoccupation of PI is the nature of language and of linguistic meaning, together with the philosophical perplexities generated by reflection upon meaning, language, and thought. Characteristically, the theme is introduced by way of error and illusion, since the later W. thought the road to sanity in philosophy lay through an understanding of madness.

The purpose of this chapter is to introduce a proto-picture (*Urbild*) of the essence of language (*Wesen der Sprache*) which, W. contends, lies at the heart of numerous misguided conceptions or 'theories' of meaning. This proto-picture, the 'Augustinian picture of language', is explored relatively perfunctorily. The initial aim is to give us a surview of its elemental characteristics. Later many of its constituents are examined in detail.

The chapter divides readily into three parts.

Part A runs from §1 to §7. It introduces the Augustinian picture of language, and in quick succession raises a variety of problems: (i) word-meaning; (ii) word/sentence distinction; (iii) diversity of types of word; (iv) different methods of explaining the meaning of a word (and their bearing on differences of logical type among words); (v) the nature of understanding and the relation between the meaning of an expression and the criteria for understanding that expression. In each case the Augustinian picture is shown to breed confusion and error, to obscure distinctions that are philosophically important, and to bring together linguistic phenomena which should be kept separate. In the course of the discussion various key notions occur, the significance of which will emerge only later: the use, application, and criteria of application, the role, function, and purpose, of words, phrases, or sentences. Similarly, key distinctions are briefly introduced: (i) the contrast between training and explanation; (ii) the distinction between ostensive teaching and ostensive definition (which exemplifies the first contrast); (iii) the difference between a complete and an incomplete language, language-game, or segment of language. Finally, a pair of crucial methodological notions occur: the conception of philosophy as a quest for an *Übersicht* (§5) and the concept of a language-game (§7). W. exemplifies the language-game method of analysis and gives a rationale for it.

The structure of Part A:

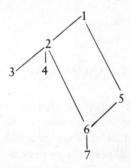

Part B runs from §8 to §17. It opens with an extension of language (2) in preparation for examining one of the ingredients of the *Urbild* of §1. This expanded language-game contains different kinds of word, i.e. the possibility of different groupings of words according to similarities and differences among their uses. According to Augustine's picture, every word signifies something and to grasp its meaning is to know what object it signifies or stands for. This, W. now argues, forces the great diversity of uses of words into a vacuous strait-jacket. (Language (8) is used to illustrate this point.) The discussion introduces the analogies between words and tools and between words and levers. Finally, W. characterizes the logical status of the colour samples in language (8), describing them as instruments of language.

The structure of Part B:

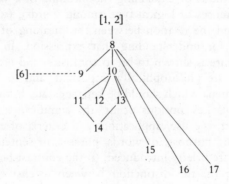

Part C runs from §18 to §27(a). It is parallel to Part B and explicitly linked with §§2 and 8. It explores the other main ingredient of the Augustinian picture, viz. that sentences are combinations of names which function as descriptions. According to this conception, to grasp the meaning of a sentence is to know what it describes, and this knowledge is the product of understanding what its constituents stand for and how they are combined. This, W. argues, misrepresents the diversity of uses of sentences and the criteria for understanding them. W. makes a number of controversial claims: (i) that a language might consist only of commands or questions and answers; (ii) that such a language would not be incomplete; (iii) that the distinctions between assertions, questions, commands, prayers, requests, etc., turns not on the grammatical forms of sentences, nor on any mental acts accompanying their utterance, but on their uses or applications; (iv) that Frege's conception of assertion, supposition, and the thought is mistaken; (v) that uttering sentences and reacting to them must be seen as part of a whole pattern of activity (or form of life); and (vi) that knowing what each of the words of a sentence signifies does not fix the use of the whole sentence (as is obvious from considering one-word sentences).

The structure of Part C:

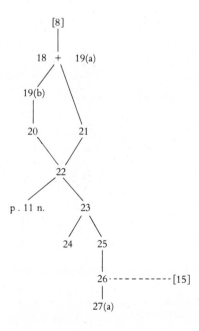

§§26 and 27(a) link the preliminary investigation of the Augustinian picture with the more thorough discussion of naming and ostensive definition in Chapter 2 (§§27(b)–64). §27(b) opens the next chapter.

Correlations

PI	PPI	PPI(R)
1(a–b)	1	1
1(c)	2	2
2(a)	3(a)	3
2(b)	3(b)	4
3(a)	4(a)	5
3(b)	4(b)	6
4	5	7
5	6	8
6	7	9
7	8	10
8	9	11
9	10	12
10	11(a–d)	13
11(a)	11(e)	14
11(b)	12(a)	15
12	12(b)	16
13	12(c)	17
14	12(d)	18
15	13	19
16	14	20
17	15	21
18	16(a)	22(a)
19(a)	16(b)	22(b)
19(b)	17	23
20(a)	18	24
20(b)	19	25
21	20	26
22(a–b)	21	27
22(c)	22	28
22(d)	23	29
23	24	30
24	25	31
25	26(a)	32
26	26(b)	33
27(a)	26(c)	34

Refers to Witt, Meaning & Understanding

Augustine's picture of language: *das Wesen der Sprache*
1. Introduction   2. The Augustinian picture   3. Augustine's picture: a proto-theory or paradigm   4. Frege   5. Russell   6. The *Tractatus*

EXEGESIS §§1–27(a)

SECTION 1

1   The book opens with a 'particular picture of the essence of human language'. This *Urbild* is held to inform vast ranges of philosophical thought in a multitude of different and frequently unrecognized ways (see 'Augustine's picture of language', pp. 13 ff.). One of the tasks of PI is to show how this picture leads to error and confusion. The general background of the passage W. quotes is as follows:

> Thus, little by little, I became conscious where I was; and to have a wish to express my wishes to those who could content them, and I could not; for the wishes were within me, and they without; nor could they by any sense of theirs enter within my spirit. So I flung about at random limbs and voice, making the few signs I could, and such as I could, like, though in truth very little like, what I wished. And when I was not presently obeyed (my wishes being hurtful or unintelligible), then I was indignant with my elders for not submitting to me, with those owing me no service, for not serving me; and avenged myself on them by tears. Such have I learnt infants to be from observing them; and, that I was myself such, they, all unconscious, have shown me better than my nurses who knew it. . . . (At my infancy's close) I could seek for signs whereby to make known to others my sensations.[1]

The immediate context of W.'s quotation is:

> It was not that my elders taught me words (as, soon after, other learning) in any set method; but I, longing by cries and broken accents and various motions of my limbs to express my thoughts, that so I might have my will, and yet unable to express all I willed, or to whom I willed, did myself, by the understanding which thou, my God, gavest me, practise the sounds in my memory. When they (my elders) named . . .[2]

These passages contain the following central points: (i) an 'inner' and 'outer' picture of the mind, (ii) a presumption of pre-linguistic self-consciousness, and *a fortiori* a presumption of the intelligibility of self-knowledge of mental states (sensations, wishes, thoughts); (iii) a conception of language according to which it is necessary only for communication, but not for thinking.

These fundamental conceptions or 'pictures' are not mentioned here by W., though later assailed. Repudiation of (i) is the keystone of his

[1] *The Confessions of St Augustine,* revised from a former translation by G. B. Pusey (Parker, Oxford, 1853), I, vi.
[2] Ibid. I, viii.

philosophy of mind; (ii) is repudiated by the notorious non-cognitive doctrine of avowals. Repudiation of (iii) is a constant theme of his philosophy of language. Here, however, he is concerned only with the points explicit in the quotation in (a). (iv) Words signify or name objects. (v) Sentences are combinations of words. (vi) That a word signifies a given object consists in the intention with which the word is used. (vii) The intention with which a word is used (i.e. the intention to *mean* that object) can be seen in behaviour, bodily movement, facial expression, tone of voice, etc.

Augustine makes two points with which W. must agree. First, he stresses bodily behaviour as 'the natural language of all people' and as a precondition of language and language-acquisition, a point W. himself emphasizes (PI §§185, 202–7, etc.). Secondly, he insists that the child's learning required hearing 'words repeatedly used in their proper places in various sentences' and hence that meaning and understanding presuppose mastery of combinatorial possibilities of expressions.

W. does not take Augustine to expound an interesting 'theory of meaning'. Consequently, it detracts nothing from the interest of W.'s discussion to discover that elsewhere in his writings Augustine's crude reflections upon language contain observations which are *prima facie* at odds with the *Urbild*. In *De Magistro* he notes that one cannot point to objects signified by prepositions (e.g. *ex*). In *Principia Dialecticae* he distinguishes between the spoken word, its meaning (as grasped by the mind), its mention (i.e. its use as a sign for itself), and its use as standing for an object. He also refers to the forces of words—the effects they have upon an audience. Neither inconsistencies in his remarks nor peculiarities in some aspects of his account of language-learning disqualify Augustine as a spokesman for a certain pervasive conception of language. What interests W. is Augustine's pre-theoretical, pre-philosophical picture of the working of language which informs Augustine's own remarks on language as well as a multitude of sophisticated philosophical analyses of meaning.

The picture of language, extracted in (b) from the quotation, involves the following main contentions: (i) words name objects; (ii) sentences are combinations of names. This very simple pair of apparent truisms provide the foundation for a more sophisticated conception (the Augustinian picture) according to which, in addition, (iii) every word has a meaning; (iv) a word is, in some way, correlated with its meaning; (v) the meaning of a word is the object for which it stands. These latter three contentions provide the main theme of §§1–59 of the book. §§1–27(a) explore (iii); §§27(b)–38 examine the primary candidate for the correlating mechanism of (iv); §§38–59 examine the ramifications of (v).

How could the Augustinian picture ever inform serious reflection upon the 'essence of language' (*Wesen der Sprache*)? After all, the obvious and immediate objections seem so powerful. How can it be said that words name or stand for objects which are their meanings when (i) some expressions (e.g. 'if . . . then . . .', 'the'), though meaningful, do not seem definable except by contextual definition; and (ii) some meaningful expressions seem to cancel out uniformly in certain combinations (e.g. double negation)? How can a sentence be a combination of names when (iii) we sharply distinguish a meaningful sentence from a mere list of names, (iv) we distinguish supposition from assertion, and assertion from order, question, expression of intention or wish, and (v) we distinguish one-word *sentences* from words?

These obvious objections are important and correct, but they are objections to full-blooded 'theories of meaning' that stem from the Augustinian *Urbild*, not objections to the *Urbild*, which is antecedent to argument. Theories which grow out of the primitive picture do indeed attempt to resolve these problems.

Objection (i) may be countered, e.g., by suggesting that logical connectives represent attitudes of mind (e.g. hesitation for alternation, denial for negation). Platonism, on the other hand, will invoke peculiar non-empirical entities (universals) for concept-words and function-names to stand for. Russell, e.g., argued that 'if p then q' is a certain propositional function of two arguments from pairs of propositions to a proposition, and the meaning of the logical constant 'if . . . then . . .' *is* this propositional function. This unrestricted Platonism leads to contradictions whose removal requires the development of a theory of categories or logical types as a way of preserving intact the underlying *Urbild*.

Objection (ii) may be countered, as in TLP, by restricting the account of the 'essence of language' to atomic propositions. In that case one will argue that there are no 'logical objects', that logical constants are *not* names and do not go proxy for or represent any objects. Alternatively, one might deny the principle that a function cannot disappear. Thus, for example, it could be argued that the equivalence in sense of '~ ~ p' and 'p' does not show that '~' lacks sense, since the sense of '~' is established by the difference in sense of 'p' and '~ p' (analogously, the identity of sense of 'q & (pv ~ p)' and 'q' does not show that 'p' lacks sense).

Possible solutions to (iii) vary. Psychologism may attribute the difference to accompanying representations or to speaker's intentions. Or one might, like Russell (PrM 40), accept the fact that a sentence is more than the sum of its constituents, but sadly admit that the difference defies analysis. The most elaborate way of tackling the matter within the parameters of the Augustinian picture of meaning involves introducing a theory of types. It can then be argued that a sentence is an articulated (complex) structure composed of parts with differentiated functions (e.g. singular referring expression and propositional function). Only well-formed sequences of names constitute sentences; all others are mere lists of names.

The characteristic solution to (iv) is to treat difference between supposals and assertions, or assertions and other moods, as being psychological.

This sketch of possible manoeuvres shows how the primitive picture can grow into complex and sophisticated theories. One task of PI is to persuade us to alter our point of view, to look upon language—and hence upon philosophical problems—from a new perspective.

In (c), W. notes that the Augustinian picture fails to distinguish different parts of speech. Its primary focus is upon personal names, sortal nouns, and mass-nouns. Names of actions and properties, and other types of words, are neglected. Elsewhere (PG 56, BB 77), W. elaborates: verbs ('eat', 'go'), indexicals ('here', 'there'), token reflexives ('today'), connectives ('not', 'but'), and modal adverbs ('perhaps') must not be assimilated to the category of proper names, nor do they have the same mode of signification as proper names (itself different from that of sortal nouns).

A preliminary illustration of different types of words is given by the shopping example in (d). 'Five', 'red', and 'apple' are words each one of which belongs to a type the use of which is fundamentally different from the use of words of the other types. To say that 'apple' is the name of a fruit, 'red' the name of a colour, and 'five' the name of a number would mask deep differences beneath superficial similarities. Again, one might think, 'apple' involves correlation with an object, 'red' with a colour, and 'five' with counting objects of a type, so all words involve correlation with *something*. The web of deception is readily woven.

The example is designed to stress the fact that the contention that the three words are of different types rests on the differences between the operations carried out in each case, and on the ordering of the operations. First, objects of a given type are identified; subsequently, a sensible characteristic is matched with a sample; finally, a 1:1 correlation of objects and numerals is carried out. It would be senseless to recite the series of numerals before identifying a range of objects.

Each of the three words in 'five red apples' has a different use, and this can be described without answering questions such as 'What is the meaning of the word "five"?'—where 'meaning' is thought to be given by specification of an entity. Of course, W.'s point is that there is nothing left to say about the meaning of 'five' (properly understood) after its use has been described (PG 321). The meaning of a word is given by specification of its use, and this can be done without answering questions such as 'Of what is "five" the name?' or 'What does "five" stand for?' There is no need to answer what, on the Augustinian picture of language, is the fundamental question. Moreover, even if it were answered, this

would not provide by itself any account of how 'five' is correctly used
(cf. PLP 157 f.).

How the shopkeeper knows what operation to carry out in each case is
brushed aside as irrelevant. W.'s standard grounds for this move are that
genesis of knowledge or of an ability, conceived of as a causal mechanism, is a matter of empirical fact. Being contingent, it stands in no logical
or normative relation to exercise of the ability or manifestation of the
knowledge.

1.1   'No such thing was in question here . . .': W. corrected this to
read 'There was no question of such an entity "meaning" here' (PPI(R)
§2).

2   (i) Vol. VI, 243: W. remarks that he should begin his projected book
with the analysis of an ordinary sentence such as 'A lamp is standing on
my table', since everything should be derivable therefrom. This, he adds,
expresses something he has long felt, viz. that he should start his book
with a description of a situation from which the material for all that
follows can be obtained. The thought reaches back to NB ('My *whole*
task consists in explaining the nature of the proposition' (NB 39)) and
TLP ('To give the essence of a proposition means to give the essence of
all description, and thus the essence of the world' (TLP 5.4711)), and forward
to PI with the example of §1 and the primitive language-game of §2.

        (ii) BT 25 f. makes three points. (a) When Augustine speaks of learning
a language, he speaks of how we name things and understand names.
Here naming is conceived to be the foundation of language. (b) This
conception is equivalent to that which takes the form of explanation
'That is . . .' (i.e. ostensive definition) as fundamental. (c) Augustine's
remarks are significant for us because they represent the conception of a
naturally clear-thinking person who is temporally far removed from us
and does not belong to our intellectual milieu (*Gedankenkreis*).

        (iii) BB 16 f. introduces the shopping example to illustrate what
'operating with signs' means and to side-step the question 'What are
signs?'

        (iv) BB 79 elaborates the introduction of numerals into this game. It
stresses the different *training* and *method of application* of each type of
word. Numerals, unlike 'brick', 'cube', 'slab', etc., require learning the
series by heart. As with other words, teaching is demonstrative; but the
same numeral, e.g. 'three', may be taught by pointing to slabs, bricks,
or columns. On the other hand, different numerals will be taught
by pointing to *different groupings* of stones of the *same shape*. The demonstrative gesture and uttering of the word is the same in all cases. But
the way the gesture is used differs, and the difference is not captured by
saying 'In the one case one points at a shape, in the other at a number.'

SECTION 2

1   The Augustinian conception of meaning is rooted in a primitive idea of the functioning of language. A primitive idea, in this sense, is one that oversimplifies the phenomena. So this referential conception of meaning is a primitive one. But, W. now adds, 'one can also say that it is the idea of a language more primitive than ours'.

(b) describes a language (subsequently referred to as a 'language-game') for which the *description* given by Augustine is right. Note that it is *not* contended that the Augustinian conception of the 'essence of language' is right for this proto-language, merely that Augustine's *description* is appropriate for it. The Augustinian conception of meaning is therefore an idea or picture (*Vorstellung*) derived from over-hasty reflection upon a linguistic phenomenon. The therapy chosen consists of isolating the phenomenon and examining in detail whether the conception is apt or not.

It is noteworthy that the description of the language specifies a context (building activities), speech community (builder and assistant), a vocabulary ('block', 'pillar', 'slab', 'beam'), criteria of understanding (bringing the requested stones in the appropriate order), and a use of the vocabulary (the words are called out when the corresponding stones are wanted). However, the 'language' (i) has no syntax; (ii) contains no rules for sentence-formation, *a fortiori* none for formation of complex sentences (and so no logical connectives); (iii) is incapable of expressing generality; (iv) has only one mood (imperative). Nevertheless, W. contends, it is a *complete* language.

In view of these serious limitations, one might well wonder whether W. rightly calls this 'a language'. For one may plausibly think that syntax is essential to language, since it is a prerequisite for the creative powers of language which distinguish arbitrary signs from symbols in a language. Equally, the possibility of truth and falsity is commonly thought to be essential to language, but, lacking logical constants and having no assertoric mood, this 'language' contains no possibility of truth and falsity, but only of compliance and non-compliance. Philosophers frequently assume that the assertoric mood and the true-false 'direction of fit' are the most fundamental, and that non-assertoric moods must be explained in terms of the assertoric. Finally, it is often thought that it is essential to language that it express thought. But does this 'language' have the power to express thoughts? Not every form of communication constitutes a language. It is not clear that a dog speaks a language, even if it is possible to derive information about who is walking up the garden path, or about the dog's desire to go for a run, from its growls, whimpers, barks, whines, etc.

A general reply to these qualms is given in §494. It may be that we would be inclined to withhold the term 'language' from this activity. But it is a rudimentary system of communication and is, in important ways, analogous to language. It shares and highlights significant features of language *stricto sensu*.

Other scattered remarks deal with the more specific objections. Whether this language-game lacks sentences, whether 'Slab' is a word or a sentence, is raised in PI §§19 f. and the general issue is discussed in §49. Certainly it lacks syntax, logical connectives, and quantifiers. Hence it lacks the generative possibilities typical of our language. That no more disqualifies it from counting as a language than does the fact that it consists only of orders (PI §§18 ff.). Z §§98 ff. and C §§396, 566 discuss the applicability of the concepts of thought and knowledge to the users of such a proto-language.

1.1   (i) 'one can also say that it is the idea of a language more primitive than ours': it would be over-hasty to conclude that the referential conception of meaning is correct for this primitive language. Rather, the picture of meaning that emerges from Augustine's description appears, at first glance, to fit the primitive language without strain (whereas further moves are necessary to make it fit a language containing numerals, connectives, second-level predicates, etc.).

(ii) 'Conceive this as a complete primitive language': not, of course, one that cannot be extended (cf. BB 77). There can be an incomplete description or an incomplete understanding of a language—but not an incomplete language. (This is an aspect of W.'s thesis of the autonomy of grammar.) No language is, as it were, incomplete *from within*—it is what it is. If it provides no means for a certain type of discourse, then it is silent. Our language was not incomplete before the introduction of the terminology and notation of chemistry. The fact that an extension of a system of communication is conceivable does not prove that in its unextended form it contains gaps. The possibility of advancing from a system of counting '1, 2, 3, 4, 5, many' to the system of the natural numbers does not show that the first system is incomplete, or contains only the possibility of an incomplete arithmetic (cf. Vol. IV, 152, PLP 78 f., BT 209). For further discussion, see Exg. §18.

2   (i) BT 25 ff.: strikingly, the language-game of §2 occurred to W. long before the method of language-games emerged. Here, the activity also encompasses specification of directions by correlation of letters and arrows in a table and of colours by a colour-chart.

(ii) Vol. X, Um. 35 (cf. PG 56): W. remarks that the concept of meaning *he* adopted in his (early) philosophy originates in a primitive philosophy of language. What we call 'meaning' (*Bedeutung*) seems to be connected with the primitive language of gestures. He crossed this last remark out, and added instead: the German word for 'meaning' 'Bedeutung' comes from the word for 'pointing' 'deuten'. It is not surprising, therefore, that the language of §2 was originally introduced here in association with pointing as an integral part of setting up the conventions of meaning. This is omitted in PI; perhaps because ostensive definition is part of the grammar of language, not of the language itself.

(iii) Z §98 ff. (in part = TS. 229, §1227, TS. 232, §§182 f. and 204; = MS. 132, 102, MS. 136, 45 f. and 99) contains a sustained discussion of thought in connection with §2. The builders may do their job thoughtfully or thoughtlessly, for thinking is not an inner quasi-verbal accompaniment of external activity.

Section 3

1.1   'Augustine . . . does describe a system of communication': an over-generous concession. Is Augustine's picture *correct* even for the language-game of §2? For reasons cited, this is doubtful.

2   (i) BT 25; PG 57: Augustine is said to describe a *calculus* of our language, only too restrictive a one. This formulation disappears as the calculus model of language is repudiated.

(ii) EBT 12 suggests, perhaps more cogently, that the way Augustine describes language-learning can show us from what primitive picture or world-picture this conception emerges. (This remark precedes what is now PI §4.)

Section 4

1   The analogy parodies the Augustinian picture. The misinterpretation of the script fails to distinguish the radically different *functions* of letters (sounds, emphasis, punctuation). So the Augustinian picture assimilates the functions of, e.g., 'red', 'run', 'perhaps', 'three', 'here', to that of words like 'cat', 'table', 'tree'.

The analogy is imperfect. The sanction for misinterpretation of the script is the production of a *false* (phonetic) reading. The sanction of the Augustinian picture is vacuity—a house of cards.

Section 5

1.1   (i) 'surrounds . . . with a haze': the shopkeeper example in §1 illustrates the ramifying confusion of conceiving of the meaning of a word as a corresponding entity.

(ii) 'clear vision', 'command a clear view' (*übersehen*): see 'Übersicht', p. 295.

(iii) 'phenomena of language in primitive kinds ˙of application': see 'Explanation', p. 32, and 'Language-games', p. 52 f.

(iv) 'The aim and functioning of the words': in §1. W. suggests that the point of a philosophical investigation of language is to get clear about the use of expressions in language. Here he adds the notion of purpose or aim. This might be interpreted to indicate his adherence to a 'communication-intention theory of meaning',[3] the view that linguistic meaning must ultimately be explained in terms of a speaker's aim or intention to communicate something to someone. This is not obviously a correct interpretation of PI. There is a general doubt whether he would allow as intelligible the notion of speakers' communicative intentions logically prior to and independent of the concept of linguistic meaning. Moreover, he ascribes aims or purposes (*Zwecke*) to *words*, not to speakers (§§6, 8; cf. §§317 (to *Sätze*), 345 (to orders)). This might be dismissed as metonymy. But it suggests that another interpretation should be sought, one that makes the purposes of linguistic expressions internal properties of the expressions.

(v) 'not explanation, but training': a crucial contrast; see 'Explanation', pp. 30 ff.

It is a philosopher's vice not to recognize the terminus of explanation and hence to continue to construct 'explanations' where none is possible (Z §§314 f., = B i. 40 and 434, = Vol. XI, 61 and Vol. XII, 39). We are unwilling to recognize that explanations and justifications come to an end, and we invent pseudo-explanations to give foundations to free-floating structures (e.g. Brouwer's intuitionist explanation of numbers in psychologistic terms (cf. PG 322)). This criticism is part of the negative force of the dictum that philosophy should be wholly descriptive (PI §109).

2   'Dispersing the fog': in BB 17 the point of the language-game method is said to be to disperse the fog of conceptual confusion.

---

[3] Cf. P. F. Strawson, 'Meaning and Truth', in *Logico-Linguistic Papers* (Metheun, London, 1971), p. 172.

Explanation
1. Introduction   2. Training, teaching, and explaining   3. Explanation and meaning   4. Explanation and grammar   5. Explanation and understanding

1   (a) is connected with the last sentence of §2. Two points are stressed: (i)
that the language of §2 can be conceived to be the whole language of a
group; (ii) that the use of the four words is integrated into the everyday
actions and reactions of the group. The whole form of life of which
communication is a part is relevant to the philosophical study of this
language. The corresponding general point is embedded in the expressions 'language-game' (cf. §7, and 'Language-game', pp. 54 ff.) and 'form
of life' (cf. Exg. §19).

        (b) introduces the primitive correlate of ostensive definition, namely
what W. calls 'ostensive teaching of words' (in BB 77 it is called
'demonstrative teaching'). The discussion applies the distinction between
training and explanation. Ostensive teaching is part of the training in the
use of words but does not amount to explanation since no doubts,
perplexities, or requests for clarification concerning word-meanings can
as yet arise. BB 77 stresses that the proto-language will indeed be
accompanied by drills as part of teaching and learning, e.g. the child may
just 'name' things when the teacher points to them or just repeat words
in order to learn to articulate them. In PI this point is deferred until §7.

        Ostensive teaching is an important part of training—*with human beings*.
It could be imagined otherwise. First, if we were born with the ability to
speak (as opposed to the ability to learn to speak), then ostensive teaching
of language would not exist. But ostensive *definition*, as an explanation of
the meaning of expressions, would still obtain in so far as giving an
appropriate one constituted a criterion of understanding. Secondly,
ostensive teaching involves pointing at objects, thereby directing the
child's attention. It is part of our nature to look in the direction of the
gesture, and not (like cats) at the gesturing limb (PG 94; PI §185). Were
this not so, the training would be different. We might go up to the object
and tap it, or smell it, etc.; or we might use illustrated tables (cf. PLP
107). Samples can be introduced other than by ostension, and ostensive
definition (as W. terms it) of proper names can be replaced by other kinds
of explanation (cf. 'Ostensive definition and its ramifications', p. 97).
W. insists upon the multiplicity of legitimate explanations.

        Ostensive teaching establishes an association between word and
object. This is a correct part of the Augustinian picture. But what is
the nature of the association? One natural conception is that hearing the
word will, by associative habit, call up a picture of the object in the mind

of the hearer. So the training is conceived of as designed to inculcate an associative habit. This picture underlies the conception of language-learning and meaning amongst many philosophers and psychologists.

It could be that such associative habits are generated. However, it is an empirical question whether or not the calling up of mental images is involved in the use of language; also whether or not mental images might facilitate the learning of such a language or increase the accuracy with which it is applied. The conclusions of such inquiries would be 'hypotheses' about the psychical mechanism underlying the use of language (BB 12). It could even be that the production of such associations is part of the purpose of an utterance, in which case uttering words *would be* like striking a note on the keyboard of the imagination. But it is not the purpose in the language of §2, which is rather to produce a behavioural response, namely to bring a slab or pillar to the builder, or, if one becomes a builder, to learn to utter these words with the intention that one's assistant should bring the object desired. Bringing a slab, using 'Slab!' in order to get another to bring a slab (as well as naming a slab, cf. §7 below) are the *criteria* for understanding the expression. (So does 'Slab' here mean the same as 'slab' in our language? cf. §20.)

On the Augustinian picture sentences are merely combinations of names, and hence understanding of a sentence results trivially from learning what objects it is that the different words in a language name. In this language, however, sentences are degenerate combinations of names; the production of the word 'Slab!' is itself a command. Hence, understanding of the order 'Slab!' should, on the Augustinian view, be the effect merely of the ostensive teaching of the word 'slab'. This, however, is not so, at least if how B reacts to orders determines whether he understands them or not. B's understanding of this order is not a trivial consequence of the ostensive teaching of the names in the slab-game. The Augustinian conception takes for granted the general structure of language and how it is used, finds that this needs supplementation by ostensive definition or teaching of names, and wrongly jumps to the conclusion that everything about language follows from the correlation of names with objects. If understanding of expressions is conceived as an effect of language-learning, then its cause is not ostensive teaching alone (cf. BB 69).

The idea that B understands the command 'Slab!' only if he acts upon it correctly by bringing a slab to A is the germ from which the causal theory of meaning grows. It suggests that the meaning of a command lies in its effects (PLP 111). The causal theory of meaning is frequently criticized by W. (e.g. Vol. VI, 94, cf. PLP Ch. VI). It seems to apply here due to a failure to grasp that behaviour in response to a command is a *criterion* for understanding it.

The mechanical analogy of (d) emphasizes the fact that ostensive teaching *alone* does not effect or bring about understanding. Only in the context of a particular training and circumstances will it be causally efficacious. There is a parallel to this for ostensive definition and explanation (and the lever analogy is invoked to illuminate a grammatical, not a causal point (cf. §12, PB 59)). Ostensive explanation gives a grammatical rule, and citing it is a *criterion* of understanding. But giving such an explanation does not *guarantee* that the hearer will understand, nor does it entail that the speaker knows the meaning of the explicandum. Here the point is logical, not causal.

2   PB 59: a lever is a lever only when connected up. This, interestingly, is a gloss on Frege's contextual dictum 'A word has a meaning only in the context of a sentence'.

2.1   'Uttering a word is like striking a note on the keyboard of the imagination': PG 152 ff. uses this metaphor to characterize W.'s earlier conception of thought. In NB and TLP language was indeed conceived to mediate between thought and the reality which it is about, and communication was pictured as playing on the keyboard of the mind.

3   It is striking that Coleridge employed a similar keyboard image in explaining what poets mean by the soul. The soul, he suggested, is conceived as a 'being inhabiting our body and playing upon it, like a musician enclosed in an organ whose keys were placed inwards' (*Letters*, i, 278).

Language-games
1. The emergence of the game analogy   2. The idea of a language-game   3. Invented language-games   4. Natural language-games

SECTION 7

1   §7(a) elaborates the point that the teaching of the language of §2 will contain the activities of naming on demand and repeating words (cf. BB 77).

§7(b) introduces the important notion of a language-game (see 'Language-games', pp. 51 ff.). Here the following points are stressed: (i) that the term 'language-game' is used to refer to the complex consisting of activity and language-use; (ii) that the training activity antecedent to the language-game of §2 is itself a language-game; (iii) that the use of language portrayed in §2 can be considered a model of initial language-learning. Indeed, it is a semiconscious prototype underlying the Augustinian picture of language in general.

Exploiting the classification of the essay 'Language-games' we can anatomize the language-game of §2.

(i) The distinction between word and sentence is drawn by reference to use. We can distinguish between ordering (in the building activity) and naming or repeating (in the learning activity). So 'slab' has a use as a word in the naming activity and as a sentence in the building activity.

(ii) The context of the game: (a) the participants are builder and assistant, adult and learner; (b) the essential activities without which the game cannot be played are building activities; (c) the essential objects are the building materials. It is curious that W. does not mention the over-all goal of the activity. There are, after all, different building activities: one may build for fun, because houses are needed, or for the glory of the gods, etc. This is not an irrelevant part of the context.

(iii) The game is to be considered complete.

(iv) The learning and training are itemized; they consist of learning to articulate and of giving the correct name on demand.

(v) Other than in teaching, the use of the elementary expressions of §2 is exclusively imperatival.

It is noteworthy that this language-game was constructed to provide a model which would exemplify the grounds for the temptation to think that a word means the object it names. Indeed it is true that if all the slabs, etc., were destroyed the language-game would be defunct. Yet even here it would still be wrong to equate the meaning of 'Slab' with a slab or the class of slabs.

1.1   (i) 'the practice of the use of language' ('die Praxis des Gebrauchs der

Sprache'), 'processes resembling language' ('sprachähnliche Vorgänge'): the intended contrast is between the use of language in the actual language-game and its similar use in training where no 'moves in the language-game' (other than in the language-game of teaching itself) are effected. W. translated 'beides sprachähnliche Vorgänge': 'both of these exercises already [being] primitive uses of language' (PPI (R) §10).

(ii) 'Spiele': 'games' in English is more restricted, see Exg. §66.

(iii) 'games like ring-a-ring o' roses': W. preferred 'nursery rhymes'.

SECTION 8

1   The expansion of language-game §2 diversifies the parts of speech of the language by adding: (i) primitive numerals, (ii) indexicals used with pointing gestures, (iii) colour samples. Consequently, a primitive syntax can be built up. Thus, 'd–slab–there', uttered while showing a colour sample, and pointing to a place when saying 'there', is grammatical. But 'slab–pillar–a–b–c–this–there', uttering 'there' without pointing, or showing a colour sample when saying 'there', are senseless.

The diversity of parts of speech introduces a further diversity of operations done by the speaker, i.e. producing samples and pointing. The amplified language-game now contains: (i) an enlarged vocabulary, (ii) syntactical structure, (iii) novel activities, i.e. matching objects to samples and pointing, (iv) new instruments, i.e. colour samples, gestures (in BB 79 numerals are also called instruments). Consequently, there are new criteria of understanding for the new parts of speech and for complex sentences thereby made possible.

1.1   (i) 'an expansion of language (2)': see Exg. §2, §18.

(ii) '"there" and "this" . . . that are used in connection with a pointing gesture': brings out the interpenetration of speech and non-linguistic activity (cf. §7). 'The pointing gesture in this case is part of the practice of communication itself' (BB 80). Cf. 'Indexicals', pp. 119 f.

(iii) 'samples': cf. 'Ostensive definition and its ramifications', pp. 97 ff.

(iv) The names in this game, unlike §15 below, are clearly sortals.

2   (i) BB 79 ff.: what in PI §8 is treated in one stage is here treated as a series of extensions, and each successive stage is discussed in some detail.

(ii) PLP 93 f. discusses a series of four language-games. The first is the slab-game of §2, and the final one corresponds exactly to the extension here in §8.

SECTION 9

1   Parallel to novel operations in the language-game involving application of the expanded vocabulary and 'instruments' are novel training tech-

niques which are relevant to philosophical concerns, e.g. memorizing the ordered series of numerals. Nothing corresponds to this in the first language-game. In W.'s view, learning the series of numerals by heart is an essential part, not only of this language-game, but also of the fully developed language of arithmetic.

Apart from this, the child must learn the use of numerals to count objects. What is the role of ostension in teaching a child to master the use of numerals? W. distinguishes two cases: first, where the number of objects can be taken in at a glance, and, second, where to establish their number one must count the objects. In the first case teaching the numerals is similar to ostensive teaching of many generic nouns and adjectives, though of course numerals are used very differently (see Exg. §§28–9, and 'Ostensive definition and its ramifications'). In the second case, however, one does not point at a group of slabs, but at each slab successively, each ostension being accompanied by utterance of a numeral (in the appropriate order). This kind of case illustrates the necessity for memorizing the series of numerals as 'one of the essential features of learning this language' (BB 79).

The role of ostension in training in the use of indexicals is again quite different, because the ostensive gesture is *itself* part of the indexical *use* of 'this' or 'there' and not merely part of teaching their use. When the child learns the use of 'slab', one exercise is to learn to *name* building elements which the teacher points out. But in learning the indexical use of 'this' and 'these', he is not learning to name anything. (Cf. Exg. §38 and 'Indexicals', pp. 123 f.)

1.1   PPI rightly inserts quotation marks around 'a' 'b' 'c' in *l*. 2.

2   (i) BB 80 alludes to Russell's view that such words as 'this', 'here', 'now' are logically proper names. Here this is deferred until §§38 ff.

(ii) PLP 105 distinguishes between the categories of 'visual number' and 'inductive number', arguing that ostensive definition of numerals is possible only for the first class.

(iii) PLP 95f. makes the point that the gesture is applied in the use of language in connection with 'here' and 'there'. But there the explanation is given that 'the gesture of pointing is part of the expression of the command, it is essential to its sense, i.e. the words of the command without the gesture would be incomplete'. The *words* 'a-slab-there!' do not express the whole sense of A's command to put a slab in a particular place.

SECTION 10

1   The moral of the two language-games is drawn. Augustine claimed that by hearing words used in their proper places in sentences, he 'learnt to

understand what objects they *signified'*. This, in philosophy, may lead one
to demand that explanations of meaning assume the form 'The word "ξ"
signifies ξ'. This in turn forces a uniformity upon diverse types of
expression, and obscures the nature of language and so of our language-
using ability. Of course, one can say '"Red" signifies the colour red',
'"One" signifies the number one', etc., but that will merely make it
appear as if all words function in a similar way (as indeed all are written
or spoken!).

There is, to be sure, *a* use of this misleading canonical form—namely
to distinguish *between* different types of expression, e.g. '"a" "b" "c"
signify numbers not building-blocks', or to distinguish *within* categories,
e.g. '"c" signifies 3 not 4'. But in both kinds of case a general grasp of the
mode of signification, the use, of the type of expression is presupposed, and
not explained, by the canonical form.

2   BB 82 argues that just as we are tempted by the canonical form 'The
word "ξ" signifies . . .', so too we are tempted by the canonical form
' "ξ" is the name of a . . .'; e.g. we talk of names of numbers, colours,
materials, nations. W. suggests two sources. One is an illusion of
uniformity of function (perhaps derived from *apparent* uniformity of
ostensive explanation). The other, more subtle, stems from noticing the
differences of function between say 'chair' and 'Jack' and between 'east'
and 'Jack', and so noticing the analogy in the lack of analogy.

SECTION 11

1   The salient point of the tool analogy is diversity of function, despite
similarities and interconnections. A screwdriver looks similar to an
auger, but one makes a hole, the other screws a screw into a hole. Both
are connected with screws (screws cannot be used without screwdrivers),
but their roles are vastly different. So too with words (cf. Vol. XII,
217).

The analogy can be criticized on the grounds that tools work on the
world in isolation, whereas words have to be assembled to constitute a
move in a language-game. Disregarding one-word sentences, the reply
which will preserve the analogy consists of noting the wide use of 'tool'
to include, e.g., screws and nails. Moreover, just as there can be a
pre-training in use of words which is antecedent to using words to any
purpose (e.g. learning the series of natural numbers), so too there is a
pre-training in the use of tools, e.g. learning to use a saw or to hammer a
nail without actually mending or making anything.

(b) connects §11 with §§10 and 12. The uniform spatial or temporal
sequence of written or spoken words makes them look alike and does not
make evident the diversity of their application. Hence it is so difficult,

especially in philosophy, to obtain a surview. For in philosophy we labour under illusions about, or hanker for, uniform explanations of meaning (cf. §10) and try to discover a unique 'name-relation'. Contrast this uniform appearance of our symbols with the language-game of §8, or the example of §1, where the application of different types of symbol *is* overt in their use.

1.1   (i) 'Werkzeuge': tools; it is unnatural, in English, to refer to nails, screws and glue as tools. Not so in German: to classify, e.g. glue, as belonging to *Werkzeug* (used as a mass-noun) is quite normal. By using the plural, 'Werkzeuge', W. indicates that what is part of your *Werkzeug* is also one of your *Werkzeuge*. He did, however, transfer this German usage to English (LA 1).

(ii) 'Denn ihre *Verwendung* steht nicht so deutlich vor uns': W. translated 'their *use* is not so clearly there before our eyes' (PPI (R) §15).

Section 12

1   This picks up the point of deceptive uniformity of appearance. The handles in the locomotive cabin look alike, since they are made to be handled, as words are made to be sequentially spoken or written; but their mode of operation differs profoundly.

2   (i) Other favoured analogies for the diversity of function of different parts of speech are: (a) lines on a map, which may indicate rivers, roads, borders, railways, isotherms, contour lines, etc., despite the fact that they look alike (PG 58); (b) chessmen, which are all similar pieces of carved wood, but have very different functions (PG 59)—a feature brought out by reflection on the fact that the *chessboard*, no less than the chess pieces, is an element in the game.

(ii) PR 59 invokes the lever analogy (a) to exemplify, as here, the diverse functions of words; (b) to exemplify the contextual dictum that a word has a meaning only in the context of a sentence (a rod is a lever only in use, when connected up; cf. PI §6 (d)); (c) to illuminate what it is to understand a proposition as a member of a system of propositions. This is akin to seeing the lever of a four-gear gearbox as *having* four (possible) positions, even though it only occupies one at a time.

(iii) PG 58 contains a noteworthy juxtaposition. While words, like locomotive handles, look alike despite their diverse functions, they are 'experienced' differently:

A man who reads a sentence in a familiar language experiences the different parts of speech in quite different ways. (Think of the comparison with meaning-bodies.) We quite forget that the written and spoken words 'not', 'table', 'green' are similar to each other. It is only in a foreign language that we see clearly the uniformity of words. (Compare William James on the feelings that correspond to words like 'not', 'but', and so on.)

This latter theme (experiencing the meaning of a word) is deferred in PI. The analogy holds, nevertheless. One might say of the locomotive driver that the brake feels different from the pump, the crank, the valve-lever, etc. Not so to the child who clambers up to play. The different experience, one might say, is an epiphenomenon of the ability to use the levers (words) correctly.

SECTION 13

1   W. stresses the vacuity of the dictum 'Every word in language signifies something', itself derived from the misleading canonical form 'The word "ξ" signifies ξ' (cf. Exg. §10). The criticism here is that no principle of distinction (contrast) is drawn by this statement, unless it is between words of the language and nonsense words like 'Lilliburlero'.

Note that the dictum is not criticized as false. For, given the canonical form, virtually every word can be put into the strait-jacket: e.g. 'red' signifies a colour, 'three' signifies a number, 'and' signifies a function. The dictum is vacuous, and also misleading, for it assimilates what should be kept apart.

2   PLP 157 significantly rejects the dictum as false since 'Oh dear!' cannot be put into the canonical form, yet it would be false to say that it is meaningless, or has no significance. It is used, he says, as a 'vocal vent'. Similarly, a full stop has a use, but does not signify an object. PLP here reflects W.'s *early* moves against the calculus model of language (cf. discussion of 'perhaps' and 'Oh!' (PG 64, 66)).

SECTION 14

1   Straightforward.

SECTION 15

1   There is, however, a natural, non-philosophical use of 'signify': a label or nameplate (*Namentäfelchen*) can be said to signify that the object to which it is attached is what the nameplate says it is.

1.1   (i) 'Am direktesten ist das Wort "bezeichnen" vielleicht da angewandt. . . .': W. preferred 'The expression "the name of an object" is very straightforwardly applied where the name is actually a mark on the object itself' (PPI (R) §19).

(ii) 'naming something is like attaching a label to a thing': this nameplate analogy is misleading. It is unclear from §15 whether the analogy concerns proper names or sortals. §41 stresses that §15 introduces proper names to the language-game of §8. But in §26 explicitly, and in §§8, 10 tacitly (as well as in PG 97, BB 69) it is evident that the analogy is intended to apply to sortals too. Given that a central criticism of Augustine's picture is its assimilation of all nouns to a misguided conception of proper names (and of throughgoing Augustinian theories of meaning that they extend this assimilative tendency to all expressions), it is strange that W. should use the nameplate analogy both for proper names and for sortals. Why does he? It is part of his strategy in demystifying the so-called 'name-relation', in particular for dispelling the illusion that it is essentially 'in the mind'. In BB 69 we are to imagine that 'objects' are labelled with names that we use to refer to them. Some of these words would be proper names, others would be generic names, others names of colours, shapes, etc. This diversity makes it clear that 'a label would only have a meaning to us in so far as we made a particular use of it.' But one can readily see that the fact that everything is labeled may so impress us that we forget that what gives the words on the labels their meanings is not that they are stuck on objects, but their use.

This employment of the label analogy is very general indeed; the point made concerns all words: to have meaning is not to stand for or signify an object, but to be used in a certain way. However, just because of its generality the labelling or nameplate analogy loses its force. In GB it is used more narrowly to cast light on the role and function of proper names and there it is powerfully evocative. It suggests aspects of proper names (especially of persons) completely neglected by philosophers and quite different from the common picture of the name/bearer relation. A name can readily be conceived as sacred to a man, for it is both the most important instrument given to him, and also akin to a piece of jewellery hung around his neck at birth (GB 32). We explore this theme in 'Proper names' (pp. 245 ff.).

SECTION 16

This discusses the status of the samples employed in language-game §8. They are supposed to have a definite role in the activity. Whenever A issues an order of the type 'd—slab—there', he shows B a colour sample, and B then selects slabs of this colour from the stock of building materials. The samples are used as part of issuing individual orders, not once for all to explain colour-words; indeed, there are no colour-words in this language-game, only colour samples.

W. recommends counting these samples as instruments 'belonging to' the language-game §8. This particular move is a special case of a general recommendation helpful for obtaining an *Übersicht* of language, especially by making a first step towards undermining the misconception that ostensive definitions, by explaining expressions by reference to samples, connect language with reality. Moreover, in certain respects W.'s proposal is entirely natural. If I send someone a sample in placing an order for cloth of a certain colour, this sample is obviously part of my communication (PR 73). It is a sign or symbol, not something symbolized or described (cf. PLP 109, 277 f.). An argument supporting this classification of such samples as symbols is that their role could be discharged by words, which are clearly symbols. Language-game §8 could be enriched, e.g. by introducing colour-words explained by reference to the samples, and thereafter these words could take over the function of the samples. It would seem counter-intuitive to deny that a colour sample is a sign if it can be replaced by a word without affecting what is communicated. Hence it is natural to call any sample playing a role in communication an instrument of *communication*, but does this mean that it belongs to the *language* or that it is an instrument of *language*? Of course, colour samples are not words, and a sample used *ad hoc* for a particular communication is not governed by standing rules and hence lacks any grammar. None the less, they are signs used in communication. W. recommends extending the term 'language' ('Sprache') to include 'everything that serves the end of expression and communication' (PLP 93), hence everything that counts as a sign (PLP 93 f., 109). This is apparent in his contrasting *Sprache* with *Wortsprache* ('language' with 'spoken language').

W. counters the natural objection to his extension of 'language' with an analogical argument. Although a colour sample, e.g. a coloured bit of paper, is not a word, i.e. it is not part of our *spoken* language (PPI (R) §20), we naturally count as a word, and hence as part of a sentence, a *mentioned* word used as a sample sound for pronunciation (e.g. 'Pronounce the word "the"'). In this use the mentioned word does not function in accord with its ordinary grammar but rather as a sample, and hence its role is exactly parallel to that of the coloured bit of paper. The inclination to think that a sharp boundary separates samples that belong to our language from those that do not can be countered by interpolating a series of intermediate cases: e.g. 'Pronounce "abracadabra"', 'Write the symbol ⬡', 'Say "per impossibile"', 'Pronounce "ἐπιθυμία"', 'Say "ugh"', 'Repeat after me "Rule Britannia, Britannia rule the waves"' [singing], 'Sing this note [singing middle-C]'. Of course, we might then deny that '"the"' in the order 'Pronounce "the"' belongs to our language since it there functions as a sample. But W. urges the opposite course, viz. to count all of these examples as parts of our language even though some are not English words and others not words (or mere words) at all. The crucial point is that no gulf divides words from samples (or patterns (cf. BB 84)).

The remark alluded to in the final parenthesis cannot be positively identified, perhaps because it was never written. There are only two clues as to its content: first, the phrase '*this* sentence', which occurs in W.'s discussion of the Cretan Liar Paradox (PR 207 f.; Vol. X, 19 = Z §691; B i. §735), and, secondly, the context, viz. the discussion of samples and of their being counted as instruments of language. This information is enough to make a reasonable conjecture about what W. had in mind. In language-game §8, A uses colour samples to tell B what colour of building stone to select from the stack. This language-game might be extended by introducing a demonstrative expression 'this colour' to be used in conjunction with a gesture of pointing at one of the colour samples or by introducing colour-words (e.g. 'red' or 'brown') by means of ostensive definitions by reference to the samples. In the first case, uttering the words 'this colour', together with a gesture and a sample, take the place of the showing of a colour sample in the primitive game. In the second, the colour-words are written signs that are *representatives* of what is pointed to in the ostensive definitions, viz. the samples (cf. PG 89). To call these words 'representatives' implies that they can, at least in certain cases, perform as well as, and hence stand in place of, what they represent (PG 89; PLP 311 f.). Conversely, what is represented must be capable of replacing the representatives; in particular, the explanation of the colour-word must be capable of replacing the word itself (cf. PG 99). In both extensions of language-game §8, the new signs (viz. demonstratives + gestures + samples and colour-words) *replace* the samples of the unextended language-game, and hence they can be 'cashed' in terms of these samples. W. applies this idea to the phrase 'this sentence'. If correctly used, it must *represent* some sentence; i.e. it must hold the place of a sentence as a card with 'Mr Jones' written on it represents Mr Jones by holding his place at a dinner table (PLP 312). Therefore, it must be possible to replace this reflexive phrase by the sentence that it represents. In some cases, this is unproblematic. Consider the sentence 'This sentence is ten centimetres long'; this is equivalent to '"This sentence is ten centimetres long" is ten centimetres long', and measuring the mentioned sentence will determine its truth-value. Similarly, 'This sentence contains five words' is clearly true, and 'This sentence is written in Gothic script', clearly false (B i. §735). But what about the paradoxical sentence 'This sentence is false'? If it has a meaning, then the phrase, 'this sentence' must represent some sentence and hence be replaceable by this sentence. But what sentence? The answer cannot be simply to repeat that it refers to *this* sentence, but it must take the form of uttering a complete sentence which will take the place of the phrase '*this* sentence' in 'This sentence is false' (Z §691). This cannot be done, for in this context

'This sentence is false' cannot be substituted once for all for the phrase 'this sentence', since the same question crops up again, viz. what sentence is represented in the new, more complex, sentence by the phrase 'this sentence'. Hence, the fundamental error lies in thinking that the phrase 'this sentence' can refer to a sentence, as it were from a distance, without having to represent it (PR 207 f.; Z §691). That idea is as absurd as the thought that a sample used to explain a colour-word could not take the place of this word in communication. W.'s view is not that all self-reference is incoherent; instead, he demands simply that it be explained how we are to use the phrase 'this sentence' in our language-game. This can be done: e.g. the sentence 'This sentence contains five words' might be used as a paradigm of the number five. Any such use of the phrase 'this sentence' involves using the sentence containing it as a sample (in a way parallel to the use of the quoted word 'the' as a sample in W.'s analogy). A sentence seems paradoxical only when it is divorced from its use (B i. §735).

SECTION 17

1   In the description of language (8), W. distinguishes different kinds of words. This turns on the degree of resemblance or difference in the function of words. It also depends on the aim of our classification and, perhaps, on what strikes us as important.

This conception of what a kind (type, category) of words is contrasts with that implicit in the Augustinian picture. There category distinctions are read off from the essential natures of the things correlated with the words of language. They are given ineluctably and independently of us. Two words belong to the same category if, and only if, they are correlated with objects sharing the same essential properties. Here, by contrast, category distinctions are the shifting product of our particular purposes in classification and of our discrimination of degree of kinship in the use of words.

This conception is also at odds with the standard construction of categories according to the criterion of substitutability *salva significatione*. That assigns two expressions to the same category if, and only if, the substitution of one for the other in the context of any sentence leaves its meaningfulness unchanged (but not necessarily its meaning). Categories so constructed are equivalence-classes. Hence, the categories to which two expressions 'x' and 'y' belong either coincide or are disjoint. (Cf. PM i. 95—'the axiom of identification of type'.) By contrast, W. envisages classification of words into kinds according to the degree of kinship in their functions. This will allow the shading off of one category into another, i.e. non-transitivity of the relation '"x" belongs to the same category as "y"'.

1.1   Different points of view from which one can classify chessmen: e.g. by
their powers; by the directions of their permitted movements; by their
order of value; not to mention 'irrelevant' classifications such as size,
constitutive material, colour, etc. (cf. BB 84). The usefulness of a given
grouping depends on our purposes and inclinations (ivory chessmen are
more costly than plastic ones).

2   PLP 96 ff. comments on 'kinds of words' (parts of speech). The test of
substitutability *salva significatione* makes the construction of categories
pointless. It has some initial plausibility: e.g. the order 'Put the ξ in the
corner!' relegates 'surface of the table' and 'table' to different categories.
But this evaporates once we note that it would segregate 'black' from
'green', 'red', and 'white' (e.g. 'The signal light flashed ξ') and each
numeral from every other (e.g. '1' from '2', '3', '4' . . . by reference to
'The playground was divided into ξ parts').

Waismann too emphasizes the analogy with tools. Tools have a variety
of different kinds of similarity, and can be differently grouped (the
hammer with the nails, or with the axe; the axe with the hammer, or
with the chisel, or with the saw; the screwdriver with the screw, or with
the auger). So too with words; different purposes and overlapping
similarities of different kinds make possible various different groupings.

The uses of sentences
1. Introduction   2. Descriptions and facts   3. Disguised descriptions
and analysis   4. Last refuge   5. The illusion of uniformity
6. Sentences as instruments   7. The uses of sentences   8. Assertions,
questions, commands make contact in language

SECTION 18

1   This is addressed to the proponent of the Augustinian picture. He might
be troubled in various ways by the fact that language-games (2) and (8)
consist only of orders. (i) Given that sentences, being combinations of
names, have a uniform use (as descriptions), how is it possible for a
language to contain orders, still less to consist only of orders? Here his
worry would be the (uniform) non-descriptive use of these sentences.
(ii) Given that all sentences are essentially descriptions, orders must themselves be capable of being exhibited as descriptions or as containing
descriptions. How is this possible within language-games not containing
any assertions? Here his worry would be the limited *resources* of these
language-games, i.e. the impossibility of paraphrasing apparently non-
descriptive uses of sentences. (iii) Given that all sentences are descriptions
or can be so analysed that they contain descriptions, how can a language
contain the possibility of constructing orders without also containing the
possibility of constructing assertions? Here the worry would be the
closure of a language consisting only of orders.
      W. envisages the proponent's objecting that the languages (2) and (8)
are incomplete. This strategy constitutes a coherent defence of the
Augustinian picture only if the objector's worry is either (ii) or (iii). W.'s
reply makes clear that he treats (ii) as the background to the objection. He
does not discuss any principle of closure (e.g. whether it must be possible
within any language containing a command to describe what would
constitute obedience to this command) and simply describes without
argument other equally problematic possibilities (§19(a)). What he
discusses are the implications of extending the resources of a language by
adding new notations or language-games to existing ones. Extending a
language does not show that it was previously incomplete. Neither does
the possibility of extending it. Any language can be extended indefinitely
by adjoining new language-games (§23) (this is an aspect of the
autonomy of grammar). If the possibility of extending a language proved
that it was incomplete, there would be no such things as a language that
was not incomplete, and hence the word 'incomplete' would be meaningless if used in this way.

1.1   (i) The symbolism of chemistry and the notation of the infinitesimal
calculus: the imaginary critic infers from the fact that something more
can be said in an extended language than could be said in its unextended
form that before the extension it contained gaps. Clearly, the invention

of the symbolism of chemistry and of the notation of the infinitesimal calculus have extended our language in such a way. They allow us to frame such questions as 'What is the valency of the carbon atom?' or 'What is the derivative of arc sin x?' But these possibilities no more show that our unextended everyday discourse about the world contains gaps than the fact that there is a possibility of extending a pawn-less form of chess to the usual variety shows that this primitive game contains gaps waiting to be filled by the extension. We think that the unextended language (or game) contains *gaps* in so far as we are prone to view it relative to the extended one. If the extension is radical (i.e. there is disruption of the preceding internal relations), then there are possibilities not permitted in the previous form, but then the disruption of internal relations shows that the language (or game) is simply *different*. And if the extension is conservative, then there is nothing but a further articulation of a pre-existing framework, i.e. antecedent permissions and prohibitions are preserved intact.

(ii) 'before a town begins to be a town': given that extending a language is not conceived as filling in gaps, the only objection left is that a language consisting only of orders is 'too small' to be a language.

2   (i) BT 209 identifies the relation of a language consisting only of commands to our actual language with the relation of a primitive arithmetic (e.g. the number system '1', '2', '3', '4', '5', 'many') to our arithmetic (of the natural numbers). The moral: 'just as the arithmetic is not essentially incomplete, neither is this primitive form of language.'

The completeness of such a primitive number system is an important point (PG 321 f.; PLP 78 f.; cf. Vol. IV, 152): there are no gaps in such a system, waiting to be filled by extending it to include all the natural numbers. Similarly, the natural numbers do not contain gaps to be filled by rationals, nor rationals gaps to be filled by reals, etc. Rather, there are, as it were, no gaps until they are already filled. (For a less paradoxical, more exact, account, see EMD 45–7, 61.) This is another dimension of the autonomy of grammar. W.'s view contrasts with the thesis that arithmetic containing natural numbers admits the possibility of defining addition, subtraction, multiplication, and division as well as the possibility of constructing the signed integers and the rationals so that these operations are well defined on every pair of natural numbers (except for division by zero). On that view the natural numbers are not a complete system of numbers because they are not closed under the four basic arithmetical operations. W.'s contention that every system of numbers is complete and self-contained amounts to a rejection of this idea that there are any mathematical closure principles for such systems. The generalization of this point is that there are no metalogical principles of closure for languages. Every language is, as it stands, complete and self-contained; it contains no gaps. Consequently, the third worry of the defender of the Augustinian picture is nonsensical.

(ii) PG 112 f. introduces a language consisting only of commands for the different purpose of repudiating the thesis that no doubt is possible about how to apply the term 'proposition' (*Satz*).

3   (i) The contention that a language could consist only of orders is a radical one because contemporary analyses of meaning make the concept of truth and the notion of truth-conditions (or assertion-conditions) the pivotal ideas for their general accounts. But the notion of truth (*a fortiori* assertion-conditions) attaches paradigmatically to the declarative sentence (or, perhaps, to an underlying 'sentence-radical'). To the extent that attention is directed to non-declarative sentences, there is a general presumption that an account of their sense can be produced by reference to the sense of the corresponding declarative sentences (e.g. descriptions of the obedience-conditions of commands). It thus seems doubtful whether we can make sense of the notion of giving orders in a language in which the obedience-conditions of the orders cannot be described with the resources of the language. For it must be possible, it is thought, to recognize the conditions in which an order is executed and to distinguish them from those in which it is disobeyed.

W. does *not* directly discuss this issue, though his remarks may have implications for contemporary developments in the philosophy of language. It does not follow, however, from the fact that a language consisting only of imperatives is conceivable that the notion of assertion is not pivotal in the analysis of the sense of sentences in *our* language.

(ii) 'an ancient city': Boltzmann (whose writings had a seminal influence on W.) uses the same analogy to illustrate the growth of science: 'In early centuries, science advanced steadily but slowly through the work of the most select minds, just as an old town constantly grows through new buildings put up by industrious and enterprising citizens.'[4]

SECTION 19

1   (a) continues the argument of §18. (They were combined into a single remark in PPI.) Any language-game is complete. Hence there is no limit to the range of possible languages. A language might consist only of orders and reports in battle; of sentence-questions and devices for

---

[4] 'On the Development of the Methods of Theoretical Physics in Recent Times', in *Ludwig Boltzmann: Theoretical Physics and Philosophical Problems,* ed. B. McGuinness, tr. P. Foulkes (Reidel, Dordrecht, Holland, 1974), p. 77.

positive and negative answers; etc. Imagining such languages requires imagining different forms of life, i.e. different patterns of activity and different ways of integrating speaking into these activities.

(b) opens a new argument. It implicitly raises an objection, viz. that 'Slab!' in language (2) does not have the same meaning which it has in our language. (BB 77 makes this objection explicit.) Is 'Slab!' in §2 a word or a sentence? If a word, it has a different use from our word 'slab'. If a sentence, it cannot have the same meaning as our elliptical sentence 'Slab!' (A speaker in §2 cannot have in his mind the sentence 'Bring me a slab!' and hence cannot mean this by 'Slab!' Therefore, 'Slab!' does not have the same meaning in §2 as in our language.)

W.'s response is that 'Slab!' is both a word and a sentence. Moreover, it *is* equivalent to our ellipitical sentence 'Slab!' (since it has the same function in language-game §2 as 'Bring me a slab!' would have in the corresponding fragment of our language).

In (b) the objector invokes the same picture of a person's meaning something or wanting something as consisting in his saying to himself a sentence expressing what he means or what he wants. This move is to support the view that a speaker of language (2) cannot mean by 'Slab!' what we mean since he cannot say to himself 'Bring me a slab!' or 'I want him to bring me a slab!'. W. queries the picture in several ways.

Although (b) raises the problem whether 'Slab!' in the language-game of §2 is a word or sentence, it does not focus on this issue nor argue for its answer. (The problem is more directly discussed in §49.) Rather, the distinction is invoked obliquely to strengthen the objection that 'Slab!' in §2 does not have the same meaning as the elliptical sentence 'Slab!' in *our* language (BB 77). The debate focuses on the question whether a person's meaning something by a sentence must always consist in his saying to himself another sentence expressing what he means.

1.1   'form of life': this notorious expression occurs in PI §§19, 23, 241, pp. 174, 226, and also C §§358 f. The actual term apart, there is no reason to associate W.'s use of it with Spranger's *Lebensformen* (the English translation of which, appropriately, has the title *Types of Men*). If we wish to search for an influence here by far the most likely is Spengler:

... the words *History* and *Nature* are here employed ... in a quite different and hitherto unusual sense. These words comprise *possible* modes of understanding, of comprehending the totality of knowledge ... as a homogeneous, spiritualized, well-ordered *world-picture* ... The possibilities that we have of possessing an 'outer world' that reflects and attests our proper existence are infinitely numerous and exceedingly heterogeneous. ... One condition of this higher world-consciousness is the possession of *language*, meaning thereby not mere human utterance but a culture-language.[5]

[5] Oswald Spengler, *The Decline of the West*, tr. C. F. Atkinson (Allen and Unwin, London, 1932), Vol. I, p. 55.

It is noteworthy that in BB 134 imagining a language is equated with
imagining a culture. Switching to 'form of life' rightly reduces reference
to the indefinitely complex superstructure which characterizes a language
together with its varied uses in the activities of a linguistic community,
and draws attention to the underlying consensus of linguistic and
pre-linguistic behaviour which is presupposed by the language.

The notion of a form of life is connected with that of a language-game,
but is more general and elemental. A form of life is a given unjustified
and unjustifiable pattern of human activity (part of human natural
history (PI §25)). It rests upon, but is not identical with, very general
pervasive facts of nature. It consists of shared natural and linguistic
responses, of broad agreement in definitions and in judgements, and of
corresponding behaviour.

A language perforce contains moves which are not justified by
reference to anything, but are simply accepted as appropriate, as a
common pattern of linguistic behaviour by reference to which other
moves are justified. Equally, any cognitive claims, as well as any doubts,
occur within a framework of propositions that are not doubted, that
belong to the frame of reference of the system of knowledge (propositions of the *Weltbild*). Training in what counts as justification, acceptance
of undoubted truths of the world-picture, is acculturation in the form of
life of a community.

2   BT 201 ff. (cf. EBT 594 ff.; Vol. XI, 81 ff.; PLP 285–8) discusses the
notion of an elliptical sentence (and the distinction between meaning 'I
have toothache' as one word or as three words, i.e. the problem of PI §20).
The discussion focuses on one-word sentences in order to criticize TLP's
conception of a proposition's 'agreeing with reality' in virtue of
isomorphism (and hence to repudiate the necessary logical multiplicity of
the atomic proposition). W. introduces a language-game in which the
expressions 'Light' and 'Dark' are taught in connection with turning an
electric light on and off, and then used to say that there is light in the
room or to express the wish that there be light in the room, etc. One
could say that 'Light' and 'Dark' are meant here as sentences. Agreement
with reality does not consist in the proposition and reality having
identical multiplicity, but in the explanation (in language) that 'This is (is
called) "Light"', or 'This agrees with "Light"' (turning the light on
when uttering 'This'). What seemed in TLP to be an ineffable ('metalogical') relationship between language and reality is now seen to be an
intra-linguistic grammatical relationship, i.e. 'to agree with reality' is an
everyday expression with an unproblematic use.

2.1   RC §302: 'Would it be correct to say that our concepts reflect our life?
They stand in the middle of it.'

SECTION 20

1   This opens with an objection arising out of the discussion in §19(b).
There W. suggested that the sentence 'Bring me a slab!' might be
considered a lengthening of the sentence 'Slab!' If so, one might now
retort, someone who says 'Bring me a slab!' must be able to mean this
whole sentence as *one* word. The rest of (a) consists of W.'s raising and
answering a series of questions that grow out of this objection. The point
of the dialogue is to establish that the contrast between a person's
meaning 'Bring me a slab!' as four words and his meaning it as one word
need not consist in anything present in his mind when he utters the
sentence. Instead, what is required is his mastery of a language in which
this sentence can be used in contrast with other sentences consisting
partly or wholly of the same words. Therefore the objection in (a), like
the previous worry in §19(b), rests on identifying meaning something
by a sentence with mental accompaniments of uttering it.
    §20(b) applies these considerations to clarify the claim in §19(b) that
'Slab!' in language-game §2 is (synonymous with) the elliptical sentence
'Slab!' in our language. Our sentence is elliptical, not because it abbrevi-
ates a 'mental utterance' of the corresponding sentence 'Bring me a slab!',
but because our language contains the possibility of contrasting the
sentences 'Bring me a slab!', 'Take away a slab!', 'Bring him a slab!', etc.,
each of which might, in certain circumstances, be shortened to 'Slab!'.
    (b) then canvasses an objection: if 'Slab!' in §2 is synonymous with
our sentence 'Slab!', and hence too with our sentence 'Bring me a slab!',
then it must be possible to say what the sense is that each of these
sentences has. How, then, is this sense to be formulated? The implicit
assumption of this objection is that there must be some privileged form
for expressing the sense of any sentence; i.e. that there must be a verbal
formulation which completely expresses the sense of a sentence simply by
virtue of its *form*. W.'s reply is that there is no such formulation: the sense
of a sentence depends on how it is used. Hence, given an understanding
of how they are used, *both* of the sentences 'Slab!' and 'Bring me a slab!'
are complete verbal formulations of their sense.
    The final parenthesis ridicules the idea that the verbal expression for
the sense of 'Slab!' is to be sought in the 'language of thought'.

1.1   (i) '*our language* contains the possibility of those other sentences': not
merely hypothetically, i.e. as something we could *calculate* if we wanted
(e.g. the possibility of iterated relative clauses, as in 'The stone which the
man whom the chicken which the boy beat pecked threw hit the tree'),
but a possibility we constantly exploit.
    (ii) Note W.'s talk of use of *sentences* in (b). (See 'The uses of sentences',
pp. 68 ff.)

2   BB 78 makes clear the connection of PI §20 with §19 and hence with
§18. BT 11, PG 51, and PI §502 indicate a harder line on the request for
the 'verbal expression' of the sense of a sentence, viz. that it makes no
sense to ask what sense is expressed by the sentence (unless this is
construed as a request for an explanation of the sentence, e.g. by
paraphrasing it). In saying that 'Slab!' and 'Bring me a slab!' have the
same sense, one has already given an answer to the question 'What does
"Slab!" mean?', viz. 'Bring me a slab!'

SECTION 21

1   W. now turns to language-games admitting contrasting uses of
sentences (as in §19(a)). If the slab-game in §§2 and 8 is extended to include
reports on the numbers, colours, and shapes of stacks of building
materials, what would distinguish such reports from orders?
      Two answers are open to a defender of the Augustinian picture.
      (i) The distinction is in the grammatical forms or intonation-contours
of these sentences. Reports must differ from commands in surface
grammatical structure. W. replies that this need not be so. We can
imagine the report and the order to have the same form (viz. 'Five slabs')
and even to be uttered with the same intonation; here the difference
would be solely in their applications. Moreover, the correlations of
orders, assertions, and questions with certain grammatical forms and
intonation-contours are quite contingent; they could easily be imagined
to be otherwise than they are, e.g. requests could have the form and
intonation typical of questions in standard English. Hence the explanation of such distinctions among sentences must be sought in some other
direction.
      (ii) The distinction is in what the speaker *means* in uttering a sentence.
He must mean something different when he uses 'Five slabs' as an order
from what he means in using it as a report. This difference is something
present in his mind, something psychological. W. does not directly
discuss this suggestion here. Instead, he states a view about the difference
between orders and reports that stands to this suggestion in the same
relation that his account in §20(a) stands to the parallel suggestion about
the difference between meaning the sentence 'Bring me a slab!' as one
word and as four. Of course, a speaker does mean something different by
uttering 'Five slabs' as an order from what he means by uttering it as a
report, but the difference consists in his mastery of the practices of using
these sentences in different ways, not in something present in his mind.
      The difference between assertions, commands, and questions lies in the
use or application of sentences, in the 'part which uttering these words
plays in the language-game'. For obvious reasons, basic distinctions in

function are commonly marked by surface features (word, word-order, intonation-contour, punctuation, etc.). But these distinctions do not consist in differences in these features.

1.1   'Behauptung' should be translated uniformly throughout §§21–4 (presumably 'assertion', as in PPI (R) §§26–31). So should 'Praxis', cf. §7.

2   (i) BT 201 ff. (cf. Exg. §19), in describing the language-game in which 'Light' can be used either to express a desire for light or to report that there is light in a particular room, raises the question whether the difference consists in what is meant in the two cases. Does meaning something consist in particular mental processes that accompany the utterance or in a pattern of behaviour in which the utterance is embedded? If I say 'Light' and somebody asks what I meant, I might reply 'I meant you to turn on the light'. But my having meant this does not consist in my having had a particular picture in mind when I said 'Light', nor in my having said to myself another sentence such as 'Turn on the light'. That would give a narrow distorted account of the variety of cases in which it is correct to say 'I meant . . .'.

(ii) Vol. XI, 82 elaborates the theme that there is a great variety of cases in which one can say 'I meant . . .', i.e. that my having meant something may consist in many different things. Perhaps in uttering 'Light' in a different tone or with a different experience; or merely in using it in a different context of activity (*Spielzusammenhang*); or in the fact that in one case I respond to the question 'What do you mean?' by saying 'I mean you should turn on the light', in the other by saying 'I mean that the light is turned on'. This text (unlike PI) treats 'I meant . . .' as introducing a family resemblance concept.

2.1   'the difference being only in the application': according to Frege's account of language, there is no such possibility. The assertoric force of a sentence is 'carried' by its form (T 22) and differences in force must correspond to differences in form (cf. Exg. §22). In contrast, W. notes that it is easy to imagine a language in which questions and commands do not have distinctive forms, but are expressed in the form of assertions (e.g. 'I want to know whether . . .', 'It is my wish that . . .' (RFM 116)).

SECTION 22

1   Together with p. 11 n., this criticizes Frege's analysis of assertion. His separation of the act of assertion from the content of assertion belongs to a sophisticated partial defence of the Augustinian picture of sentence-meaning. He purports to demonstrate that a declarative sentence used to make an assertion, the same sentence occurring in a conditional, and the

corresponding sentence-question have a common content—a thought.
The differences between these correspond to psychological differences in
the relation of the speaker to this common content. W.'s criticisms are
integral to his attack on the Augustinian picture of sentence-meaning. If
cogent, they would defeat a fuller defence of the Augustinian picture,
which unearthed a common 'descriptive content' over a wider range of
uses of sentences (e.g. orders, wishes, expressions of intention).

Background: Frege's analysis, despite various changes, was guided by
two fundamental ideas.

(i) A declarative sentence has as its content a thought which is what it
expresses. A thought is objective (cf. NS 160), exists independently of
being apprehended, and is the bearer of truth-values. It is what is grasped
when an utterance of a declarative sentence is understood and what is
believed when various people believe the same thing. As objects,
thoughts can be named; e.g. the expression 'the thought that $2 + 3 = 5$'
names a particular thought which is its reference (SR 66). But such a
name does not itself express a thought; i.e. no thought is its sense. Only a
sentence has a thought as its sense (T 20; NS 142 f., 189).

(ii) It is possible to express a thought without asserting it (FC 34; NS
201) and to entertain a thought without judging it to be true (N 119; NS
214), the first possibility being the behavioural counterpart of the second.
(Making an assertion is the externalization of the mental act of judging
(NS 150, 214).) To deny these twin possibilities breeds confusion. It then
seems impossible to make a denial, express a false belief, construct an
indirect proof or a non-trivial argument by *modus ponens*, entertain a
supposition or hypothesis, etc. Confusion is eliminated by carefully
distinguishing expressing a thought from asserting it (or entertaining an
hypothesis from judging to be true). In Frege's view, it is a defect of
natural language that this distinction is not transparent. There is no
distinct symbol to signal that a sentence is being used to make an
assertion, whose absence would then signal that it is being used merely to
express a thought (NS 201). Instead, the assertoric force of a sentence lies
in its declarative form (T 22, 22 n.; SR 64). Confusion arises because
possessing this form does not guarantee the use of a sentence to make an
assertion. A declarative sentence may be used merely to express a thought.

Assertion: to make an assertion is to assert some *thing*; viz. the thought
expressed by the uttered declarative sentence. Merely expressing the
thought that p, asserting it to be true, merely entertaining it, and judging
it to be true, are different relations of a person to an object. The thought
that p is what is common to these acts. In particular, it is the thing that is
asserted ('dasjenige . . ., was behauptet wird' (PI §22))in asserting that p.
A thought must appear as one constituent in the analysis of the act of
making an assertion. Consequently, Frege takes thoughts to be indis-
pensable for the correct analysis of indirect speech (GA i. p. x).

Assertion-sign: the assertion-sign 'ꞁ' is designed to make perspicuous the distinction between making an assertion and merely expressing a thought. An assertion in Frege's symbolism is expressed only by prefixing 'ꞁ' to a well-formed sentence (e.g. '2 + 3 = 5'); without such a prefix such a sentence is used only to express a thought (i.e. as the mere name of a truth-value). The articulation of the symbolism conforms to Frege's analysis of assertion. The expression of the assertion 'ꞁ2 + 3 = 5' subdivides into the initial vertical line (the judgement-stroke)[6] and the rest ('— 2 + 3 = 5', i.e. the 'horizontal' and the sentence '2 + 3 = 5'). A sentence prefixed with the horizontal merely expresses the thought expressed by the sentence. Adding the judgement-stroke converts this expression of a thought into an assertion. The judgement-stroke has neither sense nor reference, rather it 'contains the act of assertion' (GA i. §5). The judgement-stroke expresses the performance of the interior act of judging to be true the thought whose expression it precedes. The defect Frege discerned in natural language is remedied because the correct expression of a thought ('—p') cannot by itself be used to make an assertion, it merely designates a truth-value. Only a sentence flagged by 'ꞁ' makes an assertion.

W.'s criticisms: evidently, §22(a)–(c) is intended as a criticism of Frege's account of assertion, whereas (d) looks like a neutral comment on his use of the assertion-sign. Although the import of (c) is obvious in outline, the argument of (a) and (b) is obscure. It is unclear why Frege's analysis rests on the possibility of transforming every declarative sentence into the form 'It is asserted that p'. Since Frege would agree that a 'that'-clause is not a sentence, it is not obvious why this is a criticism of his view. Moreover, on Frege's analysis neither a 'that'-clause nor the correct expression of the content of an assertion can be used to make an assertion. W.'s criticism is so condensed that it is difficult to reconstruct his argument against Frege.

(a) criticizes Frege's claim that every assertion we make *contains* an assumption, the assumption being 'the thing asserted'. If this were so, then analysis of the sentence used to make an assertion should yield a proper part which expresses the assumption and another part which effects the act of assertion. (Since, in Frege's view, the declarative form of a sentence carries the assertive force, the expression of the assumption must be stripped of this form, and the expression of the act of assertion must endow the whole with declarative form.) We can indeed effect such a transformation by rewriting every statement in the form 'It is asserted that p'. ('It is the case that p' might be preferable.) 'It is asserted' expresses

---

[6] For notational perspicuity we will write the judgement-stroke as the assertion sign 'ꞁ'. According to Frege's principle for amalgamating horizontals, the result of prefixing 'ꞁ' to '—p' is identical with that of prefixing the simple vertical line.

the act of asserting, 'that p' expresses the assumption. One might link
this notation to Frege's *Begriffsschrift*, thus (BT 208):

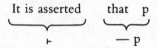

The noun clause 'that p' which, in this transformation, is 'the thing
asserted' is appropriately thought of as a sentence-radical (p. 11 n.), i.e.
something which may be part of a sentence used to make an assertion or
part of a sentence used to ask a question ('Is it the case that p?'), but which
cannot *by itself* be so used.

It now seems puzzling that W.'s immediate riposte is that this noun
clause is not a sentence, not a move (or not something that can be
independently used to make a move) in the language-game. For surely
the purpose of explicitly segregating an expression of the assumption
was precisely to produce an expression which cannot by itself be used to
make a move in the language-game? W.'s point is that whatever form of
words is chosen as an expression of the assumption must also remain a
sentence, for the assumption is, according to Frege, the sense of a *sentence*
(not of a noun clause). The two statements 'If p then q' and 'p' are held to
contain the same sentence 'p', once asserted and once unasserted. Hence
we cannot replace the antecedent of the conditional by a noun clause,
precisely because a noun clause is not a sentence. Any attempt to
represent Frege's claim that every assertion contains an assumption by
transformations permissible in language is thus subject to contradictory
demands. For the linguistic expression of the contained assumption must
both be, and not be, a sentence. The fact is that what we conceive as a
declarative sentence is something that *can be* used to make an assertion,
but *need not* be so used.

If we relinquish the noun clause as an expression of the assumption and
adopt the transformation 'It is asserted: such and such is the case' as a
form of words appropriate for making assertions, it is immediately
obvious that the prefix 'It is asserted' is superfluous. For the form 'Such
and such is the case', being a sentence (and hence a form of words that *can
be* used to make an assertion), is already fully fit for making assertions. If
a token-sentence 'p' is not used to make an assertion (but, e.g., occurs as
the antecedent of a conditional) prefixing 'It is asserted:' to it will not
make it so used; if it is used to make an assertion, such a prefix will make
no difference.

Frege would certainly reject these criticisms. First, 'that p' is not an
expression of the thought which is expressed by '—p'. On the contrary,
the noun clause names (i.e. has as its reference) that thought. Equally, 'It
is asserted' at best describes the act performed by prefixing '⊢' to '—p'.
Consequently, there is no correct translation of '⊢p' into natural lan-

guage, and no expression synonymous with either of its two constituents '⊢' and '—p'. 'It is asserted that p' is but a rough approximation to an explanation of what is ineffable. More accurately, it is a *report* in oratio obliqua of what is effected by '⊢p' (GA i. §5). Secondly, this untranslatability merely reveals the defectiveness and lack of perspicuity of ordinary language. Precisely this is remedied by a scientific concept-script.

This defence against W.'s criticism presupposes that Frege's concept-script is intelligible, i.e. that he has given a cogent explanation of the assertion-sign and of the horizontal used in expressing a thought. According to his stipulation, the horizontal is a function-name; hence, '— ξ' stands for a function whose value is always a truth-value, whatever proper name may be inserted into its argument-place. If its argument-expression designates the True, its value is the True; otherwise, its value is the False. Frege construes sentences themselves as proper names of truth-values having thoughts as their senses. Consequently, if 'p' is a sentence having a truth-value, the reference of '—p' is identical with the reference of 'p'. This stipulation entails that the sense of '—p' is identical with the sense of 'p', provided that 'p' is a sentence with a truth-value. In this respect '—p' is similar to the complex sentence 'It is true that p'. This identity of sense is equally demanded by Frege's taking '—p' as the expression of the thought that is asserted by using the sentence 'p' to make an assertion. According to his stipulation an expression of the form '—p' cannot by itself be used to make an assertion; it merely expresses a thought and names a truth-value. If, by itself, it merely names a truth-value, then it cannot, without aid from a further symbol, do anything more. In his notation no sentence appears without a prefixed horizontal, hence a special sign is necessary in order to be able to make an assertion, viz. the assertion-sign '⊢'. The complex expression '⊢p' is a proposition (*Satz*) of *Begriffsschrift*. 'It does not designate anything; it asserts something' (FC 34n). But *only* the sign '⊢', not '—p', 'contains the act of assertion' (GA i. §5). Therefore, in Frege's notation, it is always perspicuous whether a content of judgement is asserted or merely entertained, supposed, or hypothesized.

Frege's explanation of the horizontal presupposes an understanding of what constitutes a sentence, but, at the same time, it involves a gross distortion of the concept of a sentence. A sentence with a sense ('expressing a thought') is an expression that *can* be used by itself to make an assertion, though it *need* not always be so used. In one respect Frege's conception conforms to this truth of grammar. If the sentence 'p' is used to make an assertion, then this is represented in his notation by the expression '⊢p'; barring truth-valueless sentence-tokens, any sentence 'p' can legitimately be prefixed with '⊢'. But this conclusion and the route to it both embody a conception of sentences that is not in accord with our understanding of what a sentence is. His characterizing sentences as names of truth-values might be passed off as an terminological idiosyncrasy, and his normative stipulation that '—p' cannot be used by itself to make an assertion as legitimate legislation. Yet both reflect and support a misrepresentation of sentences. On his view, producing a sentence (e.g. '2 + 3 = 5' or '5 > 4') is just to 'give an expression of a truth-value' without making any assertion; writing down a sentence is never more than writing down the name of a truth-value (FC 34). Hence 'in a mere equation there is as yet no assertion; "2 + 3 = 5" only designates a truth-value' (GA i. §5). This conception of sentences is supported by the idea that they are proper names (of truth-values), since no proper name uttered in isolation can be used to make an assertion. Similarly, it is supported by construing '— ξ' as the identity-function when it is applied to sentences having truth-values, since the fact that '—p' cannot be used alone to make an assertion is then mirrored in his claim that no sentence 'p' can be so used. Frege is committed to the thesis that no sentence expressing a thought can be used by itself to make an assertion. This reappears in the interpretation that he would give of the truism that any sentence can be used to make an assertion. For, in his notation, this possibility is represented by the legitimacy of prefixing 'ⱶ' to any sentence with a truth-value; but then it is not the sentence 'p', but only the complex expression 'ⱶp', that can (and must) be used by itself to make an assertion. Since his conception of a sentence is inconsistent with our understanding of what a sentence is, his explanation of the horizontal is either incoherent or unintelligible.

The incoherence in Frege's conception of a sentence can be highlighted by bringing together two aspects of the grammar of sentences. First, *only* a sentence is the expression of a thought. Secondly, any sentence (expressing a thought) can be used by itself to make an assertion. Frege's explanation of the horizontal is inconsistent with at least one of these truths of grammar. If 'p' is a sentence with a truth-value, then '—p' is the expression of a thought; hence, it must *be* a sentence; consequently, it must be capable of being used by itself to make an assertion. Conversely, if '—p' cannot be used to make an assertion, it cannot be a sentence; therefore, if it does express a thought, the thesis that only sentences express thoughts must be false. Finally, dropping the stipulation that '—p' cannot be used to make an assertion would render both the horizontal and the assertion-sign superfluous, since '—p' would just be an idosyncratic way of writing 'p' and could be used without the prefix 'ⱶ' to make an assertion. The criticism of §22(a) applies no less to Frege's own notation than to any putative translation of it into natural language.

Not surprisingly, Frege's correlative explanation of the assertion-sign is equally defective. His claims that 'ⱶ' contains the act of assertion and that 'ⱶp' asserts something are radically confused. His introduction of 'ⱶ' manifests an incoherent conception of the relation between the form of an expression and its use. There is no such thing as embodying the use of an expression in its form in accordance with his demands on '⊢'. He explains '⊢' as a mark or indication of a use, a use which, by stipulation, can only be effected by the employment of this sign. But a sign *is not itself* a use; it must *be used.* The inscription '⊢p' does not *contain* the act of assertion, and it can only be said to assert something if it is used to assert something. If one writes '⊢5 > 4' on a blackboard as an example of a proposition of *Begriffsschrift*, one has not thereby asserted that 5 is greater than 4. In his vain attempt to concoct a form which will *contain* its own use, Frege can only produce a sign whose explanation assigns to it the role of distinguishing an assertion from a fiction or supposition (§22(c)). Moreover, even that explanation confers a use on '⊢' only provided that we possess criteria for the correct use of '⊢', i.e. only if there are criteria for determining whether the complex symbol formed by prefixing '⊢' to a sentence is used to assert something. Far from needing '⊢' to distinguish sentences used to make assertions from mere expressions of thoughts, this symbolism is intelligible only if we have mastery of the criteria for making this distinction. In so far as someone is genuinely confused in drawing this distinction, his confusion can be cleared up only by clarifying the criteria for using sentences to make assertions, not by the introduction of a magical sign that 'contains the act of assertion'.

(b) continues the criticism of the idea that every assertion really contains a 'that'-clause encapsulating its content. W.'s tactic is to reduce this analysis to absurdity by pointing out that this particular transformation of asserted sentences is not unique and therefore cannot be accorded a privileged status. Since every asserted sentence 'p' can be rewritten in the form 'Is it the case that p? Yes.', we could with equal cogency conclude that every asserted sentence contains a question! The question 'Is it the case that p?' is just as much a *part* of the asserted sentence 'p' as is the clause 'that p'. Indeed, we could mimic the schema

It is asserted   that p

⊢   *Annahme*

with the parallel schema (BT 208)

Is it the case that p?   Yes.

Annahme   ⊢

(c) opens by remarking that we can legitimately introduce the symbol '⊢' into a sentence as a punctuation mark, parallel to a question–mark, to clarify the intention to use the sentence to make an assertion rather than to ask a question, or to make a statement of fact rather than to put forward an hypothesis or to tell a fictional story. This sign would correspond to familiar surface features of utterances in natural languages which are used to signal differences in sentence-use (e.g. punctuation marks, intonation-contours, word-order, and moods of verbs). Nothing stands in the way of introducing a sign with this function. We need only specify the rules for its use, to give its grammar (PLP 302). It will not, however, possess the extraordinary property of containing its own use. Like any other sign, it will have to be used, and there will be criteria for its correct use and criteria for its incorrect use. There will also be criteria for the correct use of sentences prefixed by the assertion-sign in giving examples, in oratio recta, in jokes, in drama, etc.

According to Frege's account, the sign '⊢' in the expression '⊢p' is not a mere signal that the sentence 'p' is being used to make an assertion. Rather, he conceives it to be a constituent in the analysis of the asserted sentence, clarifying the structure of the act of making an assertion. (c) continues by criticizing this conception of the assertion-sign. Frege treats the act of assertion as the externalization of the interior act of judgement, and the act of judging a thought to be true he anatomizes into the act of entertaining a thought and the act of assigning to it the truth-value True. The function of the judgement-stroke (Urteilsstrich) is to symbolize the performance of the act of judging a thought to be true (Urteilen). Consequently, the symbol '—p', considered merely as the expression of a thought, must correspond to the act of contemplating the thought that p. The articulation of the symbol '⊢p' into the constituents '⊢' and '—p' thus reflects the articulation of the act of judgement and hence also that of the act of assertion. Producing the symbol '⊢p' manifests performance of this pair of mental acts since the symbol itself makes an assertion. Therefore, someone's reading the symbol '⊢p' which he has produced must consist in his performing these mental acts. This symbol is a signal for the performance of certain mental activities, among others the contemplating of a thought (Denken) and judging it to be true (Urteilen). Here W. dogmatically repudiates this conception. Neither meaning something (Meinen) nor understanding are mental acts accompanying uttering or hearing a sentence. Using a sentence to make an assertion does not consist in accompanying the mouthing of words by an interior act of judgement. Nor does understanding a sentence used to make an assertion require the carrying out of any mental activities correlative to hearing the words uttered. A sentence is not a set of dead signs: the possibility of communication does not rest on mental acts which give these signs meaning and life, as if meanings were always in the mind (cf. Vol XI, 87). 'One might say "Understanding a sentence means getting hold of its content; and the content of the sentence is in the sentence" ' (BB 167).

(d) gives a partial characterization of the grammar of Frege's assertion-sign, describing it as a form of punctuation marking the beginning of a sentence. It functions like the first member of a pair of parentheses, the second of which is the full stop (Vol. XI, 86), but could instead be written as a reversed assertion-sign, e.g. '⊢p⊣' (PLP 302). Together these signs distinguish a complete sentence from one which occurs as a clause within another. This observation is not a criticism of Frege; in part, it even conforms to his conception (Vol. XI, 86). Nor is the idea original with W., since Russell explicitly notes this function in borrowing the assertion-sign from Frege (PM i. 81). This comparison with punctuation marks is illuminating in several respects.

(i) There is a set of fairly definite rules governing the use of punctuation in written languages. Each punctuation mark is a symbol with a determinate use. Though we must distinguish these symbols from other symbols used in writing (especially letters and words (cf. PI §4)), we must not exaggerate the difference by supposing that they stand on a different level.

(ii) Some actual punctuation marks (e.g. the full stop and the question-mark) do serve the purpose of distinguishing complete sentences from clauses within them. If we read each full stop twice, viz. as closing the preceding sentence and opening the subsequent one, then the full stop would already perform the function of marking the beginning of a sentence. Indeed, we could describe '⊢' as having the same use as the full stop at the end of the preceding sentence (BT 206). An exact parallel with the punctuation '⊢ . . . .' for declarative sentences would be the pattern '¿ . . . ?' of punctuation for questions in Spanish.

(iii) In part, English punctuation is already used roughly for the purpose that '⊢' might legitimately serve, according to (c): viz. '.' and '?', and to a lesser extent '!', are used as surface representations of differences in sentence-use. So-called 'declarative sentences' are punctuated with full stops and typically used to make assertions, while 'interrogative sentences' are punctuated with question-marks and typically used to ask questions. There is a rough correspondence between punctuation and sentence-use in many languages. Employing '⊢' to mark sentences used to make assertions would be an extension and regularization of the familiar practice of punctuating.

(iv) The ban on using full stops within a single sentence in English is parallelled by a ban on using '⊢' within a well-formed sentence in Frege's *Begriffsschrift*: e.g. the formulae '(⊢p) v (⊢q)' and '⊢(⊢p→⊢q)' are not well formed. Similarly, if symbols '?' and '!' are introduced to mark the use of sentences as questions and orders respectively, then the formula '! p v ? q' is not well formed (EBT 599).

Comparing '⊢' with punctuation marks, especially with a full stop or a bracket (cf. PLP 302), gives only a partial account of its grammar. It leaves open many questions: e.g. whether the translation of any declarative sentence of *The Brothers Karamazov* into Frege's *Bergriffsschrift* should be prefixed with '⊢' (Vol. IX, 95 f.) or whether each sentence in the rule-book for a game should be so treated (cf. Vol. XIV under 23.9).

1.1   (i) 'Annahme': W. signified dissatisfaction with the translation 'supposal' and restored the German term in PPI (R) §27. He thus appears to treat 'Annahme' as a technical term in expounding Frege's view (cf. Exg. p. 11 n. on pp. 66 f.).

(ii) 'Behauptung', 'Behauptungssatz,' 'Behauptungszeichen': the internal connections among these terms should be preserved in the translation.

(iii) 'nach dem Zeichen des Satzes': PPI §22 reads 'nach den Zeichen. . .' and is translated 'according to the signs of the sentence' (PPI (R) §28). The sign or signs meant are the expression of an assertion in Frege's concept-script, not an everyday sentence of natural language.

2   (i) Though he derived the idea and the symbolism from Frege, Russell's explanation of the assertion-sign differed somewhat from Frege's:

> The sign '⊢' . . . means that what follows is asserted. It is required for distinguishing a complete proposition, which we assert, from any subordinate propositions contained in it but not asserted. In ordinary written language a sentence contained between full stops denotes an asserted proposition . . . The sign '⊢' prefixed to a proposition serves this same purpose in our symbolism. (PM i. 8)

Russell thus introduces '⊢' as a punctuation mark (cf. PI §22(d)), and he notes its importance by using it to explain what it is to make an inference by *modus ponens* (PM i. 8).

Later he correlated his employment of the assertion-sign with an analysis of assertion identical with that criticized in PI §22(a)–(b):

> Any proposition may be either asserted or merely considered. . . . In language, we indicate when a proposition is merely considered by '*if* so-and-so' or '*that* so-and-so' or merely by inverted commas. In symbols, if *p* is a proposition, *p* by itself will stand for the unasserted proposition, while the asserted proposition will be designated by '⊢.p.'. The sign '⊢' . . . may be read 'it is true that' (although philosophically this is not exactly what it means). (PM i. 92.)

This contains echoes of Frege's account; it puts forward 'that'-clauses as the proper expression for the content of assertions; and it intimates the reasoning underlying the claim that a proposition (i.e. an unasserted proposition) is an incomplete symbol, completed only by the *act* of judgement (PM i. 44).

(ii) BT 208 introduces another objection to the claim that every assertion contains an assumption. There are indeed assumptions (*Annahmen*), expressed by sentences of the form 'Suppose that it is (or were) the case that p'. But is such an assumption *a part* of an assertion? Is this not as if someone said the question whether p is the case is a part of the assertion that p is the case?

(iii) RFM 116 clarifies the same point:

> The great majority of sentences that we speak, write and read are assertoric sentences (*Behauptungssätze*). . . . these sentences are true or false. Or . . . the game of truth-functions is played with them. For assertion is not something that gets added to the proposition, but an essential feature of the game we play with it. Comparable, say, to that characteristic of chess by which there is winning and losing in it . . .

W.'s argument is that assertion is not something *added* to the proposition; hence, that asserting something does not contain two separable acts, entertaining a proposition and asserting it. If such a decomposition were possible, then there would be only an external relation between propositions and assertions; propositions could be characterized independently of assertion, and it would just happen that we assert only propositions (and not, e.g., WH-questions). The analogy with chess is meant to stress that the connection is internal. Just as we cannot characterize such a game without specifying what counts as winning in it, so we cannot characterize propositions (what are true and false, what we play the game of truth-functions with) independently of assertion. An assertion no more consists in an assumption and the asserting of it than a command consists in a proposal and the commanding of it.

(iv) PPI §23 (= Z §684) differs from the final version, PI §22(d): we grasp the importance of Frege's assertion-sign if we note that it marks the beginning of the sentence; this function is important since it determines what a person has asserted (e.g., in asserting 'It is not the case that p' or 'I believe that p', he has not asserted that p). Both these ideas are part of Russell's account of Frege's assertion-sign and implicit in §22(d). The corrected translation (PPI (R) §29) is happier than that of Z §684: 'Our philosophical difficulties concerning the nature of negation and thinking in a sense are due to the fact that we don't realize that an assertion "⊢not p" or "⊢I believe p", and the assertion "⊢p" have "p" in common, but not "⊢p".' What these asserted sentences have in common is the *sentence* 'p'; they make contact in language (cf. 'The uses of sentences', pp. 77 ff.).

(v) Vol. XII, 321 notes the obvious fact that it is possible to utter an assertoric sentence (e.g. 'It is raining') without making an assertion, e.g. in reading a poem. But whether or not the utterance is an assertion depends only on the 'circumstances (the spatial and temporal setting)' in which it is spoken (not on whether the speaker performs certain mental acts accompanying its utterance).

2.1   (i) 'Ungefähr wie wir nach Noten singen': W. treats singing a song as an example of a pair of parallel activities. Each (singing the melody and articulating the words) can be performed independently of the other (BB 42). Hence, singing the melody is a paradigm of something that *accompanies* saying the words. W. frequently employs the analogy of singing from a score to illustrate what he means by 'accompaniment' in arguments demonstrating that meaning something (*Meinen*) is not a psychic accompaniment of saying something (BB 35, 42; PG 130; Z §§246 f.). He even gives the analogy a role in one such demonstration: he exploits the idea (BB 5) that if meaning something were a mental accompaniment of speaking it could be replaced by an *outward* accompaniment of speaking, e.g. by putting words to a tune.

Denk' Dir Leute die alle Sätze (Behauptugen, Fragen, etc.) wenn sie sie *meinen*, sich nicht nur in ihrem Aussprechen üben, oder dergl., *singen*. Vom gesungenen Satz sagen sie, 'er lebt', vom nicht gesungenen, er sei tot.
Wenn diese Meschen über den Begriff 'meinen' philosophieren, werden sie versucht sein zu sagen: meinen heisse singen. (Vol. XII, 316.)

(Imagine people who *sing* all sentences (assertions, questions, etc.) when they *mean* them and are not only practising their pronunciation, or such-like.
Of the sung sentence they say 'it is alive', of the unsung one, 'it is dead'.
If these men philosophized about the concept 'to mean (something)', they would be inclined to say: 'meaning (something)' means 'singing (it)'.)

The absurdity of this conclusion proves that no accompaniments of speaking, *a fortiori* no psychic accompaniment, can give life to language (cf. BB 35).

(ii) 'das "*Meinen*" (Denken) des gelesenen Satzes'; the precise articulation of this thought is not clear. This unclarity persists in spite of W.'s repeated efforts to redraft this sentence. There are some half-dozen redraftings of the original version (BT 207) at BT 206v., then two further revisions in Vol. XI, 86 f. The view criticized is that reading the complex symbol '⊢p' consists of two independent activities corresponding to its two parts; one part ('—p') indicates the words to be uttered in asserting that p, the other ('⊢') signals a mental performance (an act of judgement) *accompanying* the uttering of the words in 'p'. W. replies that the signs composing '⊢p' are not signals for the performance of the mental activities of meaning or thinking in reading this sentence, e.g. signals for entertaining a thought or judging it to be true (cf. BT 206v.). If they were signals for any accompaniment of the mouthing of the words of 'p', this accompaniment must be a particular way of reading the sentence (e.g. an intonation-contour or tone of voice) that itself would be an assertion-*sign*, parallel to '⊢' and used to signal a particular use of the spoken sentence (BT 207; Vol. XI, 86). No accompaniment of its utterance makes the production of a sentence into the act of asserting something. *A fortiori*, '⊢' does not signal the performance of the mental act of judging a thought to be true whose accompanying the utterance of a sentence would make the act of uttering these words into the act of making an assertion. Moreover, although someone who uses a sentence to assert something must *mean* to make an assertion, his meaning to do so is neither a mental act nor any other accompaniment of his speaking. The scare-quotes enclosing 'Meinen' are perhaps intended to flag this misconception.

Page 11 Note

1   This remark, cut from B i. §432, is the most controversial of all those printed below the line. Before analysing it, we must emphasize that W.'s intentions in inserting these slips into the typescript of PI are not known. He *may* have meant to add these remarks as they stood to the text (just as he apparently composed §§198 ff. by inserting slips cut from B i into a collection of material from another source). Equally, he *may* have inserted them to remind himself of modifications that he intended to make to the 'final' text (perhaps deletions as well as additions). Different slips may have been inserted for different purposes and some for multiple purposes. In ignorance of his intentions, we make a mistake in principle if we make the interpretation of PI turn on the content of any of these slips. *A fortiori*, the suggestion that p. 11 n. is a key to PI should be treated with the utmost scepticism and requires weighty proof.

Location: none of the earlier versions of p. 11 n., including the text of B i. §432, contains the last sentence. It was presumably added by W. when he inserted the slip in TS. 227. This indicates that p. 11 n. belongs with PI §22(a), elaborating on Frege's notion of *Annahme*.

Background: every earlier version of this remark (Vol. IX, 56; EBT 574–6; Vol. XI, 58; BT 244 f.; cf. PLP 144, Vol. XIII, 146) and the correlative introduction of the term 'Satzradikal' occurs in a different argumentative context, viz. the discussion of what a rule is and how the formulation of a rule differs from a statement of fact (*Erfahrungssatz*). In each case, the discussion of proposition-radicals is quite separate from the discussion of the distinction between using sentences to make assertions, to ask questions, to formulate suppositions, etc. The point of the argument is to deny that the formulation of a rule (e.g the chess rule: 'Each queen stands on its own colour (in the initial position)') is as it stands an assertion of fact. (Such a sentence cannot, e.g., be characterized as true or false (Vol. XIV, under 23 September).) But this sentence forms a nucleus for constructing sentences that are statements of fact: e.g., 'In chess each queen stands on its own colour' or 'The rule that each queen stands on its own colour was not observed in Norway until 1459'. It is this fact about rule-formulations that W. meant to highlight by the analogy with the picture of the boxer. In isolation a picture *says* nothing;

it makes no assertion. But it can be used to make a variety of assertions when combined with other signs, e.g. words and gestures, and there it will be part of these assertions. The rule-formulation is similar in that it has no use by itself as an assertion, but may be a proper part of sentences that do have a use as assertions. This parallel between the picture of the boxer and the rule-formulation is captured in the simile of a radical in chemistry and encapsulated in the term 'Satzradikal' ('sentence-radical'). A sentence-radical cannot be used by itself to make an assertion, but can be part of sentences used to make assertions.

Application: the final sentence gives this old remark a new application, viz. to elucidate one aspect of Frege's conception of the 'assumption' (the thought, the content of an assertion). It is crucial to the rationale of his concept-script that the proper expression of a thought (e.g. '$-2 + 3 = 5$') *cannot* be used by itself to make an assertion. Otherwise, there would be a risk that the sign '⊢' would be superfluous, since the act of asserting something might be performed without it; and absence of this sign would not guarantee that a thought is merely expressed without being asserted. Consequently, it is an essential part of Frege's conception of assertion that the correct expression of a thought be a sentence-radical, not a sentence. The purpose of p. 11 n. is merely to emphasize this point since it is what is criticized in §22(a).

Implication: against the background of his having analysed propositions as pictures in TLP, W.'s introduction of the picture of a boxer in explaining the term *Satzradikal* might be taken to suggest a whole new outlook on his earlier ideas. Pictures are radically 'ambiguous': they can be used in a variety of ways, as illustrated by the picture of the boxer (and even when used for one purpose, they can often be interpreted in different ways: cf. PI p. 54 n. (b)). Sentences too can be used in different ways. While this strengthens the analogy of sentences with pictures, it also suggests that the picture theory of meaning must be supplemented by an account of how sentences are used. What we understand in understanding a sentence uttered in a particular context typically goes beyond grasping the picture presented by it and includes a grasp of the use to which the picture is being put. Hence a full account of understanding a sentence seems to have two components: an account of what it is to grasp the 'descriptive content' of a sentence (a picture) and an account of what it is to grasp the use of this picture. The picture theory of meaning focused exclusively on the first component, dismissing differences in sentence-use as merely psychological (NB 96). This error of TLP can be corrected by treating the picture theory as an account only of the proposition-radical, not of the proposition-in-use. The alleged purpose of p. 11 n. is to present this modified version of the picture theory. This is confirmed by its juxtaposition with §23. Both emphasize the varied uses of sentences. First, p. 11 n. introduces the idea of the descriptive content of a sentence. Then §23 suggests that we should attend to what gets added to the proposition-radical in making it into a proposition-in-use. Although W. developed this central idea no further in PI, a fuller account of understanding sentences can be given in terms of operators whose arguments are proposition-radicals and whose values are propositions-in-use. Such a theory of meaning generalizes Frege's procedure in introducing the assertion-sign, correcting his principal mistake, which was to deny that the content of judgement could be common to sentences used to give orders, to make requests, to praise and curse, etc. This one slip of paper, p. 11 n., is key to the interpretation of PI. *Mirabile dictu*, the account of the sense of sentences in TLP is a partial truth: a correct account of one component (the proposition-radical) of propositions-in-use. PI is not a repudiation of TLP, but a supplementation of its central ideas. Its flowers are borne on this ancient stock.

This interpretation is a travesty of PI. In almost every respect it is completely misconceived.

(i) The methodology pursued in constructing it is mistaken. It connects p. 11 n. with §§23 ff. in a speculative way in spite of the fact that W. apparently intended to relate it to the discussion of Frege's *Annahme* in §22(a). Moreover, an interpretation is given to p. 11 n. that is supported nowhere in the text of PI, and this is then treated as the key to the whole book.

(ii) The interpretation nurtured from the seed of p. 11 n. is inconsistent with the entire argumentative thrust of PI §§1–143. W. there criticizes many of the central conceptions of the Augustinian picture of language and thereby undermines the foundations of his thought in TLP.

(iii) Far from developing an account of meaning incorporating mood-operators and proposition-radicals, W. nowhere even mentions the possibility. Moreover, one might extract from §23 the idea that any such account of meaning is doomed to failure.

(iv) The interpretation rests on an *ignoratio elenchi*. Pictures have different uses. So too do sentences. Moreover, understanding an utterance involves knowing how a sentence is used, whether to make an assertion, to ask a question, etc. But does it follow that knowing how a sentence is used is knowing how a picture or a 'descriptive content' is used?

(v) The idea that grasping its 'descriptive content' and grasping its use are separate components in understanding an uttered sentence presupposes that the criteria of understanding an utterance decompose into two separate sets of criteria, one for understanding its content and the other for understanding its use. This contradicts W.'s description of the criteria for understanding ('The uses of sentences', p. 74).

(vi) The analysis of sentence-meaning by means of mood-operators and proposition-radicals takes as its model Frege's isolation of the

thought as the common content of an assertion and its counterpart
sentence-question. Far from concurring with Frege's analysis of assertion, W. decisively repudiates it in §22. Therefore, this putative
interpretation of PI generalizes a thesis that W. clearly rejects in PI.

1.1   (i) '(chemisch gesprochen) ein Satzradikal nennen': what W. understood
by 'Radikal' ('radical') in chemistry is what is now expressed by the term
'Gruppe' ('group'). There are certain combinations of elements that
themselves recur as constituents of more complex compounds although
they have no independent existence. For example, the ethyl group $C_2 H_5$
and the hydroxyl group OH combine together to form ethyl alcohol
$C_2H_5(OH)$. Consequently, something called *Satzradikal* must be a
combination of elements recurring as constituents of *Sätze* though not
itself a *Satz*. This characterization fits rule-formulations. They are
sentences, typically composed of several words, and, not being characterizable as 'true' or 'false', they do not express propositions, and cannot
be used to make assertions. This would not be true of typical declarative
sentences (descriptions). They do express propositions and may be used
to make assertions when uttered in isolation; they have independent
existence as *Sätze*. Therefore, the thesis that the content of every
assertion is expressed by a proposition-radical requires that the expression of its content be something other than a declarative sentence, e.g. a
sentence-question or a 'that'-clause. Far from being something advocated
in PI, this is the very thesis that W. discredits in §22(a)–(b).
        (ii) 'Annahme': the terminology is somewhat mysterious. In published
writings, Frege only once (FC 34) used the term 'Annahme' in connection
with what he initially called 'the content of judgement' and later 'the
thought'. We might suspect that W. misrepresents Frege's account of
assertion by using the term 'assumption' from *Russell*'s formulation of
Frege's semantics (PrM 503),[7] or, alternatively, that he conflates Frege's
terminology with Meinong's, since W. shows some awareness of
Meinong's views on *Annahme* (Vol. V, 26; EBT 336; PLP 301 f.). On the
other hand, W. does stick close to Frege's account. His explanation of
Annahme as what is common to an assertion and the corresponding
sentence-question conforms exactly to Frege's explanation of the
thought (BT 207). And he there adds a bracket after 'Annahme': viz. '(So
wie er das Wort gebraucht)' ('(as he uses the word)'). This suggests that
Frege sometimes used 'Annahme' as a technical term in the exposition of
his semantics. So too does W.'s insertion of the German term in
correcting Rhees's translation of PPI (PPI (R) §27). The idea would be
natural to Frege since he standardly cited the antecedents of conditionals
as examples of expressions of unasserted thoughts. The most plausible

[7] Cf. also B. Russell, *Essays in Analysis,* ed. D. Lackey (Allen and Unwin, London, 1973),
p. 44.

conjecture is that Frege did use the term in *conversation* or *correspondence* with W. Certainly, the thesis in TLP 5.54 ff. that 'A asserted that p', 'A believes that p', etc., do not describe a relation between a person and an abstract entity is directly contrary to one of Frege's central tenets. This makes it probable that their correspondence and discussions of TLP covered the topic of the content of assertion, belief, etc.

It is important to note that p. 11 n. does not assert that Frege holds there to be an assumption in common to the sentences 'You should stand thus-and-so', 'You should not stand thus-and-so', and 'B did stand thus-and-so at place C and time D', even though each of these utterances might correspond to one use of the picture of the boxer. There is only an *analogy* between the picture and the expression of Frege's assumption. W. gives a faithful account of Frege's notion of the thought, not the inaccurate account required for treating the picture of the boxer as the 'assumption' common to all the uses of it mentioned here.

2   The thesis that by itself a picture says nothing, though it can be used together with other signs to make assertions, has a parallel in illustrations to works of fiction (cf. PI §663). From such illustrations alone we can seldom draw any conclusions about the content of a story.

(Denke, ich sähe eine Illustration, wüsste aber nicht, ob sie eine Situation der Haupterzählung, oder eine Erinnerung, einen Wunsch, einen Traum des Helden, oder einer andern Person, darstellt.) (B i. §209.)

((Imagine that I saw an illustration but did not know whether it represented a situation in the main narrative, or a recollection, a wish, a dream of the hero or of some other character.))

On the other hand, illustrations can be used, together with other signs, to tell a story, and they may even form an integral part of the 'text'.

2.1   'Annahme': W. gives two other criticisms of Frege's thesis that an assertion contains an assumption as one ingredient.

(i) If we represent the sentence-question corresponding to '⊢p' by the symbol '?p', then the assumption that p is what '?p' and '⊢p' have in common (BT 207). But the question '?p' is identical with the question '?~p'; i.e. apart from the prefix 'yes' or 'no', either '⊢p' or '⊢~p' is an answer to both of them.[8] Consequently, the assumption that p must be identical with the assumption that not-p (BT 208; EBT 600; PLP 302, cf. 405 f.). This seems absurd. It also conflicts with Frege's thesis that the assertion and denial that p are the performance of the same act (assertion) on *different* 'contents of judgement' (the assumptions that p and that not-p respectively) (N 128 ff.). If positive and negative sentence-questions

---

[8] This argument is problematic. It is adumbrated in an early unpublished work by Frege (NS 8).

are identical, then Frege's account of assumptions is incoherent (PLP 302).

(ii) It is, of course, possible to express suppositions and to argue from them,[9] but Frege's distinction between assumption and assertion gives a grotesque account of these activities. An actual assumption is typically expressed by a sentence of the form 'Suppose that p is (or were) the case'. But such a sentence seems incomplete. Someone who makes a supposition must go on to do something with it, to draw consequences from it. Only by doing so does he make his utterance 'Suppose that p is the case' into a move in the language-game. Otherwise, it is as if he had said 'If p is the case, then . . .' and not filled in the consequent (BT 208; EBT 599, PLP 302). Making a supposition is not something that can be done in isolation from making inferences: a fortiori, not something derivable from an assertion by subtracting the act of assertion, as implied by Frege (FC 34). Moreover, if 'Suppose that p is the case' is the typical form for expressing a supposition, it is obvious that there is no *supposition* contained in the analysis of an asserted sentence and common to the assertion that p and the supposition that p, nor does a conditional contain a supposition in its antecedent.

SECTION 23

1   If sentence-tokens are classified into kinds according to their uses or applications, not according to their grammatical forms, then there are as many kinds of sentences as there are kinds of uses of sentences. These are very numerous: we distinguish commands, orders, requests, invitations, threats, pleas, etc., even among sentences imperatival in form. Moreover, the classification of sentences will be open-ended in two ways. (i) It will depend, like the distinction of words into types, on our purposes in making the classification; we can classify according to different sorts of similarity and difference (cf. PLP 97, 298). (ii) It will depend on how speaking is connected with the other activities of the speakers of a language, and this may evolve over time. Consequently, there is no hope of constructing a complete catalogue of the uses of sentences that would be applicable to every possible language. There are literally 'countless' kinds of sentences: not uncountably many, but indefinitely many.

W. then lists a number of language-games. His aim is to highlight the absurdity of the Augustinian picture, especially its fundamental claim that all sentences function *uniformly*, viz. as descriptions. That view, as he notes, is clear in TLP.

[9] A complication: Frege sometimes argues that it is only possible to make inferences from thoughts acknowledged to be true (e.g. N 119). Hence he treats an argument from an assumption as the assertion of a hypothetical. We ignore this complication here.

1.1   'the multiplicity of language-games': different lists are given in different texts to emphasize the variety of uses of sentences, i.e. the variety of language-games with sentences (BB 67 f.; BT 208 v.; Vol. XI, 87 f.; PLP 298 ff.). Some entries seem problematic: e.g. should 'carrying out an order' and 'carrying out positive and negative orders or disjunctive orders' be listed as distinct co-ordinate language-games (BT 208 v.)? Since nothing depends on the specification of criteria of identity for uses of sentences (for language-games), W. can afford to leave out any discussion of the matter.

SECTION 24

1   This remark discusses three distinct points about the Augustinian picture of sentences.

(i) (a) identifies the thesis that all sentences function as descriptions as the source of nonsensical answers to the question 'What is a question?' An 'acceptable' answer must have the form of saying what a question *describes*, while any plausible answers (e.g. a state of uncertainty or ignorance, a desire for information) cannot be fully general.

(ii) (b) points out that what we classify as *descriptions* are very varied; i.e. that the term 'description' does not signify a single uniform use of sentences, but can be correctly applied to sentences with different uses (cf. PI §291).

(iii) (c) and (d) make the point that the possibility of transforming every question into the form of an assertion does not prove that questions are disguised assertions. It no more shows that there is no distinction between these uses of sentences than the possibility of explaining every word by stating what it signifies shows that there are no distinctions between how words function. It is either false or vacuous that all sentences are descriptions, just as it is either false or vacuous that all words are names (cf. Exg. §10). (This is akin to the dilemma facing the solipsist.)

1.1   '. . . will become clearer in another place': This promise is not redeemed in PI, though the subject is mentioned in §402.

2   (i) PLP Ch. XX outlines the 'grammar of questions', i.e. a correct answer to the question 'What is a question?' This consists of pointing out similarities and differences between questions and other uses of sentences (especially statements of fact and requests), as well as clarifying how asking and answering questions is related to the activities of searching for and discovering something.

(ii) Vol. XII, 216 notes that even what are called 'descriptions of a house' may have different applications; e.g. the description of the location and appearance of the house of an actual person, the description of a house in a story, and the description of a house which somebody is to imagine (also an architect's plan).

2.1   (i) 'the cry "Help!" ': BT 202 and Vol. XI, 83 enlarge on this: if a drowning man cries 'Help!', is he stating the fact that he needs help? That without help he will drown?

(ii) '(Solipsism)': from the Preface to PPI, we know that this was to have been discussed in the book, as it had been in PR Ch. VI, BT §§101 ff., and BB 57 ff.

SECTION 25

1   This embellishes the theme that speaking a language is part of a whole pattern of activity (a form of life). A being, whether angel or beast, who shared too little of our natural history could not be described as asking questions, making assertions, etc. Or, more paradoxically, if a lion were to speak, we could not understand him (PI p. 223).

Instead of simply describing the fact that beasts do not use language, philosophers go on to explain this fact by reference to a lack of mental capacity. This embodies two mistakes. (i) They implicitly identify asserting something, questioning something, etc., with performing a mental act, since otherwise the question of mental capacities would not arise. (The earlier part of §25 is thus linked with §22(c).) (ii) They fail to notice that there are no criteria independent of the absence of speaking for denying to animals the ability to think, i.e. that the so-called 'explanation' is empty. In spite of a long tradition in philosophy, language is not a means that humans have discovered to be useful for the communication of thoughts.

The proper course for philosophers is to eschew explanations and instead to describe what we all know, in this case that animals do not use language. They do not make assertions, ask questions, etc. If this is not transparent, what needs to be done is to clarify the behavioural criteria for asserting that p, for asking whether it is the case that p, etc. This would make clear the conceptual connections between using language in certain ways and wider patterns of human behaviour, as well as the similarities and differences among different uses of language. The investigation of whatever underlying causal factors enable humans, but not animals, to learn a language is the concern of science.

1.1   '... they simply do not talk ... they do not use language': this switch of expressions emphasizes the integration of speaking with the varied activities of human beings (cf. PI p. 174). Moreover, parrots do talk, but they do not use language.

2   (i) Z §§518 ff. (= MS. 136, 128) notes the fact that some concepts are applicable only to beings that possess a language. Cf. PI §§250, 650, p. 174.

Z §§532 ff. (cf. MS. 136, 29, MS. 134, 56 ff.) discusses the converse dependence of some other 'linguistic' abilities on the natural history of mankind: 'The concept of pain is characterized by its particular function in our life . . . Only surrounded by certain normal manifestations of life is there such a thing as an expression of pain. Only surrounded by an even more far-reaching particular manifestation of life, such a thing as the expression of sorrow or affection. And so on.' (Cf. TS. 232, 306: the expression of remorse is related to behaviour.)

(ii) PLP 134 f. notes an important consequence of the fact that commanding is part of a form of life, viz. that the application of the concept of command becomes increasingly indeterminate the more organisms differ from human beings. 'If we . . . try to transfer what we call "command" to quite another realm of being, to organisms very unlike human beings, . . . [it] is as if the word had lost its specific meaning. . . .' As we move away from men, to dogs, then to fish, then to amoebae, any talk of 'commands' gradually loses its point.

Section 26

1   This remark extracts from §25 an important consequence for the Augustinian picture of language. (The connections between §25 and §26 is indicated in the wording of earlier versions of these remarks in BT 209 and Vol. XI, 90, and in their being grouped together in PPI §26.) Understanding an utterance requires grasping its use and hence mastery of the whole pattern of speaking and activity that constitutes using a language. ('To understand a sentence is to understand a language' (PI §199).) Understanding a word must involve knowing how it is used as part of making moves in the language-game. Therefore, grasping the technique of using sentences is fundamental for understanding the meanings of words. The Augustinian picture puts everything upside down. According to it, a complete understanding of a word is acquired by learning what it stands for, and a complete understanding of a sentence involves nothing more than knowing what each of its components names. This presupposes that the use of sentences flows from correlating its words with things. Consequently, the Augustinian picture does not leave room for the possibility that a single type-sentence can

have different uses; and it cannot account for the connection between the
uses of sentences and the natural history of mankind.

W. suggests a method for reorienting our thinking about language:
viz. to remind ourselves that naming something is a *preparation* for using
a word (or, more generally, that establishing the grammar of an
expression is a preparation for applying it (cf. PLP 13 f.)). Then we will
have to focus on what naming is preparatory *for*. Nothing has even got a
name except in the language-game (PI §49). What is basic to learning
language is learning to make assertions, ask questions, formulate
hypotheses, etc. Any importance attached to learning what words name
is subsidiary.

SECTION 27(a)

1   (a) continues §26. The defender of the Augustinian picture answers the
question 'What is naming a preparation for?' by saying 'For talking *about*
things; for *referring* to them'.

W. makes three responses mocking in tone.

(i) The possibility of referring to things does not flow, as it were, from
the mere act of naming. We do refer to, and talk about, things; but this is
merely one of a multitude of speech activities which must be learnt.
Naming is neither a preparation for this alone, nor is learning a name
sufficient for being able to talk about something. (A baby learns the name
'Mama', and learns to call its mother, long before it can *talk about* its
mother.)

(ii) There is no *one thing* called 'talking about'. Compare talking about
the weather ('Isn't it a lovely day?' 'Yes, it really cheers one up to see the
sun.'), talking about Mr N.N. ('N.N. is such a nice fellow, he ought
to . . .'), talking about our plans ('We must do so-and-so, and then, if all
goes well, we shall . . .'), talking about an outrage ('It's disgraceful! Such
things should not be allowed!'), and talking about W.'s philosophy.

(iii) The range of speech activities is enormously varied. This is even
true of *one-word* exclamations. How can the Augustinian picture account
for their different uses? Surely it is not plausible to think that these
differences in use flow from what these words are correlated with. Nor is
it illuminating to view the words employed in these exclamations as used
to refer to or to talk about things.

W. introduces one-word exclamations as a *reductio ad absurdum* of the
Augustinian picture of sentences. He presents his familiar dilemma: it is
either false or vacuous to assert that words are always used to talk about
things.

(a) and (b) are separate remarks in PPI and PPI (R). (b) opens the
discussion of names and ostensive definition.

2   What immediately follows PI §27(a) in BT 209 v. and Vol. XI, 91 f. is PI §257. This emphasizes that the act of naming a sensation makes sense only against a background knowledge of the grammar of sensation words, i.e. mastery of their uses in the language-game.

CHAPTER 2

Ostensive definition and analysis

(§§ 27(b)–64)

INTRODUCTION

§§1–27(a) were a preliminary exploration of the Augustinian picture of language. §§27(b)–64 examine in detail the concept of ostensive definition that informs this *Urbild*. The criticisms ramify into discussions of logically proper names, their metaphysical counterparts, i.e. simples, and the notion of analysis. This is a natural progression of thought. Sophistication in developing the Augustinian picture into a theory of meaning involves distinguishing apparent from genuine names. Apparent names are analysed away; their meanings are derived from the meanings of the genuine names by means of analytical definitions. The Augustinian picture describes the inner workings of language, characterizing only real names and their combinations. Although classical empiricism developed in this direction by distinguishing simple from complex ideas, the acme of sophistication was attained only in logical atomism. According to it, logical analysis is such a strong solvent that it dissolves away almost all, if not the whole, of ordinary language and the world. Very few, if any, expressions are genuine names ('logically proper names'), and very little, if anything, of what we are familiar with qualifies as a simple, i.e. as an object that is the meaning of a logically proper name. The philosophical clarification of language will be full of surprises. Since the only legitimate use of ostensive definition is, according to the Augustinian picture, to correlate real names with simple objects, the discussion of ostensive definition cannot be isolated from discussions of analysis and of the associated notions of names and simples. Although many of W.'s criticisms are aimed primarily at logical atomism and some are particularly apposite for TLP, his target is nothing less than the illusion, which has dominated European philosophy, that language has foundations in simple concepts.

§§27(b)–64 divide readily into four parts. Part A runs from §27(b) to §36 and is concerned with ostensive definition. The salient points are as follows. (i) It is a fallacy to think that only 'simple concepts' are ostensively definable. (ii) Ostensive definition can be misinterpreted. (iii) Ostensive definition does not provide the 'foundations of language' or 'link language and reality'. (iv) Understanding an ostensive definition presupposes a tacit grasp of the type of expression defined (colour-word, shape-word, etc.). (v) The characteristic experiences accompanying ostension are not what *meaning* the colour, and the shape, etc., consists in. (vi) Hence understanding the ostensive definition is not a matter of knowing, nor of recapitulating, the accompanying experiences of the person giving the definition.

The structure of Part A:

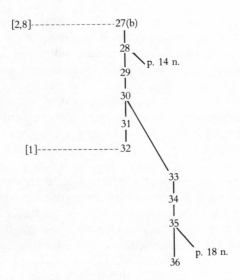

Part B consists of §§37–45 and focuses on the illusory 'real names'. According to the Augustinian picture, ostensive definitions correlate names with objects; a name has meaning in virtue of *standing for* an object. Consequently, if a name lost its correlated object, it would become meaningless. This idea generates pressure to restrict real names to expressions standing for what cannot fail to exist, i.e. 'logically proper names'. §§37–45 give the rationale for the introduction of logically proper names, criticize identifying the indexical 'this' as a real name, and expose the fallacy of equating the meaning of a name with its bearer. §43 first introduces the slogan 'The meaning of a word is its use in the language'.

The structure of Part B:

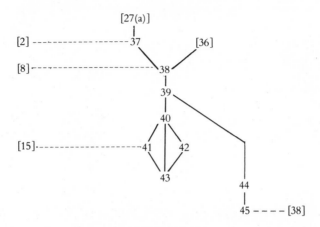

Part C extends from §46 to §59 and examines the conception of simples, i.e. the objective correlates (the 'bearers') of logically proper names. §46 uses a quotation from Plato as an archetype of the conception that simples can only be named, and it identifies Russell's 'individuals' and the 'objects' of TLP as exemplifications of this conception. §§47–8 note that what counts as simple and complex is relative to context-dependent standards of simplicity. §48 introduces a language-game of describing arrays of coloured squares which apparently conforms to the Augustinian picture and realizes the Platonic conception of simples. §§49–50 use this language-game to demystify the two characteristic theses of §46: (i) that simples can only be named, but not defined, and (ii) that simples are beyond existence and inexistence. §§51–4 discuss what the 'correspondence' between name and element in the language-game of §48 consists in: it is of philosophical interest only if it is normative, not mechanical, but both what counts as a rule correlating names with elements and how such rules enter into the applications of language are very various and complex. §55 gives a rationale for the idea that language presupposes the indestructibility of simples, viz. the possibility of using language to describe any possible state of affairs. W. suggests that samples used to explain words are things without which the corresponding words would have no meanings. §§56–7 consider two objections to this thesis. §§58–9 round off this discussion by diagnosing two sources of the illusion embodied in the Platonic conception of elements which exist 'in their own right' and remain the same through all change.

The structure of Part C:

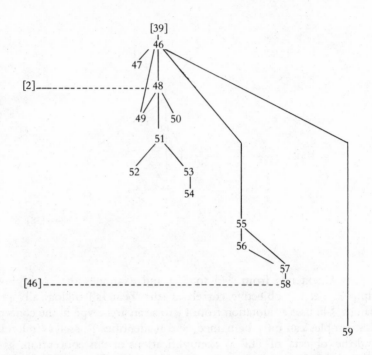

Part D embraces §§60–64 and discusses analysis. The 'deep' implica-tions of analysis, and hence too those of the theory of descriptions, are brushed aside as illusory.

The structure of Part D:

    Although the main thrust of §§27(b)–64 is critical and destructive, it would be wrong to conclude that nothing positive is achieved. W.'s account of ostensive definition and the role of samples contributes to understanding of important but neglected topics in the philosophy of language. Its ramifications even in the *Investigations* are far-reaching: it has implications for family resemblance, rule-following, explanation and understanding, and the possibility of a private language.

Correlations

PI	PPI	PPI(R)
27(b)	27(a)	35(a)
28	27(b)	35(b)
29	28	36
30	29(a–b)	37(a–b)
31	29(c–g)	37(c–g)
32	30	38
33	31	39
34	31	40
35	32	41
36	33	42
37	34	43
38(a–c)	35	44
38(d)	36	45
39	37	46
40	38	47
41	39	48
42	41	50
43	40	49
44	42	51
45	42	52
46	43	53
47(a–c)	44	54
47(d–e)	45	55
47(f)	46	56
48	47	57
49	48	58
50	49	59
51	50(a–b)	60(a–b)
52	50(c–d)	60(c–d)
53	51	61
54	52	62
55	53	63
56	54	64
57	55	65
58	56	66
59	57	67
60	58	68
61	59	69
62	60	70
63	61(a)	71(a)
64	61(b–c)	71(b–c)

Ostensive definition and its ramifications
1. Introduction   2. The range and limits of ostensive explanations
3. The normativity of ostensive definition   4. Samples   5. Samples in grammar: Wittgenstein's position   6. Samples in grammar: second-generation reflections   7. Samples and simples

Section 27(b)

1   This opens the detailed investigation of ostensive definition central to the Augustinian picture. In PPI and PPI(R) it is continuous with § 28.

The first point is that ostensive definition, like any explanation of meaning, is a correlate of requests for explanations (viz. asking what something is called). Secondly, the practice of asking for names and answering such requests is itself a language-game (absent in §§ 2 and 8), which is essentially a preparation for other language-games. Thirdly, correlative to asking for names, and answering, is the practice of stipulating names for things—and then using them.

Again it is striking how readily W. slides from talking of names in general to proper names. The parenthesis is important because of features of proper names rather than names of colours, materials, smells, etc. The example of giving names to dolls points to the great significance which we attach to personal names. Numbers, despite their impeccable individuative powers, lack the aura of proper names; giving prisoners numbers is degrading and dehumanizing; but even proper names of objects and places are significant to us ('2602, 32nd Street' belongs to a different culture from 'Sunny Corner, Rosenithon'). Once a doll has a name, one can not merely talk about it, but *to* it; this is *not* a trivial anthropological fact, irrelevant to a 'respectable semantics'. Equally important is the reminder of the vocative use of names. This familiar use strikes one as *remarkable* only when one bears in mind what philosophers have said about proper names and how they have viewed them almost exclusively as instruments for singular (unique) reference (cf. 'Proper names', pp. 229 ff.).

2   (i) PG 62 f. examines in greater detail ostensive teaching that is antecedent to definition since the learner cannot yet raise questions about meaning. Ostension has not the same role here as in more developed language-games. First, it is part of the child's training, not a response to a question about meaning. Secondly, the child cannot give an explanation by ostensive definition. But, of course, *that* the child's use *is* correct is manifest in the way its use relates to ours *and to our explanations*.

(ii) PLP 198 elaborates the parenthesis of §27(b). (i) Reflect on what particular material objects we name (the Koh-hi-noor, but not any old diamond; the Canterbury Quad, but not the front quad, etc.) and the reasons which underlie our name-conferring customs. (ii) Is it true that names (proper names) have a meaning only in the context of a sentence? They are used vocatively, and one can imagine a language in which that was the *only* way to use them (eg. all singular reference being by means of descriptions). They are used to send messages to people: the messenger (postman) must find the person whose name is on the envelope. Names are used as place-cards at dinners. One could enumerate dozens of further roles, actual and imaginable.

SECTION 28

1   With §28, W. begins the examination of ostensive definition. His aim is demystification. In particular, the idea that ostensive definition lays the foundations of language, links language to reality (thus ensuring the harmony between the two) must be swept aside. That view was associated with the idea that (i) only indefinables (the empiricists' simple ideas) were ostensively explained; (ii) the object pointed at (physically, or more commonly 'mentally') was the meaning of the indefinable expression; (iii) the correlation of indefinable and object was infallible; ostensive explanation was unambiguous and final (mental ostension, so to speak, always hits the bull's eye; for if I *mean* X by 'X'—how can I miss it?). The subsequent discussion of ostensive definition, challenging all three points, is intended to dethrone it, not deprive it of its citizenship. W. is not arguing that it is defective relative to other explanations of meaning, but rather than it is on a par with them. This point is vital, yet widely misunderstood.

W.'s first move here (against (i)) is to insist upon the wide competence of ostensive explanation. Of the kinds of term he specifies, the most outrageous, from the point of view of the current philosophical tradition, is that of numerals. Frege's response to the assertion that 'two' can be defined *perfectly exactly* by pointing at two nuts can be imagined! But reflect that instead of saying 'There are two men in the next room' one can say 'There are that ↗ many men in the next room', pointing at a pair of nuts.

The objection W. raises concerns misinterpretability. Surely one cannot define numerals ostensively, because how on earth can the addressee know *what* one is defining? W. immediately concedes that the hearer may suppose that one was naming the group of nuts. But this shows nothing, for any explanation, *a fortiori* ostensive definition, *can always* be misinterpreted. Hence the possibility of misinterpretation imposes no restriction on the scope of ostensive definitions. Moreover (iii), as well as (i), is undermined.

A Platonist who conceives of numbers as abstract objects may object that one cannot *point* at a number. To this one may reply that in so far as there is such a thing as pointing at a number, then one can so point. The only sense there is to 'pointing at a number' is pointing at a group of objects that has a number, i.e. has members (just as pointing at a colour consists in pointing at an object that has a colour).

2   PLP 104 ff. discusses the diverse range of ostensive definition. It emphasizes not only misinterpretability, but also the haziness of the borderline between what is and what is not ostensive definition, e.g. explanation by expressive gesture, calling attention to a musical note, etc.

PAGE 14 NOTE

1   This note is cut from B i. §522 (= Vol. X, Um. 138 and 197). It is impossible to say where it was meant to go. Its original home (cf. 2 below) is in the discussion of the harmony between language and reality, deferred in PI until §§429 ff. It could be viewed as a digression from §28 *à propos* the misinterpretability of ostensive definition.

Why would pointing to something green, and saying 'That is not red', not be an ostensive definition of 'red'? Not because it is open to misinterpretation, since that is generally true of ostensive definition. Even if it did generate an understanding of 'red', it would not be an ostensive definition. It plays a different part in the calculus—in the system of grammatical rules—than that played by ostensive definition. This follows from the features of an ostensive definition as an *explanation* of the meaning of a word. First, it provides, in the practices of explanation, a standard of correct use. Secondly, instead of 'red', one can substitute the deictic gesture, the utterance of 'this' and the red sample pointed at. Thirdly, giving a correct ostensive definition constitutes a criterion of a person's understanding the word thus explained. In all these respects, pointing at a green sample and saying 'That is not red' falls short of being an explanation of the word 'red'. First, in isolation, it does not constitute a standard of correctness for applying 'red'. Secondly, the partly concrete symbol constituted by the green sample, the ostensive gesture, and the utterance is *not* substitutable for 'red'. Thirdly, pointing at a green sample and saying 'That is not red' is not a criterion for a person's understanding 'red' any more than pointing at N.N. and saying 'That is not Julius Caesar' is a criterion for knowing who Julius Caesar is.

Is pointing thus at a green sample an ostensive definition of 'not-red'? This too is wrong, for we do not treat 'not-red' as a simple unitary predicate and do not accept unitary samples of 'not-red'; e.g., blue, like green, is not red—but not because it is the same colour (i.e. not-red) as green. Indeed, we explain the meaning of 'red' in 'This is not red' by pointing to something that is red (cf. PI §429).

What then is the role of 'That is not red' in the rules of colour grammar? *Qua* 'grammatical sentence' it may supplement an explanation of 'red' by contributing to determination of the boundaries of the concept. It is part of our practice of explaining colour-words not to use something employed as a sample of green also as a sample of red (although we do use a sample of white also as a sample of light-coloured). Hence we say, in the metaphysical mode, that something red all over cannot also be green all over. This utterance, as it were, gives a norm of exclusion.

1.1		(i) 'Erklärung': throughout discussion should be translated 'explanation' (cf. Exg. §70).

(ii) The final sentence is typical of W.'s repudiation of causal theories of meaning. Even if 'This is not red' had the effect that learners subsequently used 'red' correctly, this would not make the utterance a definition (any more than if hitting a person on the head while shouting 'red' brought about correct use, the blow would constitute an explanation). A correct definition must provide a standard of correctness, and giving a correct definition must be a criterion of understanding. The *practical consequences* are part of the *mechanism* of learning; an ostensive definition is part of the system of grammatical rules.

2		Following W.'s directions for stringing together these remarks from Vol. X puts PI p. 14 n. (and §446) in the context of PG 135 ff. The issue here is the problem of the 'harmony between language and reality', the illusion of which lay at the heart of the mythology of the picture theory of meaning. The connection with ostensive definition is only one aspect of this complex of problems.

SECTION 29

1		The specification of type or category might seem logically necessary and sufficient for preventing misinterpretation of ostensive definition. The fact that every ostensive definition not adorned by a category-specification can be misinterpreted (§28) shows that it must be supplemented to be complete, while the presence of such supplementation rules out the possibility of misinterpretation. W. criticizes both moves.

The claim that a category–specification is necessary is doubly misleading. (i) The ostensive definition without category-specification is not incomplete; e.g. the definition 'This ↗ is red' is not less perfect than the explanation 'This colour ↗ is red' in respect of providing a norm for applications of 'red' in standard contexts. (ii) It is clearly not necessary that we posses this categorial concept (e.g. of colour) prior to understanding fully expressions belonging to the category (e.g. 'red'); hence we need not understand the 'full' explanation in order to understand the initial one (e.g. 'This ↗ is red').

The sufficiency claim is equally misguided. (i) No explanation is proof against misinterpretation; in particular, the categorial term might not be understood or might even be misunderstood, and hence need explaining. (ii) Categorization, even by categorial terms like 'colour', is purpose-relative; correct understanding of a category term may vary with our purposes (see 1.1(i)). (W. uses neither of the expressions 'category' and 'formal concept'.)

Categorial specification is required in practice only where misunderstanding is likely (and nothing can *guarantee* success). What form is appropriate for an explanation depends on the circumstances and the learner. The possibility of misunderstanding disqualifies ostensive definitions for the role of anchors for language even when they are supplemented by categorial specifications.

1.1 (i) 'is there only *one* way of taking the word "colour"': sometimes 'colour' = 'chromatic colour', sometimes black and white count as colours too.

(ii) 'the last definition': one *can* go on explaining the words used in an earlier explanation of a word indefinitely (just as one can go on building further houses). But one *does not*; sooner or later one stops (as the explanations get farther and farther removed from the original explanandum). This finality is distinct from the finality of justification emphasized in PI §217: 'If I have exhausted the justifications I have reached bedrock and my spade is turned.'

(iii) 'ob er sie ohne dieses Wort anders auffasst, als ich es wünsche': W. preferred 'whether he misunderstands my definition if I leave out the word' (PPI(R) §36).

(iv) 'How he "takes" the definition': cf. Exg. §§85–8.

2 (i) PR 52 f. argues that colour is a categorial expression or formal concept. 'Blue is a colour' merely specifies the value of the categorial variable and gives no information about blue. This conception is closer to the TLP idea of formal concepts than to PI (cf. TLP 2.0131, 2.025–2.0251, 4.122, 4.124, 4.126–4.1274; also PT 2.0252). W. insists that expressions such as 'number', 'colour', 'shape', *need not* occur in the 'chapters' of the book of philosophical grammar. In TLP they *could not* so occur. In PI these expressions are deprived of their nimbus; they are not super-concepts, and they too need explaining (cf. Exg. §97).

(ii) PG 60 f. suggests that an ostensive definition of the form 'That is called "N"' is ambiguous. Categorial specification 'That C is called "N"', however, is wholly unambiguous. In PI, by contrast, W. studiously avoids talk of ambiguity. Certainly 'That is N' (or 'called

"N"') can be misunderstood. Certainly the misunderstanding might be eradicated by 'That C is N'. But equally, that too might be misunderstood.

(iii) BB 83 produces reasons for refusing to classify '1' with other numerals. W. invites us to reflect on our reasons for and against classifying '0' as a numeral, and black and white as colours.

(iv) PLP 98 ff. discusses the nature of categorial specification, with particular reference to 'colour'. Waismann stresses that the sentence ' "Red" is a colour-word' does not mean the same as, is not a translation of, 'Red is a colour'. A person who had been told to paint the wall some colour might say 'I had to paint the wall any colour, and red is a colour', but could not intelligibly say 'I had to paint the wall any colour, and "red" is a colour-word'.

(v) PLP 106 discusses the stratification of concepts. Understanding may begin with words like 'round', 'square', 'triangular', etc., then ascend to higher-order expressions such as 'shape', and finally to logical categories such as 'property'. With some families of concepts the particular order of learning the stratification is arbitrary, e.g. we may learn 'fir', 'pine', 'oak', first, and only later 'tree'; on the other hand, we may well learn these words in the converse order. But with other families of concepts this is not so: e.g. we could not learn the word 'number' prior to learning the numerals '1', '2', '3' . . ..

SECTION 30

1   The general thrust of §§30–1 is to present the antithesis to an element of the Augustinian picture. On that view if one knows, is acquainted with, the object for which a name stands (and knows this correlation), then one understands the name. All that one needs to do in explaining a name is to say what it stands for.

1.1   (i) 'the over-all role of the word in language': an unclear expression; W. translated 'welche Rolle' as 'what kind of role'. The suggestion is that the categorial expression, e.g. 'colour', will explain the kind of role of the word. But can every ostensively definable expression be located within the domain of a category? Is the ostensive definition without the categorial expression elliptical? Is the notion of the role or kind of role of a word in a language sharply circumscribed?

Again, it may seem that this restriction on the intelligibility or usefulness of ostensive definition is intended to reveal its defectiveness relative to other kinds of explanation. But this is wrong. Ostensive definition gives a rule for the correct use of an expression, as do other definitions. The fact that one will not commonly understand it unless one knows other rules (the rules determining the role of the word in the language) does not show that this rule is incomplete. *Any* definition can be misunderstood (PI p. 14 n.) One will not understand a *Merkmal*-definition unless one understands the words it contains. But it is not therefore incomplete. A *Merkmal*-definition of 'bachelor' is not substitutable in 'bachelor of arts', but it does not say so. Ostensive definition *differs* from other definitions but its difference does not turn on its unerring aim, nor on its being merely an *ersatz* explanation. From the normative point of view (the 'calculus'), its credentials are impeccable. From the pedagogic point of view, it depends on the circumstances.

(ii) 'um nach der Benennung fragen zu können': W. translated 'before you can ask what something is called'. This reiterates that explanation is correlative with requests for, doubts about, and misunderstandings of, meanings. Explanation presupposes antecedent training. What does one have to know already? The point is developed in §31.

SECTION 31

1.1   (i) 'without ever learning or formulating rules': presumably this means that he has learnt the game of chess, and so *knows the rules*, but has never been told them or formulated them. He might learn chess by observing the behaviour of chess-players. Though he has not been taught the rules, he must know the rules if he knows how to play the game.

(ii) 'being shown chessmen of a shape he was not used to': this seems to presuppose that the hearer knows the rules of the game.

(iii) 'the place for it was already prepared': in PPI(R), W. crossed out a similar version and wrote: 'we had in the game already prepared the place in which it was to be put'.

(iv) 'dass er in anderm Sinne schon ein Spiel beherrscht': W. preferred 'because he has in a different sense already mastered a game'. C8, 43 f. makes it clear that 'in another sense' is intended to emphasize not mere theoretical knowledge of the rules of chess, but the ability to apply them, mastery of a technique (cf. PI §150).

(v) §31(c)—'"mit Verständnis"': W. translated this '"with understanding"'. This, and '"knows what a piece in a game is"' are in scare-quotes, it seems, because knowing and understanding are problematic concepts.

(vi) §31(d): W. translated thus: 'there is only sense in someone's asking for the name if he already knows what to do with the name'.

(vii) §31(e) 'aufkommen': W. translated 'provide'.

Section 32

1   This develops §31: if one is only concerned with translation, then, assuming broad structural similarities, 'the place is already prepared', and one can often guess to what category the expression ostensively defined belongs. The Augustinian picture of language construes understanding an expression on the model of knowing its translation. To know what word in L_2 expresses what 'X' in L_1 expresses requires no more than to be told the name. To the extent that the Augustinian picture presupposes a thought-language of psychic elements, our public language is conceived as a translation of the inner language of thought.

The matter of an inner language of thought antecedent to public language will be assailed later. Here W. merely points out that although in the translation case one may guess the meaning of the ostensive definition, this presupposes a criterion for guessing right or wrong. This again reveals that understanding an expression is not merely knowing what it stands for. The criteria for guessing right lie in the anthropologist's own subsequent use of the expression and his hearer's responses, and in the 'fit' between his guess and his observations of use of the expression by native speakers.

In presupposing that the child can think (= talk to itself) but not yet speak, the Augustinian picture overlooks the role of training in language acquisition, and so the contrasts between training, ostensive teaching, and explanation.

1.1   'die Deutung dieser Erklärungen': this should be translated as 'the interpretation of these explanations', cf. §34.

Section 33

1   W. now considers an objection to the thesis of §30: surely all that is required to understand an ostensive definition is to guess what is *pointed at*, what object is *meant*, what feature is *attended to*.

(b) emphasizes that although different experiences may accompany looking at a colour from those accompanying looking at a shape, nevertheless there is no uniformity in the experiences that may accompany looking at a colour. There is no one experience (or uniform group of experiences) which necessarily accompanies looking at or attending to a feature, and it is not in virtue of any such experience that someone is rightly said to be attending to one.

1.1   'but in the circumstances that we call "playing a game of chess"': making a move in chess does *not* consist in the circumstances, nor in pushing a piece from here to there, but in moving a piece *in such-and-such circumstances*.

2   PG 63 argues that one points in a different *sense* to a body, a shape, or a colour: 'a possible definition would be: "to point to a colour" means, to point to the body which has the colour'. Analogously, a man who marries money does not marry it in the same sense in which he marries the woman who has it. This argument ramifies in two directions. First, one can point at a colour, shape, or length only in so far as one has some grasp of these concepts. Which one points at is neither determined by one's gesture, nor by one's 'mental gesture', but by the role of the sample (as a sample of colour, shape, or length) in the context—what is appropriately *done* with it. Secondly, the example illustrates the error of identifying the meaning of a name ostensively defined with what is pointed at. If we think that when we define 'blue' we 'point at the colour', we forget that to point at the colour is to point at the object which is blue, and that object (e.g. a book) is obviously not the meaning of 'blue' (and neither is its colour!).

     Cf. Z §§11 f. (= B i. 33, = Vol. XII, 31) (and BT 33), which compares hearing a piano, its sound, a piece of music, a player, his fluency; what does it mean that one hears in different senses?

SECTION 34

1   Even if there were a uniform set of experiences and actions ('I always do the same thing . . . and I feel . . .') accompanying attention to shape, those experiences and actions are not in themselves the grounds for asserting that the person was attending to the shape in saying 'That is called "a circle"'. What is crucial is what understanding the ostensive explanation 'That is a circle' consists in. If we say that it consists in having the same experiences as those accompanying the teacher's attending to the shape, then understanding becomes divorced from correct use. For as long as the learner had the same experiences (and his eyes followed the outline) when he heard the explanation, it does not matter how he subsequently uses the word. So the hearer might interpret 'This is a circle' quite differently from the teacher's intended meaning. This 'interpretation' (or 'misinterpretation') may also consist in his subsequent use of the word. W. in effect offers us a choice: *either* the learner has the same experience as the teacher, but his subsequent use is irrelevant to his understanding, *or* hearing the definition and having the same experiences is not a criterion for grasping the meaning. W.'s answer is obvious: neither intending an explanation thus-and-so nor interpreting it consist in processes which accompany giving or understanding explanations.

SECTION 35

1   §35(a) concedes that there *may* be characteristic experiences of pointing
to, e.g., a shape. Nevertheless, W. suggests two counter-moves. First,
there is no invariable 'shape-pointing experience' that always accompanies meaning the shape, any more than there is a unique 'colour-
pointing experience'. Secondly, W. invokes a tactic that will subsequently be relied on extensively in the discussion of family resemblance.
Even if there were a unique shape-pointing experience, its occurrence
would not entail that the person who had it meant that shape. Why
should not the shape-pointing experience occasionally accompany pointing at the colour? It depends upon the circumstances of pointing whether
we are entitled to assert that someone pointed at the shape. What special
experiences accompanied his pointing are not criteria of his meaning the
shape rather than the colour, even if they are regular concomitants.

    (b) intimates the point discussed in PG 63. The contrast between
pointing to the table and pointing to the chair is between pointing at two
different objects of the same general type (pieces of furniture, material
objects). But to point to a colour rather than to a shape involves a
contrast of category. In the first case we change the direction of our
gesture. In the second we need not, just because to point to the colour
(shape) *is* to point to the object which has it, and the same material object
may exemplify both colour and shape in question. This difference is evident
in the way we learn the use of words 'to point to ξ' in the various cases.

1.1   (i) 'do you also know of an experience characteristic of pointing to a piece
in a game *as a piece in a game*': this is somewhat misleading. One can
contrast pointing or attending to a carved chess piece, not even knowing
it to be a chess piece, with seeing it *as* a chess piece. This W. does not
deny. There may, for the sake of argument, even be experiences that
accompany pointing at chess pieces as chess pieces. The argument surely
should be that the experiences, if any, are so characterizable *because* the
pointing or attending is, irrespective of the experience, directed at the
piece *qua* piece rather than *qua* arbitrary carving. Hence the prior question
is what are the criteria for so pointing or attending. So far from the
experience explaining the nature of the pointing, attending, or meaning,
it is the latter which explain the nature of the former.

    On the other hand, it is evident from the foregoing that the 'experi-
ences' of pointing to the shape or attending to the colour are
activities—following the outline with finger or eye, attending to the
colour by blotting out the outline with one's raised hand, etc. Now it is
plausible—in this sense—that there are no 'characteristic experiences and
ways of pointing' or attending to a chess piece *qua* chess piece.

(ii) '(Recognizing, wishing, remembering, etc.)': these too are not correctly characterized by their accompanying experience. Cf. PI p. 231 for remembering, §§602 f. and PI p. 197 for recognizing.

2   BB 80 illuminates one source of the temptation to think that meaning the colour (as opposed to the shape) is a mental process. If asked 'What did you point at?', one can normally answer and be certain one's answer is correct.

PAGE 18 NOTE

1   It is unclear where these cuttings belong. Since §33 introduced the objection that all that is necessary to understand an ostensive definition is to know what is pointed at, attended to, or *meant*, it is possible that these remarks fit on to §35 as an amplification of what it is to mean such-and-such.

(a) and (b) come from B i. §36. This is taken from Vol. XII, 33, where they are followed by a discussion of asking for word-meanings, as in 'What colour is called "chrome yellow"?', 'What is C‴?' 'What does the word *"nefas"* mean?' (cf. Exg. §145), and the different ways of answering. This context does not illuminate the PI location. (c) comes from B i. §223 (= Vol. XII, 310).

'That is blue' can be used as an assertion about an object or as an explanation of the meaning of the word 'blue', i.e. as a 'grammatical statement'. How can this be? The word 'is' is not ambiguous between 'is' and 'is called'. 'Blue' is the name of a colour, not of the name of a name of a colour. So the fact that 'That is blue' is meant as an explanation is not accounted for by the fact that one meant by 'is'—'is called', and by 'blue'—'"blue"'. Rather, by 'That is blue', one meant 'That is called "blue"', i.e. if asked to explain what one meant one would give that paraphrase and reject the paraphrase 'The X (book, sofa, carpet, etc.) is blue'.

Of course, one could also paraphrase one's utterance by 'That colour is blue', or again 'That colour is called "blue"'. Two points must be stressed: First, the indexical 'that' is no more ambiguous than the word 'blue' (cf. 'Indexicals', pp. 123 f.); 'that' does not mean 'that carpet (sofa, book)' in the first case and 'that colour' in the second. Rather, the speaker means, by saying 'that is blue', that the colour is blue; i.e. the ambiguity of the sentence is not attributable to the ambiguity of its constituents, but to the different uses that can be made of the sentence which are manifested in the different explanations of the sentence (rather than its constituents) and the different criteria of understanding in each case. Secondly, it is not, of course, contended that 'that (colour) is blue' and 'that (colour) is called "blue"' are synonymous. Rather, one would manifest one's grasp of the fact that the sentence 'That is blue' is being used to give an ostensive definition rather than to make an assertion equally well by either explanation; giving one of these explanations is a criterion for grasping the meaning of the utterance.

If the ambiguity resides in the use of the sentence (not in its form, nor in the form of a sentence for which it is elliptical) and its meaning is to be seen in the criteria for understanding it, then paragraph (b) is clear. For a person may say 'That is blue', meaning that X is blue, but be misunderstood by the hearer to be giving an ostensive definition of 'blue'.

The marginal note: 'Here lurks a crucial superstition' is enigmatic. It may be an allusion to TLP 3.263 and the subsequent criticism of elucidations thus conceived in PR 54. In TLP, W. conceived names to be indefinable. Their meanings, however, are explained by elucidations, i.e. *propositions* that contain the indefinable. Hence these propositions can only be understood if the meanings of those signs are already known. To be sure, this is needlessly paradoxical. His point is that the meanings of indefinables can only be picked up from their use in assertions, i.e. their explanation is always extracted out of a piece of information. In PR 54 this is repudiated. 'This is A' may be a proposition (assertion) or a definition but not both. If it is a proposition it can only be understood if the meaning of 'A' is known, but if it is an explanation it is not an assertion about A. This claim is marginally qualified here, i.e. it is *possible* to get an explanation out of what was intended as information. This is not to revert to TLP, but merely to avoid dogmatism.[1] However, this does not demonstrate the possibility of eliminating explanations from language.

(c) is connected with its antecedents via the idea of being able to mean by 'is' first 'is' ('ist') and then 'is called' ('heisst'). Meaning is not a spiritual activity, nor are we free, as it were, in the domain of the mind, to mean what we wish by whatever sign we use. Meaning something by an utterance requires that the symbol employed be either predetermined as a signal (as in a code) or else possess the appropriate articulations. Whether I can mean so-and-so by uttering such-and-such depends on the general use of the sentence uttered and its relation to those sentences which would, in the language, express what I meant. It is not just a question of 'who is master'! Unlike 'to imagine' ('Whenever I say "bububu" I imagine that I am going for a walk'), 'to mean', thus used, involves *meaning something by an utterance*. And what one can mean by an utterance depends on its general use (cf. PI §§508 f.). What one means must be something representable by the sentence uttered. (Of course, one

[1] Nevertheless, *one* aspect of the TLP docrtine remains firm, namely that any explanation of a language presupposes a linguistic mastery. 'I cannot use language to get outside language' (PR 54). This point is never relinquished.

can fail to express clearly what one means. But that is not at issue here.)

2   Vol. VIII, 154 (= EBT 471) contains an interesting parallel remark:

'Dieses Buch hat die Farbe, die "rot" heisst'.
'Die Farbe, die dieses Buch hat, heisst "rot"'.
So klingen die beiden Sätze am ähnlichsten; aber wir könnten offenbar auch einem dieser Sätze den Sinn des andern geben. Aber in einem Fall setzen wir den Gebrauch des Wortes fest, verkünden // enunciate // also eine grammatische Regel, im andern Fall machen wir eine Behauptung, die durch die Erfahrung bestätigt oder widerlegt werden kann.

('This book has the colour that is called "red".'
'The colour, which this book has, is called "red".'
Put thus, the two sentences sound very much alike; we could clearly even give one of them the sense of the other. But in one case we are fixing the use of the word, hence enunciating a grammatical rule, in the other case we are making a statement, which can be confirmed or confuted in experience.)

SECTION 36

1   This concludes the first part of the discussion of ostensive definition. It characterizes the errors examined in §§33–5 in terms of a general philosophical syndrome. Faced with seemingly unanswerable philosophical problems (they *are* unanswerable—and need unravelling, not answering (MS. 158, 33)), we typically resort to mythology and mystery. Two standard strategies are employed: mentalism and Platonism. Either can be grafted on to a calculus model of language.
One exemplification of this error is examined in §§37 ff., i.e. the mystification of 'the name-relation'[2] and its pseudo-explanation by reference to the powers of the mind. Others will crop up in the sequel when W. shows how the search for mental correlates (e.g. of remembering, understanding, wishing or expecting) is a kind of philosophical displacement behaviour which replaces the examination of the multiple (not unitary) criteria for ascription of psychological predicates.

1.1   §36(b): W. preferred the translation: 'Where our language leads us to look for a physical thing and there is none: there we are inclined to put a *spirit*' (PPI(R) §42).

2   Z §§12 f. (= MS. 130, 16; Vol. XII, 277) remarks, *à propos* 'pointing in different senses to this body, its shape, colour, etc.', that here 'meaning

---

[2] Cf. R. Carnap *Meaning and Necessity* (University of Chicago Press, Chicago, 1956), Ch. III.

gets imagined as a kind of mental pointing, indicating'. We have the impression that thinking of a person is like nailing him with a thought. B i. §224 (= Vol. XII, 310) raises a similar issue. If I think of N or speak about him, how does what I say connect with N? Using N's name hardly suffices, since many people may be called 'N'. But if so, some other connection must obtain between my utterance and N, otherwise I *would not* have been speaking about *him* at all. Certainly—but not a connection of the kind we readily imagine, i.e. not via a psychic mechanism. 'I mean' is not comparable to 'I aim at . . .'.

SECTION 37

1   This complements the discussion of ostensive definition by raising the question of what it is for a name to *signify* or *stand for* an object. What is *the* relation between any name and what it names? (What is 'the name-relation'?)

§15 implied that there are many more or less similar relations described by the verb 'to signify', the most straightforward of which consists in marking the named object with its name. This implication is made explicit here: there are many possible different relations between names and what is named even in language-games as simple as that of §2. There is no single relation 'to signify' or 'to stand for', and hence there is no possibility of using 'the name-relation' to expose the essence of names. An *Übersicht* of the uses of words is not forthcoming from scrutinizing the various relations between words and what they 'stand for' in search of *the* name-relation.

This negative conclusion undermines one pillar of the Augustinian picture. That presupposes that there is a uniform relation between names and what is named. Every (genuine) name *stands for* something, and what it stands for is its meaning. Unless there is a single relation expressed by '"x" stands for y', there is neither a unitary concept of a name nor one of the meaning of a name.

The only possible defence is to sublime the logic of our language (§38). We might then suppose that the name-relation is something occult, a spiritual mechanism linking a name to what it names; but the previous investigation of ostensive definition has brought no such thing to light. Moreover, even if there were a single 'name-relation', whether obvious or 'deep', it would be irrelevant for characterizing the *meanings* of names (cf. §§51 ff.). That requires clarifying *rules* for the correct use of names, not describing what relations hold between words and things.

2   BB 172 f. stresses that the quest for 'the name-relation' is not satisfied by answers such as 'The name is written on the object' or 'When his name is

called, he comes', etc. This dissatisfaction is correct, but its correctness is masked by looking 'deeper' for some other 'non-trivial' or 'non-physical' relation, e.g. a mental or spiritual one. For this is to persist in looking in the wrong direction. 'A primitive philosophy condenses the whole usage of the name into the idea of a relation, which thereby becomes a mysterious relation.' Rather we must forget about mysteries and simply examine the use of names, their various roles in language, for the answer to our puzzlement lies here. 'It is clear that there is no one relation of name to object, but as many as there are uses of sounds or scribbles which we call names'.

PLP 199: 'What a noble role the "relation between the name and the object named" plays in the eyes of certain philosophers.'

3 Cf. Russell:

When we ask what constitutes meaning, we are not asking what is the meaning of this or that particular word. The word 'Napoleon' means a certain individual; but we are asking, not who is the individual meant, but what is the relation of the word to the individual which makes the one mean the other . . . When we are clear both as to what the word is in its physical aspects, and as to what sort of thing it can mean, we are in a better position to discover the relation of the two which *is* meaning. (AM 191.)

(Russell argues that this relation is causal.)

Section 38

1   The indexical use of 'this' would, according to the Augustinian picture, obviously exemplify 'the name-relation'. W. elaborates reasons for not assimilating indexicals to names (cf. 'Indexicals', pp. 123 f.). Even more curiously, however, the relation of 'this' to its referent has been thought to be the *only* exemplification of the genuine 'name-relation'. What are superficially classified as 'names' fail to manifest the spiritual mechanism in which the 'name-relation' really consists.

1.1   (i) 'the word "this" has been called the only *genuine* name': cf. Russell, LA 201.

(ii) Note throughout that no distinction is made here between proper names and common nouns. This is justified here since the atomists argued that ordinary proper names were not really proper names anyway, and *real* proper names could, apparently, name general characteristics as well as individuals. §38(b) stresses that *very different* things are called 'names' (e.g. names of people and places, animals and objects, colours and tastes, directions and moves in a game, numbers and proofs, etc.) but *not* indexicals. §38(c), however, seems to vacillate. W. usually uses 'N' as a dummy proper name and in PPI §35 he points out the substitutability of 'Paul' for 'this' in 'Bring this!' This makes problematic the claim that it is characteristic of a name that it can be defined ostensively, for this is *not* obviously true of proper names (cf. 'Proper names', pp. 253 f.).

(iii) 'the philosopher tries to bring out *the* relation . . .': cf. LPE 308, 'When I stare at a coloured object and say "This is red", I seem to know exactly to what I give the name "red". As it were, to that which I am drinking in. It is as though there was a magic power in the words "*This is* . . ."' (cf. also LPE 316 ff.). Striking instances of this phenomenon are NB 53, 83.

(iv) 'wenn die Sprache *feiert*': W. preferred 'when language *idles*', which fits the mechanical analogy (levers, cogwheels) better. When *is* language idling in this respect? Precisely when one stares at N and repeats the word 'N' or even 'this' to it (addressing it)—trying to fathom 'the name-relation', instead of *using* these words in a language-game. Any name-relation (as opposed to *the mythical* one) is only of interest in so far as it is apparent in the use or explanation of the name.

(v) 'baptism': the metaphor is unclear. Evidently it is a fallacy to conceive of all naming as a baptism (although baptism *is* naming an 'object'), but is *this* pseudo-naming conceived as stipulating a name or as uttering a name which already has a bearer? If the latter, in what way is it like baptism? Perhaps this: that we think that by uttering it with intense concentration we shall discover what relation actually obtains between name and object. In baptism, uttering a name—in the conventional ceremonial setting—confers a name (creates an instance of 'the name-relation'!), and the philosopher misguidedly thinks that he can discover this 'relation' by dissecting the *act* of baptism (like trying to find out what a goal really is by repeatedly kicking a ball into a net outside the context of a game).

Indexicals
Logically proper names
  1. Introduction   2. Russell   3. The *Tractatus*   4. Wittgenstein's criticism

Section 39

1   This links together three classical themes: (i) the idea of 'analysis', (ii) the 'logically proper name', (iii) the 'simple object'. These are here connected by means of the principle (adopted by Russell and TLP) that a sentence has a sense only if every expression in it has a meaning, once the logical form of the sentence is displayed. 'Excalibur has a sharp blade' has sense even if Excalibur is destroyed. Hence 'Excalibur' is not a logically proper name and must disappear when the sentence is analysed. An analysed (elementary) sentence will contain only names which cannot fail to refer, and their referents must be simple (otherwise they could decompose, i.e. cease to exist, and their names would cease to stand for anything, and hence lack meaning). Cf. 'Logically proper names', pp. 125 ff.

1.1   (i) 'Denn man ist versucht, gegen das, was gewöhnlich "Name" heisst': W. preferred 'For we are inclined to raise an objection to calling "a name" what is generally called so' (PPI(R) §46).

(ii) 'dass der Name eigentlich Einfaches bezeichnen soll': W. preferred 'a name ought really to stand for something simple'.

(iii) 'Excalibur' does not occur in the German, but 'Nothung', the name of Siegfried's sword. But W. substituted 'Excalibur' for the first occurrence of "Nothung' in PPI(R).

2.1   'as no object would then correspond to the name it would have no meaning': cf. PR 72—'What I once called "objects", simples, were simply what I could refer to without running the risk of their possible non-existence.'

Section 40

1   §40 attacks only *one* premise in the argument of §39, i.e. that a name has no meaning if there exists nothing for which it stands. The attack does not involve a direct thrust at TLP, since there the bearers of names are sempiternal (as required by the argument of §39), and so it is senseless to think of them as ceasing to exist. Hence it is nonsense to think that the TLP names have meaning when their bearers die. This is obvious, since these sublimed names and mythological objects were *expressly designed* to meet this anxiety.

One point of §40 is to undermine the doctrine of TLP by showing that the worry which led to the erection of this metaphysical edifice is groundless. The argument was that a proper name has a meaning only if there exists an object for which it stands (which is its meaning). If no such object exists the name has no meaning, and any sentence in which it occurs is thereby rendered nonsensical. But this is absurd. The meaning of a name is not its bearer, and a name may have a meaning even though its bearer no longer exists. So the demise of its bearer does not affect the sense of the sentence in which it occurs. So the supposition that 'Excalibur' cannot be a real name was groundless and the postulation of sempiternal simples needless.

Much is left unclear in the argument. The worry that destruction of complexes (changes in the facts) might affect logic (the sense of sentences) is dispelled by insistence that to have meaning is not to stand for an existing object. But W. says nothing on a topic that vexed Frege: if the sense of a name is distinct from its reference, can there be names with sense but no reference, and hence sentences with sense (expressing thoughts) but no truth-value? Certainly, W. (like Frege) claimed that fictional names have a meaning, and that there are names without a bearer (unallocated names). But it is unclear what line he would take on declarative sentences containing a referenceless name (e.g. 'Vulcan'—the supposed intra-Mercurian planet). Do they have a meaning but no truth-value? Or do they lack any meaning?

It is clear that the bearer of a proper name is not its meaning (whether we should speak of proper names having a meaning is discussed in 'Proper names', pp. 251 ff.). But is the bearer (*Träger*) the reference (*Bedeutung*) of the name? A proper name does not lose (cease to *have*) a reference when its bearer dies. Two lines of argument are open. Either '"N" has a bearer' is timelessly true or false, with the consequence that 'the bearer of "N"' cannot be substituted for 'N' in the *extensional* context 'N has died', i.e. N's death does not deprive 'N' of its bearer. This has a needlessly paradoxical appearance. Alternatively, that 'N' has a reference is timelessly true or false, but not the statement that 'N' has a bearer (referent), i.e. that the bearer of 'N' exists. While bearer = referent, to have a reference is not to have a bearer *now*. Rather, 'N' has a reference if it is used to refer to a past, present, or future particular. That that particular (the bearer or referent of 'N') no longer exists or does not yet exist (as when an author names his next book before writing it) is irrelevant to whether 'N' has a reference.

Distinguishing the meaning of a name from its bearer is a prominent theme in W.'s discussion of names. It applies both to proper names and to common nouns. One may not replace the words 'That is red' used in an ostensive definition by 'That is the meaning of the word "red"' (Vol. VII, 120).

1.1   (i) 'sprachwidrig': 'ungrammatically' (PPI(R), §47).

(ii) 'das dem Wort "entspricht" ': W. altered a similar translation to 'which the word "stands for" ' (PPI(R) §47).

(iii) 'Herr N.N.': PPI reads 'Paulus'. 'N.N.' is used in German as a dummy proper name akin to 'A.N. Other' in English.

2   PG 64 argues that 'the bearer of the name "N"' = 'N', whereas 'the meaning of the name "N"' ≠ 'N'. This synonymy thesis is incorrect; the phrase 'the bearer of the name "N"', unlike 'N' itself, is language-dependent, and these expressions may behave differently in non-extensional contexts.

SECTION 41

1   The meaning/bearer distinction is applied to the simple language-game. Whether 'N' loses its meaning after the destruction of its bearer *is not settled* by the form of introduction (bestowal) of the proper name. It is settled by the practice of its use. (A case of a person's name 'going out of circulation' in our culture is a woman's maiden name after marriage; more sharply, in the middle ages, a person's baptismal name after change of name on confirmation.)

1.1   *1*.1 states that §15 is concerned with proper names (cf. Exg. §15).

SECTION 42

1   This is an argument against the view that only what now exists or has previously existed can be named; or that a name only has a meaning if it has or has had a bearer. Such a thesis is a natural defence of an atomist (or his direct descendent) against criticism of an Augustinian picture of proper names. (But Frege is *not* the target.)

The atomists' line of defence can be generalized in the form of the thesis that it is impossible to name future or merely possible individuals. Such contentions are theory-motivated dogmas. Why is it not possible to name a future individual? Does *logic* prevent it? Is the meaning of 'name' such as to preclude it? Cannot one name an unborn or even unconceived child? Of course, if no child is born, no reference is secured. But are such medical facts going to determine whether 'N.N.' is a proper name? Cannot an author name an unwritten book? Or a dancer announce the name of the dance she is about to perform?

W. indicates the possibility of introducing names for tools that have never existed into a language-game like that of §15. All that is required is that such names have an appropriate role or use. This can easily be imagined: e.g. as a joke, asking for Cure-all whenever the work in hand is ruined.

That there is not *now* a bearer does not imply that a name has no reference. But further—that a name has no reference does not imply that it is not a name. To be sure, we can invent 'fictional universes of discourse' for Odysseus to inhabit, or even possible worlds for Zeus to rule over. But are such startling inventive powers necessary to grasp the role of such proper names? Is it not enough to describe their use and observe their affinities with uncontroversial cases of proper names?

1.1   'verwendet': 'applied' (PPI(R) §50).

·   Section 43

1   This interpolates the positive counterpart of the repudiation of identifying meaning and bearer. The slogan that the meaning of a word is its use in the language is intended to have general application. It occurs here in the discussion of proper names, stressing that we cannot conclude from the ostensive definability of a name that its meaning is its bearer. Though ostensively explained, its meaning is nevertheless its use. For explaining the meaning of a name is giving a rule for its correct use. A criterion for whether the meaning has been understood is correct subsequent use.

One might object that we do not ordinarily talk of proper names as having meanings at all (cf. 'Proper names', pp. 251 ff.).

One might also object that this slogan is not equivalent to, and hence is in competition with, W.'s other slogans, which variously associate meaning with (i) assertion-conditions, (ii) verification-conditions, (iii) role in the calculus, (iv) explanation of meaning, (v) purpose, etc. (cf. 'Meaning and understanding', pp. 368 f.).

1.1   (i) 'For a *large* class of cases—though not for all': what exceptions are envisaged? One possibility would be to exploit the antithesis 'for a large class of cases'/'sometimes', i.e. that proper names when ostensively defined are an exception. This is absurd. It would be pointless to introduce the principle into a discussion of proper names if such names were typically exceptions to it. Moreover, the only natural route to this treatment of proper names is to identify their meanings with their bearers, and this is already blocked. Finally, the thrust of the preceding argument is that whether 'X' is a proper name or not turns on its use, not on whether it has a reference. The correct interpretation is surely to look for exceptions, not to this account of the meaning of a word, but to this explanation of the meaning of 'meaning'. Meaning may be ascribed to gestures, facial expressions, natural phenomena (e.g. 'Those clouds mean rain'), signals (e.g. traffic lights), colour patterns (BB 17), events, rituals, and persons (e.g. 'He means well'). The slogan is only a partial

explanation of the meanings of 'meaning'. This interpretation is rein-
forced by PLP 155 ff.

(ii) 'dieses Wort so erklären': W. preferred 'We may . . . explain this
word thus' (PPI(R) §49). ('erklärt' in the next sentence has been translated
as 'explained'.)

(iii) 'pointing to its *bearer*': in contrast with ostensive definition of,
e.g., colour-words, where one points at a *sample*.

2   PLP 175 f. notes that 'the meaning of a word is the way it is used' is not
quite correct, for there are cases where it seems forced (e.g. 'the meaning
[of this word] has dawned on me'). To remedy this defect we need a
detailed account of the grammar of 'meaning' as it appears in various
linguistic contexts; i.e. an account of what it is to understand the meaning
of a word, to explain the meaning of a word, for two words to have the
same meaning, etc.

Section 44

1   This and §45 link the discussion with §38, showing 'why it should
occur to one' to make 'this' into a name.

Proper names can be used in the absence of their bearers, but we could
imagine names which could only be used in the presence of their bearers.
Such symbols, W. suggests, are replaceable by 'this ↗'.

This remark, and others, suggest that the notion of a proper name is at
least akin to a family resemblance concept. The use of a name in the
absence of its bearer, though a distinctive feature of proper names, is not
a necessary condition, since we can imagine a language-game with
expressions which we would unhesitatingly classify as names although
they have no such use.

2   (i) PPI §42 contains additional material: suppose we are watching a
cinema screen on which three coloured spots move about slowly
changing their shapes. Suppose we ostensively define them by 'P', 'Q',
and 'R', and we describe their changes. In this language-game the names
are used as synonyms for 'this ↗' and the coloured spot. If one of the
three spots disappears we cannot say 'P has disappeared' any more than
'This has disappeared'. But we might say 'The letter "P" is out'. In *this*
language a name *does* lose its meaning when its bearer ceases to exist (it
being assumed that we do not speak about past events, nor use some
other mode of expression for them). So here a name cannot cease to have
a bearer. But *this is not an asset* of the language-game. For a name can have
a use, a meaning, without having a bearer (e.g. 'Odysseus' has meaning).

(ii) Z §715 (cf. TS 229, §1260 = MS 133, 23) discusses a language-game
in which a name ceases to have a use on the demise of its bearer. Here the

names, as it were, have the object on a string; if the object is destroyed, the string is useless. (The strategies mentioned in Exg. §40 involve making the object indestructible or the string unbreakable.)

(iii) PLP 196 ff. stresses the family resemblance character of the concept of a name.

Section 45

1   If our convention for the use of 'this' with an ostensive gesture is that it is only correctly used in the presence of a bearer, then *of course* 'this' cannot lack a bearer. (But there are other uses of 'this', cf. 'Indexicals', pp. 119 f.) To the atomist (Russell) it thus appears that 'this' is guaranteed a reference, whether simple or complex. But that does not make 'this' into a name, since a name is not typically used with, but only explained by, ostensive gestures.

2   PPI prefixes to this remark: 'But this language-game with coloured spots can, I think, show us a reason why one might wish to say that a demonstrative pronoun is a name: for . . .' (PPI(R) §42).

Section 46

1   The quotation from *Theaetetus* 201e–202b opens the discussion of simples, providing an archetype exemplified in logical atomism. The simples are the objective correlates of logically proper names.

Not all of what is asserted of the primary elements in the *Theaetetus* is true of Russell's individuals or TLP's objects. In particular, because of conflating positive and negative predications with positive and negative existential statements, Plato, unlike the logical atomists, denies that primary elements can have even external properties. None the less, the resemblances are considerable. Primary elements cannot be defined or analysed, cannot be said to exist or not to exist, and are simple.

2   BB 31: the objects (individuals, elements) of TLP were conceived of as necessary existents; if they did not exist, we could not even imagine them. What can be imagined, though it does not exist, must be a (non-existent) combination of such necessary existents.

3   There is an unmentioned aspect of Plato's primary elements which is an important point of resemblance with W.'s early conception. This is the contention that the Forms are self-predicable, with its corollary that only a Form perfectly instantiates a property, that any other object exhibits a property only by partaking of the correlated Form, by containing part of

the Form as an ingredient adulterated with other properties. In BT 434 (cf. GB 35 f.), W. connects his erroneous conception of object and complex in TLP with this Platonic theme, expressed in such phrases as 'As dead as death', or 'Nothing is so dead as death itself; nothing is so beautiful as beauty itself'.

SECTION 47

1   There is no such thing as absolute simplicity or complexity. 'Simple' and 'complex' are attributive adjectives; hence 'Is A simple or complex?' makes sense only if it is to be understood as 'Is A a simple or complex X?' The answer depends not only on what an X is, but also on what standards of simplicity or complexity are set up for Xs. *Pari passu*, what counts as an element (constituent) also depends on our choices and interests in laying down what is to be called 'a component part'.

The analogy with the boy wondering whether 'to sleep' means something active or passive holds because of his disregard of the context of the question. Obviously, it is in the active voice: equally clearly, to sleep is not to engage in an activity.

1.1 (i) 'so wird er mit Recht fragen': 'he will rightly ask you'.

(ii) 'that would be an answer to the *grammatical* question': W. distinguishes the question 'What are here called "simple component parts"?' (i.e. what, in this context, does 'simple component part' mean?) from 'What are the simple component parts?' (i.e. 'Describe (specify) the various simple component parts').

(iii) 'the correct answer is: "That depends on what you understand by 'composite'!"': that this is a rejection of the question would be even more obvious if it were replaced by a direct question: 'What do you mean by "composite"?' This would exemplify the philosophical method of answering a question with a question (RFM 147), while the original question exemplifies the philosopher's sin of giving words a metaphysical employment outside their natural context (PI §116) and then wondering what they mean (like a child scribbling, and then asking its parent what it has drawn). Outside its proper context (i.e. in which criteria of simplicity and complexity are laid down) the question 'Is X composite, and what are its parts?' has no use, no sense.

2   (i) PR 252 f. is a remote ancestor: it argues that: (a) a larger geometrical shape is not composed of smaller geometrical structures; (b) 5 is not composed of 3 and 2 any more than 2 is composed of 5 and −3; (c) whether a chessboard is complex or not depends (in part) on what we count as complexity, for if we disregard the squares, we can see it as a unity (a large rectangle). There are, however, points of disagreement too:

(a) in actual space the figure ■□ is actually composed of the components ■ and □ ; hence, it is irreducibly composite; (b) unless we disregard the constituent squares of a chessboard, then it is incontrovertibly composite. In PR, there are options for setting up standards of simplicity, but there are also severe constraints on their range.

(ii) Cf. TS. 219, 14: after (b), W. notes that the whole picture of logical 'analysis' is misleading, for an analysis is a search for simpler components, and logical analysis, except in very special cases, is *not* concerned with that.

SECTION 48

1   This language-game gives an apparent realization of the Augustinian picture. It also approximates to the construction of a 'model' for the 'analysed language' of TLP, although it is not quite adequate (nothing *can* be) because it does not meet the atomicity requirement (e.g. 'R_1' entails '$\sim G_1 \cdot \sim W_1 \cdot \sim B_1$'). It is therefore not surprising to notice its affinity with LF's system of co-ordinates for the description of colours and shapes in the visual field. The system of numbered squares gives the method of projection to get from the sentence (the linear arrangement of names) to the complex (array) of elements. Coloured squares, by TLP's standards, would not be simples. Yet, as W. stresses, nothing could be more natural than to conceive of these as simple elements.

That there is no such thing as absolute simplicity has an important corollary: the possibility of imagining a context in which something (e.g. a monochrome square) would not count as a simple does not show that it cannot correctly be taken as simple in another (or a more restricted) context. (Cf. W.'s comments on defeasibility of descriptions in visual geometry (PR 293 f.).) Thus, e.g., the fact that a squiggly line ∿∿∿ might occur as part of a larger line that gave the visual impression under standard conditions of being straight (e.g. a boundary line on a cricket pitch), does not show that, as it stands on this page, it gives the visual impression of being straight.

1.1   (i) 'for which this account is really valid': misleading, since W. goes on to show that it is not valid.

(ii) 'Does it matter which we say . . .': as long as the principle of counting for letters is the same as that for elements, it does not matter whether types or tokens are in question—as long as we avoid misunderstandings.

2.1   'I do not know what else . . . call "the simples" ': Z §338 (=TS 229, §1273, =MS 133, 34) stresses that we can give various senses to 'This chair is complex', i.e. assign various criteria of complexity for chairs. Not so with 'Red is complex', for 'We are not familiar with any technique to which this sentence might be alluding'.

One may elaborate this theme as follows: with respect to any predicate, sortal or adjectival, we can set up criteria of simplicity or complexity. We might, e.g., determine that primary colours are simple and the others complex; or correlate simplicity or complexity of colour with causal, chemical, phenomena that produce such-and-such colours. But the fact is—*we do not*. Our philosophical confusion, however, arises thus: we see that no criteria of complexity apply to colours, and we confuse the *absence* of any criteria of complexity with the *presence* of criteria of simplicity. The truth is that the complex/simple dichotomy has, for us, no application to colours.

SECTION 49

1　　The language-game of §48 is a model for the conception of simples in the *Theaetetus*. According to that conception, simples are indefinable (§46). But what does it mean to say of the elements of §48 that they cannot be defined but only named?

That elements can only be named, not described, is a simplified representation of a salient thesis of atomism (TLP 3.221; LA 194). It did not mean that simples could not have external properties, but rather that names of simples were indefinable. For expressions for complexes were conceived to be definable by a definite description that spelt out the elements of the complex. Hence such expressions disappeared on analysis. As in §40, W. does not attack the developed doctrines of atomism, but its hidden roots. Thus he does not examine the distinction between the description (definition) of a complex and the proposition that that complex exists, a distinction which plays a central role in TLP. Rather, he undermines the basis for the distinction.

The reply to the difficulty is that a sign such as 'R' may sometimes be a word, sometimes a sentence. Or better, the sign 'R' may be used to name an element or to describe its occurrence. The difference, to be sure, does not lie in any mental act concurrent with its utterance (that way lie 'philosophical superstitions'), but in the context of utterance. If 'R' is uttered in the course of memorizing words, explaining the meaning of the signs of §48, etc., then one does not describe a configuration, but one is simply naming an element (or explaining the meaning of a name). Here 'R' is not a description. But when 'R' occurs by itself in the *application* of the signs of the language-game, i.e. in describing complexes, then it is a one-word assertion.

That one *sometimes* merely names an element by uttering 'R' is a bizarre reason for thinking that elements *can* only be named, not described. At

least three confusions are involved. (i) The use of 'R' to name and its use
to describe are 'not on the same level', the two roles do not exclude each
other (as do, say, describing and ordering). One cannot say of the
type-sign 'R' that it is a name; or better, one cannot say that every
solitary token of the type 'R' is not a description on the ground that 'R'
is a name of an element. Nor, of course, is every token really a sentence
or description. What is being done in uttering 'R' (i.e. naming or
describing) depends on the context, and this in turn determines whether
that token is a word or a one-word assertion. (ii) The atomists confused
description and definition. The elements of §48 can be described, even
when only one occurs. They cannot be defined by a *Merkmal*-definition
or a Russellian analysis (a definite description). But they *can* be explained
by an ostensive definition (which is not a description). (iii) Not only did
the atomists have too narrow a conception of definition, but they also
had too narrow a conception of description. 'R' can be used to describe
an array (a single square), but it does not ascribe a property to an object
(give an 'external description'). Is it then an 'internal description'? The
atomist is forced into this absurdity, for an external description of an
object must occur in the context of a statement of the form 'Such-and-
such is thus-and-so'. Yet 'R' used alone as a description is not, in this
sense, an external description (nor is 'It is raining').

Naming is not on the same level as describing. Not only are the two
roles not in competition (like whispering and shouting), but naming is a
preparation for describing. Assigning a name to an object, stipulating a
meaning for a sign which is thereby rendered a name, is to give the sign a
range of possible roles, including describing. *Nothing* has been done by
giving a thing a name except in so far as this *prepares* the sign for possible
moves in the language-game. If naming is akin to hanging a label on a
thing, if christening is akin to hanging a necklace around a neonate's
neck, still the label or necklace are not made names by such solitary acts.
Only in the context of a practice do these constitute naming, and the
practice determines the role of the expressions in subsequent activities.

1.1   (i) 'Satz' here would perhaps be better translated 'sentence' (PPI(R) §58).

(ii) 'memorizing the words and their meanings': W. preferred 'and
what they mean', thus removing any nuance of reification.

(iii) 'man *benennt* damit ein Element': W. preferred 'you are naming an
element with it', thus emphasizing our use of the sign.

(iv) 'This was what Frege meant too': (a) 'Satzzusammenhang'—'in the
context of'. (b) This is one of W.'s many affirmations of Frege's
contextual dictum. It is doubtful whether this is what Frege meant and
certain that it is not all he meant. The agreement between the two philosophers on this issue is slender (cf. 'A word has a meaning only in the
context of a sentence', pp. 145 ff.).

2   (i) PG 208 f. discusses the thesis that an object cannot be described. Here 'described' must mean 'defined', for of course it is not denied that the object can be '"described from the outside", that properties can be ascribed to it and so on'. Rather, what is claimed is that 'no account can be given' of the indefinables of a calculus (or language). W. then criticizes this thesis in two respects. (a) The meaning of an indefinable (e.g. 'red') can be explained ostensively. (b) Indefinables can have internal properties, expressed in 'grammatical sentences' which are 'akin to definitions'; e.g. that blue is on the bluish side of blue-red and red is on the reddish side is a proposition of grammar expressing internal relations between colours. (Colour-exclusion would be another internal property of colours.)

(ii) PLP 13 f. emphasizes the difference between the grammar and the application of language, comparing it to the difference between deciding on the metre as the unit of length and carrying out measurements of objects. Waismann uses this distinction in clarifying the nature of naming (PLP 199) and the difference between a word (name) and a (one-word) sentence (description) (PLP 318–20). Naming is the preparation of a word for use; it belongs not to the application of language, but to setting up or clarifying part of grammar. Consequently, the contrast between a word functioning as a word (naming) and a word functioning as a sentence (describing) is the difference between learning a language and the application (*Anwendung*) of a language. Even if an entry in a dictionary (e.g. 'ambulo') could function as a sentence, it does not so function there since it is not applied. A similar distinction can be made for systems of signals (e.g. railway signals), between the occurrence of signals in a chart explaining their use and their subsequent use to control the movements of trains.

(iii) The claim that naming and describing stand on different levels seems to be an instance in which W. does what he says that he always seems to be doing—'to emphasize a distinction between determination of a sense and employment of a sense' (RFM 168).

'A word has a meaning only in the context of a sentence'
   1. Introduction   2. Frege's contextualism   3. Contextualism in the *Tractatus*   4. Wittgenstein: undermining the Fregean foundations   5. Beating about the bush: meaning and understanding   6. Understanding new sentences   7. Wittgenstein's later affirmation of the contextual principle

The standard metre
   1. Introduction   2. The rudiments of measurement   3. The standard metre and canonical samples   4. At the mercy of samples   5. Uses of samples and uses of sentences   6. Conclusion

SECTION 50

1   This explores the significance of the claim in §46 that neither being nor
non-being can be attributed to the 'elements'. It ramifies into some
important remarks on samples (cf. 'The standard metre', pp. 174 ff.).
    After raising the question of what this claim means, (a) suggests a
prosaic answer. If 'being' and 'non-being' are understood in terms of the
existence and non-existence of connections between the elements, then
no sense has thereby been assigned to speaking of the being or non-being
of an element. This would require a further explanation of these terms.
(The same point holds for 'destruction', if it is explained in terms of
separation of elements.)
    (b) raises an objection to this account: the point is not merely that we
have not explained what it means to attribute being or non-being to an
element, but rather that we *could not* explain this. There is, as it were, a
logical barrier to so extending the explanation of 'being': the familiar
paradox of non-existence interpreted according to the Augustinian
picture. If 'X' names an element, it is self-defeating to deny that X exists
(i.e. to attribute non-being to X), because 'X' would not then be a name
at all and 'X does not exist' would therefore lack meaning. Correlatively,
to attribute being to X is an empty ceremony; 'X exists' says nothing
since it could not be false. This generates the illusion that elements are
what *must* exist (i.e. necessary existents), although we cannot *say* that
they exist. (The parallel argument about 'destruction', and the correlated
illusion that the elements are indestructible, is considered in §§55 ff.)
    W.'s reply invokes an analogy with the standard metre. On the
assumption that the standard metre (a particular platinum–iridium bar) is
used to determine the unit of length *one metre* in the metric system, to say
that a rod is a metre long is to say that it is the length of the standard
metre, i.e. that its ends would after suitable translation and rotation,
coincide with the ends of the standard metre. This does not include an
explanation of what it would mean to ascribe the length one metre to the
standard metre itself. But there seems a logical barrier to giving such an
explanation: if the standard metre were not one metre long, then it could
not be used to define the unit of length one metre and so we could
attribute metric lengths to nothing at all. Should we conclude that the
standard metre *must* be (exactly) one metre long? We seem to have a
metaphysical deduction of the existence of the standard metre.
Moreover, attributing the length one metre to the standard metre is an

empty gesture since it could not fail to have this length. So by reasoning parallel to that previously applied to the elements, we must conclude that the standard metre has the extraordinary property of being necessarily one metre long, although this property is ineffable. The absurdity of this pattern of reasoning is now patent.

(b) indicates W.'s diagnosis of the source of this fallacious reasoning. The argument about the standard metre explicitly rests on the fact that the standard metre functions as a (canonical) sample of the length of one metre. The putative conclusion reinterprets this as the ascription of an extraordinary and ineffable property to the metre bar. But the simple truth is that the metre bar has a special role in the practice of metric measurement. A similar fallacious argument could be constructed using any canonical sample (e.g. standard sepia).

(c) inverts this generalization. Whatever looks as if it had to exist is a sample or paradigm in our language, something that belongs to grammar or the means of representation (cf. 'Ostensive definition and its ramifications', pp. 115 f.). This is applied to the language-game of §48; its elements (the simples) are the coloured squares correlated with the names 'R', 'B', 'G', 'W', i.e. the samples used to explain these names. The illusion that these elements are necessary existents is a mis-statement of the fact that if there were no coloured squares, coloured squares would not serve the purpose of samples for explaining the words 'R', 'B', 'G', 'W'. An apparently profound metaphysical truth about the elements of language is thus deflated into a truism about how words are explained: only what exists can be used as a sample.

1.1   (i) 'the standard metre': what does the expression *Urmeter* ('standard metre') mean? Is it the length of the metre bar in Paris?[3] or is it the metre bar itself? There is scope for ambiguity.[4] Suppose I explain the term 'metre' by pointing to the metre bar in the Louvre and saying, 'That is a metre'. This might be described as ostensively defining the word 'metre' by reference to the standard metre. But there seems a double reference; for what I point to is the metre bar (a piece of metal), but what I say is that the *length* of this *bar* is called 'one metre' or perhaps that *this* length is one metre. It might well be disputed whether the demonstrative 'this' in the ostensive definition 'This is red' refers to the object or to the colour pointed at; even whether the sample *is* the object or its colour. Since the standard metre is *ex hypothesi* the canonical sample for defining the term 'metre', this apparent ambiguity in the notion of a sample might give rise

---

[3] The metre bar is now kept in the International Bureau of Weights and Measures at Sèvres, not as previously in Paris (at the Louvre). This point will be ignored henceforth.

[4] Note that the phrase 'Imperial Standard Yard' means the *unit of length* defined by means of the Imperial Standard Bar, according to the Weights and Measures Act 1856 (C. Strong, 'Plato and The Third Man', in *Plato I*, ed. Vlastos (Anchor Books, New York, 1971), pp. 188 f.).

to two interpretations in the notion of the expression 'standard metre'. If 'standard metre' is taken to mean the *length* of the metal bar in Paris (under certain standard conditions), then there are important arguments against the intelligibility of either ascribing or denying to it the property of being a metre long (see 'Ostensive definition and its ramifications', pp. 113 f.). For the length of the metre bar is a property of objects, viz. the property of being a metre long, and therefore to assert or deny this property of itself is nonsense. Though nonsense, it is the root of a powerful philosophical illusion, a form of Platonism. A property is itself treated as an individual, but as an individual exhibiting that property in its pure, unadulterated form. 'Here the image which we use in thinking of reality is that beauty, death, etc., are the pure (concentrated) substances' (GB 35 f.; BT 433 f.). By contrast, when properties are predicated of ordinary individuals, they appear as ingredients of a mixture, as constituents of something compounded (complex) (GB 36; BT 434; BB 17). This illusion ensnared both Plato and W. (in TLP). If 'standard metre' meant the length of the metre bar in the Louvre, then it would be important to recognize the nonsense of saying either that it is a metre long or that it is not a metre long. If, on the other hand, 'the standard metre' means the metre *bar* in the Louvre, then there is not *this* impropriety in ascribing it a length, nor would Platonism be the obvious outcome of failure to recognize that the standard metre is neither a metre long nor not a metre long. And W. clearly uses 'the standard metre' to stand for the metre bar, not its length. For it is the metre bar that is uniquely to be found in Paris, not its length, which may be instantiated in many different places. It is the *sample* of length (or colour) that cannot be said to have a length (or colour), not just the length (colour) of which the sample is a sample (cf. BT 241). It is the metre bar that functions as a paradigm with which comparison can be made (especially in settling disputes about standard samples used in making metric measurements). Consequently, it is the metre bar in the Louvre of which one cannot say that it is one metre long or that it is not one metre long (cf. 'The standard metre', pp. 181 f.).

(ii) 'etwas, womit verglichen wird': this is potentially misleading. Not every sample is used as an object of comparison for judging the applicability of the term it helps to define. This role is characteristic of standard samples, but not of optional ones (cf. 'Ostensive definition and its ramifications', pp. 110 f.); e.g. explicit comparison with a sample is not normally involved in describing something as red. Nor is it the case that what functions sometimes as a sample always does so; e.g., even if we cannot measure the length of the metre bar, we could weigh it, and what serves on one occasion as a sample of red can on another occasion be described as red. W.'s point is merely that objects, when being used as samples, have a normative role; as it were, they belong to the means of measurement, not to what is measured. There is a distinctive direction of fit involved in comparison with something being used as a sample; e.g., in holding a metre-stick against a table, we measure the table, not the metre-stick, as long as we are using it as a (standard) sample of one metre. W.'s own translation emphasized this point: 'the role of a standard with which comparison is made' (PPI(R) §59).

2.1   'this gives this object a role . . . it is now a *means* of representation': Vol. VII, 112 points out that if one calls green an object, one must recognize that it is part of the symbolism. To be sure, this overturns the whole TLP concept of an object. But that is as it should be. Red, left, etc., are not objects, rather the red patch, the table, etc.

SECTION 51

1   The words of §48 'correspond' to colours, but what does the correspondence consist in ('what does "the name-relation" consist in?')? The description of §48 merely set up this connection, but did not say what it was. The first response is that 'R', 'W', etc., would be taught by pointing at paradigms. This is correct. But this is to say something about the 'preparation' for the language-game. We want an explanation of what correspondence consists in *in the practice of the language*, i.e. we want to know how the teaching relates to the practice of using the signs. In particular, we must reveal the normative component of teaching that provides a standard of correct use.

Two suggestions are made. (i) 'R' corresponds to a red square if and only if the speaker always says 'R' when there is a red square. But this excludes mistakes. Surely 'R' may correspond to R even if I mistakenly say 'R' instead of 'B'. Indeed; but then what is the criterion for my making a *mistake*? (ii) 'R' stands for a red square if and only if those who use 'R' always have an image of a red square when they do so. This is equally defective; the imaging of an object is neither necessary nor sufficient for understanding its name, and mental association gives no public criterion for understanding.

What is the general point of this remark? First, there is no unique 'name-relation' or correspondence-relation such that if we understand what it consists in we will grasp once and for all how language manages to represent. Secondly, correspondence may involve many different things (connecting words with paradigms, pinning labels on things, etc.), but does not consist in any of them. We must clarify what aspect of the practice of using signs we wish to call 'correspondence', and then examine different cases, scrutinize the numerous different possibilities.

1.1   (i) 'Praxis der Sprache': better 'practice of the language', which is

sanctioned by PPI(R) and gives a consistent rendering of 'Praxis' (cf. §197).
(ii) 'a red square always comes before their minds': cf. PI §396, 'It is no
more essential to the understanding of a sentence that one should imagine
anything in connection with it than that one should make a sketch from
it.'

2   PG 97 stresses that the correlation between names and things, whether
effected by ostension, labelling, a chart or otherwise, is part of the
symbolism, i.e. is normative, not mechanical. It is not a *name-relation* that
gives 'X' its use, but explanations of its meaning, e.g. by pointing at a
sample. These are readily, if misguidedly, seen as setting up 'the
name-relation'.

SECTION 52

1   The metaphor is confusing. Is it meant to show the wisdom of looking
at things from close to? Or to reveal the source of reluctance to scrutinize
details in some cases? Or perhaps to suggest the circumstances under
which close scrutiny is not a good policy? The opacity of the metaphor
has two principal sources. First, the uncertain status of the belief that a
mouse can come into being by spontaneous generation. Is this belief to be
viewed as certainly false, and hence its negation as certainly true? If I am
convinced that spontaneous generation is impossible, is my conviction
justified? Or is *this* conviction the superstition? Perhaps even if I am
convinced of this, I should not be, and therefore I ought to examine the
rags closely. The second source of unclarity is what question it is that is
under investigation. Is it whether or not this mouse was generated out of
rags and dust? Or is it rather where this mouse came from? If the first,
then we can answer the question without examining the rags if it is
certain that mice cannot be thus generated; and otherwise this will be an
open question. But if the question is where the mouse came from, then
close examination of the rags will be necessary whether or not spontaneous generation is a possibility; indeed, it will be more necessary the more
convinced we are that this is *not* a possibility.
     Despite this confusion, the point of the metaphor can be clarified. In
PPI, §§51 f. formed a continuous remark, whereas here the metaphor is
separated off from §51. This suggests a closer link of the metaphor with
the following sentence ('But first we must learn . . .') than with the
preceding one ('In order to see more clearly . . .'), even though it is
linked with both. Dropping the metaphor gives a clear line of argument:
we must learn to focus on the details of what goes on, but first we must
understand why we (wrongly) think this to be superfluous (in philosophy). What the metaphor does is to give an answer to a general form of

this last question. We think investigation of details unnecessary when the answer to a question is already known prior to any such investigation by deduction from a 'theory', whether this 'theory' be well founded or merely an entrenched superstition. The role of 'theories' is to exclude possibilities. (This insight is the root of hypothetico-deductive accounts of scientific explanation.) This is true *in philosophy* too. What opposes the examination of details in philosophy is adherence to philosophical 'theories'. The obscurity of §52 is that it consists of a question and an answer. But the question comes after the answer, and the answer itself is an opaque metaphor. Morever, the answer is not an answer to this question, but to another one that is not stated. A full reconstruction of W.'s thought has four parts, only two of which are explicit: (i) the general question, what opposes the examination of details; (ii) the answer, couched in metaphor, that it is 'theory'; (iii) the question, what opposes the examination of details *in philosophy*; (iv) the answer, not given here but inferred from the metaphor, that it is philosophical 'theory', whether this be explicit or merely implicit in a picture.

The merits of this interpretation of §52 are the following. (i) It makes sense of the separation of this remark from §51, especially of grouping the metaphor with the subsequent (indirect) question. (ii) The metaphor does suggest at least one correct answer to the question what opposes examination of details in philosophy. (iii) There is no need to resolve the ambiguity about the status of the belief that mice are not spontaneously generated from rags and dust, for, whether superstition and prejudice or a well-founded scientific law, it has the same function in excluding a possibility from serious consideration. (iv) It removes the need to 'cash' the metaphor in a detailed way.

3   Cf. PI §340 and also Schopenhauer:[5]

> What is most opposed to the discovery of truth is not the false appearance that proceeds from things and leads to error, or even directly a weakness of the intellect. On the contrary, it is the preconceived opinion, the prejudice, which, as a spurious *a priori*, is opposed to truth. It is then like a contrary wind that drives the ship back from the direction in which the land lies, so that rudder and sail now work to no purpose.

SECTION 53

1   The two possibilities canvassed in §51 were defective. Nevertheless, the language-game of §48 is such that various conditions could justify us in saying that a sign is a name. W. mentions two, concerned with teaching that embodies grammatical rules, namely ostensive definition ('. . . were

[5] A. Schopenhauer, *Parerga and Paralipomena,* Vol. §17, tr. E. F. J. Payne (Clarendon Press, Oxford, 1974).

taught the use of the signs in such-and-such a way') and correlation in a table (chart). In §51 the method of introduction of an expression was taken for granted, and the question was what does correspondence consist in. Here the answer is given, not in terms of a correspondence-relation, but in terms of the various roles a rule might have in the practice of using an expression. The existence of such practices of explanation and application does justify claiming that these signs are names of coloured squares.

§53(b) examines a case where one might say that the rule 'enters into' the actual practice of the language, taking over, as it were the role of memory and association. The parenthesis acknowledges that this is the abnormal case for ordinary colour ascriptions.

1.1   (i) 'Gebrauch': W. translated this as 'practice' (PPI(R) §61), bringing it into line with 'Praxis der Sprache' in §51.

(ii) 'This table . . . the role of memory and association': when it comes to fine shades of colour, for example, we may well find, if asked to purchase peach-blossom pink cloth, that we cannot remember which colour peach-blossom pink is, i.e. which colour is called 'peach-blossom pink' (or, what 'peach-blossom pink' means). We might then use the colour-chart as an *aide-mémoire* in respect of the meaning of this colour-name. If one cannot remember the colour, one can carry the chart around with one and consult it when necessary.

Clearly every process of imagining alleged to be involved in understanding, e.g. 'red', can be replaced by looking at public patches of red on a colour-chart. This manoeuvre is used by W. to dispel the illusion that the life of signs resides in the mind (BB 4, 89).

2.1   'This table . . . the role of memory . . .': PI §265 exploits this comparison in attacking the supposition that a table which exists only in a speaker's imagination might constitute a rule for the use of a sign in a private language. For the role of remembering the meaning of a word is taken over by a table, not by an imagined table, let alone by a *remembered* table.

SECTION 54

1   Developing the final point of §53, W. illustrates various roles rules may fulfil in language by reference to games. In particular, he hints at the answer to the question what distinguishes a regularity from a normative activity. A counter-instance falsifies a statement of a regularity. The behavioural criteria for a mistake (the normative reactive, corrective, behaviour) confirm the existence of a rule.

2   PLP 129–35 is a fuller discussion of the role of rules in games and the distinction between rule and regularity.

SECTION 55

1   §50(a) raised the issue of what it means to say of the primary elements of
§46 that they are beyond existence and inexistence, and it alluded to a
parallel claim that these elements are indestructible.
        §55(a) gives a rationale for the idea that language presupposes the
indestructibility of simples. The reasoning is summarized in the
metaphor of not sawing off the branch on which one is sitting.
Abandoning the metaphor, we are left with the claim that we must be
able to describe the state of affairs in which everything destructible is
destroyed. Presumably this description must involve the ascription of
certain properties to some objects. Hence it will make sense only if these
expressions have meanings. If their having meaning is conceived of as
their corresponding to something, as on the Augustinian picture, then
what they correspond to must be indestructible.
        §55(b) is a rejoinder to this reasoning. If the description of the state of
affairs in which everything destructible is destroyed is to be true, then
what gives its words their meaning cannot be destroyed. But *that* is not
what we naturally think of as the object corresponding to a name. In one
sense of 'correspond', the man N.N. is what corresponds to the name
'N.N.', but 'N.N.' retains its meaning even after N.N. dies. In another
sense of 'correspond', a paradigm used together with a simple predicate is
what corresponds to this word (e.g. 'red'). Here what corresponds to a
word does give it its meaning since such a paradigm is both used with
and plays an essential role in explaining its meaning.
        The implication of this rejoinder is that the original thesis of indestruc-
tibility is false. The samples used in defining simple predicates and
invoked in their applications are no more immune from destruction than
any other objects. These are possibilities that we can describe (e.g.
'nothing is a metre long' or 'nothing is ultramarine'). So if samples are
identified as simples in virtue of their role in assigning meanings to
words, it is not the case that simples are indestructible.
        This conclusion might seem to undermine the claim that a sample used
to explain a simple predicate is something without which the word
would have no meaning. This is an illusion. It does not follow from the
fact that it must be possible to describe the state of affairs in which
everything destructible is destroyed that it must be possible *in that state of
affairs* to describe how things are. That is a separate thesis—a hidden
assumption of the reasoning of §55(a) and apparently an ingredient of
TLP's contention that whether one sentence has sense is independent of
whether others are true (TLP 2.0211).
        If there were nothing that could function as a sample for explaining a
word actually explained only by reference to samples, then this word

could not be explained as it now is and hence it would not have the meaning it now has. This point is made clear if we follow W. in saying that samples are part of grammar. Our language does not *have* to contain the samples that it does, but if it did not do so, it would be a different language (cf. PG 143).

1.1   'ein Paradigma, das im Sprachspiel in Verbindung mit dem Namen gebraucht wird': it is unclear what kind of use W. has in mind here, i.e. use in application, in explanation or both. C 8, 61 reads: 'ein Muster oder Paradigma welches in unserem Sprachspiel zusammen mit den Worten gebraucht wird.' ('A sample or paradigm which, in our language-game, is used together with the words.')

SECTION 56

1   This starts from an objection to the final sentence of §55 and then develops a fresh argument for the indestructibility of simples. Is it false that a paradigm is 'something corresponding to a name . . . without which it would have no meaning'? Is it not enough for a word like 'red' to have a meaning that we bear in mind the colour that it stands for, i.e. that we can call up a mental image of red? If this is conceded, then what corresponds to 'red' is the possibility of calling up an image of red (i.e. remembering what red is). This is something indestructible since it is always possible for us to remember what red is. According to this form of imagism, the indestructibility of primary elements is identified with a permanent possibility of recollection.

W.'s reply does not attack the presuppositions of this reasoning, viz. that public samples can be replaced by mental (private) ones and that understanding sometimes consists in associating an image with a word. Instead, he queries whether the indestructibility of simples can be established even granted these premises. Red is proved to be indestructible only if I can always remember what *red* is, i.e. only if I can always call up an image of *red*. But even if I can always form some image if I ask myself what 'red' means, how do I know whether it is correct (i.e. whether it is red)? There must be a distinction between producing a mental image of red and one of green (or square). For the objector cannot claim that 'red' means the same as 'whatever image occurs to me when I hear or speak the word "red"' (PG 70; PI §239). What then is his account of the criteria for imaging red correctly?

There are criteria for correctness of memory images. If a patch of colour may change (e.g. become darker), so may an image of a colour. Images are no more immune to change than physical samples. We can, of course, check images against public samples or standard recipes for producing samples (e.g. chemical reactions). But the objector cannot avail himself of these criteria without surrendering his supposition that the meaning of 'red' is independent of samples. Hence, on his account, we are at the mercy of memory. Not only does this fail to establish his thesis that red is indestructible, but also it is at odds with our practice in that we do not always regard what memory tells us as the verdict of the highest court of appeal.

1.1   'zur Sprache gehört': W. preferred 'is used in the language' (PPI(R) §64).

2   The development of this line of argument is complex. (i) PR 60 discusses how one knows that something is the same colour as before: one's ground is simply recognition. Hence, on the reductivist principle that 'One source only yields *one* thing', 'That is the same' *means* that I recognize it again, and the question of mistake or misrecognition cannot arise, i.e. it cannot make sense to suppose it to be the same even though I do not recognize it or that I am wrong though I seem to recognize it. (This reductionism is later repudiated, and multiple criteria for recognition acknowledged; also denied is the idea that there are *any* grounds for simple colour ascriptions, *a fortiori* that recognition is a ground.)

We may say that the colour is the same on the grounds that no chemical change has occurred. But this 'physical' sense of 'colour' (i.e. detectable by scientific tests) and the sense of 'colour' in which I recognize colour immediately (i.e. 'phenomenological' colour) are quite different. Similarly (cf. WWK 97), particular colour-words like 'red' and 'yellow' will each have a pair of senses. (Here too W.'s views change: there are not two senses of 'colour', only one; 'objective' colour is indeed recognized immediately, but not infallibly; and photoelectric-colorimeters do not detect colour *per se*, merely wavelength of reflected light, i.e. a symptom of colour.)

(ii) PG 95 states the lack of finality of memory more explicitly and perspicuously than PI §56. Can one say that the word 'red' needs a supplement in memory in order to be a usable sign?

> If the use of the word 'red' depends on the picture that my memory automatically reproduces at the sound of this word, then I am as much at mercy of this reproduction as if I had decided to settle the meaning by looking up a chart in such a way that I would surrender unconditionally to whatever I found there.
>
> If the sample I am to work with appears darker than I remember it being yesterday, I need not agree with the memory and in fact I do not always do so. And I might very well speak of a darkening of my memory.

The point of this passage is that the illusory requirement for something indestructible corresponding to each name is no better satisfied by the possibility of forming mental images than by physical samples.

SECTION 57

1   This introduces a second objection to the claim of §55 that a sample is 'something corresponding to a name . . . without which it could have no meaning'. All red things can be destroyed, but red itself cannot be destroyed, and *that is why* the meaning of 'red' is independent of the existence of red things, *a fortiori* independent of the existence of samples used to explain 'red'. (On the assumptions that every red thing can be destroyed and that 'red' is a name, this argument is the inverse of that in §55(a). That inferred metaphysical truths from the apparent requirements of logic, whereas this draws conclusions about logic from putative metaphysical truths.)

W. concedes that we cannot say that the colour red is torn up or pounded to bits. But these are only particular modes of destruction. We do say, e.g. of a sunset sky, 'The red is vanishing'. So why should 'all the red there is' not vanish? Seeking refuge in our capacity to produce mental images of red or the capacity to produce a chemical reaction yielding a red flame is futile. How can we be sure that we have such capacities? Might we not tomorrow be unable to produce the required chemical reaction? Or might it not yield anomalous results? But surely 'red' does not mean 'whatever colour the flame has when X reacts with Y in such-and-such conditions'. Similarly, unless 'red' means 'whatever image occurs to me (including none!) when I try to remember what red is', we must admit the possibility that we can no longer remember what colour red is, i.e. that we can form no image or only the wrong image of what red is. If this were to happen, 'red' would indeed have lost its meaning according to the imagist conception of meaning in §56. A speaker who assigned meaning to 'red' by reference to mental images and then forgot what colour red was would be just as badly off as one who assigned meaning to 'red' by reference to a single physical sample which he later lost.

This argument has two consequences. (i) The interlocutor has no cogent defence of his premise that red cannot be destroyed and hence no valid demonstration that the meaning of 'red' is independent of the existence of red things. (ii) The possibility of bearing in mind what a name stands for is no better a candidate than a physical sample for being 'something corresponding to the name . . . without which it would have no meaning'.

1.1   The translation omits '(color, nicht pigmentum)' in *l*. 4.

2   BB 31: a complex, e.g. my watch, exists if it has not been pulled to pieces, i.e. destroyed. But what could be meant by 'destroying redness'?—destroying everything that is red? But that would not prevent us

imagining red things! This is correct; the ability to use 'red' would not be destroyed by painting all red things green.

His interlocutor then queries, 'Surely, red objects must have existed and you must have seen them if you are able to imagine them?', and W. responds by suggesting that our initial (and perhaps only) 'acquaintance' with red might be imagining or having an image of red. (This position is rejected in LPE, PI, and Z.)

SECTION 58

1   Beginning from a further argument for the indestructibility of simples, §58 draws together the elements of the preceding remarks and diagnoses the roots of the misleading metaphysical picture sketched in §46.

The interlocutor now says that the term 'name' should be restricted to what cannot occur in the argument-place of the expression 'X exists'. His implicit reasoning depends on one component of the Augustinian picture, viz. that a (genuine) name has meaning simply in virtue of being correlated with something. If it made sense to say 'X exists', then it would also make sense to say 'X does not exist', i.e. it would be possible for X not to exist (to be destroyed). But if red did not exist, nothing would correspond to 'red' and therefore the sentence 'Red does not exist' would be meaningless. (This recapitulates the argument of §50(b).) Consequently, the defender of the Augustinian picture will want to confine 'name' to expressions which do not make sense in the combination 'X exists'. And this move seems to guarantee the indestructibility or sempiternality of the simple objects that are the meanings of names.

This restriction is an explicit part of Russell's characterization of logically proper names and an implicit part of the conception of names in TLP (cf. 'Logically proper names', pp. 127 ff., 135 f.).

W.'s response in §58(a) reinterprets the interlocutor's view in accordance with the Augustinian picture. If ' "X" has meaning' is equivalent to 'something corresponds to "X" ', i.e. to 'X exists', then the equivalence can be inverted: the sentence 'X exists', which looks as if it states something about the world, is really just a statement about language, i.e. about the use of the word 'X'. Consequently, the metaphysical thesis that red necessarily exists and is indestructible boils down to the trivial claim that the word 'red' has meaning.

(b) elaborates the standard contrasting view: it seems that in saying that 'Red exists' makes no sense we are enunciating metaphysical truths about the essential nature of red, viz. that it exists 'in its own right', that it stands outside time or that it is indestructible.

(c) diagnoses the source of the idea that logic forces us beyond the bounds of sense into metaphysics. Anyone in the grip of the Augustinian picture wants to take as equivalent the pair of statements 'Red exists' and '"Red" has meaning', and also the pair 'Red does not exist' and '"Red" has no meaning'. For it is the existence of red (and nothing else) that makes 'red' a name (i.e. gives it a meaning). But there is an obstacle to taking them as equivalent. Although the sentence '"Red" has no meaning' seems unproblematic (it is simply a contingently false statement about an English word), the 'equivalent' sentence 'Red does not exist' seems to contradict itself. For, if it were true, 'red' would lack a meaning, and then so too would the sentence 'Red does not exist'. At this juncture, we erroneously conclude that 'red' is a real name, standing for a necessary existent of which we cannot *say* that it exists or does not exist. The apparent contradiction in this picture stems from two incompatible thrusts: the metaphysical and the linguistic. In fact, sentences of the form 'Red exists' do have a role, but it is neither to make metaphysical statements nor to make metalinguistic ones.

1.1   'Namely that red does exist "in its own right"' ⎫
       'because red exists "in its own right"'   ⎬ These are allusions
                                                        ⎭
to Plato's claim (§46) that each primary element is something that exists in its own right.

2   (i) PG 137: '"the colour brown exists" means nothing at all; except that it exists here or there as the colouring of an object, and that is not necessary in order for me to be able to imagine a brown stag.'

       (ii) RFM 64: 'Red *is*' has no use. But if it were to be given one, it would be appropriate to use it as an introductory formula to statements about red objects—a formula to be pronounced when looking at a red sample, i.e. 'reminding oneself' that 'red' has meaning. What is misleading about this pseudo-sentence is that one is tempted to pronounce it when looking attentively at a sample, i.e. in a situation similar to one in which one observes the existence of an object, e.g. an insect. And so one thinks that one is plumbing metaphysical truths about the necessary existence of universals.

Section 59

1   This links the preceding discussion of simples with the brief examination of analysis of complexes in §§60–4.

       A name, on the atomists' account, signifies an unchanging, indestructible element of reality. Change is the rearrangement of constant elements, which are the 'substance of reality'. But *experience does not show us* these elements. Rather, this metaphysical picture is a misguided projection of the mundane fact of the constitution of spatial complexes of smaller (simpler) components, and such complexes are commonly destroyed by being disassembled—in which case their component parts remain unchanged 'in themselves'! (It is, no doubt, aided and abetted by the permissibility of talking of 'combinations of colours and shapes' (Vol. VII, 19).)

1.1   (i) '*Namen* bezeichen nur das . . .': W. preferred 'A name only stands for what is an . . .' (PPI(R) §67).

(ii) *ll.* 3–4: W. preferred 'While we were saying the sentence it was already before our minds. We expressed an entirely definite idea' (PPI(R) §67).

(iii) 'experience does not show us these elements': this is true of the objects of TLP, for nothing seemed to fit the bill made out by the insistent demands of 'the picture we want to use'. Analysis would, sooner or later, uncover the real objects (LF 171). This conception is criticized as 'dogmatism' (WWK 182 f.)

2.1   'These are the materials from which we construct that picture of reality': the *Urbild* out of which atomism is constructed is that of destroying a whole by dismantling it into its constituents which themselves remain intact. This picture, taken together with the doctrine of logically proper names, can be sublimed into a striking metaphysical panorama. In TLP the argument ran as follows.

First, W. rejected Frege's analytical account of definite descriptions in ordinary language. Frege thought that there are propositions which are defective in that they lack truth-value if their existential presupposition is false. But, (i) there can be no defects of logic in any language since logic is a condition of sense. Ordinary language is in good logical order, otherwise it would not be language at all—would not be capable of representing reality. (ii) '. . . "true" and "false" are not accidental properties of a proposition, such that when it has meaning, we can say it is also true or false: on the contrary, to have meaning *means* to be true or false: the being true or false actually constitutes the relation of the proposition to reality which we mean by saying that it has meaning [*Sinn*]' (NB 112). Hence to have sense, yet to be neither true nor false, is incoherent. (iii) Given (ii), Frege's account makes logic dependent on the facts. But, 'The question whether a proposition has sense can never depend on the *truth* of another proposition [a Fregean presupposition] about a constituent of the first' (NB 116).

Secondly, W. rejected Frege's stipulative account of the description-function (GA i. §11), since it presupposes that ordinary language contains truth-value gaps.

Thirdly, W. accepted Russell's theory of descriptions (but modified it to eliminate the identity-sign from the analysans (NB 4; TLP 5.53, 5.5303, 5.5321)). This enabled preservation of bivalence.[6] Accordingly,

---

[6] The stronger principle of bipolarity was secured by additional steps.

expressions denoting complexes are eliminable. A complex, e.g. a-standing-in-the-relation-R-to-b, may have a certain property. But 'every statement about complexes can be resolved into a statement about their constituents and into the propositions that describe the complexes completely' (TLP 2.0201), and 'A complex can be given only by its description, which will be right or wrong. A proposition that mentions a complex will not be nonsensical, if the complex does not exist, but simply false' (TLP 3.24). W. gave an example of the notation for such kinds of analysis in 1914 (NB 4): 'Φ(a) . Φ(b) . aRb = Df Φ [aRb]'.[7] Here 'aRb' (a-standing-in-the-relation-R-to-b) describes the complex and 'Φa' and 'Φb' are statements about its constituents. A statement about a non-existent complex is therefore false but not meaningless.

Russell harnessed the theory of descriptions and his antecedent commitment to the doctrine of logically proper names (now freed of the trammels of denoting concepts) to his epistemological distinction between knowledge by acquaintance and knowledge by description. 'Every proposition which we can understand', he argued, 'must be composed wholly of constituents with which we are acquainted.' The theory of descriptions showed how to eliminate apparent referring expressions in favour of sentences containing only quantifiers and predicates. Analysis will terminate when reduction to logically proper names and simple predicates is achieved. At this level two crucial requirements must be satisfied: (i) names must have reference, (ii) we must know the meanings of the simple predicates. Assurance is given by epistemology. Logically proper names have as their meanings sense data, whose existence (in our own case) we cannot doubt, for we are acquainted with our own sense data. Simple predicates have as their meanings universals, with some of which we are immediately acquainted.

Where Russell pursued analysis to the alleged point of coincidence of the foundations of language and knowledge alike, W. sought a metaphysical guarantee for determinacy of sense. The foundations of language do not consist of *indubitabilia* but of the substance of reality—the totality of objects whose possible concatenations provide the language-independent limits of possible worlds. Various considerations converge on the conclusion that analysis must terminate thus. (i) Sense must be independent of the facts, in particular of existence and inexistence. The simple names that are the product of analysis must denote simple things, for if they denoted complexes, the complex might not exist. But the non-existence of a complex does not prevent an expression denoting a complex from contributing to the sense of a proposition—so such

---

[7] It seems to follow that properties of wholes that are not properties of their parts are themselves constituents of the complex, e.g. shape. Moreover, if 'a' and 'b' are genuine names, but 'aRb' is an expression designating a complex, then it appears that 'Φ' is type-ambiguous.

expressions are not fully analysed. Analysis will terminate with names whose reference is metaphysically guaranteed. (ii) Termination of analysis is required by W.'s conception of determinacy of sense. If it did not terminate, the entailments of propositions would not be 'once and for all complete' (NB 64), and since their sense is given by their entailments (truth-conditions), their sense would not be determinate. (iii) Truth is objective, dependent upon objectively existing realities. The truth of propositions containing complex expressions is dependent upon the truth of the propositions entailed by them from which the complex expressions have been eliminated by analysis. But if truth is objective and ascertainable by comparison with reality, then analysis must terminate in propositions whose truth depends *only* upon agreement with reality.

SECTION 60

1   The doctrines of analysis lay at the heart of logical atomism. Analysis would reveal the hidden logical form of propositions, and also of the world. Indeed, it would reveal explicitly the hidden sense of sentences. The philosophical significance of the theory of descriptions did not lie in the fairly trivial method of grammatical paraphrase of definite descriptions, but in its vindication of a sophisticated Augustinian picture of language and in its (apparent) metaphysical and epistemological implications. These lent the theory its depth. Once they are seen to be illusory, W. has no further interest in the workings of the singular definite article in English or German. Contemporary concern therewith would, one may surmise, have struck W. as lacking philosophical interest.

The preceding discussion has undermined the doctrines which lent analysis its aura of profundity. Less explicitly, it has made clear the radical separation of meaning and understanding involved in logical atomism. For to the extent that analysis revealed the hidden sense of sentences, either (i) what we understand in understanding sentences in advance of analysis falls short of their meanings (which is absurd) or (ii) what we explain in our ordinary explanations falls short of the correct explanations of what we mean, and our understanding is, in advance of analysis, transcendent. According to (ii) correct use is compatible with total inability to give a correct explanation of meaning; the latter is a programme for future 'scientific' philosophy, which *no one* has yet executed. So if we do understand what our sentences mean, *what* we understand is not something we can say, not even to ourselves. (This conception informs current endeavours to construct a 'theory of meaning' for a language.)

§§60–4 treat of the residue of analysis, what is left of it once purified of logical atomism. §60 involves two moves. The first is to stress that what one means by 'p' and what 'p' means are not independent of what one says one means and of what is a correct explanation of 'p'. The second move meets the immediate objection to the first, namely that the correct explanation is given by analysis. The response to this resembles the argument of §19(b). The unanalysed sentence is no more elliptical for the analyzed one than the analysed one is a lengthening of the unanalysed one. The analysed sentence does not mirror a hidden, mental, articulated process that accompanies the order 'Bring me the broom'. Nor is it a better explanation of 'Bring me the broom' than 'Bring me [accompanied by a gesture] that [pointing at the broom]!'

1.1   'ausgesprochen': W. translated as 'said' (PPI(R) §68).

2.1   The style of analysis of 'The broom is in the corner' dates back to NB 4: '$\Phi(aRb) = Df \Phi(a). \Phi(b). aRb$'.

3   Lest it be thought that the conception of analysis under attack is a parody, compare:

> . . . definitions which describe the real nature of the object or notion denoted by a word . . . are only possible when the object or notion in question is something complex. You can give a definition of a horse, because a horse has many different properties and qualities, all of which you can enumerate. But when you have enumerated them all, when you have reduced a horse to his simplest terms, then you can no longer define those terms. They are simply something which you think of or perceive . . . [W]hen we define horse . . . we may mean that a certain object, which we all of us know, is composed in a certain manner: that it has four legs, a head, a heart, a liver, etc., etc., all of them arranged in definite relations to one another . . . We might think just as clearly and correctly about a horse, if we thought of all its parts and their arrangement instead of thinking of the whole.[8]

and also:

> The only kind of unity to which I can attach any precise sense—apart from the unity of the absolutely simple—is that of a whole composed of parts . . . [I]f the parts express the whole or the other parts, they must be complex, and therefore themselves contain parts; if the parts have been analysed as far as possible, they must be simple terms, incapable of expressing anything except themselves . . . All complexity is conceptual in the sense that it is due to a whole capable of logical analysis, but is real in the sense that it has no dependence upon the mind, but only upon the nature of the object. Where the mind can distinguish elements, there must *be* different elements to distinguish; though, alas! there are often different elements which the mind does not distinguish.[9]

[8] G. E. Moore, *Principia Ethica* (Cambridge University Press, Cambridge, 1960), pp. 7 f.
[9] Russell, PrM 466.

SECTION 61

1   We might agree that a particular order in (a) says the same as one in (b),
i.e. they 'achieve the same' in the respective language-games. But that
does not establish a general agreement over identity of sentence-
meaning. For identity of meaning turns on identity of functions in the
different language-games and on the similarities and differences between
the language-games.
      This point is indeed exemplified in the Frege/Russell controversy over
definite descriptions. We may agree that a sentence containing a Russellian expansion *says* the same, in a given context, as a corresponding
'unanalysed' sentence, yet deny that in general any two such sentences
are synonymous. We may agree, e.g., that the two imperatives 'achieve
the same' but deny that the 'unanalysed' one 'contains' an assertion, as it
might be thought to do when 'analysed'.

SECTION 62

1   The criteria for whether a person does *the same* in executing an order in
(a) and (b) is not determined in advance of our fixing criteria of sameness
of action, and that depends, *inter alia*, on our interests. Even where we
agree on such criteria (e.g. identity of *point*), the determination of what,
e.g., counts as part of the point is both unclear and also context-
dependent (hence may vary in different language-games). (If we are
concerned, e.g., with intelligence tests involving measurement of discriminatory powers, obeying an order in (a) with a chart is *not* the same
as doing so in (b).)

SECTION 63

1   Perspicuous.

SECTION 64

1   This elaborates the final sentence of §63: not only is it false that the
'analysed' sentence is more fundamental (e.g. understanding 'b' implies
understanding 'a' but not vice versa, or knowledge of 'b' implies
knowledge of 'a', but not conversely) but analysis may disguise an aspect
of the matter. (The *Gestalt* of a complex configuration, such as a human
face, is 'more than the sum of its parts'.)
2   RFM 425 ff. examines language-games with names for colour-
complexes.

Determinacy of sense

(§§65–88)

INTRODUCTION

§65 marks an ostensible break in the flow of argument in the *Investigations*. §1–64 have criticized the central contentions of the Augustinian picture, thoroughly undermining both its conception of ostensive definition and the buttressing notion of analysis. At this point a critic is bound to complain that W. owes us an account of the essence of language to put in place of the discredited Augustinian picture. So W. breaks off the argument to deal with this criticism. §§65–142 are subservient to this purpose. In effect, W. argues that the objection itself has its foundations in elements of the Augustinian picture, in particular in the idea that revealing the essence of language must take the form of giving a *Merkmal*-analysis of the term 'language'. For essences seem to be given only by specification of necessary and sufficient conditions. So the essence of language must be given by a delineation of its sharp boundaries. In repudiating this conception by introducing family resemblance, W. actually continues the criticism of analysis begun in §60. Hence the apparent discontinuity at §65 masks an important continuity in the argument.

§§65–142 can be seen as a single long response to the challenge in §65. W. explains and vindicates the notion of family resemblance, suggesting that it is applicable to the concepts of language and of a sentence or proposition (*Satz*). He then elaborates a conception of philosophy according to which it is a search for essence (§92), even though the clarification of a concept need not have the form of a *Merkmal*-analysis. Finally, he turns to the concept of a proposition; he argues that there is nothing common to all the things called propositions, i.e. nothing that 'fits' the concept proposition (§134), and hence seeing philosophy as the search for the general form of proposition is a fundamental misconception. The unity of this material and its articulation into three main divisions is visible in the text of §§65–142. Moreover, this line of argument is sketched in BB 16–20. The tendency to conceive of philosophy as a form of science manifests the prejudice that there must be something common to all entities subsumed under a general term.

Some respects of contrast between §§65–142 and §§1–64 are apparent. These earlier sections described a variety of language-games each of which is used to highlight particular difficulties in the Augustinian picture or logical atomism. This procedure is challenged in §65, and the sequel is a defence of it, not further applications of it. Is the contrast also one between remarks primarily destructive and those primarily constructive? This seems a doubly misleading oversimplification. The earlier material, though presented in the framework of a criticism of a kind of theory of meaning, contains important constructive ideas, especially about ostensive definition and the uses of samples. On the other hand, the insistence that only *Merkmal*-analysis is admissible in explaining concept-words is an essential ingredient of sophisticated versions of the Augustinian picture; hence the discussion of family resemblance is a continuation of the criticism of §§1–64. W. himself suggests that logical atomism reflects an underlying conception of philosophy as a super-science, and therefore the criticism of the philosophical preconceptions that come to full fruition in logical atomism might be seen as extending as far as §142. The destructive force of the *Investigations* does not peter out after §64. The constructive nature of §§65–142 is also much exaggerated. All these remarks are subordinate to the negative aim of rebutting the accusation of §65. This colours the interpretation of these sections. It casts doubt on the idea that W. intends to sketch a general theory of proper names, a new theory of universals, or a theory of meaning making room for vague concepts (see 'Family resemblance', pp. 192 ff., 'Vagueness and determinancy of sense', pp. 214 ff., and Exg. §79).

Another important point of contrast has not generally been noticed. The remarks of §§1–64 are perspicuously articulated and for the most part polished and definitive. Subsequently their articulation is less perspicuous, occasionally even misleading. Some, especially in the discussion of philosophy, have been pruned to the point of being unintelligible. Most important, some are merely provisional; the framework of thought in which some of the issues of §§65–88 are ultimately to be viewed has not been clearly set out there; indeed, W. explicitly makes this point (§81(b)) in respect of the whole discussion of family resemblance and vagueness, and it implicitly holds for his accounts of the relation of understanding to the ability to give definitions and explanations. Failure to comprehend this aspect of §§65–88 is the most important contributory factor to misconstruing them as proposing modifications to a Fregean calculus model of meaning.

§§65–88 can be split into two parts. Both focus on the dogma that there must be something common to what falls under a concept. The first emphasizes the conflict between this dogma and a plain description of how we explain and use concept-words. The second traces the roots of the dogma to a misconception about the nature of understanding and meaning something.

Part A consists of §§65–74. First, the notion of family resemblance is introduced, clarified, and applied (§§65–7(b)). Then three objections are refuted. (i) A family resemblance concept has a disjunctive common property (§67(c)). (ii) It is a logical sum of sub-concepts each of which has a *Merkmal*-definition and hence sharp boundaries (§68). (iii) Since it is explained by paradigms, it has no sharp boundaries and is therefore useless (§69). This third objection has two versions. The first, associated with Plato (PPI §67 and C 8, 77), is that a person who cannot give a *Merkmal*-definition of a word does not fully understand any sentence containing it. But, W. counters, it is possible to explain *exactly* what a sentence means without defining each of its constituent words (§70 and p. 33 n.). The second version, associated with Frege, is that any concept, like an area, must have a definite boundary. But, W. counters, explaining a concept-word may be analogous to pointing to a location (§71). Finally, W. criticizes three replies to this last argument. (i) Understanding an explanation by examples consists in seeing what is common to them though this is not put into words (§72). (ii) It consists of having a mental sample of what is common to them (§73). (iii) It consists in seeing them in a particular way (§74). Each of these proposals mistakenly identifies one of the psychological accompaniments of understanding with its essence. The intended conclusion of §§65–74 is that we should take explanations by example at their face value; we do give them for many concept-words, and they successfully introduce legitimate concepts. Consequently, the demand that every explanation have the form of a *Merkmal*-definition is unjustified; not every explanation (*Erklärung*) is a definition (*Definition*).

The structure of Part A:

```
              65
              |
              66
              |
           67(a)–(b)
          /   |   \
     67(c)   68    69
       |          /
      70        71
       |       /  |
   p. 33 n.  72  73
                |
               74
```

Part B consists of §§75–88. This can be seen as a continuation of the previous argument, an exploration of a rehabilitation of the dogma that there *must* be something common to everything that falls under a concept. The fundamental idea is that our understanding of what an expression means may transcend our ability to say what it means (§75). Our use of it might manifest possession of knowledge of common properties, while our inability to define it would merely reflect that this knowledge is not explicit and conscious. W. turns first to consider the content of this putative knowledge. Must it not be equivalent to an unformulated definition that I would acknowledge as the expression of my knowledge (§75)? This cannot be so, for it would give a sharp boundary to concepts whose blurredness is an intrinsic feature of what we understand (§§76–7). Two further parallel suggestions are similarly criticized: first, that the meaning of any proper name should be identified with that of some particular definite description (§79), and secondly, that the meaning of a term like 'chair' must settle every possible application of the word, however bizarre the circumstances (§80). The verdict from all these cases is that no definition *could* be acknowledged as an expression of the content of one's understanding. Then W. diagnoses the source of the illusion that understanding transcends the ability to explain and hence too of our reluctance to accept this conclusion: our conception of understanding or meaning something as operating a calculus according to fixed rules (§81). (We misconceive the point of comparing the uses of words with moves in a calculus.) This conception is then criticized. First, there is no guarantee that our ordinary criteria for following a rule will yield the verdict that whoever uses a word and understands it is following a definite rule (§82). Secondly, as in games, it must be possible to describe an action as not following a rule unless the expression 'following a rule' is vacuous (§83). Thirdly, the idea of an activity everywhere bounded by rules is incoherent if it requires that there be no possibility of doubt about how to apply them (§§84–5). Hence the idea that definiteness of what is meant or understood can be captured in a set of meaning-rules about whose application there can be no doubt is incoherent (§§86–7). These arguments undermine the dogma that understanding and meaning consist in operating a calculus of meaning-rules. Therefore, the way is open to accepting the suggestion that my understanding of what a game is is *completely* expressed in the explanations (*Erklärungen*) I can give of 'game' (§75), and that undermines the thesis that understanding transcends the ability to say (i.e. explain). Of course, explanations by examples might be called 'inexact' by comparison with definitions, but this is no defect; they may none the less be complete, correct, and successful (§88). Although §§75–88 criticize a misconception of understanding, they barely hint at the correct conception of understanding (cf. §81).

The structure of Part B:

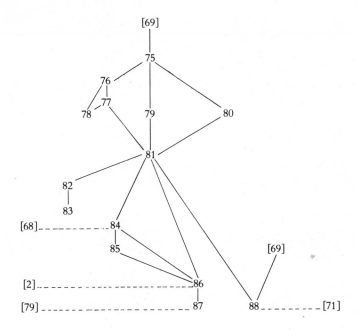

Correlations

For PI §§ 65–86 the correlations are uniform:
    PI § n = PPI § (n–3)
    PI § n = PPI(R) § (n + 7)
Thereafter:

PI	PPI(R)	PPI
87a–b	94	84
87c ⎫		
⎬	95 ⎫	
88a ⎭	⎬	85
88b–c	96 ⎭	

Family resemblance
  1. Introduction 2. Background 3. Family resemblance: a minimalist interpretation 4. Sapping the defences of orthodoxy 5. Problems about family resemblance concepts 6. Psychological concepts 7. Formal concepts

SECTION 65

1   A perspicuous introduction to the discussion of family resemblance and
to the topics of §§65–142.
Discussion of the general form of propositions is resumed at §134.

1.1   (i) 'Here we come up against the great question . . . .': this connects the
topic of analysis with the search for essences in the guise of *Merkmal*-
definitions.
(ii) 'anzugeben': the translation 'producing' has misleading connota-
tions of inventing or conjuring up. Preferable is W.'s translation 'pointing out' (PPI(R) §72). (Common properties are things to look for; and
we sometimes see them (cf. §66).)
(iii) 'weswegen wir . . . verwenden'; 'dieser Verwandtschaft, oder
dieser Verwandtschaften wegen': W.'s interest is not in what brings it
about that we use the word 'language' when we do, but in what
constitutes the grounds justifying its applications. The question is
normative, not causal.

2   (i) The search for the general form of proposition (and of language) in
TLP was treated as equivalent to the search for the essence of the world
and of thought (cf. MS. 157(a), 48). Each of these concepts—proposition,
language, thought, world—is supposed to be equivalent to each of the
others, so that the essence of one is the essence of all (cf. §96). This view
is also rejected (§§96–7). Consequently, even if the concepts of proposition (*Satz*) and language were not family resemblance concepts,
this would not have the significance that W. had earlier thought: 'Der
Begriff "Sprache" ist zwar eine Familie, aber auch wenn er es nicht wäre,
so wäre unser jetziger Standpunkt dennoch ein anderer als der der Lg.
Phil. Abh.' (MS 157a, 48) ('The concept "language" is a family, but
even if it were not, our present standpoint about it would be different
from that of the *Tractatus*.')
(ii) Part of the point of searching for the essence of language (or of
propositions) is also undermined by W.'s conception of philosophy. In a
rigorous science any lack of precision in the definition of the key
theoretical terms would lead to uncertainty and inaccuracy in what could
be explained by its hypotheses. But in philosophy a rigorous demarca-
tion of such concepts as language, proposition, number, object, property,

etc., is otiose precisely because, in this sense of 'explain', philosophy explains nothing. It should not be seen as a system of hypotheses from which deductions are to be made. This takes away the main reason for seeking a strict definition of language (PLP 93).

(iii) The claim that 'proposition' ('Satz') and 'language' each stand for a family of structures is supported by a vast amount of earlier writing. See especially BT 60–74, PG 112–27, and PLP 93 f., 280–303, 364–76.

SECTION 66

1   The concept of a game is examined to refute the philosophical dogma that a concept-word is correctly applied to each of a set of objects only if these share some common property in virtue of which they fall under this concept. W.'s strategy is to take the word 'game' and exhort us to see whether it conforms with this dogma. If we do this with care, we will *see* that there is *nothing* common to all the activities called games, instead, only a complicated network of similarities.

Two difficulties crop up immediately.

(i) Is the presence or absence of a common property something open to simple observation? Might it not be determined by complex calculation? These worries might have been forestalled by a lower-key exposition. The question is whether we now *know* of any properties common to all the things called games, not whether we can, with sufficient ingenuity, concoct some (as in §67(c)), nor whether we know that we will never discover any. We are not to speculate, but to describe what we know.

(ii) Does W. prove that there is *nothing* common to all games? That we can *never* discover a common property? By running through various kinds of games, he marshals inductive support for this negative existential statement, but might it not be refuted by a more penetrating analysis of games? His claim seems precarious, but also unnecessarily strong. He need defend only the claim that there are no properties common to all games *on account of which* we apply 'game' to them all; i.e. that justifications and criticisms of applications of 'game' do not mention any such common properties. Or perhaps only the still weaker thesis that the practice of explaining 'game' does not include singling out properties necessary for an activity to be a game. No discoveries could overthrow these statements since they can be established by careful observation of what is explicit in the practice of using and explaining the word 'game'.

The game analogy makes this discussion of the concept of a game indirectly relevant to the contention that 'language' introduces a family resemblance concept (§65).

1.1   (i) 'die Vorgänge, die wir "Spiele" nennen': the activities characterized as *Spiele* are a wider and more varied set than those called 'games'. 'Spiel' is used as an internal accusative of 'spielen', so any activity which can be characterized as playing, like throwing a ball in the air or ring-a-ring o'roses, is called 'ein Spiel'. This does not affect W.'s point.

(ii) 'Ähnlichkeiten im Grossen und Kleinen': not 'over-all similarities' and 'similarities of detail', but 'similarities in the large and in the small' (as in PPI (R) §73). (How would over-all similarities among games be distinct from properties common to all games?) The expressions 'im Grossen' and 'im Kleinen' (also 'in the large' and 'in the small') are used in mathematics, and they are probably meant to be compared with this technical usage (as indicated by W.'s correction to Rhees's original translation: 'similarities in large respects and in small').

The mathematical distinction can be clarified by considering a series of simple two-dimensional manifolds. Take three strips of paper (preferably a good deal longer than they are wide). Tape or paste the narrow ends of the first strip together to form a cylinder. Do the same with the second, but twist one end 180° before joining it to the other; this makes a Möbius strip. And the same with the third, but twist one end through 360° before joining it to the other; we could call this a twisted cylinder. Topologists say that these three structures are alike 'in the small'. By this they mean that any small enough piece (say a square) cut out of one of these structures has exactly the same structure as a small piece cut out of any other one. Each such fragment is isomorphic with a small piece of the plane. (This is why all three structures are classified as two-dimensional manifolds, along with the surface of spheres and tori, of prisms and cubes, etc.) The differences between the structures (and also some other similarities) are said to be differences (similarities) 'in the large'. The Möbius strip, e.g., has only one side; it is possible to get from any point on it to any other point along a path that does not cross the edge. And it has only one edge (though it looks as if it had two). Whereas the cylinder and the twisted cylinder each have two sides and two edges. Similarly, each structure behaves quite differently if cut all the way around along its middle parallel to its edge (edges). These similarities and differences are said to be 'in the large' because they cannot be described except by reference to the whole manifold. (The whole has properties not shared by any of its sufficiently small parts.)

This distinction has an intuitive application to many of the concepts W. considers. Why is war not a game? It certainly shares many characteristics of games. It is (usually) more or less rule-governed and competitive; it has winning and losing; and it is very absorbing. What makes the crucial difference is the status of the whole activity in the context of the way people live: the global role of making war in the human economy. Similarly, why is the dancing of bees on their hive not a language? The answer seems to turn not on detailed features of what they do, but rather on considerations of how their dancing is coordinated with the whole pattern of their behaviour. This brings out how games and languages are linked by similarities in the large as well as similarities in the small (cf. 'Family resemblance', pp. 334 f.).

2   Several parallel texts (cf. PG 74–6, PLP 179–83, BB 16–20, 86 f.) avoid the difficulties generated by §66. Instead of the exhortation to look and see whether there are any common properties, there is a description of the error to be avoided. When we notice that what we would naïvely take as the hallmark of games is not present in every case, instead of concluding that there is no common property, we postulate one. It is something difficult to grasp and still awaits discovery. In such a case, essence is hidden (cf. PG 74). This line of thought betrays a dogmatic prejudice about the rationale for applying concept-words and it also exhibits the error of proceeding from descriptions to explanation (hypothesis) in philosophy. Instead of the dubious claim that there is nothing common to games, W. suggests that even if some common feature is discovered it need not define 'game' (PG 75). Indeed, it might have no part whatever in the explanation of the word.

3   W. refers to Jean Nicod's 'Geometry in the Sensible World'[1] (Vol. I, 43 ff.; PR 252 f.; BT 202; Vol. XI, 81; C 8, 41, 45; PPI §115; cf. Exg. §130). This monograph contains a discussion of resemblance among sense data that may be one of the germs of some ideas elaborated in W.'s account of family resemblance. Three parallels are noteworthy.

(i) Nicod distinguishes global resemblance (*la ressemblance globale*) from partial similarities (then subdivides the latter into local and qualitative similarities) (pp. 78 ff.). The contrast between 'global' and 'local' similarities is at home in discussion of topological spaces and is there equivalent to the contrast between similarities 'in the large' and similarities 'in the small'.

(ii) Nicod notes that two things may be partially similar in one respect but dissimilar in another. As a consequence, it may happen that '*two overlapping structures or networks of similarities cross each other* and arrange the same data in two different ways' (p. 84).

(iii) He remarks that a particular relation of partial resemblance may form the nucleus of a set of relations forming a *family* (*une famille*) around it; e.g. that the relations of inclusion, encroachment, and separation form a family around the relation of 'local resemblance' (p. 85).

---

[1] In J. Nicod, *Foundations of Geometry and Induction* (Kegan Paul, Trench, Trubner, London, 1930).

SECTION 67

1   §67(a)–(b) complete the exposition of family resemblance. They introduce two important analogies: the resemblances among members of a
family and the construction of a thread out of many overlapping
fibres. The notion of family resemblance is applied to the concept of a
number.

Then §67(c) introduces the first of a series of arguments in defence of
the orthodox demand for *Merkmal*-definitions of concept-words. The
objector uses disjunction to manufacture a common property out of the
various respects of resemblance mentioned in explaining a family
resemblance concept. This tactic can be exploited provided that the set of
such resemblances is in every case surveyable (and finite). W.'s retort is
contemptuous: that is just playing with a word. This is not transparent
(below).

1.1   (i) 'Gebilden': W.'s translation is 'objects' (PPI (R) §74).

(ii) 'hier spielst du nur mit einem Wort': to be translated 'with a word',
not 'with words'. With what word? Presumably 'gemeinsam'. W.'s
objection is to characterizing a disjunction of common properties as itself
a 'common property'. On what grounds?

One possibility is to repudiate such a property as a genuine property.
Yet if being red and being square are each properties, then surely so must
be being red or square, since to say that something has the property of
being red or square is just an elevated way of saying that it is red or
square. How could this be denied? Only, it would seem, if we were to
distinguish genuine properties from artificial ones in terms of complexity. The property of being red or square—indeed, any disjunctive
property—might be called an artificial property because its explanation
gives its fabrication from genuine properties. This seems mistaken for at
least three reasons. First, the fabrication argument can be inverted. The
properties of being red and of being square can be synthesized from the
properties of being red or square, being not red or square, and being red
and not square. Secondly, there is no other way to distinguish simple and
complex properties for this purpose, nor does W. suggest any. Thirdly,
the objection would then turn not on the term 'gemeinsam', but on the
term 'property' (*Eigenschaft*) which does not even appear in the text! The
argument is not that it would be wrong to say that the disjunction of all
the common properties is itself a *property*, *a fortiori* that it is a common
property; but rather, that it would be wrong to call it a *common* property
(or something common) even if it were admitted to be a property.
There is no evidence that W. denies that disjunctive properties are
properties.

W.'s objection is less recondite than this. The expression 'to have something in common' is a quite ordinary one with a tolerably determinate use (cf. §72). It makes perfectly good sense to say that a certain collection of books have in common that they have blue bindings or that they are written in English, or to say that a yellow ellipse painted on my wall and a London bus have nothing in common. But the intelligibility of such statements presupposes that it is possible to specify sets of objects that have nothing in common, for otherwise to say of any set of objects that its members have something in common is to say nothing at all. W.'s objection is simply that this presupposition would be undermined if we accepted the disjunction of all the shared properties of a family resemblance concept as itself something *common* to all the objects falling under this concept. In this case, *any* set of objects, however heterogeneous, would necessarily have something in common with each other. This would make the concept of having something in common vacuous; i.e. it would make any application of the expression 'gemeinsam' mere playing with a word, an idle ceremony without significance. That this is W.'s point is indicated by his next comment. It would be absurd to say that the continuous overlapping of the fibres is something running through the whole thread just because this would make unintelligible the contrast between there being and there not being something running through the whole thread. This contrast is presupposed in speaking of the overlapping of the fibres in a thread!

2   (i) The idea that the concept of number is a family resemblance concept was developed in earlier texts, and it is the cornerstone of one phase of W.'s philosophy of mathematics (best known from F. Waismann's *Einführung in das mathematische Denken* (Vienna, 1936), which was based on conversations with W. and copious notes that he took from TS. 211). Some of its consequences are reflected in PI (e.g. §§18, 555), and many were elaborated in the original continuation of PPI. Indirectly, W.'s treatment of the concept of number is relevant to much of the material of PI, though many commentators have been reluctant to acknowledge this.

(ii) The recognition that certain concepts (e.g. number, language, game, proposition) are family resemblance concepts is not just a refutation of the single dogma that every legitimate concept must be given a *Merkmal*-definition. It has much more extensive importance. It is a prophylactic against a myriad of dogmas. This is clear from W.'s diagnosis of dogmatism in philosophy (Vol. XI., 56–7; BT 259 f.). Our thinking is often guided by setting up an object of comparison (*Vergleichsobjekt* or *Vorbild*), e.g. for languages or propositions. We reason by reference to paradigms. Dogmatism arises when we confuse the properties of the paradigm with the properties of the objects we are using it to illuminate. We read off the characteristics of the paradigm and assert that they characterize all those other objects. We argue, e.g., that languages *must always* contain assertions because this is true of the language we take as a paradigm. This is a confusion about the role of a paradigm in an investigation. A paradigm is similar to a unit of measurement. The dogmatic use of a paradigm is parallel to the claim that every object must measure an integral number of units when measured against our chosen unit of measure (Vol. XI, 57). Such misuse of paradigms can be avoided by bearing in mind their proper function as objects of comparison. If we think of problematic concepts as held together by similarities to paradigms, we are less likely to fall into false generalizations, for similarities are variable and must be inspected individually. Perhaps the only sure method to avoid dogmatism is to abstain from generalizations altogether, merely presenting a varied set of paradigms and letting them speak for themselves (cf. PLP 71 f., 77–81). Such a strategy in philosophy would be an exaggerated response to the dangers of dogmatism, and it is certainly not what W. practised, even if he preached it in moments of despair. (See 'The nature of philosophy', pp. 488 ff.)

2.1   'thread': as alternative metaphors, W. used a rope (BB 87) and a chain (PG 75). The metaphor of the chain is linked with the method of constructing connecting links (*Zwischengliedern*) between cases which fall under a concept (§122).

SECTION 68

1   This explores a second line of defence for orthodoxy. The objector concedes that the disjunction of all the respects of resemblance among different kinds of numbers is not itself something common to all numbers. But he need not defend that position. It is enough that every concept-word be defined by means of logical operations alone from a (finite) set of concepts each of which is itself either indefinable or capable of being given a *Merkmal*-analysis. This requirement is met by such otherwise problematic expressions as 'prime' (of integers), 'elastic', 'square or yellow', and also by 'number'. The concept of number is a well-defined complex concept provided it is the logical sum of well-defined sub-concepts, even though it cannot directly be analysed in terms of properties common to all numbers.

Unless the 'etc.' in the objector's definition of 'number' (*l.*3) is the 'etc.' of laziness, he has not defined 'number' as a logical sum of sub-concepts. We are to assume that 'number' is defined by a closed list of sub-concepts. W.'s objection is that this explanation would give the concept of number a range of application laid down once for all. The list of sub-concepts would exhaustively determine the kinds of thing that are to be counted as numbers. It would put an iron curtain around the extension of 'number', making the concept parallel to the concept of primary colour. This, W. contends, is not how we use 'number'. Its extension is open, not sharply bounded. Mathematicians from time to time discover (or invent) new kinds of entities (e.g. quaternions) which may be subsumed under the concept of number though distinct from any previously recognized sub-concept. We do not treat such additions to the extension of 'number' as altering its meaning.

The objector counters with the suggestion that the notion of an essentially open concept is incoherent. If the application of 'number' is not everywhere bounded by rules, how can there be a determinate practice of using this word or a distinction between correct and incorrect uses of it? The reply exploits the game analogy. This points to the objector's misconception of what it is for a set of rules to be complete. (Discussed in §§84–8, and 100.) He confuses actual vagueness of an expression with failure of its explanation to satisfy the demand for determinacy of sense. (See 'Vagueness and determinacy of sense', p. 376.)

2   It is assumed here that the sub-concepts, e.g. cardinal numbers, do have extensions closed by a frontier; that they contrast in this respect with the concept of number. PG 113 f. draws this contrast explicitly. The concept of cardinal number, whose extension is determined by the formal series [1, ξ, $\xi + 1$], is 'a rigorously circumscribed concept'. Whereas we are free to decide just what constructions to count as numbers in virtue of their degree of similarity to cardinal numbers, rationals, irrationals, etc., it 'depends on us' whether we draw the boundary here or there. Each of the concepts number and cardinal number is, he concludes, 'a concept in a different sense of the word' (TS. 302, 25). This conclusion is implicitly repudiated in PI §61. (Otherwise, the objection would be correct that a blurred concept is not really a concept at all.)

SECTION 69

1   This opens with the challenge to explain how we do explain 'game' (given that we cannot give a *Merkmal*-definition nor an explanation in terms of a logical sum of sharply defined sub-concepts). W.'s answer is that we give an explanation by examples, perhaps with the rider 'These and similar things are called "games"'. This explanation accords with the observation (§ 68) that we so use the word that its extension is not closed by a sharp boundary. (Cf. BT 68, quoted at Exg. §76.)

The objection is then raised that such a concept, since it lacks a sharp boundary, is useless. This is dogmatically rejected here (then reconsidered in §71): such a concept is no more useless than the unit of measure 'one pace' was before it was given the metric definition '1 pace = 75 cm'. The supplementary objection that such a concept or such a system of measurement is not exact is met by a demand for an explanation of what 'exact' means (further explored in §§70 and 88). What is in need of clarification is the relation of degrees of exactness to degrees of usefulness.[2]

. §69 also hints at a further objection to W.'s account of 'game': viz. that what we understand by 'game' transcends what we explain in explaining 'game', that we know more about what a game is than is embodied in our explanations. (This issue is the topic of §§75–88.) §69 suggests W.'s answer (tentatively sketched in §75) that our knowledge of what a game is is completely expressed in the explanations we can give of 'game'. In particular, there are no sharp boundaries to our concept of a game precisely because we have drawn none in explaining 'game' by examples.

2   C 8, 76 f. clarifies the intended focus of §69. There, amid draftings of remarks for PPI, §69 is immediately preceded by §68(a) and succeeded by §71(b). Therefore, the topic under consideration is perspicuous: viz. whether concepts without sharp boundaries are useless.

Further objections might be raised against W.'s explanation of 'game'.

(i) The explanation incorporates a similarity clause, and it is taken to determine the extension of 'game' by means of overlapping similarities among activities called games. But could a transition not be made from anything to anything by a sufficiently large set of intermediate links each of which exhibited many overlapping similarities with its immediate neighbours? Hence, would W.'s explanation not make 'game' senseless since its extension would be all-embracing (cf. PG 76)? Would any family resemblance concept have any frontier at all? There are three lines of reply to this objection. (a) We do explain 'game' by reference to overlapping similarities with paradigms. Moreover, we do not treat everything whatever as falling under this concept; charging a machine-gun emplacement, e.g., is not a game (cf. PG 240). From what vantage point can we judge this pair of descriptions of our linguistic activities to be incoherent? (b) The claim that the family resemblance explanation of 'game' would make its extension all-embracing presupposes a contrast between what this explanation determines as the extension of 'game' and what we determine as its extension by appeal to this explanation. Obviously so, since we accept and use the explanation but do not conclude that everything whatever falls under the concept game. Is this contrast coherent? (See §§185 ff.) (c) The possibility that somebody

---

[2] 'I asked him for a bread knife and he gives me a razor blade because it's sharper!' cf. Vol. XVI, under 9 April 1938.

might use W.'s explanation of 'game' to conclude that everything whatever is a game does not show that it is defective. Any explanations can be misunderstood (cf. §§85–7). (The usual formalistic responses share the same errors as the original objection: the claim, e.g., that an explanation by paradigms is essentially incomplete without the stipulation of anti-paradigms, or that only direct resemblances with the original paradigms support the applicability of the concept-word, not resemblances via intermediate links.)

(ii) The explanation of a concept-word must provide a means of distinguishing what falls within its extension from what falls outside. But how can an explanation by paradigms do so even with a similarity-clause? Would such a definition of 'number' (§67) by itself determine whether Julius Caesar is a number (cf. Frege, FA §56)? If not, is it not incomplete or defective? This objection rests on a superstition. There is no need to draw a boundary between what we call numbers and *everything* else (days of the week, symphonies, cabbages and kings) (BT 60, cf. PG 117). If nobody would mistake the Conqueror of Gaul for a number, then the explanation of 'number' need not provide a safeguard against making this mistake (cf. PI §87). We typically draw boundaries only where they are needed (PG 117).

SECTION 70

1   This continues the argument of §69. There it was assumed that we do know what a game is, i.e. that we do understand 'game', even though the concept of a game has no sharp boundaries. W.'s interlocutor here challenges this assumption: the fact that the concept has no sharp boundaries proves that there is nothing to understand, i.e. that we do not know what we mean by 'game'.

W.'s initial reply is an ironic counter-question: is it claimed that somebody does not know what the description 'The ground is covered with plants' means unless he can give a definition (*Definition*) of 'plant'? At first sight, this manoeuvre seems pointless. First, it changes the example, from 'game' to 'plant', and thereby appears to be a *non sequitur*. Secondly, it does not advance the argument, since the interlocuor is no doubt prepared to transfer the objection from the case of 'game' to that of 'plant'.

§70(b) accomplishes more by indicating how to justify a negative answer to the counter-question. It is false that I do not know what I mean by the description 'The ground was quite covered with plants' if I can give an explanation of what I mean by using it. And I might give such an explanation (*Erklärung*) independently of giving a definition (*Definition*) of 'plant', e.g. by drawing a picture and saying 'The ground looked roughly like this'. There are criteria for understanding sentences that are distinct from explaining its constituents.

The rest of §70(b) treats an unstated objection to this explanation of the description: viz. that it is a vague or inexact explanation because it contains the word 'roughly' ('ungefähr') (cf. BT 249 v., quoted at Exg. §88). But this is easily circumvented, for I could draw a picture and say 'The ground looked *exactly* like this'. To this the interlocutor retorts: so just *this* grass and *these* leaves were arranged just like *this*? But that, W. answers, is not what this explanation means. The explanation explains not what was on the ground but how the ground *looked*, and that could be exactly described without giving an accurate description of what was actually on the ground. (Though W. still owes us an explanation of 'exactness' in this context.)

There remain two puzzles about §70. (i) What is the connection between knowing what 'plant' means and understanding sentences incorporating the word 'plant'? Does it follow from the concession that a person who can give a picture-explanation of the quoted description understands this sentence that he also knows what 'plant' means (what a plant is)? If not, W.'s whole reply fails to refute the interlocutor's original objection. (ii) What is the connection between knowing what 'plant' means and being able to explain (say) what it means? Is being able to explain 'plant' a necessary condition of understanding it? W. himself links meaning very closely with explanation, e.g. suggesting (in §75) that a person's understanding of a word is completely expressed in the explanations that he can give of it. So why should we concede that a person understands 'plant' when he cannot define it?

The first puzzle can be set aside. The interlocutor is defending the Augustinian picture, and according to it a person's understanding of a sentence can be no better than his understanding of each of its constituents. Unless he surrenders this fundamental tenet, he must admit the cogency of W.'s argumentative strategy.

The second puzzle is perhaps not as intractable as it seems. W. makes a distinction here between 'definition' (*Definition*) and 'explanation' (*Erklärung*). What he calls 'definition' is a species belonging to the genus of explanations. In fact, it is a delineation of conditions necessary and sufficient for applying the defined expression; hence, in the case of a concept-word, a definition will typically have the form of a *Merkmal*-analysis. Explanations may take other forms, e.g. ostensive definitions, explanations by example or by sample, recursive definitions, and exhaustive enumeration. This contrast 'definition'/'explanation' is familiar from Frege's writings; it recurs in PI (e.g. §75) and elsewhere (e.g. LSP 241, 246 f., 261 f.; PG 208); and it is presupposed in §70. The word 'game' has been *explained* (by example) in §69; the objection is that we do not understand it because we are not able to *define* it. It is W.'s purpose to challenge that inference. It is explanation, not definition, that is the 'correlate' of understanding (BT 11). Being able to *explain* what it means (i.e. to answer the question 'What does this mean?') is a criterion of understanding a word, but being unable to *define* it is not a criterion for not understanding it.

1.1   (i) 'was du mit "Spiel" meinst': not 'what you mean by a "game"', but what you mean by "game"' (PPI(R) §77)—or perhaps, 'what you mean by "a game"'.
(ii) 'Eine Erklärung dessen, was ich meine': more literally, 'an explanation of what I meant' (PPI(R) §77).

2   (i) PPI §67 helps to confirm this interpretation of PI §70; for it contains an additional paragraph inserted between §70(a) and (b):

Sokrates (im   ):[3] 'Du weisst es und kannst hellenisch reden, also musst Du es doch sagen können.'—Nein. 'Es wissen' heisst hier eben nicht, es sagen können. Nicht *das* ist hier unser Kriterium des Wissens.

(Socrates (in   ): 'You know it and you can speak Greek, so you must be able to say it'.—No. 'To know it' does not here mean to be able to say it. *This* is not our criterion of knowledge in this case.)

Socrates, as depicted in Plato's dialogues, did make the inference that W. challenges in §70(a). He inferred from the fact that someone could not give a definition of 'justice', 'piety', 'courage', etc., that this person was ignorant of what justice, piety, courage, etc., were. W. contradicts this claim: to know what justice is (to understand 'justice') is not equivalent to being able to define 'justice' (i.e. being able to give what Socrates would take as a correct answer to the question 'What is justice?', i.e. being able to say what justice is). Since there is no such definition, giving it is not the criterion for our ascribing understanding of what justice is to anybody. But we can see from their *explanations* (e.g. by examples) that some of Socrates' interlocutors do manifest understanding of the terms that they are being challenged to define (cf. BB 20, PG 120 f.). Socrates distorts the concept of understanding by refusing to acknowledge giving any explanations apart from definition as criteria of understanding. (Note that 'able to say' ('sagen können') in PPI §67 must be read as equivalent to 'able to *define*'.)
BT 248 ff. also confirms this interpretation by linking PI §70 with §75, where the contrast between definition and explanation is prominent:

---

[3] W. did not fill in the reference. Perhaps it is Plato, *Charmides* 159a.

Was heisst es, zu wissen, was eine Pflanze ist?
Was heisst es, es zu wissen und es nicht sagen zu können?
'Du weisst es und kannst hellenisch reden, also musst Du es doch sagen
können.'
Müssigkeit einer Definition, etwa der, des Begriffs 'Pflanze'. (BT 248.)

(What does it mean to know what a plant is?
What does it mean, to know it and not be able to say it?
'You know it and you can speak Greek, so you must be able to say it.'
Uselessness of a definition, say of the definition of the concept 'plant'.)

Note, particularly, that it is a *definition*, not an explanation, of 'plant' that
is characterized as useless. Its dispensability is what PI §70 demonstrates,
viz. that the criteria for understanding 'plant' include giving explanations
of 'plant' and of sentences in which it occurs.

(ii) BT 248 criticizes the thesis that understanding a sentence incorporating the term 'plant' presupposes the ability to *define* 'plant'.

Wer uns sagen würde, wir wissen nicht, was wir reden, ehe wir eine Definition
der Pflanze gegeben haben, würden wir mit Recht für verrückt halten. Ja, wir
könnten auch mit einer solchen Definition uns in den gewöhnlichen Fällen nicht
besser verständigen. (BT 248.)

(Somebody who told us that we don't know what we are talking about until we
have given a definition of a plant we would rightly take to be mad. Surely we
would not be able to make ourselves any better understood in ordinary
circumstances had we such a definition.)

Indirectly, this challenges one of the fundamental principles of the
Augustinian picture and its corollary that vagueness is infectious. Bio-
logists may well puzzle over how to classify certain very simple organisms,
whether to count them as plants or animals (cf. BT 69, 250), but the
resolution of such puzzles by a definition of 'plant' would not sharpen
our understanding of *every* sentence in which this word occurs (BT 69;
cf. 'Vagueness and determinacy of sense', pp. 224 f.).

(iii) Vol. XI, 41 notes that a precise verbal definition of a concept like
game or plant that has no sharp boundary introduces a *new* concept,
different from but akin to the original one explained by resemblances to
paradigms (cf. PI §76).

PAGE 33 NOTE

1   The point of this and its relation to the text are obscure. The slip was cut
from B i. §545, derived from Vol. X, Um. 194, and inserted in TS. 227,
p. 60, which begins with the last three sentences of PI §69 and ends with
§71(a). Its original context is printed as PG 117–20.
Its immediate context (PG §75) is a refutation of the idea that the

meaning of a word is something that comes before our mind when we hear a word. Certainly what comes before our minds is characteristic of the meaning, but only in this sense—that what comes before our mind is an example, an application of the word. This coming to mind does not consist in an image being present whenever one hears or speaks the word, but in the fact that when asked what the word means, applications of the word occur to one. PI p. 33 n. follows this, then: 'Suppose someone said: "No. I didn't mean that sort of game; I used 'game' in the narrower sense"' (PG 119). To this W. has two responses. (i) How does it come out that he used the word in the narrower sense? There are two obvious moves: first, to deny that there are multiple senses (that 'game' is ambiguous). What the speaker means by so saying is that he did not mean that sort of game, *tout court*. Secondly, that he did not mean a gambling game does not consist in the antecedent occurrence of images, but is shown by what he subsequently says (the past tense of 'I meant' here is deceptive (cf. Exg. §178)). (ii) Can one then use 'game' in its broadest sense? There is no 'broadest sense'; no boundaries are drawn unless we fix them. By implication narrower and broader senses can be *stipulated* for special purposes, but in the case of family resemblance terms they are not implicitly determined in advance, nor, when stipulated, do they finally reveal the essence of the definiendum.

This suggests that p. 33 n. is related primarily to §70, though thematically (cf. PG 118–20) to its environs. The connection with §70 is specifically to 'Eine Erklärung dessen, was ich meine . . .' ('An explanation of what I meant'). For it blocks off the suggestion that an explanation of what I meant consists in describing something that I had before my mind, e.g. an image. This criticizes an argument that W. had earlier constructed around the example of §70. Suppose I tell a story containing the description 'The ground was quite covered with grass and herbs'. Definitions of 'grass' or 'herb' would be lengthy and complicated. Substituting them in the original sentence would produce a sentence of considerable length and complexity. Would this analysis express what I meant by the original description? EBT 48 suggests that this is false *because* I did not have all that in mind when I said 'The ground was quite covered with grass and herbs'. But that inference is fallacious.

Section 71

1   The target of §71 is Frege's requirement of 'completeness of definition' for concept-words (GA ii. §56)—a particular form of what W. had called 'the demand that sense be determinate' (TLP 3.23). This is rejected for several reasons. (i) Its being met is not a presupposition for a predicate to be usable in communication. (ii) It is not met by many actual explana-

tions of concept-words. (iii) Its being met in the explanation of a concept-word 'Φ' would not make the term 'Φ' more useful than it would otherwise have been; on the contrary, there may be advantages to concepts with blurred boundaries.

Although clear in purpose and structure, §71 fails to lay out the rationale for the demand for determinacy of sense (see 'Vagueness and determinacy of sense', p. 218 ff.). Without this background, Frege's requirement seems a gratuitous blunder. Whereas it is not a blunder at all, but an expression of his commitment to the functional analysis of the sense of sentences. W. does not make clear the depth of Frege's requirement of completeness of definition.

1.1   (i) 'Is it even always an advantage': this seems a *non sequitur*. W. counters Frege's contention that a vague concept is not a concept at all with the question 'Is an indistinct photograph a picture of a person at all?' The intention is simply to ridicule Frege's thesis as dogmatic. (Clearer, perhaps in BT 248v.; 'Was wenn Einer sagen würde: "ein unscharfes Bild ist eigentlich gar kein Bild"?!' ('What if someone were to say: "a blurred picture is no picture at all"?!') But then of what relevance is the further suggestion that an indistinct picture may be better than a sharp one? W. gives no *reason* for thinking that a vague concept is ever advantageous.

(ii) Frege compares a concept to an area: viz. GA ii. §56. This is a metaphor. Frege would cash it by appealing to his conception of concepts as functions from objects to truth-values. Any function is specified only if its value is determined for every admissible argument. (This explanation too might be thought metaphorical, but not by Frege.)

(iii) 'This presumably means that we cannot do anything with it': it is here that W.'s argument seems most open to challenge. If a concept is compared to a function, then a vague concept could be only one incompletely defined, i.e. one whose values are stipulated for only part of the domain of admissible arguments. But a partial stipulation of values is no less useful than the restriction of a complete definition to this part of the domain of arguments. For these arguments values are stipulated, and hence application of the partially defined concept-word to these objects yields sentences with determinate truth-values. The usefulness of a concept does not depend on its being completely defined; only on its being defined for some cases, so that some things do fall under it in certain circumstances and some others do not (cf. PR 264, PG 240). This conclusion is certainly compatible with Frege's conception of a concept as a function. So what justification has W. for ascribing to him the thesis that a vague concept is (generally) useless? The answer lies elsewhere, in Frege's contention that vagueness is contagious, i.e. that indeterminacy in the sense of any expression infects with indeterminacy the truth-conditions (sense) of every sentence in which it occurs. We need to uncover the rationale for this view.

(iv) 'intends them to be taken in a particular way': not as a means for seeing something common that I cannot put into words, nor as hinting at a definition of 'game' that I cannot express. Instead, the examples themselves are supposed to function as we conceive a rule as functioning, viz. to establish a definite practice of using the term explained ('game'). We use them to teach a practice. This is, as it were, the trajectory of the paradigms. The possibility of explaining a term by paradigms (or examples) presupposes agreement in judgement; if others generally did not agree in applying a term explained by paradigms, the explanation would be useless. The intention to explain a word by reference to paradigms is not the intention to convey a rule that is not stated.

(v) 'das Gemeinsame sehen': italicized in PPI to highlight the relation of §72 to §71.

(vi) 'jede allgemeine Erklärung': In view of the importance of the contrast *Definition/Erklärung*, this should be translated 'every general explanation' (PPI (R) §78). (Definitions are a species of 'general explanation'.) No form of explanation, not even definition, guarantees understanding. Any explanation can be misunderstood (cf. §§26, 86 f.).

2.1   (i) 'And this is just how one might explain . . . what a game is': W. had earlier used the analogy between different ways of indicating a place and different ways of explaining words. The place of a word in grammar is its meaning (PG 59), and this is what explanations of meaning explain. Explanations by examples are compared with rough specifications of a place, e.g. with saying that a meeting will take place *beside* such and such a tree (PG 118).

(ii) 'he is now to *employ* those examples in a particular way': when he earlier conceived understanding a word as a matter of operating a calculus, W. had described the intention by saying that the examples were to be taken as 'the point of departure for further calculation'. Hence, what interested him most was 'the *exact* relationship between the example and the behaviour that accords with it . . . the geometry of the mechanism' (PG 273). (Now what interests him is the architecture of the practice.)

(iii) '*indirect* means of explaining': This expression would be intelligible only if there were such a thing as a direct means in this case (cf. BB 125). Moreover, the multiplicity of the examples would then not be essential to the explanation, since it would be no more than a mechanical device for getting someone to see what they had in common. This would be equally visible in a single example when properly understood (PG 272).

(iv) 'in default of a better': they are not something second best. 'Examples are decent signs, not rubbish or hocus-pocus' (PG 273).

SECTION 72

1   This comments on §71, but it bears on arguments in §66 and §67. The
point made is that there is a variety of criteria for seeing what is common
(cf. BB 135), even for the case where what is seen to be in common is a
colour. Three cases are sketched. Reflection on them is supposed to
establish the conclusion.

The point of noting the diversity of criteria for seeing what is common
to a set of objects is to correct part of the misconception underlying the
demand for *Merkmal*-definitions. We think of seeing what is common as
an intermediate stage in the process of coming to understand expressions
defined by paradigms or samples. First, somebody points out some
samples of the colour blue or some paradigm games; *then* (if we come to
understand 'blue' or 'game' at all) we see what is common to these
objects; and, finally, as a result of this, we acquire the ability to apply
'blue' or 'game' correctly to further objects. We take having seen what is
common as an explanation for our having this ability. We may concede
that we sometimes do frame explanations of words by reference to what
is common to a set of objects (as in all three examples of §72). We
recognize too that there is sometimes an intermediate process of seeing
what is common to these objects. The learner may manifest his arrival at
this intermediate stage, e.g. by pointing out what is common or by
producing it on request. The criteria for his seeing what is common to a
set of paradigms for 'x' are independent of whether he goes on to use 'x'
correctly. Hence it makes sense to suppose that his ability to use 'x'
correctly depends on his having seen what is common to the paradigms.
This is an hypothesis, not part of an explanation of what it means to 'see
what is common'. But in many cases there is divergence from this
pattern in one of two respects. (i) Although the explanation of 'x' (e.g.
'blue') may refer to a common property of some paradigms (as in
§72(c)), we do not recognize any intermediate process of seeing what is
common to them. More precisely, we treat nothing as a criterion of
someone's seeing what is common apart from his going on to use 'x'
correctly. This is the sole criterion we appeal to in support of the claim,
e.g., that someone has seen what is common among the samples of
shades of blue in §72(c) (cf. BB 130). (ii) The explanation of 'x' may not
refer at all to properties common to the paradigms, as in W.'s explanation
of 'game' in §69. Here going on to use 'x' correctly, though a criterion
for understanding 'x' and so too for understanding the explanation of 'x',
need not be treated as a criterion for seeing something common among
the paradigms (or among what 'x' applies to), since common properties
of the paradigms are not relevant to the explanation of 'x'. In neither case
does it make sense to say that the ability to use 'x' correctly is a

consequence of having seen what is common to the paradigms used to explain 'x'. In the first case, because there is no criterion independent of the correct use of 'x' for seeing what is common; in the second, because no sense at all has been assigned to the expression 'seeing what is common among the paradigms'. The hypothesis is indefensible that understanding an expression explained by paradigms *always* depends on seeing what is common to the paradigms. Nor, of course, could we meet this argument by claiming that seeing what is common may be unconscious.

To put the matter differently, the purpose of § 72 is to remind us that 'seeing what is common' is an ordinary expression with a well-understood use. There are criteria for seeing what is common to a set of objects, and a wide range of criteria at that. Lacking an *Übersicht* of these, philosophers distort the notion of seeing what is common (and its relative 'common property': cf. §67).

If understanding 'x' need not depend on a process of recognizing what is common to paradigms of 'x', then this weakens the case for thinking that *being* 'x' is always a matter of having a set of properties common to all objects that fall under 'x'. (Indeed, if the meaning of 'x' is limited to what we understand in understanding 'x', this case is completely exploded.) This supports the original thesis that there *is* nothing common to all games (§66). It thus explains the resemblance between W.'s position and nominalism. (Cf. MS 129, 193, quoted below p. 265).

1.1   (i) 'various multicoloured pictures': W. substituted 'a coloured comic' (PPI (R) § 79).

(ii) 'eine Erklärung': this is not a definition (*Definition*), but an explanation (since it uses a set of samples); (cf. PPI (R) §79).

2   (i) PG 118 criticizes the statement 'We understand the word "chair", since we know what is common to all chairs' in the context of an argument for eliminating causal connections from a description of learning and explaining the meanings of words. The suggestion is that this statement is meant to be causal, but that it cannot be because the sole criterion for attributing to a person knowledge of what is common is that he applies the word 'chair' correctly.

(ii) BB 130–5 amplifies and clarifies §72. It is directed at showing how illusory is the idea that there must be an intermediate step of seeing what is common on the way to understanding words explained by paradigms. It makes two major points: (a) there are all sorts of phenomena used as criteria for seeing what is common; (b) using a word correctly (e.g. responding appropriately to the order to bring something red) may itself be the criterion for his having seen what is common to what he was shown.

(iii) BB indicates how to develop a parallel between nominalism and

W.'s account of family resemblance concepts. 'To say that we use the word "blue" to mean "what all these shades of colour have in common" by itself says nothing more than that we use the word "blue" in all these cases' (BB 135). The point is not that being blue is not a property common to all objects coloured any shade of blue; for that would be a paradigm for explaining the expression 'common property'. Rather, that the presence of a common property does not *justify* applications of 'blue'. Seeing this common property and applying 'blue' correctly have the same criteria. Hence it would be better to say that nothing justifies a person in applying 'blue' as he does (cf. PI §381). 'If, pointing to patches of various shades of blue, you asked a man "What have these in common that makes you call them blue?", he'd be inclined to answer "Don't you see?" And this of course would not be pointing out a common element' (BB 131—with 'blue' substituted for 'red').

The presence of a common property among objects which are Φ does not always justify the applications of 'Φ'. Consequently, there is no reason to suppose that absence of a common property would make the use of 'Φ' capricious or unintelligible. To that limited extent nominalism is correct.

SECTION 73

1   This introduces a comparison between ostensive definition of a colour-word by reference to a sample and explanation of certain sortals by reference to paradigmatic examples. W. subsumes both kinds of explanation under the heading 'explanation by samples (or paradigms)'. The connection between them is that in both cases we use particular 'objects' in giving explanations of words and intend them to be employed in a particular way.

Ostensive definition of colour-words can be compared to putting a table, i.e. a colour-chart, in somebody's hands (cf. §§53, 265). We intend him to use it (the samples) in a particular way: we may, e.g., intend him to use samples as objects for comparison in deciding the applicability of colour-words (e.g. §1), and we will certainly intend him to read the table in a certain way (e.g. as correlating the words and the samples according to the pattern ⇉ or ⏐⏐⏐⏐ : cf. §86). His coming to understand the defined colour-words in virtue of this explanation is shown by how he employs the samples that we have given him, i.e. by his 'playing the game' with them in accordance with our practice.

This comparison of ostensive definition with explanation by a table aggravates two general problems about ostensive definition.

(i) How is explanation by reference to a sample involved in applications of the explained expression? What is it to follow the rule embodied in such an explanation? What is the continuing role of the sample in the use of the explicandum? Must we refer to any sample in the way that we refer to a colour-chart in language-game (1) if it is not to be dismissed as of merely historical interest in describing the use of the explained word?

(ii) A sample is something particular, whereas the rule for using an expression contained in an explanation by a sample must be general. It must provide a standard of correctness for applying the word over an indefinitely large range. How is this generality conjured out of correlating a word with a concrete particular? How is generality *contained in* an ostensive definition? How in a colour-chart?

For ostensive definitions a traditional solution to the first problem is to locate the 'real' sample in the mind; it is not a correlation of the colour-word with an object exemplifying a colour that explains the meaning of the word, but rather a correlation with an idea or image of the colour exemplified by the so-called 'sample'. Such mental furniture, being easily portable, is always at hand when we apply the defined expression. The solution to the second problem is to invoke the notion of resemblance. The general rule implicit in an ostensive definition of a colour-word is that anything resembling *this* object in colour can have the explained word predicated of it. Combining these two solutions yields the familiar idea that applying 'blue' in accord with an ostensive definition of it consists in comparing the colour of a perceived object with that of the mental sample correlated with 'blue'.

§73 suggests extending this account from perceptual predicates explained by samples to sortals explained by examples. 'Leaf', e.g., is explained by pointing to various leaves and saying '*This* is a leaf, and *this* and *this* too'. The proposal is that someone understands the term 'leaf' when given this only if he comes to have a general image of the shape of a leaf, so his following the explanation in applying 'leaf' consists in his referring to this mental sample of the shape of a leaf. (This idea is akin to the one criticized in §71(b).)

Although there are objections to this second idea distinct from those to the first (see 2), W. here concentrates on a single objection that holds against both. This amounts to Berkeley's familiar criticism of the notion of abstract general ideas. In accordance with his usual strategy (BB 4), W. replaces imagining a schematic leaf with looking at a picture of a leaf. What shape will a picture of a leaf have if it is to exhibit only 'what is common to all shapes of leaf'? Or what shade is the sample of what is common to all shades of green? W. argues that the difference between a picture of a particular leaf and a picture understood as a schema of leaf-shape lies in how these pictures are used. A schematic picture is not a special kind of thing with extraordinary properties, but a picture used in a special way. The use made of a schematic figure does not flow from its properties, but is something extrinsic (a method of projection). Nor, conversely, do its properties flow from its use as a schema. The schematic figure of a leaf can be of any size or colour, and this 'slack' could be taken up by a convention, e.g. that every shape-sample should be one square inch in area and coloured scarlet (cf. BB 131). Parallel conclusions hold of an object or picture used as a sample in explaining a colour-word.

2   (i) BB 17 f. mentions as a typical philosophical confusion the idea that someone who understands a general term, e.g. 'leaf', must possess a kind of general picture of a leaf as opposed to pictures of particular leaves. Explanations by example are thus conceived as mere means to produce in the learner the appropriate general image of a leaf. W. traces this confusion to the idea that every word is a name whose meaning is the object named.

(ii) PG 272 f. emphasizes that the generality of an explanation by samples (or examples) is a matter of the 'geometry of the mechanism' relating these objects to the behaviour that accords with the explanation. This depends on the rules governing the samples. W. adds two further criticisms of the position sketched in PI §73.

(a) There is typically no general picture before my mind when I utter or hear such words as 'egg' or 'plant'. Rather, 'I make the application as it were spontaneously' (PG 273).

(b) The *multiplicity* of examples used in explaining such words as 'leaf' and 'plant' (and 'game') would be no more than a mechanical device for getting somebody to see what he could in principle see in a single example. But this is not so (PG 272). The multiplicity of examples is essential to explanations of such words; i.e. we treat giving explanations by examples as criteria of understanding these words only if the explanation refers to a number of suitably diverse examples. (This argument distinguishes the two different kinds of explanations by paradigms in PI §73.)

2.1 'general' samples: BB 18 alludes to the possibility of taking a Galtonian composite photograph of leaves to be a picture of what is common to all leaves. But this picture is just another kind of schematic figure whose generality lies in how it is used.

SECTION 74

1   According to W.'s translation (cf. 1.1), this comments on the different ways of seeing *drawings* or pictures and hence is subordinate to §73. Whereas the printed translation treats it as commenting on the different ways of using objects (viz. leaves) as samples and hence suggests that it, like §73, is subordinate to §71. Although this may not be true to W.'s

intentions here, this interpretation is consonant with his thought (cf. 2).

The idea introduced in §74 constitutes a possible objection to the argument of §73(b). The difference between interpreting a drawing of a leaf as a sample of 'leaf-shape in general' and taking it to be a picture of a particular leaf (or a sample of this particular leaf-shape) is not a difference in how the drawing is used or in the rules for applying it, but rather a difference in how it is experienced, i.e. how it is *seen*. In one case a person sees it in one way, in another someone else sees it in another way, and *that* is why they treat it differently. A schematic drawing is not a peculiar kind of drawing, but a drawing seen in a special way. Moreover, its being used in the way characteristic of schematic drawings is a consequence of its being seen in this particular way.

W.'s riposte is brief and dogmatic. There are cases in which we can see a drawing in different ways, e.g. the figure ⃛ (cf. PI p. 193). Differences in how someone sees it will be manifested in how he reacts to orders such as 'Bring me something like this' or 'Make a model of what you see here' (PI p. 196). But the drawing of a leaf is not such a case.

W.'s reasoning rests on two basic ideas.

(i) Only in special circumstances does it make sense to speak of seeing different aspects of a drawing (cf. PI pp. 195, 199). Not every drawing resembles the schematic figure of a cube in having multiple visual aspects; in particular, a typical drawing of a leaf does not.

(ii) Although we may speak of the 'experience of seeing a drawing as a sample of leaf-shape', this describes something very different from the experience of seeing an aspect of the drawing of the cube. Seeing a drawing as a sample presupposes mastery of a technique, viz. of using a drawing as a sample. 'It is only if someone *can do*, has learnt, is master of, such-and-such, that it makes sense to say he has had *this* experience' (PI p. 209). Knowing how to use objects as samples is the logical condition for having the experience of seeing a drawing as a sample of leaf-shape in general (cf. PI p. 208). The objection in §74 inverts this logical dependence.

1.1   'Blatt' (*ll*.2 and 6): W. substituted 'drawing' for 'leaf' in both occurrences (PPI(R) §81). This alteration affects the interpretation of the entire remark.

2   (i) TS. 229 and PI pp. 193 ff. discuss the phenomena of 'seeing as' and seeing aspects.

(ii) PG 270 ff. (Vol. VII, 90 ff. and EBT 53 ff.) criticizes the idea elaborated in the printed translation of §74, viz. that a person who grasps an explanation of 'plant' by examples does not see these examples in the same way when he 'sees the concept in them' as when he sees them merely as representatives of particular shapes or colours and that his understanding of 'plant' consists in his experience of seeing each example as an example illustrating the concept 'plant'. W. cites three arguments against this conception, which he confesses that he once held.

(a) The idea of 'seeing something in' something (or seeing something in a particular way) is taken from cases where we see different aspects of a figure, e.g. different 'phrasings' of | | | |, and this cannot be transferred to understanding the examples used in explaining 'plant'. (This point is later elaborated as the difference in sense between the two uses of 'the experience of seeing something as' distinguished in the discussion of drawings.)

(b) W. queries whether a person who uses the sign '| | | . . .' as a sign for the concept of number sees these three strokes differently from someone who uses '| | |' to denote the number three. If he saw in them the concept of number in the first case, then he would have to see them *in the same way* that he saw '| | | | . . .', for that too is a sign for this concept. Would that mean that he could not distinguish between '| | | . . .' and '| | | | . . .'?

(c) On this conception, too, the multiplicity of examples used in explaining 'leaf' or 'number' would be no more than a mechanical device, for the learner could in principle see the explained concept in a single example. But the multiplicity of examples is an essential part of these explanations.

W.'s general diagnosis of this misconception is that it treats a particular experience (seeing the examples in a particular way) as belonging to the essence of understanding, whereas what matters is the system of rules governing these examples. It is the geometry, not the psychology, of the mechanism relating the examples to the use of the explained word that concerns philosophy. We need to grasp the rules governing the example which make it into an example, whereas any mental process accompanying understanding is of no interest.

(Some arguments from PI pp. 193 ff. bear on this conception. In particular, seeing a particular leaf as a sample of leaf-shape in general presupposes a mastery of the technique of using objects as samples. This blocks off the possibility of appealing to such an experience to explain what it is to use an object as a sample.)

Vagueness and determinacy of sense
   1. Introduction   2. Determinacy of sense in Frege and the *Tractatus*
   3. Wittgenstein's Copernican revolution   4. Preliminary objections
   5. The centrality of determinacy of sense   6. Rejection of the demand
   for determinacy of sense   7. Vagueness and meaning

SECTION 75

1   The discussion now moves off in a new direction. Previously W. has argued that we do not explain the concept of a game by means of a *Merkmal*-analysis (*Definition*), but rather by means of examples (a form of *Erklärung*); further, that our acceptance of explanations by examples as legitimate explanations does not presuppose that they are known to bring about a mental state causally necessary for understanding the explained expression (e.g. seeing what the examples have in common). Explanations by example are rules to be taken at face value. Now he suggests a new move: that what is understood in understanding 'game' transcends what is explained in explaining it. Someone who understands 'game' on the basis of an explanation by examples must employ these paradigms in a particular way if he is to apply 'game' correctly. Hence, must his understanding not go beyond the examples, incorporating also a grasp of how to use them? This is not 'put into words' in the explanation. Therefore, if explanations by example are the only legitimate form of explanation of 'game', does this not prove that what we explain is only part of what we understand? It seems that we know what a game is but cannot say (explain) it. This apparent contrast is the topic of §§75–88.

     This picture of understanding as transcending the ability to explain is strongly reinforced by the truism that a person's practical abilities often outrun his ability to explain what it is that he knows how to do and his ability to teach others how to do it. Indeed, the 'paradox of analysis' is standardly tackled by applying this general distinction to the practical ability to use the definiendum correctly. We test proposed definitions of words against our practical (intuitive?) grasp of how to apply these words. The same idea dominated the background of TLP (cf. PI §81). What we mean or understand by any sentence (e.g. 'The book is lying on the table') must be perfectly sharp and definite (NB 67 f.), even though we are unable to give any general explanation of what its words mean (NB 70). The task of logic is to produce analyses of the expressions of language that can be used to close the gap between what we understand and our explanations (cf. NB 69 f.).

     Though plausible and widespread, this conception of the connection between understanding and explanation is one of W.'s main quarries. It is the target of the fundamental contentions that understanding is the correlate of explanation (BT 11) and that meaning is what is explained in explanations of meaning (BB 1). §75 is the opening of an argumentative campaign in PI, merely hinting at two points developed later. First, it is problematic whether there is any definition encapsulating what is understood by certain words (cf. §§76–80). Secondly, explanations by example are *complete* explanations of what is understood by certain words (cf. §§84–7).

It is important to note the contrast in §75 between definition and explanation. The conception mentioned and here tentatively repudiated is that the content of understanding 'game' is equivalent to a *definition*. (Of course I cannot now formulate it, but I would perhaps acknowledge it as correct if presented with it; that would suffice to give a behavioural criterion for the content of my understanding.) The contrasting conception, tentatively endorsed, is that it is equivalent to the *explanations* that I can give of 'game'—explanations that do not amount to definitions. Unless we distinguish definition from explanation, §75 is internally incoherent.

It is equally important to note the contrast between §75 and §70 in the treatment of the distinction between knowing and being able to say. The point of §70 was to argue against the identification of understanding 'game' with the ability to say (define) what a game is. There the interlocutor wished to conclude that being unable to define 'game' entails absence of understanding, and that was a mistake. The presupposition of §75 is that understanding and being able to define 'game' are distinct. Here W.'s adversary wishes to conclude that a person's understanding transcends what he is able to say in answer to 'What is a game?' But it does not follow from the fact that he cannot define 'game' that he cannot explain it. To expose this fallacy a clarification is needed of what it means 'to know and be unable to say'. Thus §70 and §75 focus on different contrasts bundled together in the distinction knowing/being able to say.

1.1　　'wie man nach Analogie dieser auf alle möglichen Arten andere Spiele konstruieren kann': W. corrected a similar mistranslation to read: 'how you can construct other games analogous to these in all sorts of ways' (PPI (R) §82).

SECTION 76

1　　This continues §75, criticizing the idea that knowledge of what a game is is equivalent to an unformulated definition. The underlying assumption is that this knowledge is something definite, and hence that a definition embodying it would have to draw a sharp boundary around the concept of a game. But, W. objects, we would refuse to acknowledge any such definition as a correct explanation of 'game' just because it would draw a sharp boundary where there is none (§68). We know in advance that no definition will correspond exactly to what we understand by 'game', because absence of a sharp boundary is an intrinsic feature of this concept. Consequently, what we understand cannot in this case correspond to a definition.

The claim that a sharply bounded concept and the concept of a game could not be the same, but at best akin, raises the general issue of the criteria of concept-identity. W. does not discuss this. No doubt he would think this unnecessary here, for we might well agree with his judgement in this instance without thereby coming to any *general* agreement about concept-identity and concept-difference (cf. PI §61).

2   (i) BT 250 f. confirms the interpretation of §76 as a continuation of §75.

'Ich weiss, was eine Pflanze ist, kann es aber nicht sagen'. Hat dieses Wissen die Multiplizität eines Satzes, der nur nicht ausgesprochen wurde? So dass, wenn der Satz ausgesprochen würde, ich ihn als den Ausdruck meines Wissens anerkennen würde?—Ist es nicht vielmehr wahr, dass jede exakte Definition als Ausdruck unseres Verstehens abgelehnt werden müsste? D.h., würden wir nicht von so einer sagen müssen, sie bestimme zwar einen, dem unseren verwandten, Begriff, aber nicht diesen selbst? Und die Verwandtschaft sei etwa die, zweier Bilder, . . .

('I know what a plant is, but I cannot say it.' Has this knowledge the multiplicity of a sentence that is as yet unformulated? So that, if the sentence were formulated, I would recognize it as the expression of my knowledge?—Is it not rather the case that every exact definition must be set aside as an expression of what we understand? i.e., would we not have to say of such a definition that it determines a concept that is akin to ours, but not this concept itself? And the kinship is perhaps that of two pictures . . .)

This makes it explicit that §76 objects only to the *initial* proposal of §75.

(ii) BT 68 f. (cf. 254) enlarges on the idea that lack of a sharp boundary is an intrinsic feature of the concept of a game:

Ich nenne daher 'Spiel' das, was auf dieser Liste steht, wie auch, was diesen Spielen bis zu einem gewissen (von mir nicht näher bestimmten) Grade ähnlich ist. Im übrigen behalte ich mir vor, in jedem neuen Fall zu entscheiden, ob ich etwas zu den Spielen rechnen will oder nicht.

(I thus call 'game' whatever belongs to this list, as well as anything that has a certain degree of similarity (that I have not further specified) to these games. Moreover, I reserve the right to decide in each fresh case whether or not I count something as a game.)

This is not a definition or even an explanation of the word 'game', but rather a description of the practice of using the word, in particular of how applications of it relate to the explanation of it by examples. The voluntarism in this description is perhaps an optional extra, emphasizing the idea that the explanation of 'game' leaves free play in so far as it does not make explicit the degree of resemblance with a paradigm requisite for an activity to qualify as a game.

(iii) PG 257 ff., derived from Vol. VII via EBT 3̄4 ff., connects the topic of explanations of concepts by examples with the analysis of generality. W. criticizes his earlier assumptions that all general propositions have one of two definite logical forms (represented by the two quantifiers ($\exists$x) and (x)) and that every proposition of the form ($\exists$x)Φ(x) (or (x)Φx) can be analysed as a logical sum (or logical product). He considers the sentence 'The cross is between the lines' describing this state of affairs: ├──✗──┤ (PG 257). After remarking 'we don't have any disjunction ready to take the place of the general proposition' (PG 258), he dispatches his earlier conception: 'It is clear that I do not recognize any logical sum as a definition of the proposition "The cross is between the lines". And that says everything that is to be said' (PG 274).

This strategy exactly parallels the argument in PI §76 rejecting putative *Merkmal*-definitions of a concept-word explained by examples.

SECTION 77

1   This continues the simile of §76, arguing that there are degrees of kinship among concepts as among pictures. The kinship is insignificant between a very blurred concept (as in ethics or aesthetics) and a sharply bounded concept given by a definition. (Consequently, no definition will illuminate such a concept, even by comparison, since none is more fitting than any other.) The terms of ethics and aesthetics have 'families of meanings'; e.g. moral goodness is really a 'family of concepts' (cf. PLP 179).

What does W. mean by remarking that a word such as 'good' has a 'family of meanings'? Is this intended as a description of the general practice of explaining and using it? Or is this a description of what each person understands in understanding such a term? The first interpretation would treat §77 as a novel phrasing of moral relativism or of the idea that goodness is an essentially contested concept (there being disagreement about the paradigms to be used for explaining it). This would, however, imply that the stylistic continuity between §76 and §77 masks a change of topic. More likely, therefore, is the second interpretation, viz. that each of us attaches a family of meanings to 'good' so that each of us has a family of concepts of moral goodness. This coheres with the implication of §77(a) that the concept of moral goodness is exceptionally blurred. It hardly matters whether we say that no definition of 'good' is correct or that many different definitions are correct; everything—and nothing—is right. The point is that no definition (giving the word 'good' sharp boundaries) closely fits our concept of moral goodness and that a large number determine concepts that equally resemble our concept.

1.1   'How did we *learn*': not child psychology, but an invitation to explore how a word (e.g. 'good') is *taught* or *explained*, for its meaning is what is explained in teaching how to use it. (But see LA 1 f.)

2   (i) Vol. XI, 47 f. confirms this interpretation of §77(b):

Welches ist die Bedeutung eines Wortes wenn der Redende sie nicht angeben kann? Nun, wir werden vielleicht sein (tatsächliches) Verhalten als ein Schwanken zwischen mehreren verwandten Bedeutungen beschreiben können.

(What is the meaning of a word when the speaker cannot state it? Well, we could perhaps describe his behaviour as a fluctuation between various related meanings.)

(Here, it seems, being unable to specify the meaning of a word is equivalent to being unable to give a *Merkmal*-definition of it.) The individual speakers' use of the word is described as a fluctuation between different meanings, and hence he could be described as attaching a number of different related meanings to the word, i.e. a family of meanings.
      (ii) EBT 492 indicates an early reservation about this form of description:

Nun, wir werden sein tatsächliches Verhalten durch ein 'Schwanken zwischen mehreren Bedeutungen' beschreiben können.
Es ist wohl wesentlich, dass ich ihn fragen kann: was hast Du eigentlich gemeint. (EBT 492, cf. BT 255.)

(Well, we could describe his actual behaviour as a 'fluctuation between several meanings.'
It is absolutely essential that I can ask him, 'What did you really mean?')

W.'s point is that the phrase 'fluctuation between several meanings' fits the case of ambiguity which the speaker could remove by an explanation if he were made aware of it. Hence, the phrase is misleading as a description of a person's use of the word if he cannot say what the word means, i.e. if he cannot give the definitions determining the meanings between which his use of the word is said to fluctuate; for he cannot answer the question 'what did you really mean?'
      (iii) PI §79(c) incorporates the idea of using a word with multiple related meanings. I use the name 'N' without a fixed or rigid meaning; its meaning shifts, vacillates, or wobbles. Alternatively, we might describe it as having a fluctuating meaning ('die Bedeutung . . . eine *schwankende* nennen' (LSP 116)).

2.1   (i) 'concepts in aesthetics or ethics': W. alludes to them elsewhere, but

nowhere does he develop the idea that they are families of concepts.
(Beauty (*Schönheit*) is discussed in MS. 157a., 25 ff. and asserted to be a
family resemblance concept, but the analysis of it is perfunctory.)

(ii) '("good" for instance) . . . a family of meanings': contrast PG 77,
which asserts that 'good' (in an ethical sense) introduces 'a single concept'
whose unity lies in the interrelatedness of the large number of games that
constitute facets of its use.

SECTION 78

1   At first glance this seems perspicuous: it pinpoints three cases in a
spectrum, ranging from the first, where knowing and being able to say
seem indistinguishable, to the third, where knowing seems compatible
with being unable to say. It seems to imply that knowing how the word
'game' is used (or what a game is) occupies an intermediate position, and
it clearly implies that knowing what a game is does not entail being able
to say what it is. Consequently, §78 establishes the possibility of the
contrast introduced in §75.

But what is the point in placing this remark here? It is inconclusive
since it does nothing to establish that knowing what a game is differs in
respect of being able to say from knowing the height of Mont Blanc. All
it shows is that we should not dismiss this possibility as absurd. But this
is not a tactic that appeals to someone who supposes that understanding
what a game is transcends what is said in explaining what a game is.
Rather, it would appeal to someone who followed Socrates in identifying
knowing with being able to say and advanced the initial objection of
§70. Although §78 is an effective polemic against the Socratic position
of §70, it has no point in the different argumentative climate of §75.
Unless, perhaps, it is meant as a prophylactic comment on §§76–7, i.e.
on the demonstration that understanding a word is not equivalent to
being able to give a definition of it.

§78 seems worse than pointless; it is misleading as a sequel to §75.
There W. suggested that my concept of a game is *completely* expressed in
explanations that I can give of 'game'—an idea that is central to his
accounts of meaning and of understanding. Since it is natural to describe
my explanations of 'game' as my *saying* what a game is (or as my saying
how I use the word 'game'), §75 implies that my knowing what a game
is *is* my being able to say (=explain) what a game is, whereas the
ostensible point of §78 is to undermine this identification. This inconsistency could be avoided only by putting a particular gloss on 'saying'
in §78, e.g. that 'saying' means 'giving a *Merkmal*-definition' or 'putting
into words (without the help of concrete samples, examples, or gestures)'.
But there is no hint of this. Consequently, §78 is misleading because it

is naturally taken to be a comment on §75 and yet undermines the fundamental point that W. there tentatively formulates and elsewhere supports.

To remedy this defect and give §78 a point would require careful unpacking of the different ingredients of the notion of saying, e.g. distinguishing defining from explaining (as in §75) or the different kinds of things called 'describing'. I can, e.g., explain how a clarinet sounds by imitating it, by relating its sound to the sound of other woodwinds, or by putting on a record of a clarinet concerto and saying '*That* is the sound of a clarinet' when the instrument makes its entry. Whether such explanations fall under our intuitive notion of saying how a clarinet sounds is neither important nor interesting. What matters is a detailed account of the reasons for and against assimilating explanations of these various forms with *Merkmal*-definitions, descriptions, specifications of height, etc. None of this is done in §78.

§78 is misleading in another respect. It implies that one cannot say how a clarinet sounds, since otherwise there is no contrast between the first case and third. This idea is, of course, a philosophical commonplace. It is natural to imagine that the sound of a clarinet, like the colour red or the taste of a pineapple, is something that cannot be 'put into words', i.e. something indescribable and indefinable. Indeed, this assumption underlies the empiricist contention that such simple ideas must be derived from acquaintance (since no words can convey them into the mind). But W., far from accepting this conception, attacks it. Indeed, one of the main thrusts of his discussion of ostensive definition is to destroy the idea that terms explained by reference to samples are, in any important sense, indefinable (for they *can* be explained). The parallel idea that certain experiences, tastes, colour, shapes, etc., are essentially indescribable is also criticized (cf. 2.1). Consequently, one will accept §78 as indicating contrasting cases only to the extent that one has failed to learn the lesson that it is mistaken to think of the sound of a clarinet as something indefinable and indescribable. §78 will have to be thrown away by someone who has achieved a correct understanding of what it discusses.

The most favourable treatment of §78 is to isolate it from the constructive suggestion §75 by taking it as a comment only on §76–7. This makes it irrelevant for the important question of whether understanding may transcend explanation. It also isolates §78 from §§79–80.

2　§78 originates in Vol. XI, 40 ff. This confirms that it should be read as a comment on §§76–7 and isolated from the discussion of explanation in §75 (which did not occur in that context). This part of the revision of BT has the following structure: it opens with the question of what it means to know what a plant is and of what it means to know this and not be able to say it. Then Socrates is quoted (cf. Exg. §70) without comment.

Then the suggestion is made that this knowledge is equivalent to an unformulated sentence which, if expressed, I would acknowledge as an expression of my knowledge. Immediately follows the objection of PI §76: '—Ist es nicht vielmehr so, dass jede exacte Definition als Ausdruck unseres Verstehens abgelehnt werden müsste? D.h.: müssten wir nicht von so einer sagen, sie bestimme zwar einen, dem unsern verwandten, Begriff, aber nicht diesen selbst?' (Vol. XI, 40.) ('Isn't it more like this, that every exact definition must be rejected as an expression of our understanding. That is, must we not say: it determines a concept, related to ours, but not this one itself.') This paragraph concludes with the picture analogy of PI §76, as in BT 250 f.

At this point occurs the ancestor of §78. Hence there is no previous mention of the idea that understanding of 'plant' is to be identified with what is explained in explaining it. The point of the remark is simply to query the conception exemplified by the quotation from Socrates and its development as a disposition to acknowledge a correct definition. Only after the precursor of §78 does W. indicate the correct conception of understanding with a single pseudo-quotation. 'Ich weiss, was eine Pflanze ist: ich kann Dir Pflanzen zeigen, aufzeichnen, beschreiben' (Vol. XI, 41). ('I know what a plant is: I can show you plants, draw them, describe them.')

2.1   (i) 'how the word "game" is used': Vol. XI, 41 distinguishes four cases (instead of the three in §78) by splitting this case into two: viz. distinguishing what a plant is and how the word 'plant' is used. For purposes of contrasting knowing and being able to say, this distinction seems unimportant.

(ii) 'how a clarinet sounds': MS. 162(b) contains a long discussion of describing shades of colour, aromas, the atmosphere of a piece of music, facial expression, memory experiences, etc. Much of this focuses on the idea that descriptions leave out certain features which are essentially indescribable (e.g. atmosphere (cf. PI p. 66 n.), the aroma of coffee (PI §610, derived from MS. 162(b), 58 via B i. §664)). He criticizes this conception:

> Wenn ich sage: ein bestimmter Farbton sei unbeschreibbar, so habe ich natürlich eine bestimmte Art der Beschreibung im Sinn. Ich sage mir z. B.: nicht so, wie ein einfaches Ornament mit einfachen Farben *beschreibbar* ist.
>
> Ich denke an eine bestimmte Methode der Beschreibung und sage: 'sie passt nicht'.
>
> Dann denken wir an Beschreibungen, die der gewünschten Beschreibung noch am nächsten kommen . . .
>
> Von allen diesen Beschr[eibungs]methoden fühlen wir dass sie in die Nähe dessen kommen wovon wir reden; es aber doch nicht treffen. (MS. 162(b), 31 f.)

(If I say: a particular shade of colour is indescribable, then of course I have a

particular mode of description in mind. I say, e.g., not as a simple ornament with simple colours is describable.
I think of a particular method of description and say 'it doesn't fit'.
Then we think of descriptions which come nearest to the desired description . . .
We feel that all these methods of description come close to the one we are talking about; but they do not get there.)

The idea that indescribability is not absolute, but relative to a particular norm of description, is elaborated in the atomists' terminology of decomposition into elements. Indeed, W. interpolated into the discussion just quoted a remark on the sentence 'Der Farbton ist nicht weiter zerlegbar' ('The shade of colour is not further analysable'). Similarly, he appended this comment to PI §610(a), which discusses describing the aroma of coffee:

> Ein bestimmtes Ideal der Beschreibung sitzt uns im Kopf. Etwa das einer Zusammensetzung des Aromas aus exacten Mengen von Aromaelementen. (B i. §664.)
> (A particular ideal [norm] of description is fixed in our mind. Perhaps that of a composition of an aroma from a precise set of aroma-elements.)

Philosophers divorce the notion of description from particular language-games of describing (*Beschreibungspiele*) and thereby create the illusion that there is a single form of description and an absolute notion of indescribability.

> 'Das Aroma beschreiben' nennen wir eine bestimmte Sprachverwendung. Z.B: 'Das Aroma dieses Kaffees ist ähnlich diesem aber stärker gebrannt'. Wenn man glaubt, es gebe abgesehen von solchen Beschreibungen noch etwas anderes, was in einem eminenteren Sinn die Beschreibung des Aromas wäre: so läuft man einer philosophischen Schimäre nach. (MS 162(b), 59.)
> (We call 'describing the aroma' a particular use of language. E.g. 'The aroma of this coffee is similar to that but it smells more darkly roasted.' If one believes that there is, irrespective of such descriptions, also something else, which would be in a more distinguished sense the description of the aroma: then one is chasing a philosophical chimera.)

Given this criticism of philosophical employment of the notion of indescribability, it is odd that §78 apparently subscribes to the idea that the sound of a clarinet is indescribable.

Proper names
   1. Introduction   2. Frege: the general principles   3. Frege and Russell: simple abbreviation theories   4. Cluster theories of proper names 5. Wittgenstein: the general principles   6. Wittgenstein: some critical consequences   7. The significance of proper names   8. Proper names and meaning

SECTION 79

1   This discussion of proper names has an important place in contemporary
philosophy. It is generally treated as the definitive exposition of W.'s
account of proper names and interpreted as advancing a modified version
of Russell's theory that names are disguised descriptions (the so-called
'cluster theory of proper names').

Current interpretations of §79 suffer from the defect of treating it in
isolation from its immediate context and from W.'s other remarks about
proper names. It does not open with W.'s declaring that he is about to
delineate his general account of names. Far from this being so, it starts
with the preamble 'Consider this example'. This surely suggests that
W.'s aim was to illustrate some point made or implied in the immediately
preceding remarks and that §79 should be interpreted in relation to that
specific purpose (whatever it may be: cf. 1.1). Similarly, it is odd to treat
§79 as the whole of W.'s analysis of proper names. There are other
important remarks about names even in PI (e.g. §§40–3), let alone
elsewhere, and this subject is closely related to his account of ostensive
definition and of explanation (cf. 'Ostensive definition and its ramifications', pp. 81 ff.) and to his criticisms of the Augustinian picture and of
logical atomism (cf. 'Logically proper names', pp. 138 ff.). Consequently,
it is clear that §79 is not the whole truth about W.'s conception of proper
names, and it is not even clear that it contains nothing but the truth.

Given the dense mist of controversy surrounding §79, it is important
to start from a careful description of what the unprejudiced eye must see
in the text.

§79(a) introduces as an *example* the sentence 'Moses did not exist'.
This may mean various things, and we do ask, in such a case, 'What do
you mean? Do you wish to say that . . . or . . . etc?' Possible answers are
suggested. Then, W. remarks, it would accord with this variety of
answers to follow Russell's practice of saying that the name 'Moses' can
be *defined* by means of various descriptions. For that would assign
different senses to the sentence 'Moses did not exist' (and also to every
other proposition about Moses) according to which definition is given to
the name 'Moses'. (Note how little W. subscribes to: nothing more, in
fact, than the idea that 'Moses does not exist' may have various
meanings. Note also the use of the terms 'define' and 'definition' in the
sketch of Russell's position.)

(b) raises an objection to Russell's conception that the meaning of

'Moses' (what I mean or understand by 'Moses') is given by a *single* description which is used to define the name—or even by a conjunction of such descriptions. This point is generalized by discussing the sentence 'N is dead', incorporating a schematic proper name. W. suggests that the definition of 'N' would be a conjunction of all the descriptions used to explain 'N' on different occasions. According to Russell's theory of descriptions, this would make the sentence 'N is dead' false if a single one of these descriptions were not satisfied by N (since, according to this definition, 'N' would have no reference). This is absurd. For if I had explained the name 'N' in this way I should now be ready to alter this explanation. (Note that W.'s argument is that *no definition* of a name 'N' captures what I mean by 'N'; every definition by means of a description, however complex, would be rejected in certain circumstances, and hence none can be acknowledged as expressing what I mean and understand by 'N'. This conclusion is parallel to §76.)

(c) summarizes (b) in the statement: 'I use the name "N" without a fixed meaning'. And it adds that this does not make 'N' useless. (This looks parallel to the conclusion of §77(b). Using 'N' without a fixed meaning might be phrased as using 'N' with a family of meanings or with a set of meanings between which it fluctuates.)

(d) dismisses the objection that (b) should be summarized in the statement that I am using a word whose meaning I do not know and so am talking nonsense. (This objection restates for proper names the Socratic position discussed in §70.) W.'s reply is ironic.

(e) draws an analogy, presumably between the fluctuating definitions of scientific concepts and the use of proper names without fixed meanings. (This is not directly relevant to the discussion of proper names in (a)–(d).)

The upshot of this investigation seems to be that §79 discusses proper names in a way parallel to the discussion of the concept of a game in §§76 and of aesthetic and moral concepts in §77. The thrust is negative: no sharp *definition* of a name 'N' encapsulates what I understand by 'N' because I do not use 'N' rigidly in conformity with a single definition. 'N' has either a family of meanings (§79(c)) or no meaning (at least none that I know) (§79(d)), since either many definitions are correct or else none is (§77(a)). The positive points of §79 are few and humdrum. (i) Sentences of the form 'N did not exist' may have various meanings. (ii) What I understand or mean by 'N' may be explained by descriptions specifying who N is. (iii) Explanations of 'N' by descriptions may vary from occasion to occasion, and they may be revised in the light of further information. (iv) The variability and revisability of explanations of 'N' does not detract from the usefulness of 'N'. None of these ideas is an arresting discovery, and the conjunction of them hardly merits the title of 'a theory of proper names'. Moreover, other points about names are not mentioned at all in §79, e.g. that a proper name may be explained by ostension (§43).

1.1   (i) 'Consider this example': what point is the discussion of names supposed to illustrate? One possibility would be the contrast between knowing and being able to say (§78). But does §79 establish this contrast for names? Does it demonstrate that there is more to our understanding of a name than we can say? It shows only that no *definition* by descriptions matches what we understand by a name, not that our understanding outruns our ability to *explain* names. The latter thesis would be inconsistent with §75 and with W.'s whole general account of the relation of explanation and understanding. Consequently, §79 must be meant to illustrate some other point. The obvious candidate is the one mentioned at the beginning of §75 and criticized in §§76–7, viz. that knowledge of who N is (or of what I mean and understand by 'N') is equivalent to some *definition* of 'N'. That is the position sketched out and criticized in §79. The discussion of what it is to know who Moses is parallels the earlier discussions of what it is to know what a game is and what it is to know what moral goodness is. 'Moses' is another example to illustrate the shortcomings of the initial proposal in §75. Therefore, the preamble reinforces the idea that the thrust of § 79 is negative. (Slight further confirmation is found in Vol. XI, 43. There, after discussing the example of 'plant' and establishing the criticism of PI §76, W. introduces 'a further example', viz. the term 'egg-shaped' ('eiförmig'), and shortly thereafter moves on to consider the name 'Moses'.)

(ii) 'Nach Russell können wir sagen': interpreting §79 as advancing a cluster theory of names presupposes W.'s initial attraction to the idea of construing proper names as disguised descriptions. For then it would be plausible that W., unable to follow directly in Russell's footsteps, followed him at a respectful distance. Hence it is crucial whether the text of §79 expresses any commitment to Russell's analysis of names. This is doubtful. The phrase 'nach Russell können wir sagen' is neutral. W. himself gave an antiseptic paraphrase of it: 'in Russell's terminology' (PPI (R) §86). Far from expressing his approval, this simply introduces a (correct) statement of Russell's view. What W. does is to cite Russell's *explanation* of the fact that the sentence 'Moses does not exist' may have various meanings. Given the background idea that the meaning of a sentence is a function of the meanings of its constituents, this ambiguity of the negative existential sentence must be traced to ambiguity of the name 'Moses', and Russell's disguised description theory of names exposes this ambiguity by producing numerous distinct *definitions* of 'Moses'. Not only is Russell's account a distortion of our understanding of names (as argued in §79(b)), but also the movement of thought evident in it, i.e. the substitution of quasi-scientific explanation for description, is antithetical to W.'s views of proper philosophical procedure. This is an additional reason against taking §79 to be proposing a modification to Russell's theory.

(iii) 'and so does every other proposition about Moses': this is an (implausible) consequence of the principle that the meaning (or sense) of a sentence is a function of the meanings (or senses) of its constituents. We might follow Frege in trying to allay disquiet by claiming that this ambiguity is practically so unimportant that it altogether escapes our attention in everyday uses of language (SR 58 n., cf. Z §438).

(iv) 'Unter "Moses" verstehe ich'; 'was ich unter "N" verstehe': W. translated 'verstehen' by 'mean' in both instances (PPI (R) §86).

(v) 'eindeutig bestimmten Gebrauch': perhaps 'unambiguously settled use' (only words, not uses, can be said to be 'univocal' or 'equivocal'). This phrase is equivalent to 'used without a fixed meaning' (§79(c)).

(vi) 'ohne feste Bedeutung': W. preferred 'without a rigid meaning' (PPI (R) §86).

(vii) '. . . I am using a word whose meaning I don't know . . .': although this is misleading, it is no more so than saying that 'N' has a family of meanings (cf. §77(b)) or that 'N' has a meaning that fluctuates (cf. LSP 116). The facts are that the use of 'N' does not exactly match that of any single descriptive definition of 'N' and that its use equally resembles that of a number of different descriptive definitions of 'N'. If what we call 'meaning' is tied rigidly to definitions (rather than to the wider class of explanations), then to say that 'N' has no meaning is no more, and no less, misleading than to say that it has many. What is required to escape from this impasse is a more adequate conception of meaning, viz. one that relates meaning to understanding and to explanation; only then will we see proper names aright (cf. §81(b)).

(viii) 'The fluctuation of scientific definitions': this alludes to the fluctuation between criteria and symptoms in relation to scientific concepts (cf. PI §354, Z §438). In such a case the meaning of the relevant expression can be said to fluctuate, although for the most part this is not noticed (Z §438). Presumably, this fluctuation in definitions is mentioned as an analogy for the use of 'N' without a fixed meaning (§79(c)), since in that case too the meaning of 'N' can be described as fluctuating (LSP 116). The varying explanations by description of 'Moses' and 'N' could be called fluctuating definitions of these names. It is not clear that anything more is intended by the analogy; in particular, W. need not be taken as claiming that there is a fluctuation between criteria and symptoms associated with our understanding of names.

2   The origin of §79(a)–(d) is very early. It first appears in Vol. VIII, 186 ff., and then recurs with only minor modifications in EBT 489 ff., BT 251 ff., and Vol. XI, 43 ff. (cf. also PLP 69 ff., C8, 77 f.). The stability of this

discussion of proper names is remarkable given the considerable
development in W.'s conception of meaning between writing Vol. VIII
(late in 1931) and composing PPI (late in 1936). It suggests that we might
be well advised to treat §79 as a relic of an earlier conception of language
and to discount its importance in so far as it seems problematic in the
context of PI.

This strategy would be mistaken. There is another aspect of the
precursors of §79 that is also remarkable for its stability: the immediate
argumentative context. In each version the remark introduces discussion
of the mistake of thinking of understanding or meaning something as
operating a definite calculus of rules and a reference to the sins of TLP in
respect of its subscribing implicitly to this dogma (i.e. the substance of PI
§81). Consequently, the immediate purpose of every precursor of §79 is
to illustrate a negative thesis: reflection on proper names is supposed to
demonstrate that their use cannot be accounted for on the assumption
that it is the output of a rigid meaning-calculus whose rules are
definitions by means of descriptions. The closest defensible approximation to this assumption is the idea that the use of a name fluctuates
between the output corresponding to the different definitions of it by
means of descriptions, i.e. that it is not used with one fixed meaning (if
meaning is conceived to be the correlate of definitions). Since the purpose
of the precursors of §79 is negative, and since W. continues to criticize
the idea that understanding consists in operating a calculus according to
definite rules, the presence of this 'ancient' remark in PI is apposite; §79
is not obsolete or in need of discounting.

Of course, the negative thrust of §79 and its precursors is com-
plemented by a positive account of what it is to understand or to mean
something, and *that* did undergo substantial change. In accord with the
conception of meaning in WWK and PR, the meaning of a name 'N' is
identified with a method of procedure for determining of something
whether it is the bearer of 'N', and a definition of 'N' is a signpost
pointing at N; different definitions of 'N' specify different methods for
determining the bearer of 'N', and hence confer different senses on every
sentence in which 'N' occurs. Remnants of this conception are still
evident in Vol. VIII and EBT. Different definitions by description confer
different meanings on the defined name so that a sentence having a sense
according to one may have none according to another definition.

Ich erzähle jemandem von einem Herrn N.; er habe mit mir studiert; sei dann in
das und das Geschäft gekommen, etc. Und nun zeige ich ihm eine Gruppe von
Leuten und sage: schau, ob einer von diesen Herr N ist.—Das ist doch so sinnlos,
wie die Aufgabe, das Alter der Kapitäns zu bestimmen, wenn die Dimensionen
des Schiffs gegeben wurden. Nicht mehr und nicht weniger sinnlos.—Hätte ich
das Aeussere des N beschrieben, so wäre die Aufforderung nicht absurd. (EBT
494.)

(I tell somebody something about Mr N; we were students together; then he went into such and such employment, etc. And then I point to a group of people and say: look and see if one of these is Mr N—That is as senseless as the problem of specifying the age of the captain[4] when only the dimensions of the ship are given. Neither more nor less senseless.—Had I described the appearance of N then the request would not have been absurd.)

The same conception of meaning is evident in W.'s endorsement of Russell's account of the ambiguity of names and its consequence.

Ich will doch wohl das sagen, was Russell dadurch ausdrückt, dass der Name Moses durch verschiedene Beschreibungen definiert sein kann. . . . Und je nachdem wir die eine oder andere Definition annehmen, bekommt der Satz 'Moses hat existiert' einen andern Sinn und ebenso jeder andere Satz, der von Moses handelt. (BT 252.)
(I wish to say just what Russell expresses by saying that the name 'Moses' can be defined by different descriptions. . . . And according as we assume one or another definition, the sentence 'Moses existed' takes on a different sense—and so too does every other sentence about Moses.)

(Cf. LSP 388: 'Wie B. Russell bemerkt hat, erweisen sich sehr viele Namen bei näherem Zusehen als abgekürzte Beschreibungen.' ('As B. Russell has noted, many names show themselves on close inspection to be abbreviated descriptions.')) Far from deploring it, W. still welcomed and insisted upon the consequence that sentences incorporating ordinary proper names are radically ambiguous. However unambiguous they may seem, such sentences really are equivocal; there is a degree of free play or fluctuation in what constitutes verification of them, and this can be traced in part to the fact that names are not unambiguously defined and hence fluctuate between different meanings (WWK 47 f.).

According to this early conception, the meaning of any word is its role in the calculus of language. The implication of the discussion of the name 'Moses' is that a name does not typically have a single completely defined role in the calculus; rather, it has a number of different but related roles each of which is pinpointed by a particular definition of it. The negative consequence is the indefensibility of the dogma that a person who means something by a name must be operating a calculus of meaning-rules in which the name corresponds to a single invariable definition. The positive consequence might be drawn that we can treat language only as an approximation to such a calculus. The 'vagueness' of a name like 'Moses', i.e. the fact that it fluctuates between various meanings, is of crucial importance (PLP 71). It block the *identification* of using language with operating a calculus by forcing the concession that there are no

[4] This is an allusion to a traditional children's joke: 'There was a ship of such-and-such length, height, breadth, width, etc. Now, what is the age of the ship's captain?'

exact rules laid down for the use of names (PLP 70). At the same time, however, the 'vagueness' of names is revealed by *comparing* language with a calculus, and we can do justice to it by treating language as an approximation to various calculi of meaning-rules (cf. PLP 71 ff.).

PI §81(a) explicitly criticizes the strategy of treating language as an approximation to a calculus. This development from his earlier conception is associated with W.'s substituting the notion of language-game for that of a calculus (cf. 'Language-games', pp. 49 ff.), and with his critical scrutiny of the notion of the ideal (§§89 ff.). It is also related to his emphasizing the concept of explanation in contrast to that of definition. This makes the positive implications that might be drawn from the precursors of §79 inconsistent with fundamental ideas of PI. In particular, the fact that the use of 'Moses' is not exhaustively described by any *definition* is not in itself a reason for concluding that 'Moses' is ambiguous, that it has no meaning, or that its meaning fluctuates (that it is vague). Rather, this fact should be treated as an invitation to look into what count as legitimate *explanations* of names and how explanations are related to the content of our understanding of names.

Shifts in W.'s conception of meaning and the correlative change in the putative positive purpose of the discussion of 'Moses' contrast with the invariability of its negative purpose. Its link with the criticism of the calculus model of meaning and understanding corresponds to a definitive grouping of a set of books which survives intact through the general reorganization of a library (cf. BB 44 f.).

Its history counts strongly against interpreting §79 as an argument intended to reconcile the variability of definitions of names with invariance in what we understand by them. The earliest versions, far from being employed for this purpose, were used to establish the opposite conclusion, viz. that proper names as ordinarily used are very ambiguous and vague and that it is illusory to think of them as having a single invariant meaning. What this shows is that, if PI does reconcile variability of explanation with invariance of understanding, the key to this achievement must lie outside §79 itself. (It is the notion of criteria of understanding, about which §79 is silent. Cf. 'Proper names', pp. 244 f.)

BT 253 confirms the connections of §79 with §§76–7 as criticisms of the initial proposal of §75. After concluding that we use 'N' without a fixed meaning it continues: 'Das erinnert an das was ich früher einmal über die Benützung der Begriffswörter, z.B. des Wortes "Blatt" oder "Pflanze", geschrieben habe.' ('That is reminiscent of what I once wrote about the use of concept-words, e.g. of the word "leaf" or "plant".') (The concept of a plant, rather than that of a game, was discussed in the precursors of §§75–6.)

2.1 (i) 'Ich gebrauche den Namen "N" ohne *feste* Bedeutung': cf. BT 252 f.—'Das kommt nun darauf hinaus, dass wir den Namen "N" in gewissem Sinne ohne feste Bedeutung gebrauchen, oder: dass wir bereit sind, die Spielregeln nach Bedarf zu verändern (make the rules as we go along).' ('That comes down to this, that we use the name "N" in a certain sense without fixed meaning, or that we are ready to alter the rules if necessary (make the rules as we go along).') This reformulation makes clear that W. saw §79 as a criticism of the idea that understanding consists of operating a calculus of rules (§81(b)), and it also connects §79 with the criticism of the 'ideal' that the application of a word be everywhere bounded by rules (§§83–4).

(ii) 'wie dem eines Tisches, dass er auf vier Beinen ruht, statt auf dreien': Vol. XI, 45 makes use of an alternative analogy in which the 'defect' is purely theoretical: 'wie einer Brücke, dass sie kein absolut starrer Körper ist' ('as it does from that of a bridge that it is not a perfectly rigid body').

SECTION 80

1 This parallels §79. If the conception of a person's being able to say what a chair is, is that he should be able to state a rule that unambiguously settles every possible application of 'chair', then there is room for a contrast between knowing what a chair is and being able to say what a chair is. The alternative would be that we do not know what 'chair' means because we are not able to state rules for every possible application of the word.

1.1 'we do not really attach any meaning': this point is raised in §70(a) in connection with 'game', and in §79(d) for proper names. It embodies a mistaken conception of understanding (§81(b)) and of explanation (cf. Exg. §87).

2 W.'s strategy is to describe bizarre circumstances of perception to undermine the conviction that our understanding of 'chair' consists in explicit knowledge of a rule that settles the truth-value of 'There is a chair' in every conceivable circumstance. This is pursued elsewhere too. It is particularly familiar from Waismann's writings (PLP 75–6, 222–3, 'Verifiability',[5] and LSP Appx. B).[6] He elaborates such cases more fully and draws the conclusion that there are no complete sets of rules for the

---

[5] F. Waismann, 'Verifiability', in *Logic and Language*, ed. A. Flew, First Series (Blackwell, Oxford, 1960).

[6] An English translation appears as Ch. V in F. Waismann, *Philosophical Papers*, ed. B. McGuinness (D. Reidel, Dordrecht and Boston, 1976).

applications of such ordinary words as 'chair' and 'table' (e.g. PLP 76, 223). This reflects a phase of W.'s thinking (cf. BT 249, LSP *Nachwort* pp. 647–55).

The parallelism between Waismann's arguments and the material of §80 suggests that the moral of §80 might be taken to be that the concept of chair is open-textured. This would be a fundamental mistake, however plausible it may seem. The very concept of open texture is not consistent with the framework of thought of the *Investigations*. There are two reasons for this verdict.

(i) Open texture is inseparable from the notion of an hypothesis (*Hypothese*). It is the correlate of hypotheses. The open texture of 'gold' or 'chair' consists in there being no conclusive verification or falsification of such sentences as 'This is (a piece of) gold' or 'This is a chair'. What is the ground for that claim? Just that any such (material object) statement is an hypothesis relative to descriptions of immediate experience and hence can never be conclusively verified (or falsified). It is part of the grammar of such sentences that their verification is incomplete; i.e. they are *essentially* unverifiable (and unfalsifiable), though experience makes them more or less probable (or improbable). In this way, the empirical content of an hypothesis transcends all possible experience. This notion was elaborated by W. for a considerable period (PR; EBT; BT; cf. LSP), but then criticized and repudiated (BB 48; Z §260; cf. C §§3, 105, 342 f.). Since there is no such thing as an hypothesis (in his technical sense), there is no such thing as open texture.

(ii) The characterization of open texture presupposes a distorted conception of what it is for a set of rules to be complete (or incomplete). Describing the concept of a chair as open-textured implies that the rules governing the application of 'chair' are not complete; that the grammar of 'chair' is incomplete (cf. PLP 76); that there are many 'directions in which we have not limited our concept' of a chair (PLP 223; cf. 'Verifiability', p. 120). Implicit in these remarks is a conception of what it would be for the rules defining 'chair' to be complete; viz. that mere inspection of them would explicitly decide the truth-value of 'There is a chair' in every imaginable situation, however bizarre. Hence the mere possibility of imagining cases where a definition leaves us in the lurch is taken as sufficient to demonstrate that this definition is incomplete. This need not be a defect of language, and it typically is not so, since the grammar of our language has been shaped to conform with the prevalent conditions of our experience. The demand for completeness of definition for all our words would be utopian (PLP 223, cf. 76), as long as concepts fulfil the practical purposes for which they were devised (PLP 223). Any concept can be further refined by providing rules for further possibilities should the need arise (PLP 76; BT 249). From the perspective of the *Investigations*, this is a muddle. The impossibility of satisfying *this* demand for completeness of definition shows not that the demand is utopian, but rather that it makes no sense. It is a complete distortion of what it is for a definition or explanation to be complete. Since the concept of open texture is introduced as correlative to such a concept of completeness, there is no such thing as open texture either. To say of a concept that its application is left open in certain respects is to say something substantial about it. To say that it is open-textured is to say nothing. (For a correct conception of what it is for explanation of words to be complete, see 'Explanation', pp. 38 ff., and 'Vagueness and determinacy of sense', p. 225).

PG 220 f. discusses 'Here there is a chair' as an hypothesis relative to mere description of what is perceived, e.g. relative to systematic series of views from different angles.

C8, 79 subjoins to the ancestor of PI §80 the crucial question 'Was ist ein komplettes Regelverzeichnis für ein Wort. . .?' ('What is a complete set of rules for a word?'). This discussion is developed in Vol. XI, 50–3, from which PPI §114 (cf. Z §440) is derived. Serious attention to this question is what exposes the incoherence of the currently popular and influential concept of open texture.

2.1   'we do not really attach any meaning to this word': instead of saying this, we might say that we use 'chair' without a fixed meaning, or even that we make up the rules for using 'chair' as we go along. These comments about proper names (cf. §79(c)) seem equally applicable to concept-words such as 'leaf' or 'plant', also presumably to 'chair' or 'game' (BT 253).

SECTION 81

1   This fundamental remark diagnoses the ultimate source of the reluctance to acknowledge the legitimacy of family resemblance concepts, i.e. of the unshakable conviction that everything falling under any concept-word *must* do so in virtue of properties that it shares with everything else within the extension of this word. This is a particular conception of what it is to mean or understand something by a word. The fact that what I mean and understand is something definite seems to entail that I use the word according to a quite definite rule, whether or not I can state this rule. The task of philosophy is to bring to light by analysis the rules hidden away in the medium of the mind and underlying all the uses that we make of language. If inspection reveals that we do not appeal to *Merkmale* in explaining a particular concept-word (e.g. 'game'), that simply shows by how much what we mean and understand by this word transcends what we explain and how fallible a guide actual explanations are to the content of our understanding. The definiteness in the pattern of

our using the word shows that we do *know* what are the properties common to all objects falling under it even though we cannot *say* this. By falling back on considerations about meaning (*Meinen*) and understanding, i.e. on the 'psychological' correlates of meaning (*Bedeutung*) and explanation, the defender of the demand for *Merkmal*-definitions seems able to turn the previous rout (§§65–74) into a victory. §81(b) pinpoints the mistake in his reasoning as the misconception that meaning or understanding words consists in operating a calculus according to definite rules. Calling attention to this misconception is the main purpose of §81.

§81 is the keystone of the surrounding arguments. §§75–80 have prepared for its diagnosis by arguing against the thesis that the content of understanding is invariably given by a definition (i.e. a definite rule for applying a term in every conceivable circumstance); in many cases, we could acknowledge no definition as a correct expression (analysis) of what we mean and understand. §§82–8 criticize some of the ingredients of our mistaken conception of operating a calculus according to definite rules. The whole of §§75–88 is intended to clarify the misconception diagnosed in §81(b).

There are further important points made in §81.

(i) All of the matters discussed in §§75–88 can appear in the right light only when one has attained greater clarity about the concepts of understanding, meaning, and thinking. In particular, the earlier discussion of family resemblance concepts like 'game' or 'plant', the account of proper names, and the discussion of 'chair' are merely *provisional*, not definitive, and must be reconsidered after later clarification of the 'psychological' concepts of understanding and meaning something. So too must the discussion of completeness, finality, and exactness of explanations.

(ii) §81(a) implicitly criticizes as dogmatism the idea that using language is playing a game with fixed rules. It is a mistake to think that we *must* be operating a calculus with definite rules whenever we mean or understand a sentence. This dogmatism was, according to §81(b), embedded in the idea of analysis in TLP. W. uses Ramsey's remark that logic is a normative science to signal the repudiation of this dogmatism.

(iii) §81(a) criticizes seeing actual language as an *approximation* to a calculus with definite rules. This view is liable to mislead us since it suggests that actual languages fall short of the ideal and that they would be improved by being brought more closely into conformity with such a calculus. One is apt to be dazzled by the idea of this ideal (cf. §100).

(iv) §81(a) does not deny that it is useful to *compare* the uses of words with games or calculi with definite rules. Comparison may reveal important differences as well as similarities, and it may aid in obtaining an *Übersicht* of part of our language (cf. 'Übersicht', pp. 305 ff.).

1.1   'für den luftleeren Raum': W. paraphrased this: 'not taking into account friction and air resistance' (PPI (R) §88). This makes a connection with PI §130.

2   (i) Vol. V, 281 (cf. EBT 141) elaborates the criticism of TLP:

Man möchte sagen: 'Man muss nur etwas mit dem *meinen*, was man sagt, dann ist alles Wesentliche gegeben'. Und ich betrachte also 'etwas meinen' und 'einer Regel folgen' als gleichbedeutend.
Kann ich sagen: Wenn ich etwas *meine*, so habe ich meine Worte nach einer gewissen Regel gewählt?

(One would like to say: 'One must merely *mean* something by what one says, then everything essential is given'. And thus I consider 'meaning something' and 'following a rule' as synonymous.
Can I say: if I *mean* something, then I have chosen my words according to a certain rule?)

The illusion indicated here is that meaning something is following a definite rule; and its corollary, that not following a rule in using words to say something would be to string words together aimlessly (cf. BT 254). The parallel illusion about understanding is discussed in EBT 144.
    BT 253 relates this criticism specifically to TLP:

War es nun nicht ein Fehler von mir (denn so scheint es mir jetzt) anzunehmen, dass der, der die Sprache gebraucht, immer *ein bestimmtes Spiel* spiele? Denn, war das nicht der Sinn meiner Bemerkung, dass alles an einem Satz—wie beiläufig immer er ausgedrückt sein mag—'in Ordnung ist'? Aber wollte ich nicht sagen: alles müsse in Ordnung sein, wenn Einer einen Satz sage und ihn anwende? Aber daran ist doch weder etwas in Ordnung noch in Unordnung—in Ordnung wäre es, wenn man sagen könnte: auch dieser Mann spielt ein Spiel nach einem bestimmten, festen Regelverzeichnis.

(Was it not a mistake of mine (for so it now seems to me) to assume that someone who uses language is always playing *one definite game*? For, was this not the meaning of my remark that everything in a sentence—however loosely it may be expressed—'is in order'? But didn't I want to say: everything must be in order if someone says a sentence and applies it? But there is nothing in order or in disorder in it—It would be in order if one could say: this man too is playing a game according to a definite fixed set of rules.)

This obviously alludes to TLP 5.5563. It identifies the idea that a sentence is in order with the proposition that a speaker means something by it, and both of these are identified with the statement that he is playing a definite game with fixed rules (cf. PI §81(a)). The implicit criticism is that it makes no sense to speak of being in order or being in disorder if *whatever* a person may do is described as his playing a game with fixed rules.

EBT 491 contained an extended version of the previous remark, relating this misconception that every use of language manifests the hidden operation of a definite set of rules with a general misconception about what it is for an action to be in accord with a rule.

Und setzt das nicht wieder voraus, dass dieses ganze Regelverzeichnis irgendwie schon in jedem einzelnen Zug des Spiels gegenwärtig ist? Ist es nicht vielmehr so, dass sich zwar zu jeder Handlung//Spielhandlung//ein Regelverzeichnis aufstellen liesse, dem sie entspricht, dass wir aber dann in gewissen Fällen den Gebrauch der Sprache als eine fortwährendes Wechseln des Spiels (des Regelverzeichnisses) beschreiben müssten//müssen// . . .?

(And does this not in turn presuppose that this whole set of rules is somehow already present in every single move of the game? Is it not rather that to every action//action in the game//a rule can be set up that corresponds to it, but that in certain cases we must describe the use of language as a continuous alteration of the game (of the set of rules)?)

The idea that the whole set of rules for a game are somehow present in every move has a 'psychological' counterpart; viz. that intending to play a game or even to make a move in a game presupposes having in mind the whole set of rules of the game (cf. PI §205). This indicates at least one respect in which clarification of the concept of thinking might help to expose the illusion of supposing that meaning and understanding consist in operating a calculus of rules.

(ii) BT 253 links Ramsey's remark with the criticism of the implicit dogmatism of TLP about understanding or meaning something. Although it indicates a reservation about the dictum, it does not develop this into a criticism of the misleading idea that a calculus of meaning-rules is an *ideal*.

Wenn man damit meint, sie stelle ein Ideal auf, dem sich die Wirklichkeit nur nähere, so muss gesagt werden, dass dann dieses 'Ideal' uns nur als ein Instrument der annähernden Beschreibung der Wirklichkeit interessiert. Es ist allerdings möglich, einen Kalkül genau zu beschreiben und zwar zu dem Zweck, um dadurch eine Gruppe anderer Kalküle beiläufig zu charakterisieren.

(If that is meant to say that it [logic] sets up an ideal to which reality only approximates, then it must be said that this 'ideal' interests us only as an instrument for an approximative description of reality. It is of course possible to describe a calculus exactly and for the purpose of thereby roughly characterizing a group of other calculi.)

Hence it may be as useful to compare language with a calculus, just as it might be useful to convey what board-games are by describing a particular game.

(iii) PLP 71–81 elaborates on how it may be useful, and how misleading, to compare the use of words in language with a calculus with fixed rules ('a grammatical model'). Waismann emphasizes that such calculi should not be seen as parallel to scientific theories, i.e. as systems of propositions intended to function as explanations of the phenomena of language. Rather, they should be used as objects of comparison that may illuminate certain aspects of the uses of words. He compares their use with Boltzmann's conception of the use of models in scientific theories (PLP 77), and he connects the employment of grammatical models with the purpose of obtaining an *Übersicht* (PLP 80 f.) (cf. 'Übersicht', p. 306).

2.1   'Logic. . . "a normative science"': this dictum served as a focal point for W.'s reflections about meaning. It occurs, e.g., in the heading of BT §58 (p. 248), introducing a discussion of much of the material of PI §§65–88. But it is open to differing interpretations, some of which W. criticizes and others of which he applauds.

BT §58 uses the dictum to clarify the idea that philosophy is a descriptive study of how language works. There is a tension in that claim:

> Die strikten grammatischen Spielregeln und der schwankende Sprachgebrauch.
> Die Logik normativ.
> Inwiefern reden wir von idealen Fällen, einer idealen Sprache. ('Logik des luftleeren Raums'.) (BT 248.)

> (The strict rules of grammar and the fluctuating use of language.
> Logic normative.
> To what extent we speak of ideal cases, of an ideal language. ('Logic of a vacuum'.))

The point of stressing that logic is normative is to emphasize the contrast between the clear, rigid rules of 'grammar' and the fluctuating, fuzzy concepts of actual language. The logician studies language in the guise of calculi proceeding according to fixed rules (BT 258; PG 63). He constructs calculi corresponding to the actual fluctuating use of language. His activity parallels the task of sketching a sharply defined picture to correspond to a blurred one (BT 258; PI §77). His rules, like his picture, cannot be said to be descriptions of what he finds; at least, that would be misleading in view of the clear divergence between the copy and the original (cf. BT 258; Vol. IV, 160). Does that mean that he produces an ideal to which actual language more or less closely approximates? That too would be misleading: the point of constructing the 'ideal' is simply to have something to compare with actual word-use. Our purpose in producing it is to heighten our sensitivity to language in the hope that our worries and puzzles will thereby disappear (BT 258). The procedure is analogous to clarifying what a board-game is by describing draughts in detail (BT 253). The purpose in constructing calculi of meaning-rules is not to criticize actual language-use nor to propose modifications to bring

it into line with operating calculi, but rather to characterize, by way of
similarity and contrast, how we operate with words.

BT 257 gives a different interpretation of the dictum, employing it to
highlight the distinction between descriptions of 'grammar' and descriptions of the world. W. considers someone who describes the shapes of the
objects in his room by comparing them with solid polygons. In doing
this, he would not be asserting that everything in his room has the form
of a solid polygon. Nor would his noticing that there were spherical
objects there make his procedure erroneous.

Es wäre auch irreführend, den ebenflächigen Körper ein 'Ideal' zu nennen, dem
sich die Wirklichkeit nur mehr oder weniger nähert. Aber die Geometrie der
ebenflächigen Körper könnte man mit Bezug auf diese Darstellungsweise//Dar-
stellung//eine normative Wissenschaft nennen. (Eine, die das Darstellungsmittel
darstellt; gleichsam eine, die die Messgläser eicht.) (BT 257.)

(It would also be misleading to call a plane-sided body an 'ideal' to which reality
more or less closely approximates. But the geometry of solid polygons could be
called a normative science in relation to this manner of representation//this
representation//. (A science that represents the means of representation; as it were,
one that calibrates measuring cups.))

Though there is reason to call them both 'descriptions', the descriptions
of the shapes and sizes of objects are *toto mundo* different from the
descriptions of a system of geometry or of a system of measurement.
Calling the descriptions of the 'grammar' of a language a normative
science is meant to emphasize how unlike a natural science a philosophical account of language is.

Later revisions of BT are more critical of Ramsey's dictum.

'Die Logik ist eine normative Wissenschaft' sollte doch wohl heissen sie stelle
Ideale auf denen wir nachstreben sollen. Aber so ist es ja nicht. Die Logik stellt
exacte Kalküle auf. (BT 252v.)

('Logic is a normative science' should really mean that it sets up ideals which we
should try to emulate. But this is not so. Logic sets up exact calculi.)

The only legitimate role of such calculi is as objects of comparison, but
that is not what Ramsey's dictum suggests. W. criticizes the related idea
that we must banish vagueness in order for language to be fit for
scientific purposes.

Wenn Frege sagt, mit unscharfen Begriffen wisse die Logik nichts anzufangen so
ist das insofern die Wahrheit//wahr//, als gerade die Schärfe der Begriffe zur
Methode der Logik gehört. Das ist es was der Ausdruck, die Logik sei normativ,
bezeichnen kann. (BT 68v.)

(In saying that logic does not know how to deal with fuzzy concepts, Frege is
speaking the truth//truly // in so far as the sharpness of concepts belongs directly to

the method of logic. That is what the expression 'Logic is normative' can be used to designate.)

This is a stipulation of the means for describing language, not a proposal for improving language (as Frege wrongly thought). And, of course, it is not the only possible means of representation for the 'grammar' of a language.

3   (i) a 'normative science': it is uncertain what Ramsey meant by this phrase, and it is not known in what context he called logic a normative science. But Ramsey did criticize as a piece of 'scholasticism' W.'s view that all our everyday propositions are completely in order and that it is impossible to think illogically.[7] That view is explicitly criticized in early versions of §81 (cf. BT 253) because it is a form of dogmatism, not a description of language. This criticism might be recast by appeal to the contrast descriptive/normative. Consequently, it *may* be the case that Ramsey's remark belonged to a discussion of the TLP thesis implicitly criticized in §81.

(ii) 'normative Wissenschaft': this terminology has been traced (by C. S. Peirce, *Collected Papers* Vol. I, p. 314 and Vol. II, p. 5n. (Harvard University Press, Cambridge, 1960)) to the school of Schleiermacher, and to Wundt in particular. The conception of laws of logic as normative laws dictating how we *ought* to think if we wish to attain truth in our inferences was widespread in the nineteenth century. It posed a difficulty for psychologicians who conceived of the laws of logic as *also* constituting descriptions of how we are constrained to think in virtue of the constitution of our minds. Frege saw this as a point in favour of a Platonist conception of logic as a normative science (cf. NS 139; GA i. pp. xv–xvi). W. thought that both conceptions misunderstood the normativity of logic.

SECTION 82

1   This initiates criticism of the conception of meaning or understanding an expression as operating a calculus of fixed rules. The point here established is that given what we understand by the expression 'The rule by which he proceeds' there are expressions in language which are applied in the absence of any rule stating conditions for their correct application. The example which shows this is that of a proper name 'N' (§79). First, the name is not applied by invoking any such rule. Secondly, although the speaker offers explanations of 'N', he is willing to withdraw and alter his explanations of 'N' in certain circumstances. (Note that it

---

[7] F. P. Ramsey, *The Foundations of Mathematics* (Routledge and Kegan Paul, London, 1931), p. 269.

does not follow that there are no criteria for whether the speaker knows who N is or for whether he uses 'N' correctly.)

How do we determine the rule by which a person proceeds? W. suggests various possibilities: (i) the hypothesis that fits his observed use of the expression in question (see below); (ii) the rule he overtly consults when using the expression; (iii) the rule he cites when asked. There are yet further means, especially the statement of rules in teaching, criticizing, or justifying the use of expressions.

This sketch of what we call 'the rule by which he proceeds' suffices to undermine the thesis (§81(b)) that meaning and understanding always involve 'operating a calculus according to definite rules'. Explanations that the speaker is prepared to withdraw or alter cannot be the *definite* rule that he *always* follows. When he says 'N is dead', he consults no rule; when asked he gives varying explanations but no definite rule. This leaves the burden of the claim that he is following a defnite rule on the supposition that observation of his behaviour will always disclose that it conforms to some rule that we can formulate. But why may it not happen that observation brings no rule to light?

To this it will be objected that all that we need to justify describing him as following a particular rule is an hypothesis that fits his use of the expression and that we cannot fail to find such an hypothesis because *any* (finite) set of observations can always be subsumed under a general explanatory hypothesis (indeed, under indefinitely many such hypotheses). But this objection would prove too much. According to its conception of following a rule, no use of a word by a speaker could fail to be an instance of his following a rule. There is no such thing as not following a rule in speaking. Hence to assert that meaning or understanding something consists in using words according to *definite* rules is to say nothing whatever. Unless we could describe what it would be for him not to proceed according to a definite rule, the thesis about understanding criticized in §81(b) is empty. (And if we can do so, the thesis is. simply false (cf. §83(b)).)

1.1   (i) 'keine Regel klar erkennen lässt': better—'does not enable us clearly to see any rule'.

(ii) 'Erklärung': 'explanation' (not 'definition').

iii) 'Was soll der Ausdruck ". . ." hier noch besagen': W. preferred the paraphrase 'What use is there left for the expression ". . ."' (PPI (R) §89).

2   BT 253 (quoted at Exg. §81) makes explicit the relation of §82 to §81(b). This precursor of §81 criticizes the dogma implicit in TLP that anyone who uses language is always playing a definite game with fixed rules, and it ends by suggesting the criticism that this would make sense

only if a person could fail to play a game 'nach einem bestimmten, festen Regelverzeichnis' ('according to a definite, fixed list of rules'). A precursor of §82 immediately follows: 'Denn ich habe zur Feststellung der Regel, nach der er handelt, zwei Wege ange[ge]ben' ('For I have specified two ways to ascertain the rule according to which he acts').

SECTION 83

1 The game analogy is exploited to cast doubt on the dogma that whenever we use words we must be operating a calculus according to definite rules. That idea is as absurd as the contention that whenever a person plays with a ball he must be playing a particular game governed by definite rules. In fact, we contrast playing a particular ball-game according to definite rules both with playing aimlessly with a ball and with playing games whose rules we make up or change as we go along. In any of the latter cases, observation of the players' behaviour will not bring to light the rules by which they have all along been proceeding because there are none (cf. §82).

Many philosophers would argue that *any* behaviour whatever of a group of people playing with a ball can be described as proceeding in accord with a (sufficiently complicated) set of game-rules, just as *any* set of observations of phenomena can be fitted under some suitably complicated natural law. But, according to this conception, the notion of players proceeding according to a definite set of rules is vacuous. Of course, this is *not* the everyday conception of proceeding according to definite rules.

The purpose of the game analogy in §83 is to indicate a parallel argument against the dogma (§81) that whenever someone uses language and means or understands it he must be operating a calculus according to definite rules.

2 BT 252–4 clarifies the argumentative context of §83. First, it dovetails the game analogy with the criticism (§81(b)) of the conception of what it is to use language which was characteristic of TLP. On that conception, the thesis that every sentence is 'in order' as it is amounts to the assumption that in using language a person is always playing a game proceeding according to a definite invariable schedule of rules. Secondly, BT 254 makes explicit the purpose of the analogy in §83 by continuing immediately with a discussion of the use of the proper name 'N' in the sentence 'N is dead' (§79(b)); the implication of the game analogy for language is drawn out and considered. Thirdly, BT 254 concludes that the uses of words are not everywhere bounded by rules (cf. §§80 and 84).

Aber—wird man einwenden—der den Satz 'N ist gestorben' gesagt hat, hat doch nicht planlos Worte aneinander gereiht (und darin besteht es ja, dass er 'etwas mit seinen Worten gemeint hat').—Aber man kann wohl sagen: er sagt den Satz planlos, was sich eben in der beschriebenen Unsicherheit zeigt. Freilich ist der Satz von irgendwo hergenommen und wenn man will, so spielt er nun auch ein Spiel mit sehr primitiven Regeln; denn es bleibt ja wahr, dass ich auf die Frage 'wer ist N' *eine Antwort* bekam, oder eine Reihe von Antworten, die nicht gänzlich regellos waren.—Wir können sagen: Untersuchen wir die Sprache auf ihre Regeln hin. Hat sie dort und da keine Regeln, so ist *das* das Resultat unsrer Untersuchung.

(But—somebody will object—whoever said the sentence 'N is dead' did not string words together aimlessly (and that is what his 'having meant something with his words' consists in).—But one could well say: he said the sentence aimlessly, and this is manifested in the above-mentioned uncertainty [cf. §79(b)]. Certainly he got the sentence from somewhere and, if you like, he is also playing a game according to very primitive rules; for it is certainly true that I got an answer to the question 'Who is N?', or a series of answers that were not altogether random.—We could say: Let us investigate language in respect of its rules. If here and there it has no rules, then *that* is the result of our investigation.)

The difficulty in philosophy is to recognize that this result is the *end* of the matter.

SECTION 84

1   §§84–7 discuss the issue of what it is for a set of rules to be complete. §84 introduces it with a back-reference to §68 (explicit in PPI). There W. remarked that the application of certain words, viz. 'number' and 'game', is not everywhere bounded by rules. Here he takes up a more general thesis, that the application of any word is not everywhere bounded by rules.

This can be interpreted in two ways by exploiting the game analogy. First, a game can be described as not everywhere bounded by rules if not every aspect of playing it, or not every activity involved in playing it, is explicitly mentioned in the rules and regulated by them. This form of unboundedness seems rather anodyne. Secondly, a game could be said to be not everywhere bounded by rules if all possible doubt about how to apply these rules is not closed off, i.e. if there can be cases about which the rules leave doubts. This is the interpretation discussed in §84. Reflection suggests that for any game there are countless bizarre possibilities each of which raises irresolvable doubts about how to apply its rules (cf. PPI §114, Z §440). Therefore, there is no such thing as a game 'everywhere bounded by rules' (in this sense), hence no answer to the question 'what does a game look like that is everywhere bounded by rules?'

It detracts nothing from a game that it is possible for us to imagine doubts about how to apply its rules. A game has rules in spite of this. Moreover, it will typically be *certain* how its rules apply to a given situation. This is all that is required for the possibility of playing it. What would be damaging for a game is not the mere possibility of doubting how to apply its rules, but the existence of real doubt about how to apply them in important or frequently recurring situations. For in this case the game would break down into arguments or quarrels. The possibility of doubting how to apply a rule does not demonstrate that it is actually not certain how to apply it in particular cases (cf. PI p. 224). Actual doubts are important and can be treated one by one, perhaps by extending the rules of a game. Possible doubts are inexhaustible and harmless.

1.1   'sie sei nicht überall von Regeln begrenzt': this allusion to §68 demands harmonization of the translations, preferably by substituting 'bounded' for 'circumscribed' in §68 (as in PPI (R) §75).

2   (i) C8, 80: a cancelled sentence applies the analogy of §84(b) directly to applying rules. 'Ich kann mir sehr wohl denken, dass einer Zweifel über die Anwendung einer Regel hat, aber deswegen zweifle ich selbst nicht.' ('I can very well imagine that someone has doubts about how to apply a rule, but I do not myself have doubts because of this'.)

(ii) PPI §114 uses the game analogy to discuss the equivalent question what it would be to have a *complete* set of rules for the application of a word. It is always possible to construct doubtful cases not clearly decided by the manual of rules for a game. In chess, e.g., the rule that black and white make moves alternately would be problematic in its application if players did not ordinarily agree in their memories of who had made the last move. If such possibilities were taken to show that the rules of a game are not complete, then there would be no such thing as a complete set of rules for a game.

(iii) Vol. XI, 51 f. explores a different response to the possibility of doubt about how to apply the rules of chess. After describing the case in PPI §114, it continues with two questions: 'Macht aber die Möglichkeit eines solchen Zweifels das Schachspiel zu einem nicht ganz idealen Spiel? und welchen Begriff haben wir von diesem Ideal?' ('But does the possibility of such a doubt make chess into a game that is not altogether ideal? and what conception have we of this ideal?') In trying to answer this question, we are driven into a paradox. 'Es scheint da als wäre alles was wir "Ideal" nennen nur ein angenähertes Ideal gegen das ideale Ideal.' ('It seems as if everything that we call "ideal" is merely an approximation to the ideal in contrast with the ideal ideal.') We have no concept of what is ideal here (cf. LSP 221), and we find it impossible to construct one that satisfies us (cf. §88 (e)). Hence, invoking the concept of the ideal is a pointless shuffle (cf. §100).

SECTION 85

1   A perspicuous comparison of a rule with a signpost (continued in §87(c)).

1.1   'querfeldein': W. preferred 'over hedge and ditch' (PPI (R) §92).

SECTION 86

1   §§86–7 apply the conclusions of §§84–5 about what it is for rules to be complete to the special case of explanations of expressions in a language.

§86 considers only the case of an explanation by a table correlating written signs with pictures of the building materials used in language-game (2). Against a background of the players' having been trained to use tables in a certain way, appeal to such a table effectively guides applications of the explained expressions and yields general agreement in judgements. The possibility of introducing different ways of using a table (i.e. different schemata for 'reading' it) does not show that such an explanation by a table was incomplete. Otherwise *every* explanation by a table would be 'incomplete'; i.e. there would be no such thing as 'completeness' and hence no such thing as 'incompleteness' either. (This is one instance of a more general conclusion: the possibility of extending a system of rules does not show that the system in its original form was incomplete.)

1.1   'Und sind es die andern Tabellen ohne ihr Schema?': W. paraphrased this question: 'And so, are the other (abnormal) tables incomplete without their diagrams?' (PPI (R) §93).

2   (i) §86 invokes the idea that any explanation has its foundation in training (Z §419). See BB 90, Z §318, PLP 150, PI §6, and 'Explanation', p. 31.

(ii) The possibility of interpreting an explanation by a table in different ways, e.g. according to different schemata of arrows, is mentioned in many other texts (BT 54; PG 93 f.; BB 90 f., 123 f.; PI §163; PLP 149 f.; PPI §83). But the moral drawn from this 'ambiguity' of tables changes. Originally we were to conclude that there are no final or conclusive explanations (*endgültige Erklärungen*) of words; no table is a conclusive explanation of the symbols contained in it, but rather an explanation only for those who understand it in a certain way (PLP 149; LSP 219; cf. PG Ch. IV). Later W. criticized this notion of understanding a table in a particular way, since this merely introduced an extra step between teaching by means of a table and the actual use made by the learner of the symbols he had been taught (cf. BB 124). Finally he concluded that it is a misconception of what it is for an explanation to be complete (or conclusive) to deny that any explanation by a table is ever complete (or conclusive) (PI §86). (An excellent instance of how the significance of a remark depends on, and alters with, its argumentative context.)

(iii) Introducing alternative schemata for reading a table exemplifies in respect of explanation of words by charts the general thesis that any course of action can be made out to accord with any rule (§201).

SECTION 87

1   This generalizes the tacit conclusion of §86 and spells out W.'s reasoning. No explanation can avert every possible doubt about to apply the defined expression. This is illustrated for the case of an explanation of 'Moses' which specifies a necessary and sufficient condition for someone to be Moses. Although this explanation leaves less room for doubt than typical explanations of proper names by descriptions (cf. §79(b)–(c)), it does not remove all possible doubts. Nor would the possibility of doubt come to an end in the case of 'indefinables' like 'red', 'dark', and 'sweet', which would be explained by using samples. Hence, no expression can be so explained that we cannot imagine circumstances in which its application would not be open to doubt.

Does this mean that no explanation is complete, final, or conclusive? W.'s antagonist makes this (erroneous) assumption. But to call an explanation incomplete or inconclusive is to criticize it for failing adequately to serve its purpose. This means that it does not convey a correct understanding of the explained expression. W.'s antagonist invokes this conception, drawing the paradoxical conclusion that no explanation can convey what someone understands by an expression since none can avert every possible doubt about how to apply the defined expression.

W. rightly ridicules this objection. An explanation no more hangs in the air unless supported by further ones than a building hangs in the air because its foundations do not themselves rest on further foundations. The purpose of an explanation is to convey an understanding of the explained expression, and it fulfills this purpose provided it guides speakers correctly in applying the expression when it is applied in accord with the general practice of using similar explanations. Whether or not it is complete must be judged in relation to this practice, not by reference to its intrinsic 'geometry'. It is complete, like the rules of a game, provided that it does not, in the context of the practice, lead to misapplications. The practice gives each explanation, as it were, a trajectory; provided this trajectory leads to hitting the target, no correction of its course is necessary, and the explanation is complete. An explanation, like a signpost, is in order if, under normal circumstances, it fulfils its purpose. This does not imply, however, that it is invariably successful even if circumstances are normal (some people sometimes may need extraordinarily complicated explanations to understand an expression), nor that it directs the application of the defined expression in extraordinary circumstances (especially if the background practice of applying the kind of explanation to which it belongs is disturbed or abrogated, e.g. the practice of reading charts normally (§86)). (Cf. 'Explanation', pp. 38 ff.)

§87(b) intimates criticism of a philosophical search for the ultimate foundations of language (cf. PLP 149) modelled on a search for the foundations of knowledge according to the Cartesian method. This search rests on a misconception about certainty, here manifested in adherence to the mistaken dogma that an explanation cannot be final, complete, or conclusive if it leaves open any possibility of doubt about applying the explained expressions. Language does not rest on explanations immune to Cartesian doubt.

§87 is pivotal in the argumentative structure of the *Investigations*. It is the key to the structure of §§65–88. In expressing the misconception of what it is for an explanation to be complete, it reveals the root of the misguided demand for determinacy of sense and the associated denigration of ordinary forms of explanation, especially of family resemblance concepts and of proper names.

§87 is also the gateway to W.'s constructive exploration of the relation of meaning and understanding in §§143–84. A proper account of completeness of explanation must focus on the relation of explanation to understanding.

1.1   (i) 'als *zeigte* jeder Zweifel nur': W. preferred 'as if every doubt were just a symptom of' (PPI (R) §94).

        (ii) 'ein sicheres Verständnis': W. preferred 'well-founded understanding' (PPI (R) §94).

2   PLP §149 f., in contrast to PI, advances a form of pragmatism applied to explanations. Waismann argues that every explanation really is incomplete. None the less, many do serve to set up an agreed practice of using words. Human nature being what it is, there is no *need* for further explanations; the actual ones are good enough provided they work. In this way we get a glimpse into the connection between 'logic and life'.

2.1   (i) 'Aber wie hilft mir dann eine Erklärung zum Verständnis?'; this
question embodies a misconception. An explanation is not merely a
means for achieving understanding nor just a *vehicle* for conveying it,
hence explanations cannot be said to *help* people to understand words, at
least not in the sense in which a gin and tonic helps one relax (EBT
255(=Vol. VI, 213)). Rather, there is an internal relation between
explanation and understanding. '"Verständnis" nenne ich aber gerade,
was mir eine Erklärung gibt' (Vol. XI, 54). ('"Understanding" is just
what I call what an explanation gives me.') (Cf. BT 11 ff. and 'Explanation, pp. 41 ff.)

(ii) 'hung in the air': the dissatisfaction with an explanation apparently
left hanging in the air is typical of the philosophical malady of failing to
recognize the terminus of explanation (Z §314).

SECTION 88

1   This rounds off the argument of §§65–87 by closing off the last avenue
of retreat for someone who defends the demand for determinacy of sense
by contending that understanding and meaning something involve
operating a calculus according to definite rules. Strategic withdrawal
might take the form of contrasting the ideal with the actual. It is
conceded that explanations of concept-words need not have the form of
Merkmal-definitions, and that we can make use of words without sharp
boundaries (i.e. words whose explanations do not remove every possibility of doubt about their applications). None the less, explanations are
inexact or imperfect to the extent that they deviate from *Merkmal*-
definitions, and concepts diverge from the ideal to the extent that their
boundaries are not sharp. Similarly, it is conceded that understanding and
meaning something need not involve operating (even unconsciously) a
calculus according to definite rules. Yet our understanding of language is
imperfect to the extent that our use of it is not informed by a calculus of
meaning-rules, and hence our actual use of language should be considered as a more or less close approximation to this ideal. All that the
arguments of §§65–87 have shown, W.'s antagonist claims, is that actual
language and our understanding of it do not perfectly correspond to
what is ideal in language and understanding. This line of retreat was left
open in §69 and mentioned disparagingly in §81.

W.'s response centres on two points (§88(c)–(d)). First, the terms
'exact' and 'inexact' (and such related terms as 'perfect', 'imperfect',
'complete', 'incomplete', and 'ideal') have explanations that mention
goals; hence, particular applications of them presuppose the specification
of particular goals. There is, e.g., no such thing as an absolutely exact
time-determination; what provides a standard for the exact specification

of a time for one purpose (e.g. starting dinner) may be inexact for another purpose (e.g. navigating by time-differences between radio signals), and conversely, what is requisite for exactness in one case may be pointless for exactness in the other. Secondly, these terms are terms of praise and blame; what is inexact does not attain the relevant goal as well as what is (more) exact. Consequently, particular applications of such terms presuppose truths about efficacy (or inefficacy) in attaining goals.

These two points have implications for explanations of meaning which are alluded to in §88 (a)–(b). This considers the order 'Stand roughly here', coupled with pointing at a particular spot; and that use of this sentence was explicitly compared with explaining by examples what a game is (§71(b)). The implied point is that an explanation like 'Chess, cricket, patience, backgammon and similar things are games' may be called inexact (cf. §69), but that this does not mean that it is unusable. Moreover, unless it is shown how such an explanation is defective in comparison with others in securing mutual understanding, this application of 'inexact' will not carry the customary pejorative connotation of 'inexact'. Accordingly, there is no ground for taking substitution of a *Merkmal*-definition for an explanation by examples to be an improvement in explaining 'game'. This undermines the case for treating *Merkmal*-definition as the *ideal* explanation of meaning. Deviation from the 'ideal' of completeness of definition is not an imperfection, nor, conversely, is extending an explanation to remove a mere possibility of misunderstanding an improvement to it.

These points about 'exact', 'inexact', and related terms clarify W.'s criticism of discussing understanding language as if it were an approximation to operating a calculus according to strict rules (§81). If we use that terminology, we suggest that understanding would be more perfect if it consisted in operating such a calculus of meaning-rules, and this implication is just what cries out for justification. We dazzle ourselves by such deployment of the concept of the ideal and therefore fail to focus properly on what it is to understand or mean something by an expression (cf. §100).

1.1   (i) 'Stand roughly here': PPI §85 includes a back-reference to PI §71 (=PPI §68).

(ii) §88(c) and (e): these discuss the contrast 'genau'/'ungenau', whereas (b) and (d) discuss 'exakt'/'unexakt'. These discontinuities are masked by the uniform English translation 'exact'/'inexact'. (PPI §85 includes a bridging sentence joining (d) and (e).)

(iii) '"Unexakt", das ist eigentlich ein Tadel': W. paraphrased this: '"Inexact"—that really suggests blame' (PPI (R) §96).

(iv) 'at least any that satisfies you': this is a patient-oriented bit of philosophical therapy (cf. §79 (d)).

2   (i) In earlier writing, W. had treated inexactness (and vagueness) in a
very different way. It stood for an intrinsic property of certain objects and
certain experiences. (This is perhaps most familiar from some of
Waismann's articles.) It was used to distinguish the geometry of the
visual field from Euclidean (or even non-Euclidean) geometry (PR 263,
269; WWK 55 f., 55n.; PLP 49; PG 236–9). It was an essential feature of
memory images (PLP 209) and also of some visual experiences (PLP
208–10, 211). W. had even argued that the 'inexact' words of everyday
language were often better suited to express the blurredness (*Verschwom-
menheit*) of experience than the symbols of an 'exact' language would be;
that they can often describe *exactly* what we experience (PLP 210 f., cf. PR
260). This defence of the thesis that ordinary language is 'in Ordnung' is
no more intelligible than the very different one given in TLP.

(ii) Vol. XI, 52 considers the objection that the task of the philosopher
in clarifying the grammar of language would be pointless if there were
not an ideal of exactness that stood in contrast with ordinary standards of
exactness.

Wir wollen Verwirrungen & Beunruhigungen beseitigen die aus der Schwierig-
keit entspringen, das System unsrer Ausdrucksweise zu übersehen. . . .
Dadurch kann es allerdings den Anschein haben als setzten wir uns vor die
Sprache zu reformieren.

(We wish to remove the confusions and disquiet that arise from the difficulty of
surveying the system of our modes of expression. . . . Because of this it may
look, however, as if we set ourselves the task of improving language.)

This is an illusion. There are many paths that lead to particular
confusions; hence, as many ways of removing a mistake as there are
roads back from error to truth. There need not be a single explanation
that will invariably remove a particular confusion independently of how
it may be arrived at. A single ideal of exactness is not necessary for
philosophy to be possible.

(ii) C8, 86 f. mentions a third important point about 'exact' and 'inexact',
viz. that exactness is a matter of degree. Relative to a fixed purpose, some
ways of determining time may be characterized as *more* or *less* exact than
certain others. This aspect of exactness is also distorted by the objections
in §88(b)–(c).

2.1   'why shouldn't we call it "inexact"?': the justification for calling this
explanation 'inexact' is just that it contains the word 'roughly' ('ungefähr').

'Was ist eine "exacte" Definition im Gegensatz zu einer unexacten?'—Nun etwa,
eine Definition in der nicht das Wort 'ungefähr', 'beiläufig', oder ähnliche
vorkommen (BT 249v. = Vol. XI, 42).

(What is an 'exact' definition in contrast with an inexact one?—Well, perhaps a definition in which the word 'roughly', 'approximately', or a similar one does not occur.)

This is a formal criterion for whether an explanation is exact or inexact. It corresponds only roughly with a functional criterion, and it obviously provides no justification for calling every explanation by examples, by descriptions, or by samples 'inexact', *a fortiori* none for calling them all 'unusable'.

———————————————

CHAPTER 4

Philosophy

(§§89–133)

INTRODUCTION

§§89–133 constitute a sustained, if disorderly, discussion of the nature of philosophy. Disorderly, inasmuch as these sections display less argumentative structure than the preceding ones. The manuscript sources of the text date *primarily* from two periods: 1930–1 (Vols. IV–VI, VIII) and 1937 (MS. 157). Only two remarks appear to have a later source (§§117 and 125 derive from PPI(B) §125 and MS. 130, 12–15 respectively). It is noteworthy that the general conception of philosophy that dominates Wittgenstein's later work emerged so early, namely in 1930–1. (The 1937 reflections are largely concerned with criticizing the idealization of logic and language that characterized TLP; these dominate PI §§89–108.)

The main *polished* sources of these remarks are BT Ch. 12 and PPI §§86–116. These, especially the latter, are illuminating source material. The PPI text contains almost all the remarks embodied in the final version of PI, but it is more than twice the length and very differently arranged. PPI (A) and (B) are substantially rearranged versions of PPI, shorter, but with occasional handwritten additions and modifications. They converge on the final text, and occasionally illuminate it.

The most striking feature of PPI's discussion of philosophy is the extent to which the remarks are explicitly directed against positions wittingly or unwittingly adopted in TLP. For many of the sibylline pronouncements of §§89–133 are, in PPI, embedded in detailed discussions of errors and misconceptions in the early philosophy.

The pruning of PPI has increased its obscurity by removing so much of the original context and targets of many of the critical remarks. The process whereby this happened is clear enough. In PPI (B) the reference to TLP is reduced, with the purpose of generalizing the remarks. Thematic unity is restored by exemplifying the diagnosis with philosophical puzzles about time, thus referring back to the quotation from Augustine in PI §89. In TS. 227 even this is eliminated.

In content the chapter divides, very roughly, into two topics:

(i) dialectical remarks about the nature of philosophical illusion, which are phenomenological, diagnostic, or analytical-argumentative, and (ii) methodological remarks varying between prognostic ones, indicating the ways of combating philosophical illusion, and dogmatic ones, stating the nature and limits of philosophy.

In structure the chapter splits into two parts. Part A runs from §§89–107 and is almost wholly concerned with philosophical dialectic. It explores the apparent sublimity of philosophy (logic), conceived of as an enquiry into the essence of the world (the *a priori* structure of what is possible). This part splits up into two groups: (α) §§89–97; (β) §§98–107.

Group (α) opens with §89 and raises the question of the sublimity of logic. §§90–2 explore from a fresh angle the ideals of analysis and of exactness (cf. §§60–4, 88). §§93–6 examine a different range of illusions—the strangeness of the proposition, the uniqueness and mysteriousness of thought. These remarks, when amplified, obviously have as their target TLP—as representative of a particular type of pervasive 'disease of the intellect'. §97 is transitional, linking group (α) to group (β) and also to Part B (§§108–33).

The structure of Part A, group (α):

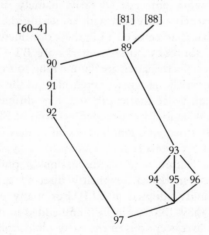

Group (β) of Part A runs from §§98–107. §§98–100 examine TLP's misguided interpretation of the truth that ordinary language is in good logical order, namely the demand for determinacy of sense. §§101–7 explore the phenomenology of the craving for the 'ideal' logical structure which 'must' obtain and hint at the misguided ways in which philosophers try to satisfy it.

The structure of Part A, group (β):

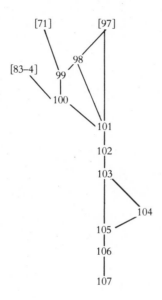

Part B (§§108–33) divides untidily into two large groups: (α) §§108–121; (β) §§122–33. Untidily, because the second (largely methodological) group is linked with §109.

Group (α), excluding §109, examines the consequences of the need to return to the examination of ordinary language in order to resolve the problems of philosophy. §108 is the key section of the group, linked with §97 through the repudiation of construing 'proposition' and 'language' as 'super-concepts' with a formal unity and with §89 via rejection of the 'crystalline purity of logic'. The argument has four 'branches'. §§110–15 again dwell upon the captivating illusions of philosophical depth, the 'compulsion' of preconceived pictures, and the projection of forms of representation onto reality. §§116–17 repudiate the philosophical sublimation of words (e.g. 'knowledge', 'being'). §§118–19 stress the negative, critical, nature of philosophy and its importance as destroyer of idols. §§120–1 stress the ordinariness of the language which philosophy describes, as well as the ordinariness of the language with which it describes it.

The structure of Part B, group (α):

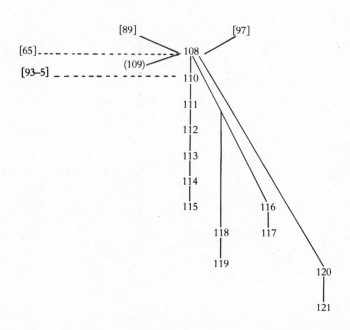

Group (β) contains a wide range of dogmatically asserted claims about the nature and limits of philosophy. §109 is the first substantial elaboration of the new conception of philosophy. It has three 'branches': §§122–3 are concerned (briefly) with the notion of a surview (cf. 'Übersicht', pp. 295ff.). §§124–5 emphasize the 'detachment' of philosophy (it only describes, giving other subjects neither foundation nor explanation) and contain a brief excursus into the philosophy of mathematics. §§126–9 are linked to both §123 and §125, emphasizing again the purely descriptive, elucidating role of philosophy, its neutral quest for surveyability of grammar. The final remarks (§§130–3) are concerned with the 'non-ideality' of invented language-games, including artificial calculi and the nature of the 'order' which philosophy seeks (and hence are linked with §109).

The structure of Part B, group (β):

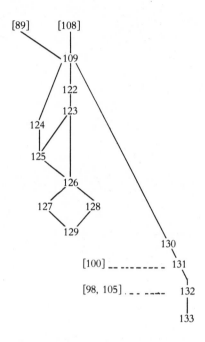

The nature of philosophy
1. Russell's conception of philosophy 2. Wittgenstein: the 'Preliminary' and *Notebooks 1914–16* 3. The *Tractatus* 4. The later conception of philosophy (The source of philosophical problems; Language, philosophy, and mythology; The nature of philosophical problems; Philosophy and common sense; The status of philosophy; The difficulty of philosophy; Methods of philosophy; Is systematic philosophy possible?)

Correlations

PI	PPI	PPI(R)	PPI*	PI
89	86	97	86	89
90	87	98	87	90
91	88	99	88	91–2
92	88	100–1	89	93–6
93	89	102–3	90	97
94	89	104	91	98–100 (Z §§441–2)
95	89	105	92	101–3 (Z §445)
96	89	106	93	Z §444
97	90	107–8	94	105(b)–6
98	91	109	95	107–8(a)
99	91	—	96	109–10
100	91	111	97	111
101	92	112	98	112
102	92	112	99	—
103	92	112	100	122
104	110	—	101	124
105(b)	94	114	102	126(a)
106	94	115	103	126(b)
107	95	116	104	127–8
108(a)	95	———	105	129
109	96		106	—
110	96		107	131
111	97		108	—
112	98		109	115
113	110		110	114 (Z §443)
114	110			113, 104, (Z §448)
115	109			116(a)
116	110		111	116(b). 118–19
117	—†		112	120(b) ff.–121
118	111		113	132
119	111		114	133(a), (Z §440)
120(b)ff.	112		115	130, 133(b)
121	112		116	133(c), (Z §447)
122	100			
123	—†			
124	101			
125	—			
126(a)	102			
126(b)	103			
127	104			
128	104			
129	105			
130	115			
131	107			
132	113			
133(a)	114			
133(b)	115			
133(c)	116			

* This table gives an inverse correlation of PPI with PI. It helps to reveal the originally conceived structure. Individual paragraph correlations have been omitted here because the extensive rearrangement would complicate the table excessively. All significant rearrangements and omissions are discussed in the exegesis.

† The PI versions are added in pen to PPI (A) and (B) and numbered §125 and §133 respectively.

EXEGESIS §§89–133

SECTION 89

1   §89(a), which raises the problem of the apparent sublimity of logic, is linked to §§81 and 88, in which the 'language' of logic is said to appear to be better, more perfect, than our everyday language.

The first half of §89(b) gives reasons for this apparent sublimity. Logic appears to have a universal significance in that it gives the foundation of all sciences. It does this, for it investigates the nature of all things; it is a universal, not a particular science. It is not concerned with contingent events, but seeks to see to 'the bottom of things' (why they must be as they are).

The rest of (b) is W.'s response. It is true that logic is not concerned with contingent facts or causal connections, but with the 'essence' or 'nature' of everything empirical. This search for the 'essence' of reality, *properly understood*, is not chimerical, nor absurd (cf. §92). But to grasp the essence of reality, thus understood, requires no new facts, nor discoveries. What we want to understand is already *in plain view*.

§89(c) exemplifies the point by reference to Augustine's phrasing of his puzzlement about time. It could not be said of an empirical, scientific question that we know the answer when no one asks us, but no longer when we are asked. But that is how it is in philosophy: we need to *remind* ourselves of something—of the rules of grammar, of the way we use words. But an *Übersicht* of our use is difficult to obtain.

1.1   'something that we need to *remind* ourselves of' echoes Plato's *Meno* and *Phaedo*.[1] The remark links up with §127.

2   BB 26 ff. discusses the Augustinian puzzle about time. It is not, W. argues, a request for a definition—although the question 'What is time?' makes it look so. Nor is it a quest for causes or reasons, but rather an expression of typical philosophical puzzlement which, W. intimates, illustrates Hertz's point:[2]

---

[1] Compare also Boltzmann when he argues *against* his own earlier ideal of a philosophy that clearly defines each concept introduced: '. . . [W]hat wealth of experience, as well as of words and ideas used for denoting it, must be presumed as known if we are to understand each other at all . . . [W]e shall begin by examining what facts constitute the basis and precondition for knowledge. We shall honestly admit that with these facts we cannot and should not do more than recall them to memory by known signs, nor shall we be amazed that it is precisely these facts that have till now been regarded as the most difficult to explain.' ('On the Question of the Objective Existence of Processes in Inanimate Nature', in *Ludwig Boltzmann: Theoretical Physics and Philosophical Problems*, p. 57.

[2] Hertz, *The Principles of Mechanics*, p. 9.

. . . the answer we want is not really an answer to this question. It is not by finding out more and fresh relations and connections that it can be answered; but by removing the contradictions existing between those already known, and thus perhaps by reducing their number. When these painful contradictions are removed, the question as to the nature of force will not have been answered; but our minds, no longer vexed, will cease to ask illegitimate questions.

The apparent contradiction in Augustine's case (i.e. how can one *measure* time if the past has already gone, the future has not yet arrived, and the present is an extensionless point?) stems from different methods of application of 'measurement' in respect of length on the one hand, and time on the other (cf. PLP 40 f).

2.1   (i) The first half of §89(b) echoes NB (and TLP), e.g. logic is an investigation into the *a priori* order of the world (NB 53), the nature of the world (NB 79); logical propositions show the logical properties of the Universe, every real proposition mirrors some logical property of the Universe (NB 107).

(ii) '. . . something we need to remind ourselves of': cf. BT 419: 'Das Lernen der Philosophie ist *wirklich* ein Rückerinnern. Wir erinnern uns, dass wir die Worte wirklich auf diese Weise gebraucht haben.' ('The study of philosophy *really* is a recollection. We remind ourselves that we really did use words in this way.')

SECTION 90

1.1   (i) '. . . *penetrate* phenomena': it seems to us as if we had to penetrate or see through phenomena in order to explore the nature of all things. But our investigation is not one into phenomena, but into the possibilities of phenomena. Is W. affirming this latter contention? Is philosophy a super-science of the possible? The answer is brought out in the sequel. Philosophy is, in a sense, an investigation into the possibilities of phenomena, but not by way of 'seeing through' them, discovering their ultimate constituents, etc., but rather by examining the grammar of the language.
   Cf. MS. 157(a), 46:

Dieses *Verständnis* schienen wir durch eine besondere Art des *Einblicks* gewinnen zu müssen aber es wurde uns klar dass wir mit diesem Einblick nicht die Tatsachen // die Erscheinungen // durchschauen wollten // versuchten // sondern unsere Sprache von diesen Tatsachen // nicht die Erscheinungen sondern die Sprache in der wir von ihnen reden durchschauen wollten.

(It seemed that we must achieve this *understanding* through a special kind of *insight*, but it became clear to us that we did not want // were not trying // to see through the facts // phenomena // with this insight, but our language about these facts // wanted to see through, not the phenomena, but the language in which we talk about them.)

PPI(R) translates 'durchschauen' as 'see through' (and 'richtet sich nicht auf' as 'not one into'). *Durchschauen* should be contrasted with *übersehen*; the former is a chimerical ideal, the latter is the proper concern of philosophy.

(ii) The kinds of statements Augustine recalls to mind are that we say 'a long time' or 'a short time' only of time past or to come; that a long time past we call 'a hundred years ago', that a long time to come we call 'a hundred years hence', etc. These are not philosophical statements, but their use is a source of philosophical confusion. It is, however, worth bearing in mind that having 'reminded himself' of the way temporal expressions are used, Augustine does not think that the problem dissolves. On the contrary, he proceeds to construct a 'theory of time', according to which there are three times: a present of past things, a present of present things and a present of future things. Time, according to Augustine, must be 'explicable' in terms of the mental functions of memory, attention, and expectation (cf. *Confessions*, XI, 20). This in no way affects W.'s point.

(iii) The misleading analogies of language in this case are the analogies between measuring time and measuring length.

(iv) 'Analysis', in the last sentence, links this discussion with §§60–4. Some misunderstandings stemming from misleading analogies can be eliminated by substituting one form of expression for another. A paradigm example of this is clearly Russell's theory of descriptions, in which worries about subsisting entities, arising from analogies between proper names and singular definite descriptions, are eliminated by translation of 'The Φer . . .' into 'There is one and only one . . .'. This can be called 'analysis'.

SECTION 91

1   In PPI this is continuous with §92; in PPI(R) with §90. It continues the topic of 'analysis' and the illusions it breeds. (Thus linked to §§60–4, in particular §63.) The application of the notion of 'analysis' to the theory of descriptions (in conjunction with the quest for logically proper names) was an aspect of the illusions of *complete* and *final* analysis which would reveal what is *hidden* in the structure of language.

§91(b) links up with §88. The atomists' ideal of analysis was coupled with the illusion that there exists an *absolute* ideal of exactness, which it was the goal of analysis to achieve. But exactness, like simplicity, is a relative and variable notion (§88).

2.1   '. . . something hidden . . . that had to be brought to light':
       (i) BB 81 accuses Russell of this confusion, for he thought that analysis

will reveal which kind of things are real 'individuals'. This applies to TLP too, for there analysis was to yield, at the ultimate stage, the real 'objects'.

(ii) MS. 157(a), 55: 'Die Rolle der "logischen Analyse". Wie kann ich den Satz *jetzt* verstehen, wenn die Analyse soll zeigen können, *was* ich eigentlich verstehe. // was es ist was ich verstehe. // Hier spielt die Idee des Verstehens als seltsamen geistigen Vorgangs hinein.' ('The role of "logical analysis". How can I understand a proposition (sentence) now if it is for analysis to show me *what* I really understand. // what it is that I understand. // Here there sneaks in the idea of understanding as a peculiar mental process.') Part of this remark (= Z §445) is a segment of PPI §92, which follows on directly to PI §103.

SECTION 92

1   The illusions of 'final analysis' and 'complete exactness' are expressed in the quest for the essence of language. *This* is not illegitimate; philosophy does indeed seek to lay bare the essence of language (cf. 'The nature of philosophy', pp. 290 ff.), but by an *Übersicht*, not by analysis. When the problems of the essence of language are approached from the standpoint of the illusory ideals of a sublimed logic, they are misconceived. The essence is thought of as hidden, to be revealed by future analysis. The questions are formulated in the misguided form of 'What is language?' or 'What is a *Satz*?' (cf. Exg. §93), which look like quests for sharp definitions. But neither 'language' nor 'Satz' are definable (non-trivially) by *Merkmale,* nor are their limits sharply determined.

1.1   (i) 'Denn wenn wir auch in unsern Untersuchungen . . .': W. translated 'For although in our investigations we are trying . . .' (PPI(R) §100), which makes it clearer that his investigations *are* an attempt to understand the essence of language, though that essence is not given by *Merkmale.*

The point is even clearer in MS. 157(b), 8: 'Denn wenn wir auch, in einem (hausbackene) Sinn, das Wesen der Sprache . . .' ('For although we, in a (homely [plain]) sense . . .')

(ii) '*übersichtlich*': W. paraphrased as 'becomes transparent. I mean capable of being seen all at a glance' (PPI(R) §100). Here W., like his translators (cf. 'Übersicht', p. 295), felt the difficulty in translating 'Übersicht' and its cognates.

(iii) 'And the answer to these questions is to be given once for all; and independently of any future experience': some light is shed on this by MS. 157(a), 47: 'Und es war wesentlich dass sich jene Antwort *ein für allemal*, also unabhängig von zukünftiger Erfahrung geben lassen müsse. Und es durfte also in dieser Antwort nicht heissen es gibt 13 Arten von

. . . Und morgen finden wir also vielleicht eine 14te. Es durfte also überhaupt nicht von Arten die Rede sein.' ('And it was essential that that answer must be capable of being given once and for all, hence independently of future experience. And so this answer could not say there are thirteen kinds of . . . And then perhaps tomorrow we find a fourteenth. So there was to be no talk whatever of kinds.') This is obviously an allusion to TLP 5.554 ff.

This does not dissolve the puzzle, however. Certainly this was a requirement of TLP. But is W.'s suggestion *now* that future experience *will* answer, or change the answer, to the question 'What is a *Satz* [language]?'? §108 suggests, as we might expect, that the error of the atomists, of those who sublime logic, is to think, as W. once did, that these concepts have a formal unity. But what does this point have to do with future experience?

Possibly Z §447 (= Vol. VIII, 143 and = PPI §116) throws some light. It stresses the endlessness of the task of philosophy, perhaps alluding to the essential historical dimension of philosophical analysis. Philosophical problems are resolved, *inter alia*, by a 'quiet weighing of linguistic facts'. But these change from epoch to epoch as language and grammar respond to a multitude of pressures. New forms are grafted on to language, new grammatical articulations evolve, old concepts are modified and new ones introduced. Of course, a correct description of language as it now is is not vitiated by unforeseeable innovations; it merely becomes obsolete. So how does the historicity of the task of philosophy affect the quest for the essence of language, and in particular the search for a definitive answer to the demand for essentialist definitions of formal (categorial) concepts? In TLP, 'language', 'proposition' and related terms were conceived as expressing formal concepts with a trans-historical validity. These were the essential structural elements of any possible language at any time or place. Their nature, therefore, must be capable of being given once and for all. It is this conception that W. now undermines. These expressions do not express 'super-concepts' (PI §97); the concern of philosophy is not with non-spatial, non-temporal *Undinge* (PI §108) but with the spatio-temporal phenomenon of language. Not only are these concepts not 'super-concepts', they are not even explained by *Merkmale*, but are rather family resemblance concepts explained by examples. They are no more immune to change than any other human artefact, or any other concepts.

SECTION 93

1   Notoriously, the German term 'Satz' is problematic for W.'s translators. This is largely due to the corruption of the term 'proposition' in the

hands of English-speaking philosophers. Traditionally, 'proposition' meant a significant sentence, hence a linguistic entity. However, philosophers in this century have commonly used 'proposition' to mean a non-linguistic entity, the sense of a sentence (akin to Frege's *Gedanke*). To translate 'Satz' by 'sentence' is misleading, since a sentence is commonly conceived as a syntactical entity. To translate it by 'proposition' is also misleading, since a proposition is now commonly conceived to be a non-linguistic entity.

W.'s use of 'Satz' is usually captured by 'sentence with a use', and in this broad sense includes not only declarative, but also interrogative, imperative, and deontic sentences. More narrowly, 'Satz' is often restricted to a sentence with a sense, i.e. a meaningful sentence which is bipolar (true or false, and capable of being either). When he is concerned with the assertive use of such a sentence with sense he often employs the term 'Behauptung'. There are, however, passages in which 'Satz' is used simply to mean 'sentence' (the syntactical notion), although here he often uses 'Satzzeichen' (sometimes ironically). It should also be borne in mind that W. includes as constituents of *Sätze* items which would not normally be so classified, e.g. gestures and samples. Not only does he conceive of gestures and samples as symbols belonging to language, but also the overt expression of thought in a *Satz* will obviously often include gestures and samples.

Utterances of expressions of the following kinds can all be said to be *Sätze* in the appropriate contexts: 'The book is on the table', 'This is here', '2 + 2 = 4', 'I am tired', 'Business is business', 'F = m.a', 'John', etc. But they are not *Sätze* in virtue of sharing a common essence. Rather, *Satz* is a family resemblance concept. This is not captured by saying that 'sentence' is a family resemblance concept, and to say that 'proposition' is a family resemblance concept wrongly suggests that we are talking of non-linguistic entities.

Philosophers have not recognized that the concept of a sentence with a sense ('proposition' in its traditional use) is a family resemblance concept, and this has exacerbated existing flaws in their reasoning. Already inclined, for Platonistic and other reasons, to conceive of the proposition as an abstract, non-linguistic entity, they have met the difficulties generated by the family resemblance character of a sentence with a sense by multiplying entities. Hence we have a plethora of bizarre entities, *Gedanken*, statements (which may be unstated), assertions (which may be unasserted), eternal sentences, propositions (variously defined), etc. They then commonly pick upon one of these as the *primary* bearer of truth-values, or the *correct* argument of truth-functions, or the real object of thought. And others are typically chosen to fill other roles. The sharp boundaries they thus draw 'will be related to the fluctuating boundaries of the natural use of language in the same way as sharp contours in a pen-and-ink sketch are related to the gradual transitions between patches of colour in the reality depicted' (PG 120, cf. PI §76). This activity is not in principle illegitimate, although it carries with it characteristic dangers (cf. 'Family resemblance', pp. 207 f.). In particular, it must not be thought to be an explanation of our common-or-garden use of 'proposition' ('Satz', 'sentence with a sense'), nor does it tell us what we 'really mean' by 'proposition'.

Why should a sentence with a sense strike one as a queer thing or as 'doing' something queer? The answer is given in §§94–6; sentences—miraculously—express thoughts, enable us to communicate; they picture the world, tell us how things are; even more remarkably, they tell us also how things are *not*. Reflection on the matter leads to a strange conception of propositions, which, conceived as the sense of sentences, appear to be ethereal entities, beyond space and time (cf. Exg. §108), and independent of any language which 'expresses' them.

1.1   'die Formen unserer Ausdrucksweise': better rendered 'the forms of our modes of expression'.

SECTION 94

1   This amplifies §93. When, for reasons given above, propositions (i.e. sentences with a sense) strike us as queer, we are inclined to sever the senses of sentences from sentences. Propositions then become Platonic entities of a pure transcendent kind, the soul of the sentence. Sentences are then conceived as mere propositional signs, the dead corporeal matter of thought. Our forms of expression send us in pursuit of chimeras. What forms? Presumably locutions such as 'They both said the same thing (he in English, she in German)' (cf. BB 7), or 'This sentence expresses the same as . . .', as well as some locutions employing the term 'proposition' itself (cf. 'The uses of sentences', p. 77 ff.). A different kind of 'sublimation' is a psychologistic correlate of the Platonistic one (cf. Exg. §108).

Was W. himself guilty of this? The TLP conception of language can with justice be said to 'sublime the signs themselves', and the *Gedanke* discussed in the correspondence with Russell is a psychological (not Platonic) intermediary between the signs and the facts.

'. . . But a *Gedanke* is a *Tatsache*: what are its constituents and components, and what is their relation to those of the pictured *Tatsache*?' I don't know *what* the constituents of a thought are but I know *that* it must have such constituents which correspond to the words of Language. Again the kind of relation of the constituents of thought and of the pictured fact is irrelevant. It would be a matter of psychology to find out . . .

> Does a *Gedanke* consist of words? No! But of psychical constituents that have the same sort of relation to reality as words.[3]

1.1   'a pure intermediary': W. substituted 'a pure (immaterial) entity mediating between' (PPI(R) p. 104). This makes it clear that the *Gedanke* of TLP, no less than Frege's, lies in the target area.

2.1   BB 32 emphatically makes the point that the (English) terms 'proposition', 'sense of a sentence' are misguidedly introduced to designate an hypostatized shadowy intermediary.

SECTION 95

1   This provides yet another aspect of the 'queerness' of the proposition. At first glance the section is obscure: what is meant by saying that our thought does not 'stop anywhere short of the fact'? The metaphor indicates the impression that by means of the thought 'we had caught reality in our net' (PI §428; cf. BB 37), that we anticipate, encapsulate, the fact in our thought. This idea seems bewildering!

> 'Thought is a remarkable process, because when I think of what will happen to-morrow, I am mentally already in the future.' If one doesn't understand the grammar of the proposition 'I am mentally in the future' one will believe that here the future is in some strange way caught in the sense of a sentence, in the meaning of words . . . (PG 155.)

This 'proximity' of thought to reality is expressed in the way we conceive of *meaning* someone or something (as a kind of 'reaching out' to the very object itself (cf. PI §428)).

> What makes us think that a thought, or a proposition we think, contains the reality? It's that we're all ready to pass from it to the reality, and we feel this transition as something already potentially contained in it (when, that is, we reflect on it), because we say 'that the word *meant him*'. (PG 154.)

The paradox, expressed as a truism in the formulation 'When we think such-and-such is the case we mean such-and-such is thus-and-so', is indeed better expressed in the form 'It is possible to think of what is not the case'. If I think that something is red, to use a favoured example (PG 135, 163; PI §429), and it is not red, it is *red* that it is not.

The 'puzzle' is no other than that which dominates TLP: the proposition is a model of reality as it may or may not be. Being bipolar, it provides room for two kinds of 'harmony between language and reality', the 'fit' that consists in reality fitting or not fitting its description, and the two-way *direction* of fit that distinguishes statements (descriptions) from

---

[3] *Letters to Russell, Keynes and Moore*, p. 72.

expressions of will (intentions, commands, requests, etc.). Only the former is of concern to TLP, but the latter issue is raised in the discussions in the early 1930s.

The queerness of the impression of thought 'meeting' reality is equally pronounced in reflection upon expectation. Indeed, W.'s preoccupation with the puzzles of negation and harmony in TLP switch to the virtually identical type of puzzle regarding expectation, wish, and intention in the 1930s. 'The wish that he should come is the wish that really *he* should really *come*' (PG 143). The expressions of will, intention, expectation seem to contain within them their own satisfaction (even if, ultimately, they are disappointed). And so, indeed, in a sense, they do. For the linguistic expression of will or expectation is internally related to the description of its satisfaction, and so too to that of its non-satisfaction (since the latter description is simply the negation of the former). But, of course, that a noise is not as loud as I expected is not because it was louder 'in my expectation' (PG 135).

1.1   (i) 'do not stop anywhere short of the fact': no intermediary is required betwixt the thought and what makes it true (cf. BB 31 f.).

We may now be inclined to say: 'As the fact which would make our thought true if it existed does not always exist, it is not the *fact* which we think' . . . The next step we are inclined to take is to think that as the object of our thought isn't the fact it is a shadow of the fact. There are different names for this shadow, e.g. 'proposition', 'sense of the sentence'.

The temptation, which is the source of much of the philosophical mythology of language, arises equally for expectation, intention, and command. An order, wish, or expectation completely anticipate their execution. But what if they are not fulfilled? The issue is exhaustively debated in PR Ch. III, PG Ch. VII, BB 31 ff., and in PI §437 ff.

        (ii) '*This—is—so*' is an inappropriate translation of '*das und das —so und so—ist*'. The ordinary use of 'This is so' is for propositional reference. What we need here though is a linguistic correlate of a propositional variable, i.e. '*Such-and-such is thus-and-so*' (cf. 'The general propositional form', pp. 314 f. and Exg. §134).

        (iii) '*Thought* can be of what is *not* the case': W. replaced this by 'It is possible to *think* what is not the case' (PPI(R) §105).

MS. 157(a), 49 elaborates the point. Why do we say that *thought* is unique? Why not speaking or writing? It is thought that gives meaning to the spoken or written propositional sign. The thought is not only a picture, but a picture and interpretation simultaneously ('Bild und Deutung zugleich'). It is the thought which captures reality ('Im Gedanken wird die Wirklichkeit eingefangen'). The proposition is not the thought, but the understood propositional sign, and in understanding we go right up to reality. When we *mean* that things stand thus we do not stop anywhere short of the fact, but mean that such-and-such is thus-and-so.

2   (i) PG 108 f. emphasizes the fact that thought must be something ordinary, but we are inclined to think otherwise because we misunderstand its grammar and hanker for a substance to correspond to the substantive.

(ii) PG 154f. contains a long discussion of the strangeness of thought. A thought does not seem queer when we are thinking it, only when we reflect upon thinking it. Then it seems strange because: (a) it seems to connect objects in the mind, e.g. the substance and its property, the person and his act; (b) it is *not* a sign or a picture, since they are lifeless unless I know how they are meant; (c) thought, unlike signs, is not dead, because *for me* what I think really happens ('in thought'); (d) thought seems to contain reality, in that it 'points' right at it ('that word *meant him*'); (e) thought seems an extraordinary way of producing pictures and signs; (f) thought can be *of* the future, and so in a sense projects the thinker into the future. This discussion comes at the end of a whole chapter (Ch. VII) concerned with intending, expecting, wishing, etc., in which the related issues of harmony between language and reality are discussed in great detail.

2.1   'Thought must be something unique': cf. PI §110 and §428.

SECTION 96

1   This concludes the scrutiny of the thought that propositions are strange and mysterious. It is clearly a portmanteau of TLP doctrines. The *Gedanke*, belief (TLP 5.542), the sentence, the fact are indeed lined up behind one another as logically isomorphic structures. Thought mediates between language and reality, projecting one on to the other. The sources of these illusions are complex and varied—and not discussed here.

The final, parenthetical, remark is 'a reminder' to examine the actual use of these apparently 'super-concepts' and so to destroy the illusory grandeur which envelops them and leads to metaphysical nonsense. This theme is picked up in §97(b).

2.1   'Thought, language, now appear to us as the unique correlate, picture, of the world': cf. NB 82 'Now it is becoming clear why I thought that thinking and language were the same. For thinking is a kind of language. For a thought too is, of course, a logical picture of the proposition, and therefore it just is a kind of proposition.' Compare also TLP 4.014 (the fairy-tale alluded to is Grimm's 'Golden Children').[4]

---

[4] We owe this reference to R. W. Newell.

SECTION 97

1   This picks up the themes of §§89–92 (i.e. the sublimity of logic (§89), its concern with the *a priori* order of possibilities (§90), its simplicity once analysis brings all to light (§91)) and in (b) links them with the preceding discussion of the queerness of thought and proposition (§§93–6) via the illusions of a super-order between super-concepts.

That logic reveals the *a priori* order of the world was, of course, a dominant theme of NB, and—after due transformation into the doctrine of showing and saying—of TLP. The order of possibilities common to both world and thought was, in TLP, determined metaphysically by the combinatorial possibilities of objects and *reflected*, as a condition of sense, in language. This conception of language-independent possibility is, of course, repudiated in the later philosophy.

The metaphor of the adamantine crystalline structure of logic is reminiscent of a passage in Łukasiewicz:

> Whenever I am occupied even with the tiniest logistical problem, e.g. trying to find the shortest axiom of the implicational calculus, I have the impression that I am confronted with a mighty construction, of indescribable complexity and immeasurable rigidity. This construction has the effect on me of a concrete tangible object, fashioned from the hardest of materials, a hundred times stronger than concrete and steel. I cannot change anything in it; by intense labour I merely find in it ever new details, and attain unshakable and eternal truths. Where and what is this ideal construction? A Catholic philosopher would say: it is in God, it is God's thought.[5]

(b) is a quick allusion to a large topic, which needs more extensive treatment. The profundity of philosophy is misunderstood if it is thought to be derived from the endeavour to grasp the essence of language by grasping the order that obtains between categorial concepts conceived of as 'privileged' and fundamentally different from others.

Philosophy is profound; it is an endeavour to grasp the essence of language, but not by way of revealing a super-order between super-concepts. The words 'language', 'experience', 'world' are *words*, they have currency in our language as much as 'table', 'lamp', and 'door'.

What is at issue here? In TLP category-names were treated as super-concepts. They were the formal, pseudo-concepts of the book, represented by variables and *excluded from language*. What one tries to express by their use is shown by sentences in which the constituent names have the form represented by a given variable. It is *this* which is repudiated.

---

[5] J. Łukasiewicz, quoted and tr. by P. T. Geach in C. Cooper, P. Geach, T. Potts, and R. White, *A Wittgenstein Workbook* (Blackwell, Oxford, 1970), p. 22.

W. is not denying that there are words (e.g. 'colour', 'shape', 'tone', as well as 'proposition', 'fact', 'object') which can with justice be thought of as categorial. But there are now six claims which he makes which run contrary to TLP doctrines. (i) Categorial words are words in our language and have legitimate uses. (ii) A sentence such as 'Blue is a colour' or 'Square is a shape' are indeed merely 'grammatical', but, in the terminology of TLP, they are senseless, not nonsense. They do not violate the rules of language any more than do tautologies (although they do not give any information, any more than do tautologies). (iii) There is no 'ineffable' theory of types: in TLP, W. argued that a theory of types was neither necessary nor possible, but what the theory of types tried to express was shown in ordinary language. He still thinks that such a theory is neither necessary nor possible, but now also denies that there is anything ineffable which it tries to express. *There is no mystery.* (iv) Though some words may rightly be dubbed 'categorial', there is no sharp division of words into those which are, and those which are not, categorial. (v) The concepts which we are inclined to conceive of as categorial do not have sharp boundaries (PG 120). 'Colour' sometimes is used to include black and white, sometimes not. Such concepts as 'proposition', 'language' are family resemblance concepts. (vi) Items falling intuitively within the extension of a categorial term do not possess the same 'logical form', and their names are not always substitutable *salva significatione*; e.g. one is no less a number than two or three, but it makes no sense to substitute 'one' for 'two' in the order 'Divide the playground into two parts' (PLP 97).

1.1   (i) 'halo': W. substituted 'nimbus' (PPI(R) §107).

        (ii) 'Schliessens': should be translated 'inference', not 'proof'.

2.1   (i) 'the purest crystal': MS. 157(a), 69 echoes Schiller's response to Goethe's conception of the Primal Plant (cf. 'Übersicht', p. 302).

> Die Kristallreinheit der Logik hatte sich mir ja nicht *ergeben*, sondern ich hatte sie gefordert.
> Die Logik musste rein sein: denn was sollte rein sein, wenn nicht sie?
> 'Die Logik muss einfach sein': das ist eine *Forderung*, nicht ein Ergebnis.

> (The crystalline purity of logic was not given me in experience, but rather was something I demanded.
> Logic had to be pure; for what should be pure if not it?
> 'Logic must be simple': that is a *requirement*, not an experience.)

        (ii) '. . . logic, presents . . . the *a priori* order of the world . . .': MS. 157(b), 4:

> Die Idee, dass die Logik in irgendeiner Weise das *Wesen der Welt* zeigt, muss verschwinden.

Das *a priori* muss zu einer Form der Darstellung werden, D.h. es muss diesem
Begriff auch sein Nymbus [sic] genommen werden'.

('The idea that logic in some way shows the *essence of the world* must disappear.
The *a priori* must become a form of representation. i.e. this concept too must
have its nimbus removed.')

SECTION 98

1.1   '. . . our language "is in order as it is"'': an allusion to TLP 5.5563 (see
2.1). This contention was propounded in opposition to Russell and
Frege. As §98 notes, we are not striving after an ideal language that
awaits construction by us. In the Preface to TLP Russell revealed the
depth of his incomprehension.

> Mr. Wittgenstein is concerned with the conditions for a logically perfect
> language—not that any language is logically perfect, or that we believe ourselves
> capable, here and now, of constructing a logically perfect language, but that the
> whole function of language is to have meaning, and it only fulfils this function in
> proportion as it approaches to the ideal language which we postulate (TLP p. x).

This view W. repudiated, both in TLP and later. What was wrong with
TLP's conception of the 'good order' of ordinary language was its
forcing the requirement of determinacy of sense upon language. The
theme is pursued in §§98–107.

2   BB 28: the only point of *constructing* 'ideal languages' is for therapeutic
purposes (cf. Exg. §131).

2.1   Of TLP 5.5563, W. wrote to Ogden: 'By this I meant to say that the
propositions of our ordinary language are not in any way logically *less
correct* or less exact or *more confused* than propositions written down, say,
in Russell's symbolism or any other "Begriffsschrift". (Only it is easier
for us to gather their logical form when they are expressed in an
appropriate symbolism.)'[6]

SECTION 99

1   This continues §98. If the good logical order is conceived to consist in
absence of vagueness, then even the vaguest sentence must be in order; it
must be determinately indeterminate. A sentence with a sense may leave
this or that open, undetermined, but what it leaves open must be
determinate; otherwise it has no sense at all, for its truth conditions are
not settled. This thought echoes NB:

[6] *Letters to C. K. Ogden,* ed. G. H. von Wright (Blackwell, Oxford, 1973), p. 50.

Every proposition that has a sense has a COMPLETE sense, and it is a picture of reality in such a way that what is not yet said in it simply cannot belong to its sense . . . If a proposition tells us something, then it must be a picture of reality just as it is, and a complete picture at that.—There will, of course, also be something that it does *not* say—but what it does say it says completely and must be susceptible of SHARP definition.

So a proposition may indeed be an incomplete picture of a certain fact, but it is ALWAYS a complete picture[7] (NB 61.) . . . if possibilities *are left open* in the proposition, *just this* must be *definite*: *what* is left open . . . What I do not know I do not know, but the proposition must show WHAT I know. (NB 63.)

Such claims are, W. now contends, akin to Frege's claim that an indefinite boundary is not a boundary at all (cf. PI §71). So indeed they are, being derived from Frege and motivated by a demand for determinacy of sense interpreted in the Fregean mode.

The response here is in low key: it is not true that a vague boundary is *no* boundary. If there is only one hole in an enclosure then there is only one way out, and we need to keep an eye on one point only.

2   The ancestor of §99 in PPI extends the argument for determinate indeterminacy (PPI §91(b)–(c) = Z §§441 f.): the claim might be made that the rules of a game (and so, by analogy, the rules of language) may allow a degree of freedom, but must nevertheless be definite. That is like claiming that a prisoner is allowed a certain freedom of movement in his cell, but the walls must be perfectly rigid. Yet the walls could be elastic, and still imprison him!—But do they not have to have a determinate degree of elasticity? What, W. queries, does that amount to? That it *must* be possible to state it?—It is not always possible. So the Fregean is forced back upon a realist contention that it must have a determinate elasticity independently of our cognition (and of the possibility of cognition). *This* claim, however, is not a truth about reality, but a commitment to a form of expression, to a certain interpretation of the Law of Excluded Middle. Of course, the claim does not *look* like that; it appears to be about the necessary structure of objective reality, not about language. But any avowal of adherence to a form of representation formulated in the material mode must be *a priori*, since its opposite can only be expressed by a form of words which is being excluded from language.

SECTION 100

1   This is linked with both §84 and §99. §84 contends that rules are needed only where they are *needed*, not where it is logically possible that they might be needed. §100 adds that if we think that a game with rules

[7] Cf. TLP 5.156.

providing for every logically possible contingency (is there such a set?—a finite one?) is, in some sense, an *ideal* game, then we misunderstand the notion of the ideal. The philosopher may be inclined to think that we call something a game only because it resembles or approximates to the ideal game. But the explanation of 'game' does not involve reference to an ideal game as a paradigm. The role of the 'ideal' in our mode of expression is not as a paradigm useful in grammatical explanations in virtue of approximation. Nor is the ideal 'contained', in its pure form, within the impure variety manifest in ordinary language—as if every ordinary game like cricket or chess *really* contained a complete and perfect set of rules, since otherwise it would not be a game at all. ('There must be perfect order even in the vaguest sentence' (§98).)

What then *is* the role of the ideal in language? The matter is settled elsewhere. First,

Aber das Ideal is Deine Ausdrucksform und ein Missverständnis verführt Dich das Ideal *falsch anzuwenden.*
　Es ist, als wenn Du sagtest: 'Der Umfang dieses Rades is *wirklich* Dπ' (so genau ist es gearbeitet). (MS. 157(a), 65 f.)

(But the ideal is your form of expression and a misunderstanding tempts you to misapply the ideal.
　It is as if you said: 'The circumference of this wheel *really* is πD' (it has been so exactly wrought).)

(The last sentence is retained in PPI §91.)

Secondly, MS. 157(b), 10 ff., contains many redraftings of an early form of PI §100, *ll.* 5–8. The points are clear throughout. The ideal is the form of representation itself. Misunderstanding the function and grammar of 'ideal', we misapply it. The ideal itself is no more than the glasses we wear, but we misguidedly think that it reveals the nature of reality. You too, W. continues, would call it a game, only you are dazzled by the ideal and so do not see the actual application of the word 'game'. But how did you ever arrive at this ideal, from which material did you form it? Until you can resolve this, you will not shake yourself free of the fascination of the ideal. The roots of error must be uncovered. (This discussion is embedded in PPI §107.)

It is important that the early version of PI §131 (cf. Exg.) follows on shortly afterwards. The 'ideal', the form of representation, is a measuring rod, *an object of comparison*, something by reference to which we judge reality, not something *we find in reality* (cf. Exg. §81).

1.1　'die Rolle, die das Ideal in unsrer Ausdrucksweise spielt': literally 'the role played by the ideal in our mode of expression'.

2　In PPI §91 this remark is continuous with Z §442.

Section 101

1   §§101–4 apply the thought of §100 to the concept of a sentence with a
sense (thus connecting the discussion with §98). They explore the
illusory conception of the role of the ideal in language.

§98 characterized W.'s early insistence that ordinary language is in
good logical order in terms of absence of any vagueness. Now, having
castigated the distorted conception of the ideal in language as leading to
deep confusion, W. applies the same thought to his early conception of
a proposition. Starting from the preconception that there cannot be any
vagueness in logic, we become convinced that language *must* satisfy our
preconceived idea, even if we cannot see how it does so. NB manifests
this tendency again and again, e.g. 'But the sense must be clear, for after
all we mean something by the proposition, and as much as we *certainly*
mean must surely be clear' (NB 67). The author of these remarks did 'not
as yet *see* how it occurs' nor did he 'understand the nature of this "must"'.

1.1   (i) 'there can't be any vagueness in logic': cf. MS. 157(b), 4: 'Was heisst
es: "Eine Vagheit in der Logik kann es nicht geben"? (Vor allem kann es
dann auch keine *Bestimmtheit* geben.)'—('What does it mean: there can't
be any vagueness in logic? Above all there cannot then be any *exactness*
either.')

(ii) '"must" be found in reality' and 'must be in reality': the ideal of
absolute determinacy must actually obtain in existing language—in its
depth grammar if not on the surface. This interpretation is confirmed by
MS. 157(a), 55, which occurs in the context of the discussion of the
myth of the hidden super-order concealed in language (the source for PI
§105). We feel that this super-order—the ideal—must be found in
language (or, at any rate, in the mind: cf. Exg. §105).

(iii) 'nor do we understand the nature of this "must"': its nature is
clarified by the comparison of the form of representation with spectacles
(§103), and by the statement that we predicate of the thing what lies in
the method of representation (§104). Cf. also MS. 157(b), 11 f.: the ideal
lies in your form of expression (*Ausdrucksform*), but you misunderstand
the role which it plays in your expression.

Section 102

1   This attempts to capture at a stroke one of the well-concealed roots of
the TLP conception of the relation between thought and language. This is
clear from PPI. There it came after PI §103[8] and Z §445 (= PPI

---

[8] The final rearrangement was indicated in W.'s hand in TS. 227.

§92(b)): 'How can I understand a proposition *now*, if it is for analysis to show *what* I really understand?—Here there sneaks in the idea of understanding as a special mental process.' §102, therefore, was intended to exemplify one line of thought which results from the irresistible obsession with the ideal in our form of representation. Given our intoxication with a particular picture of the underlying ideal structure of language, which is in effect a misguided conception of our form of representation and its consequent *projection* on to reality, then the ideal 'is unshakable' (§103). A consequence of this 'fixation' is that it forces questions to the surface which rest upon the illegitimacy of this conception of the ideal. But the questions call out for answers, and we invent a mythology of language to answer them.

Given the apparent necessity of an ideally sharp and determinate logical structure of language, and given that the *appearance* of language is so far removed from this ideal, how can we understand language at all? Analysis will, *must*, reveal the sharpness of the underlying structure, but it has not yet been carried out (cf. LF 171). Consequently, in TLP, understanding, grasping the hidden, ideal, structure of the proposition must be something carried out by the mysterious operation of a hypothetical mental mechanism.

The strict rules of logical syntax were, in TLP, hidden in the medium of the understanding, for it was thought that mediated between language (propositional signs) and reality. In ordinary language the form of a thought is concealed by the lack of perspicuity of surface grammar; there is enormously much added in thought to each sentence and not said explicitly (NB 70; TLP 4.002), there is a multitude of tacit conventions which do not lie on the surface of what is said. But in the medium of the mind the structure of thought corresponds to the structure of reality.

PPI §92 adds to PI §102 this remark: 'Der ideal strenge Bau erscheint mir als etwas Konkretes:—Ich hatte ein Gleichnis gebraucht; aber durch die grammatische Täuschung, dem Begriffswort entspräche *Eines*, das *Gemeinsame* aller seiner Gegenstände, erschien es nicht als Gleichnis.' ('The ideal, strict construction seemed to me like something concrete. I used a simile; but due to the grammatical illusion that a concept-word corresponds to *one thing*, that which is common to all its objects, it did not seem to be a simile.') This was cancelled in TS. 227.

This is followed (PPI §93 = Z §444) by a remark beginning 'We now have a *theory*, a "dynamic theory" of the proposition'. This is singularly apt, for the TLP conception of the relation between thought and propositional sign could indeed be called a 'dynamic theory' of the proposition analogous to Freud's 'dynamic theory' of dreams.[9] Ordinary language stands to its depth structure (analysed form) as the phenomenal

---

[9] There is a brief explicit discussion of Freud's 'dynamic theory of dreams' (every dream is a wish-fulfilment) in MS. 157(a), 56. W.'s point is simply that it is a *theory*, an *hypothesis*,

dream to its underlying explanation (revealed by analysis). TLP too attributes to the unseen mechanisms of the mind the *explanation* of the *apparently* strange and unique phenomena of propositions of language.

The end of PPI §93: 'For we are under the illusion that what is sublime, what is essential, about our investigation consists in its grasping *one* comprehensive essence' echoes the omitted passage just quoted from PPI §92.

PPI §93 is followed by an early version of PI §105.

1.1   (i) 'hidden in the medium of the understanding': (cf. Exg. §105), i.e. in the ethereal medium of the mind (BB 3, 47).

      (ii) '(even though through a medium)': i.e. indistinctly, at one remove. I see them in as much as I understand, but their nature remains to be discovered.

SECTION 103

1   This precedes §102 in PPI and continues straight on to Z §445 (cf. Exg. §102).

The metaphor of the inescapability of the ideal, the airlessness of what lies beyond, represents, of course, the bounds of sense; beyond these there is no thought. What is the ideal in this context, and why does it seem so inescapable? The ideal, with respect to the structure of the proposition, is the general propositional form (cf. Exg. §104). It seems inescapable because any form of words which expresses a sense will possess that form, and if we try to describe that form by means of an expression which lacks it, all we can produce is nonsense.

The section involves an unhappy mixture of metaphors. The ideal is first said to be unshakably embedded *in* our thought; then it is conceived as the imprisoning walls, immediately compared to the limits of space ('There is no outside'). Finally, the idea of the ideal is compared with spectacles.

1.1   (i) 'in unsern Gedanken': in our thoughts or in our conception, not 'as we think of it'.

      (ii) 'sitzt unverrückbar fest': 'unshakably embedded' might be better than 'unshakable'.

      (iii) 'It is like a pair of glasses . . .': the idea of the ideal.

---

a *supposition*. But if one were to ask 'What is a dream really?' the right answer would be—'Have you never dreamt? Don't you know?'

    The analogy with 'What is a proposition?', the *Tractatus* 'dynamic theory', and the correct way of answering, (i.e. making fun of the question and then surveying grammar) holds!

    PPI(B) §109 n. makes explicit W.'s intention to draw an analogy to Freud's dynamic theory of dreams.

1   §§98–107 are concerned with the illusory requirement of hidden sharpness, which will ensure complete determinacy of sense. If §104 is to fit smoothly into the argument of these sections, we must take it to be concerned with projecting misguided demands upon ordinary language, demands which lie in our method of representing language. On this interpretation 'the thing' ('der Sache') is language or the proposition, and the 'method of representing it' ('Darstellungsweise') is the representation of propositions as pictures. This interpretation receives some support from the fact that PI §105 was preceded, in PPI, by Z §444 (cf. Exg. §102). That remark concludes:

The tendency to generalize the case seems to have a strict justification in logic: here one seems *completely* justified in inferring: 'If *one* proposition is a picture, then any proposition must be a picture, for they must all be of the same nature'. For we are under the illusion that what is sublime, what is essential, about our investigation consists in its grasping *one* comprehensive essence. (Z §444.)

On this reading, 'the possibility of comparison' is the comparison of a proposition to a picture, and the 'state of affairs of the highest generality' is the generalization that *all* propositions are pictures.

Against this interpretation speaks the fact that W. does not commonly use 'Darstellungsweise' to speak of a philosophical 'theory' about language or propositions. It is language itself that is commonly said to be our form of representation. Further evidence against the above reading stems from the location of §104 in PPI §110. There it occurs at the end of a lengthy discussion of the errors of TLP.

If we interpret §104 in the light of its location in PPI, it is evident that there 'the thing' is reality (or its constituents) and 'the method of representation' is language, as we conceive it under the spell of a misguided vision. We predicate of reality the correlate of the hidden sharpness we demand in order to ensure determinacy of sense. This seems necessary if the hidden structure of language is to exclude any indeterminacy, or at least render any indeterminacy determinately inde-terminate. This requirement is illusorily satisfied by projecting on to reality a metaphysical means of satisfying it, namely simple objects that are the meanings of simple names. Accordingly, the 'state of affairs of the highest generality' is the general propositional form which gives the general form of facts of which the world consists. The 'possibility of a comparison' which so impresses us can be taken to be either the comparison of propositions with pictures, or the possibility of compar-ing propositions with reality.

This interpretation is supported by examining the context of §104 in

PPI. PPI §108 begins an explicit discussion of some of the confusions of TLP: W. commences with points now familiar to us from the appendices to PG Part I. The conception of an atomic sentence as a concatenation of names standing for objects, the whole describing a state of affairs,[10] is under attack. In the correct use of 'object' and 'complex', spatial relations are not said to be objects, and locations are not part of the constitution of complexes (a complex of buildings does not consist *inter alia* of its location, nor of the spatial relations of its part). One can speak of combinations of shapes and colours, and of combinations of different shapes or bodies. But this form of words was, W. confesses, the source of his wrong expression: 'a fact is a complex of objects'.[11] It is a misuse of words, and mistaken, to say that a red circle consists of red and circularity. The fact that this circle is red does not consist of anything.

The theme is continued in PPI §109, which confirms the anti-nominalist interpretation of TLP. He was, W. avows, looking frantically for a unity underlying all propositions, and so became a prisoner of certain forms of expression of our language. He gives two telling examples: we can replace 'The bottle is blue' by 'The bottle has the property blue', or 'The bottle is to the right of the glass' by 'The bottle stands to the glass in the relation to-the-right-of'—and so it can appear that every sentence is really a combination of names. For here all words with a 'material' meaning seem to be distributed in a network of purely logical relations. Similarly, one is brought to think that all words correspond to objects, since 'Paul' signifies *this*, 'eats' signifies *this*, 'three' *this* and 'apples' *this*.

This revealing passage was followed by an early version of PI §115, which casts light on 'the picture' which 'held us captive'.

PPI §110 continues the exorcism of the ghosts of TLP. Every proposition says: 'This is how things stand' ('Es verhält sich so und so')—here is a *form* that can mislead us and did mislead W. So too Plato's remark (*Theaetetus* 189a)[12]: 'When someone means something, he means

---

[10] W. uses the term 'complex' here—misleadingly, since in TLP the expression 'complex' was reserved for the denotation of definite descriptions, and sharply distinguished from facts and states of affairs. This does not however vitiate the critical points he makes, since facts, no less than complexes, were said to be composed of objects. Indeed, in MS. 127, under 1 March 1944, having copied out TLP 4.22, 3.21 f., 3.14, 2.03, 2.0272, and 2.01, W. makes the same point without using the misleading term 'complex', but rather 'configuration': 'What a misuse of language [*Die sprachwidrige Verwendung*] of the words "Object and Configuration" [*Gegenstand und Konfiguration*]! A configuration can be made up of 5 balls which are spatially related in a certain way; but not of the balls *and* their spatial relations. And if I say "I see here three objects", I do not mean: two balls and their mutual position.'

[11] He did not say this, but rather that a fact is put together (*zusammengesetzt*) out of objects, has objects as components (*Bestandteile*), is a combination (*Verbindung*) of objects. But the criticism goes through despite the shift of terminology.

[12] Also referred to at PG 137, Z §69, etc. We have translated W.'s German 'Wer etwas meint, meint doch etwas Seiendes' rather than the original.

something that is.' This is the kind of sentence that one repeats to oneself countless times (cf. PI §114), confusing the nature of an object with the form by means of which we represent it.

This curious aberration of projecting form on to reality, which is the concern of §104, is caricatured in the subsequent passage in PPI (= Z §443). Suppose that one pointed by means of a gesture encircling the indicated object. A philosopher might then claim that everything is circular, since the table looks like *this*, the stove like *this*, the lamp like *this*, etc. Thus form of representation is projected on to the objects represented.

So too with the form of words 'This is how things are' (cf. PI §114). It is a picture which holds one captive, and until this optical illusion is removed, one cannot see language simply as it is (cf. 'The general propositional form', pp. 311 ff.).

'The expression of this illusion', PPI §110 concludes, 'is the metaphysical use of our words. We predicate of the thing what lies in the method of representation. Impressed by the possibility of a comparison, we think we are perceiving a state of affairs of the highest generality.' Here, at last, we have PI §104 back in its early dwelling place;[13] and there, we can recognize its more general implications.[14]

The phenomenon of projecting on to reality features of our grammar characterizes numerous facets of TLP. The simplicity of the object is a projection of a feature of *some* paradigmatic samples, its sempiternality a projection of the role of a sample in explanation of the meaning of some types of predicate. That all non-logical words are names is a sublimation and projection of the possibility of ostensive explanation; that the sentence is a concatenation of names is a projection of the possibility of formal transformations of sentences in grammar. The general propositional form is a projection of one kind of quasi-propositional variable.

This exercise in philosophical archaeology may, however, seem to have purchased enlightenment at the price of generality. Interesting as TLP is, it is not the culmination of the march of 'Spirit' through the ages. Nevertheless, the phenomenon under examination is characteristic of metaphysics in general, not just of W.'s early philosophy. Frege's conception of numbers as objects is, *inter alia*, a projection on to reality of the grammatical feature that numerals resemble names. His distinction between concept and object, allegedly 'founded deep in the nature of

---

[13] It is noteworthy that it is followed by the remark 'Denn, "Gegenstand" hat man doch nie, z.B., die Lage eines Dinges genannt.' ('For no one has ever, e.g., called the position of a thing "an object".') And then follows Z §448 (which further emphasizes that the target is the general propositional form). So did the 'objects' of TLP include locations? Who knows! But cf. LF 165 ff.

[14] The final rearrangement is entered in ink in TS. 227.

things', is a projection (and sublimation) of the subject/predicate form of grammar (PG 202 ff.). The abstract *Gedanke* occupying a transcendent 'third realm' is a projection of such innocuous forms of speech as 'He is saying the same as I am, only in different words'. Similarly, Russell's theory of types, conceived as a theory about the construction of reality (e.g. that properties 'cannot have' first-order properties) is a projection of grammatical conventions. Likewise, Russell's unflagging adherence to the 'existence of universals' stems, in part, from certain uses of the word 'meaning'. General words have meaning, Russell observes, so there must *be* meanings for them to *have*.

Nor would it be correct to conclude that the intellectual malady is a local phenomenon—infectious only at the end of the nineteenth century and the beginning of the twentieth. Cartesian simple natures are prototypes of TLP's objects. The classical preoccupation with simple and complex ideas is an idealist projection of definition by *Merkmale*. The doctrine of the simplicity of the soul is attributable to misunderstood features of the use of the first-person pronoun, namely that certain sentences containing 'I' are immune to error through misidentification of the subject (BB 66 ff.). The epistemological doctrine of the transparency of the mind and the attendant conception of 'inner sense' is a projection of the groundlessness of certain first-person psychological sentences.

The list could continue almost indefinitely, for the phenomenon is ubiquitous in metaphysics. Indeed, from the vantage point of W.'s later philosophy, it is only to be expected. For metaphysics is an attempt to describe the structure of reality prior to experience. But, in W.'s view, the 'structure of reality' is merely the shadow of grammar. So philosophers' efforts to describe what they take to be the structure of reality must consist in their projecting grammar on to reality, and then describing what they find as if it were there independent of language and thought—but, miraculously, derivable therefrom.

That W. had the full generality of the phenomenon in mind is evident from PPI(B) §§121 f. The sentence 'The expression of this illusion is the metaphysical use of our words' which opens this version of PI §104 is attached, as in PPI, to PI §113. But the latter remark has been generalized (cf. Exg. §113).

2   MS. 157(b), 4: 'Ein Satz a priori entsteht dadurch, dass ein Satz der von der Darstellungsart handelt eingekleidet wird in die Form einer Aussage über die dargestellten Gegenstände.' ('An *a priori* proposition results from dressing up a proposition which is concerned with our mode of expression in the form of a statement about represented objects.') This theme is developed in BB 48 ff.

SECTION 105

1   This continues the discussion from §103. Its ancestor in PPI (§94) came after an extended version of PI §102 and Z §444, whereas §104 occurred in a different context.

The pure signs after which we hanker are evidently the 'real' names[15] of TLP and the general propositional form. But these are not to be found in ordinary language. So the philosopher, in the grip of this obsession, retreats to the idea of the sign, or the idea at the present moment, i.e. a mental correlate of the physical sign.

1.1   '*Vorstellung* vom Zeichen': this is clarified by MS. 157(a), 52f.:

> Wir scheinen jene Überordnung in der wirklichen Sprache finden zu *müssen*. So fragen wir uns auch was das *eigentliche* Wort, der eigentliche Satz unserer Sprache sei, denn die geschriebenen und gedruckten Wörter und Sätze besitzen in ihrem Wesen nicht die Klarheit die die sublime Sprache erfordert. So gehen wir auf die Suche nach dem eigentlichen Wort und glauben es etwa in der Vorstellung des Worts zu finden.
>
> Und so kommt es dazu, dass wir Idealbegriffe haben und sagen, sie *müssen* auf die Realität der Sprache anwendbar sein, aber nicht sagen können wie.

> (It seems that we *must* find this super-order in actual language. So we ask ourselves what the *real* word, the real sentence [proposition] of our language is, for the written or printed words and sentences do not have in their nature the clarity which the sublime language demands. So we go in search of the real word, and believe that it may be found, e.g. in the idea of the word.
>
> And so it comes about that we [think that we] have ideal concepts and say that they *must* be applicable to the reality of language, but cannot say how.)

This is, indeed, just what W. did in his early work (cf. NB 70).

Cf. also Vol. XI, 49: 'Unsere alltäglichen Begriffe "Satz", "Wort", etc. sind viel zu wüst, zu ungeklärt. Sollte man nicht von den Sinnesdaten der Sätze etc. reden?' ('Our everyday concepts "sentence", "word", etc., are far too muddled, too unclear. Shouldn't one talk of the sense data of sentences, etc.?')

SECTION 106

1   The therapy for projection and sublimation alike is to return us to everyday matters, to what we ordinarily call 'things', 'objects', 'words',

---

[15] Cf. MS. 157(a), 58: 'Der ideale Name soll so funktionieren: Diesem Namen entspricht *das*. Und das "*das*" soll einfach sein, ganz einfach.' ('The ideal name should function thus: to this name corresponds *this*. And the "*this*" should be simple, completely simple.')

'signs', and so forth. For it is characteristic of the metaphysical use of words that key terms, such as 'language', 'object', 'fact' are ripped out of their ordinary, humble, contexts and inflated to the grandiose status of 'super-concepts' (cf. PI §116).

The extreme subtleties are the apparent fine-grained structures of reality which ordinary language seems unable to capture (cf. LF). The torn spider's web is ordinary language—torn, it seems, because of the apparent lacunae in it (its vagueness and indeterminacy). We feel, in philosophy, that our task is to show how these apparent faults are remedied. But it is impossible to do so, for there are none.

1.1   'den Kopf oben zu behalten': W. crossed out 'to keep our heads up' (they are not hanging in shame!) and substituted 'to keep the head above water' (PPI(R) §115).

SECTION 107

1   This concludes the discussion of the illusory sublimation of logic, linking it with the subsequent treatment. The 'ideal language' which seemed to contain explicitly the required structure of language constantly conflicts with ordinary language. The workings of ordinary language will not fit the Procrustean mould prepared for it. They must be described as they are, without the preconceptions of a theory which dictates how they must be.

1.1   The metaphor of friction is reminiscent of Kant's metaphor of the dove (*Critique of Pure Reason*, A5/B9). In both cases the 'absence of friction' represents the lack of empirical conditions of application of expressions.

The metaphor also makes contact with §81: an 'ideal language' appears to be a logic for a vacuum, i.e. no logic.

3   Unto a mill the mind compare,
That grinds whatever grain is there;
But if no more of it is brought,
The stones on one another caught
Mere splinters, dust and sand prepare.[16]

SECTION 108

1   §108(a) begins the treatment. Returning to 'the rough ground' consists

---

[16] Grillparzer, quoted by Boltzmann, 'On a Thesis of Schopenhauer's', in *Ludwig Boltzmann: Theoretical Physics and Philosophical Problems*, p. 197.

in an impartial description of the facts of language and its use. In TLP the formal unity of the categorial concept of 'sentence' or 'proposition' was thought to be captured by the general propositional form 'This is how things are', and of 'language' by the principle of extensionality. Now, however, W. sees this as an illusory theory-based requirement grossly at odds with ordinary language. 'Proposition' and 'language' are not super-concepts. As we employ these terms, they are family resemblance concepts (cf. 'Family resemblance', pp. 206 ff.).

To the prejudiced eye, this seems to deprive logic of its rigour, and so to destroy it altogether. Clearly many considerations appear to point in that direction. If language really does contain vague predicates (and not just apparently vague ones), then the Law of Excluded Middle cannot, it seems, apply to well-formed sentences of the language. If sentences such as 'The so-and-so is red' really are the elementary (non-compound) sentences of language, then the principle of independence and of truth-functional composition cannot be correct because, e.g., of colour-exclusion. If there is a serious asymmetry between first- and third-person psychological sentences, then the classical criteria for propositional identity must be defective. If generality is as ambiguous as the subject/predicate form (PG 269), then the classical analysis of quantifiers has only limited application.

But, of course, logic cannot lose its rigour as a result of philosophical transactions; it does, because it must, 'take care of itself'. The rigour it has, it has. All that is lost are our preconceived ideas about what rigour we are inclined to demand of it. We must examine logic from the vantage point of an unclouded vision of ordinary language, rather than looking at ordinary language through the sharp lattices of a preconceived crystalline logic. This is, indeed, to rotate the axis of the investigation around the fixed point of our need for an *Übersicht*, a correct 'logical point of view'.

§108(b)–(c): the first step towards wisdom is the realization that 'word' and 'sentence' in the philosophy of logic (or language) have a perfectly mundane use. There are two fallacies to guard against: the first is the sublimation of these concepts, their elevation to super-concepts. This draws in its wake three misconceptions: (i) that such a super-concept is a form (a variable), (ii) that it is sharply defined (has a determinate range of values), and (iii) that the *real* sign 'lies behind that which is ordinarily called "sign"' (cf. PPI §94 and Exg. §105). The second fallacy concerns what it is to be a sentence with a sense. Two related misconceptions are involved. (i) We readily conceive of a sentence as a string of signs with an associated sense and conceive of the associated sense as a mental accompaniment. So, we are prone to think, what distinguishes a series of meaningless marks or sounds from a significant sentence is the thoughts it evokes (PG 152). (ii) (§108(c)) We readily think that logic is interested in words and sentences only in a sublimated, abstract sense. So the proposition (*Satz*) is conceived as a strange abstract entity, a denizen of a Platonic world (e.g. the 'class of all synonymous sentences' (PG 121)).

Frege, because of his awareness of the defects of the psychologistic type of analysis, reified propositions (*Gedanken*) for the following reasons.
(i) It must be possible for different people to think the same thoughts, otherwise agreement and disagreement would be impossible. So thoughts, unlike ideas, must be identifiability-independent of owners.
(ii) Consequently, thoughts are not properties, since instantiations of a property are identifiability-dependent upon the substance whose property they are. Thinking is a complex property, but *what* is thought is not. Thoughts are, therefore, objective entities existing 'in their own right'.
(iii) Hence propositional attitudes are relations to objective entities (otherwise how could A and B believe the same?). Thus far the anti-psychologistic pressure to reification. Further arguments stem from his realist conception of truth. (iv) Truth and falsity are properties of objective entities, otherwise there could be no rational debate about truth and objective knowledge. (v) Truth-values are objective and independent of cognition. A thought is true independently of whether it is known to be true. (vi) The truth of thoughts is timeless. Apprehension of truth is temporal, but the truth apprehended is not. These considerations led Frege to conceive of propositions ('thoughts') as objective, non-spatial, atemporal entities belonging to the 'third world' of abstract entities.

But this Platonistic view is no less objectionable than its predecessor. We are concerned, in logic, with the spatial and temporal phenomena of language, but only from a certain point of view, and it is this that can mislead one. We are not interested in the physical shape of written sounds, any more than when describing the game of chess we are concerned with the shape of the pieces. Nor are we interested in the *particular* language to which the sentences belong (Z §322 = PG 190), any more than a description of chess concerns itself with the difference between wooden, ivory, or bone chess pieces. Of course, local differences in grammar (e.g. a number system consisting of '1', '2', '3', 'many') may be philosophically highly interesting, but the interest is focused on the particular grammatical structures, not on the signs whose uses embody the structures.

Nor is our concern philological or genetic (the history of development of chess is irrelevant to its current description). Rather we are concerned with the use of the expressions of language, which is determined by the rules for their employment and our practices of applying these rules (as the description of chess is a description of the powers of the pieces and the permissible, possible, transformations in the game). This makes it *look* as if we are talking about an ideal entity, but 'Is the chess king that the rules of chess deal with such an ideal and abstract entity too?' (PG 121).

§108(d): the analogy between language and chess is discussed in 'Language-games' (pp. 48 f.).

PPI(B) §110 instructs the insertion of PI §108(b)–(d) from Vol. X, Um. 108 f.

1.1   (i) 'was wir "Satz" . . . nennen': 'Satz' is indeed a family resemblance concept, but this is not the same as saying that 'sentence' is (cf. Exg. §93).

(ii) '(Man könnte sagen: . . .)': better translated '(One might say: the examination must be turned about, but around the pivotal point of our real needs.)'

(iii) 'Unding': poorly translated as 'phantasm' since that has psychologistic (ghostly, ethereal) echoes inappropriate here (since Platonism, not psychologism, is the target). 'Non-thing' is hideous, but nearer the sense.

2.1   (b) and (d) occur in an early form in PR 61 (cf. also BT 71, PG 121). What does logic understand by a word? W.'s answer would have outraged Russell: 'Here, the crudest conception must obviously be the only correct one', and 'This can only be dealt with from the standpoint of normal common sense. (It's extraordinary that that in itself constitutes a change in perspective.)'

PAGE 46 NOTE

1   It is unclear where this note belongs, and exactly what point it is meant to illustrate. It is cut from B i. §340 (= MS. 127, under 10 January 1943; = MS. 124, 133, under 16 March 1944; = MS. 129, 177). The latter context is suggestive; the quotation from Faraday comes after the following remark: 'Man könnte sagen: wir sehen, was wir beim Folgen nach der Regel tun, unter dem Gesichtspunkt des *immer Gleichen* an. Man könnte dem, den man abrichtet sagen: "Sieh, ich tue immer das Gleiche: ich . . .".[17]('One could say: we look at what we do when we follow the rule from the perspective of *always the same*. One could say to the person one instructs: "Look, I always do the same; I . . .".') The point concerns the internal relation between following a particular rule (e.g. the rule for a series) and the determination of act-identity, i.e. if we call this behaviour 'following the rule of a series', we will also call the various actions 'doing the same'. Faraday's insistence that water is always the

---

[17] This remark, in TS. 227, was typed in between PI §223(a) and (b), and then deleted.

same despite its transformations ('it never changes') expresses his determination to fix the concept of water thus. (It is, one might say, an idea, not an experience; to be sure, it is a scientifically fruitful idea.)

The thought is also expressed in the following remark (MS. 125 under 18 May 1942). 'Wenn Weiss zu Schwarz wird, sagen manche Menschen "Es ist im Wesentlichen noch immer dasselbe". Und andere, wenn die Farbe nur einen Grad dunkler wird, sagen "Es hat sich *ganz* verändert". ('When white changes to black some people say, "It is essentially still the same". And others, when the colour darkens the slightest bit, say, "it has changed completely"'). What counts as the same is a function of our decisions and purposes.

Faraday's remark, in his lecture,[18] occurs in the following context

> Here in this bottle, is a quantity of water—pure distilled water, produced from the combustion of a gas-lamp[19]—in no point different from the water that you distil from the river or ocean or spring, but exactly the same thing. Water is one individual thing—it never changes. We can add to it by careful adjustment, for a little while, or we can take it apart, and get other things from it; but water, as water, remains always the same, either in a solid, liquid or fluid [*sic!* gaseous?] state.

It is perhaps noteworthy that this remark is comparable to Goethe's incessant (but ultimately unsuccessful) attempts to find a principle of unity which will yield an understanding of plants (cf. 'Übersicht', pp. 301 ff.) and a principle of ordering for them:

> Es mag nun die Pflanze sprossen, blühen oder Früchte bringen, so sind es doch nur immer *dieselbigen Organe*, welche in vielfältigen Bestimmungen und unter oft veränderten Gestalten, die Vorschrift der Natur erfüllen. Dasselbe Organ, welches am Stengel als Blatt sich ausgedehnt und eine höchst mannigfaltige Gestalt angenommen hat, zieht sich nun im Kelche zusammen, dehnt sich im Blumenblatte wieder aus, zieht sich in den Geschlechtswerkzeugen zusammen, um sich als Frucht zum letztenmal auszudehnen.[20]

> (However plants may sprout, bloom or bear fruit, it is always just the *same organs* that in manifold ways and many variable forms manifest nature's pattern. The very same organ that unfolds on a stem as a leaf and assumes the greatest variety of forms is contracted into a bud, develops into flower petals, is contracted into the sexual organs, in order to develop finally as the fruit.)

Both remarks reveal how the quest for scientific insight, for a surview of a range of diverse natural phenomena, is expressed in the endeavour to

---

[18] M. Faraday, *The Chemical History of a Candle* (Hutchinson, London, 1907), p. 44.

[19] This being the experiment Faraday has just conducted.

[20] Goethe, 'Die Metamorphose der Pflanzen', §115, in *Goethes Werke*, Hamburger Ausgabe, Band 13 (Wegner, Hamburg, 1955). W. was well acquainted with Goethe's essay and the corresponding poem.

find a principle of unity in terms of which the diversity of phenomena can be *explained*. Whether water is everywhere one and the same, whether the organs of the plant are all the same (transformation of leaves), whether we will *accept* these contentions, turns on the fruitfulness of the paradigm and the hypotheses one can construct by reference to it. Boltzmann sapiently remarked: 'Only half of our experience is ever experience, as Goethe says. The more boldly one goes beyond experience, the more general the overview one can win, the more surprising the facts one can discover but the more easily too one can fall into error.'[21] That ice, water (in its fluid state), and steam are 'one and the same' has proved a fruitful determination. That the organs of plants are all leaves led Goethe into a cul-de-sac, although his passionate endeavour to develop a theory of plant metamorphosis is an exemplification of the nature of creative scientific inspiration.

How does this relate to our text? One possibility is this: in TLP, W. strove to find a *formal unity* underlying proposition and language (PI §108). But an *Übersicht* in philosophy, unlike that of science (PI §109), is *not* a matter of theory construction, *not* a search for unifying paradigms leading to fruitful hypotheses. It is a grammatical investigation, not a quest for *explanation* in the form of model-building. We are not trying to explain phenomena or discover new facts by hypothetico-deductive means, but to understand our form of representation *as it is*. So our method is *descriptive*, and our puzzlement is to be dissolved by a correct arrangement of what we already know.

SECTION 109

1   The points made here are as follows. (i) Philosophy is not a science; this links the section with §89. (ii) Empirical discoveries of the possibilities of thought are irrelevant to philosophy. (iii) Philosophy contains no hypotheses. (iv) It constructs no theories. (v) It explains nothing. (vi) Philosophy describes language in order to resolve philosophical, conceptual problems. (vii) The method of resolution is the rearrangement of familiar linguistic facts. (Cf. 'The nature of philosophy', pp. 285 ff. and 'Übersicht', pp. 305 ff.)

1.1   (i) 'It was true to say . . . ': an allusion to TLP 4.111 ff.

(ii) 'It was not of any possible interest to us . . .': even TLP adhered to this view of the irrelevance of experience (cf. 6.1222), although the discussion of the application of logic (5.5541–5.557) is obscure. The matter of the relation of sense and possible thought is well discussed in

[21] Boltzmann, 'On the Development of Theoretical Physics in Recent Times', in *Ludwig Boltzmann: Theoretical Physics and Philosophical Problems*, p. 96.

PLP 37 f. Why might one think that the claim 'It is possible to think such-and-such' is philosophically relevant? Many philosophers have indeed conceived of grammar as reflecting the laws (and hence the possibilities) of thought. We cannot imagine, conceive such-and-such—and that is why we don't *say* it, why it is *senseless*; and if we *can* conceive it, *then* it makes sense! If this were the case, then grammar would have to be readjusted as people's conceivings improved. If a certain string of words seems senseless this *may* be because we have not tried hard enough to imagine, conceive, them to be true. And, conversely, if an inference seems valid, this may be because we have not tried hard enough to imagine a possibility that verifies the premises and falsifies the conclusion (Russell). But this is absurd. The bounds of sense, and so of thought, are set by the rules of grammar, not vice versa.

(iii) ' "that, contrary to our preconceived ideas, it is possible to think such-and-such" ': This 'pseudo-quotation' seems to allude to Ramsey. For in Z §272, *à propos* 'I can surely imagine a row of trees going on without end . . . it makes sense to say it never comes to an end . . .', W. remarks: 'Ramsey used to reply to such questions: "But it *just is* possible to think of such a thing." ' (cf. B i, §42 = Vol. XII, 51). Compare also PR 304 (and thence 165f.): 'I once said there was no extensional infinity. Ramsey replied: "Can't we imagine a man living for ever, that is, simply never dying, and isn't that extensional infinity?" . . . What a peculiar argument: "I can imagine . . ."!'

The underlying conception here is typical of Russell too. That Ramsey and Russell are in the target area is confirmed by PG 309 ff., which discusses the absurdity of 'getting logic ready' for the existence of many-placed relations (which we can 'think of', and so might encounter).

(iv) '(The conception of thought as a gaseous medium)': if the classical conception of introspection (conceiving, imagining) as the source and ground of the logically possible were correct, then thought would have to be conceived as an ethereal medium open to mental inspection for it to be possible to *discover* that it is possible to imagine so-and-so (cf. BB 47).

(v) 'We must do away with all *explanation*': some ramifications of this contention are pursued at Z §314 (= B i. 434 = Vol. XI, 61). One characteristic difficulty in philosophy is recognizing a solution for what it is and not vainly trying to go beyond it. The reason for this is our hankering for an *explanation* in philosophy as in science, but in *that* sense, there are no explanations. When we reach the bottom of the matter, describe language as it is, *then that is how things are*. Since grammar is autonomous there can be no explanation, and the search for one is misplaced.

Presumably an example of what W. condemns here would be his search in TLP for a philosophical (metaphysical) explanation of the 'harmony between language and reality' by reference to the metaphysics of logical atomism. Whereas the 'harmony' is a datum of language; it can be described, dissected, but not explained by reference to anything further: 'It is *in language* that it is all done' (PG 143). Such metaphysical explanation is condemned no less than putative hypothetico-deductive explanation in philosophy. WWK 182 f. criticizes TLP for the 'scientism' of thinking that we must wait on experience to discover the ultimate forms of propositions.

Noteworthy is the origin of some of these remarks in W.'s criticism of Frazer's 'scientific explanations' of customs and rituals of primitive societies, cf. GB 30, 35 (and the similarity of these criticisms to Paul Ernst's 'Nachwort' to Grimm's *Märchen*).

SECTION 110

1   This is linked to §§93–5, the discussion of the uniqueness of thought and proposition. The slogan 'Thought is something unique' encapsulated the contention that thought 'captures reality', does not 'stop short of it', that expectation 'anticipates its fulfilment', that thought about the future 'transports us into the future'. This is a mythology of symbolism—a superstition, not a mistake. If these obscure metaphorical claims were mistaken, their negation would be true, but affirmation of their negation would not slay the chimeras.

In the grip of a multitude of grammatical illusions, thought appeared unique, mysterious, impressive; now that the illusions are recognized, the impressiveness retreats to the illusions themselves. The nature of philosophical illusion is unique, extraordinary, and a fit subject of study. Indeed, it is this preoccupation with dialectical illusion which gives all W.'s later work its negative tinge.

SECTION 111

1   Though philosophy is concerned, *inter alia* with the illusions of reason, and though these have their roots in grammar, it is in no sense trivial. The problems are deep, since they stem from the fundamental structure of our form of representation. The depth of philosophy is akin to that of grammatical jokes (e.g. Lewis Carroll's).

1.1   'Let us ask ourselves . . .': W. does not answer here the question 'Why is a grammatical joke deep?' But he does in PPI §97 (cancelled only in TS. 227). There he considers two jokes: Lewis Carroll's 'We called him "tortoise" because he taught us' (from *Alice in Wonderland*, Ch. IX) and an instance from Lichtenberg's 'Letters from a Maid on Literature' in which one hundred is written '001'. W. stresses two points. The depth of a grammatical joke is lost if one thinks that since signs are arbitrary one could, e.g., use 'taught us' as a substantive (as with Czech forenames, e.g. 'Zaplatil' means 'he counted') or '001' instead of '100'. The depth of absurdity is only revealed if one keeps in mind the correct use of the appropriate signs, sees what their consequences are, and notes the conflicts and incongruities which would stem from a change in notation, e.g. if '001' replaced '100', but everything else remained the same. We have the feeling of depth when we thus look at the system of language, it is as if we could see the whole world through its net. (Cf. PI p. 216 on primary and secondary sense in metaphor.)

SECTION 112

1   This exemplifies §111. Examples of misinterpretation of forms of our language are similes absorbed into language. This generates apparently conflicting demands.

W. does not give examples of such similes here. But in PPI §98 he does: we can measure the duration of an event, but the event is never present (in its totality); the rose is red, yet it is not (is not identical with) red; time seems a medium, but it is not anything. Such similes may mislead, and we are sent in chase of shadows.

1.1   (i) '*this* isn't how it is' . . . 'Yet *this* is how it has to *be*': this intense sense of irresoluble conflict characterizes philosophical disquietude. The form of the response is present in NB, e.g. 17: 'On the one hand my theory of logical portrayal seems to be the only possible one, on the other hand there seems to be an insoluble contradiction in it.' And again at NB 45: 'It keeps on looking as if the question "Are there simple things?" made sense. And surely this question must be nonsense!'

Vol. XV, 59 ff. reports that Russell often said, in the course of their discussions, 'Logic's hell!' This, W. continues, expresses what they both experienced when thinking about logical problems—their difficulty, hardness and smoothness. The main source of this experience was that each new aspect of language of which one might think seemed to render all the previous explanations useless (just as Socrates' arguments seemed to force constant revision of definitions). Language appeared continually to be making new and impossible demands. But Socrates' difficulties are only rendered more complicated when he tries to give the definition of a concept. For he continually gives up what he has achieved whenever he comes across a different application which does not fit. One says, W. concludes, 'But this *isn't* how it is!—But this *is* how it is!'

SECTION 113

1   This elaborates the point made in §111 that philosophical problems arise through misinterpretations of the forms of language. A feature of the illusion is its irresistible, ineluctable, pressure.[22]

In PPI §110 this remark occurs in a quite different context, i.e. in the discussion exemplifying, and leading up to, the claim that in philosophy we 'predicate of the thing what lies in the method of representation' (Exg. §104). It is thus *preceded* by §114, as well as by Z §443; so 'But *this* is how it is' was there directed at the obsessive notions of the general propositional form.

PPI continues:

Denn es scheint eben im Innern der Sache zu liegen. Erst wenn diese optische Täuschung entfernt ist, können wir nun die Sprache einfach sehen, wie sie ist.
   Der Ausdruck dieser Täuschung aber ist die metaphysische Verwendung unsrer Wörter.

(For it seems to lie at the heart of the matter. Only when this optical illusion is dispelled can we see language simply as it is.
   The expression of this illusion is the metaphysical use of our words.)

This is then succeeded by PI §104.

In PPI(B) §121, W. prefixes a generalizing remark: 'Ob wir über das Wesen des Satzes, des Verstehens, des privaten, nur mir selbst bewussten Erlebens nachdenken: "Es ist doch *so*—" . . . ('If we think about the nature of the proposition, of understanding, of private experience of which only I am conscious: "But *this* is how it is—" . . .')

SECTION 114

1   This occurs in PPI §110, before PI §113, after the following:

'Jeder Satz sagt: Es verhält sich so und so'. Hier ist so eine Form, die uns verführen kann. (Mich verführt hat.)
   Bei Plato: 'Wer etwas meint, meint doch etwas Seiendes.' (Theätetus.)
   Das ist die Art [von] Satz, . . .

('Every proposition says: This is how things are.' Here is such a form which can mislead us (did mislead me).
   Plato: 'Whoever means something, means something which is.'
   This is the kind of proposition . . . etc.)

[22] MS, 158, 37 f.:
   In phil. puzzlement what plays a role besides disorder is a kind of mirage of a language which isn't there.
   What is your disease? You ask the question again and again.—How can one make you stop doing this?

1.1   'tracing round the frame through which we look at it': an apt simile to connect this section with the succeeding paragraph in PPI (= Z §443). Cf. Exg. §104.

SECTION 115

1   In PPI (§109) this precedes PI §113 and §114. It is located towards the end of the discussion of the illusions of TLP (cf. Exg. §104). So the particular picture ('das Bild' in PPI) which held him captive was that associated with the view that a sentence is a combination of names (since 'Fa' can be rewritten as 'a has the property F', etc.), and with the view that all 'material' words stand for objects (since, for any 'a', 'a' means *this*). It 'lay in our language' inasmuch as it derived from a misconception of our form of representation.

2   RFM 42 discusses the fact that 'pictures' *force themselves* upon us.

SECTION 116

1   In the grip of a picture, philosophy sublimes certain key concepts. Knowledge, in the hands of Cartesians and their empiricist successors, becomes something unachievable, for it seems that we only really know something if all *possibility* of doubt (as opposed to all doubt) is excluded. Being becomes, in the early Russell's hands, a property belonging to everything thinkable, whether it exists or not (if it did not 'have being', one could not think of it). 'Object', for the young W., was transformed into a super-concept under which properties, relations, times, and spatial locations were included (PPI §§108–10); for Frege likewise, objects encompassed every 'referent' of singular referring expressions, including numbers, locations, simultaneous occurrences of events[23] (cf. PR 137), ways of doing things, etc. The first-person pronoun, in the hands of 'rational psychologists', appears to be the name of a spiritual entity, the *real* self, which resides in the body but is quite distinct from it (since 'I' is not in general substitutable for descriptions of the body) (BB 69, 74); from the use of this humble pronoun a host of grandiose facts seem to

----

By drawing your attention to something else.
    You are under the misapprehension that the phil. problem is *difficult* whereas it's hopeless.
    I want you first to realise that you're under a spell.
    If I leave the original example and pass to a different one I do it because in this example the philosophic pressure is not so high as in the original one.
    [23] See also Russell, 'Theory of Knowledge', p. 143.

follow: the simplicity of the soul, its independence from the body, its immortality. The sublimation of 'proposition' here mentioned has already been discussed, as has that of 'name'.

The therapy for the illusions generated by this 'metaphysical use of words' is to examine, with unbiased vision, the ordinary use of these words. It will then be evident that we have been misusing them.

In PPI this section is divided into two. §116(a) occurs at the end of PPI §110, following PI §104 and Z §448. Z §448 exemplifies the therapy prescribed here. If we are obsessed by 'the general propositional form' and the resonances of 'this is how things are', we should ask ourselves whether a simple sentence such as 'It is raining' says: this is how things are. How do we actually use the sentence 'This is how things are' (cf. PI §134)? Certainly not as an expression of 'the general propositional form'. The philosopher, as it were, plays draughts with chess pieces and thinks the game retains something of the spirit of chess. §116(b) opens PPI §111, which continues with an important passage concerning the apparent triviality of philosophy (quoted in 'The nature of philosophy', p. 287).

§§116–17 are reminiscent of TLP 6.53, which discusses the 'correct method' in philosophy: whenever someone wants to say something metaphysical the philosopher must demonstrate to him that he has failed to give a meaning to certain signs in his propositions. However, there is at least one important difference even here. For PI argues that 'proposition', 'object', 'name' are not super-concepts (formal concepts) but ordinary concepts with well-established uses. We must eradicate their misguided metaphysical use by examining their ordinary use. But in TLP these expressions were not conceived to have any ordinary use at all. They were conceived as formal concepts, and as such debarred from occurrence in well-formed sentences.

1.1   'Sprache': not 'language-game' but 'language'.

SECTION 117

1   (a) contains W.'s antagonist's response to the suggestion: you know what the word 'knowledge' or 'object' or 'name' means—it is being used in philosophy in just that sense! But its sense is not *glued* to the word, and in the 'philosophical' context of application, it loses its ordinary sense. The sense of an expression is not an accompaniment of the expression which is, as it were, stuck to the expression irrespective of the circumstances in which it is used.

To Russell, 'This is here', said while pointing to a present object (or even to the 'impression' of the object), seems to express a peculiarly secure kind of knowledge and to have a peculiarly 'solid' kind of meaning. But 'This is here' has an ordinary use (in rather special circumstances, e.g. leafing through documents in a drawer, and handing the relevant ones to a friend), and it is *not* to convey an item of Cartesian knowledge to oneself.

1.1   (i) Cf. PI §514 and C §348 for the philosopher's understanding of 'I am here'.
(ii) Cf. Z §139 (= B i. 72, = Vol. XII, 85) for repudiation of the view that the sense is an accompaniment of the sentence.

SECTION 118

1   The importance of philosophy comes from the dispelling of illusion and the clarification of the structure of language. (The former, so prominent in W., should not make one overlook the latter.)

2.1   (i) 'all that is great and important': BT 407—traditional Western philosophy distinguished two kinds of 'scientific' or cognitive problems, the essential, great, universal ones, and the non-essential, contingent ones (and took the former kind as its proper domain). W.'s conception runs contrary to this for in the cognitive sense of 'problem' there are no great, essential, problems.
(ii) BT 413 remarks that all philosophy can do is to destroy idols.

SECTION 119

1   This develops §118: the value of philosophy lies in ridding us of the compulsion to try to transgress the bounds of sense.

2   WWK 68 f. discusses the need to run up against the limits of language (à propos Heidegger and Kierkegaard) in connection with ethics (cf. LE 11 f.).
EBT 171:

Die Grenze der Sprache zeigt sich in der Unmöglichkeit, die Tatsache zu beschreiben, die einem Satz entspricht // die dem Satz gemäss ist // (seine Uebersetzung ist) ohne eben den Satz zu wiederholen.
(Wir haben es hier mit der Kant'schen Lösung des Problems der Philosophie zu tun.)

(The limit of language shows itself in the impossibility of describing the fact to which a given sentence corresponds // which conforms to the sentence // (is its translation) without repeating that very sentence.

(We are concerned here with the Kantian solution of the problems of philosophy.))

3   The metaphor 'Anrennen an die Grenze der Sprache' is similar to an aphorism of Karl Kraus: 'If I cannot get further, this is because I have banged my head against the wall of language. Then, with my head bleeding, I withdraw. And want to go on.'[24]

SECTION 120

1   This reverts to the therapeutic theme: we combat the metaphysical urge by attention to the ordinary use of those words which philosophy misguidedly sanctifies. When we talk of words and sentences we employ the words 'word' and 'sentence' in their ordinary sense, and the language we use to do so is our ordinary language—we have no other. We could invent another kind of language, but the philosophical questions arise out of *our* language, and the problems must be expressed in our language, for in a language with a different structure they would not arise (though other problems might) and could not be raised (cf. §§130–2).

1.1   (i) 'Is this language somehow too coarse and material . . .' might be directed against advocates of an ideal language, such as Russell (e.g. in his Introduction to TLP, p. x) and the young W. (although the latter thought that the coarseness of ordinary language was apparent rather than real). Less general, but equally to the point, is the view that our language is inadequate to describe experiences. W. mentions in this connection William James (cf. PI §610), who wrote: '. . . our psychological vocabulary is wholly inadequate to name the differences [between trying to recall the name of A and trying to recall the name of B] that exist, even such strong differences as these.'[25] But if language is too coarse, how are we to construct another? How are we to say, to think, that which we cannot express in our language, and which we want to be able to express in an improved language?

(ii) 'Dass ich bei meinen Erklärungen': these 'explanations' are the clarificatory remarks of PI, not the kind of explanations which are 'on the Index' in philosophy.

(iii) 'dass ich nur Äusserliches über die Sprache vorbringen kann': 'Äusserliches' here contrasts with 'Wesentliches'. The legitimate explanations employ ordinary language—the genuine article, not something preparatory or provisional. Presumably the contrast is in part with TLP,

---

[24] *Beim Wort genommen* [Munich, 1955], p. 326: cf. E. Heller, *The Artist's Journey into the Interior and Other Essays* (Secker and Warburg, London, 1966), p. 219.

[25] W. James, *The Principles of Psychology* (Holt, New York, 1980), Vol. I, p. 251.

where the explanations used are allegedly provisional language involving systematic violation of logical syntax, and, like TLP itself, ultimately to be discarded.

Why does the fact that legitimate explanations use language full-blown show that one can only adduce externalities (*Äusserliches*) about language? The reasoning harks back to TLP. There the *Wesentliches* was expressed by the pseudo-propositions of the book. Strictly speaking, nothing concerning the essence of things could be said, but only shown. This is now repudiated. There are no ineffable metaphysical structures. What seemed in TLP to be pseudo-propositions about essences are mere 'grammatical propositions' which are reflections, not of the structure of reality, but of grammatical rules. Since they say nothing, they will not occur in legitimate explanations, although the explanations will lead us to recognize these grammatical propositions for what they are.

BT 413 throws further light on the matter. What is the difference between the philologist's and the philosopher's concern with grammar? We are interested, for example, in translation from one language into another, even into languages we have invented; the grammarian is not. We are concerned with rules which the grammarian does not even notice. But it would be a mistake to say that we are concerned with the (hidden) essence of grammar, and he only with its accidental features. His interlocutor remarks that this difference between the philologist's and the philosopher's investigation is surely only an external, superficial difference. W. replies, 'I don't believe there is any other.'

The antagonist's position is that philosophy is concerned with the essence of language (all possible languages), and, by a natural extrapolation, with the essence of the world which it reflects. So the antagonist resembles the young W. The retort of the older, wiser W. is that this is erroneous. He describes grammatical facts just as the grammarian does; distinguishes different uses of 'is', reminds us that the pronoun 'I' is used in such and such a way, points out that a verb meaning 'to believe falsely' would not have a significant first-person present indicative, etc. And this is the only way to achieve what has to be done. The way of TLP, the high road of *a priori* metaphysics, leads to darkness. What seemed *there* to pertain to essences were merely knots in the thread of grammar, which he now unravels.

(iv) §120 (f): the antagonist views 'externalities' of grammar as trivial, for his interest is in the *meanings* of words, not in the words. And he thinks of meaning as a thing (like a word), separable from the word which is, as it were, accidentally attached to that 'independent' meaning. But words do not stand to meanings as money stands to purchasable goods, but as money to its use.

2.1   (i) 'your scruples are misunderstandings': cf. PG 121: 'We are not justified in having any more scruples about our language than the chess-player has about chess, namely none.'

(ii) 'Is this language . . . too coarse': cf. PG 169, PI §436; it is easy, in philosophy, to get into the position of thinking that ordinary language is too crude to capture the 'elusive, subtle and ephemeral' experience or phenomenon. But the phenomena and experiences are in fact perfectly ordinary.

SECTION 121

1   This is linked with §120(e). (In PPI §112, it directly succeeds it, prefixed by 'Hierher gehört auch:'.)

§121 is not meant to block what would be a harmless regress, but to undercut the view that metaphilosophy justifies or gives a foundation for philosophy, as Hilbert thought metamathematics gives the foundations of mathematics. But Hilbert's metamathematics is just another calculus (PG 296), and philosophical reflection upon the nature of philosophy is just more philosophy. In neither case do we 'give foundations' for, or justify, anything.

2   PG 116: the non-existence of metaphilosophy, W. claims, could be presented as a leading principle of all his philosophy. Vol. VI, 189 insists that just as there is no metaphysics, so too there is no 'metalogic'. In particular, 'understanding' and 'understanding a proposition' are not metalogical expressions, but expressions like any other in language.

Übersicht
1. Introduction   2. Precursors   3. The surveyability of grammar

SECTION 122

1   See 'Übersicht', p. 295 ff.

1.1   (i) 'übersehen': 'to survey', in the sense in which one can survey a scene
from the heights of a mountain.
(ii) 'Übersichtlichkeit': 'surveyability'.
(iii) 'übersichtlichen Darstellung': 'surveyable representation'.
(iv) 'Er bezeichnet unserer Darstellungsform': 'it signifies our form of
representation.'
(v) '(Is this a "Weltanschauung"?)': this stems from Vol. VI, 257
(= BT 417 (cf. GB 35)) which mentions Spengler: '(Eine Art der
"Weltanschauung", wie sie scheinbar für unsere Zeit typisch ist. Spengler.)' ('(A kind of "Weltanschauung" that seems to be typical of our time.
Spengler.)'). This remains in PPI §100, but is cancelled in PPI (A).
What is it that is a kind of *Weltanschauung*? There are two possibilities.
The first is that our form of representation is a kind of *Weltanschauung*
typical of our times, and it is the task of philosophy to obtain a surview
of it. For this possibility speaks Spengler's conception of the various
Weltanschauungen of different cultures. The Magian, Egyptian, Apollo-
nian, Faustian, etc., cultures all have different conceptions of space, of
number, of time, etc. A surview of such key concepts in each culture will
arguably yield different results[26] and the task of philosophy, in this
respect, never ends (Z §447). Against it can be pitted W.'s ironic remarks
about progress in philosophy (BT 424, cf. 'The nature of philosophy',
p. 278). As long as languages contain verbs like 'to be', adjectives like
'true', 'false', 'probable', figures of speech like 'the stream of time', the
same philosophical problems will continue to baffle us. These seem to be
trans-cultural to a greater degree than the ingredients of Spengler's
Weltanschauungen.

---

[26] Cf. Spengler: '. . . the operations of the systematic philosopher are subject to constant and
serious error through his assuming the permanence of his results. He overlooks the fact that
every thought lives in a historical world and is therefore involved in the common destiny of
mortality. He supposes that higher thought possesses an everlasting and unalterable
objectiveness, that the great questions of all epochs are identical, and that they are capable in
the last analysis of unique answers.
But question and answer are here one, and the great questions are made great by the very
fact that unequivocal answers to them are so passionately demanded, so that it is as life
symbols only that they possess significance. There are no eternal truths. Every philosophy
is the expression of its own and only its own time . . .' (*Decline of the West*, Vol. I, p. 41.)

The second possibility is that the fundamental significance of a perspicuous representation is a part of, or a kind of, *Weltanschauung* typical of our time. Almost all the thinkers to whom W. explicitly acknowledged an intellectual debt display precisely this hankering for surveyability, a profound belief that the deepest problems are resolved or grasped or laid to rest, not by scientific hypothesis or research, but by seeing connections, arranging what is known, looking at what is there in the right way. This is typical of Hertz, Boltzmann, Ernst, Kraus, and, of course, Spengler himself.[27] They all emphasize the immense importance of analogical thought, stress that the hankering for depth is only quietened by an *Überblick* or *Übersicht*, not by analysis or hypothesis. They all strove for a certain type of clarity and perspicuity which would yield an understanding unlike that pursued by scientific thought (though some qualification here is needed in respect of Hertz and Boltzmann (cf. 'Übersicht', pp. 296 ff.)). So is W. perhaps suggesting that this quest for surveyability is part of the *Weltanschauung* typical of the times? It is certainly characteristic of one group of intellectuals whose work lent pathos to the death throes of the Austrian empire. On the other hand, it could not in any sense be said to be typical of our times. On the contrary, twentieth-century culture, intoxicated with the achievements of science and technology, has moved more and more away from this kind of *Weltanschauung*. Moreover, all those members of the intelligentsia who can, loosely, be grouped together in respect of this conception of understanding were intensely aware that they were swimming against the tide, and no one more so than W. (cf. PR, Preface). Nevertheless, it is particularly *necessary* in our times.

Further support for this interpretation comes from LA 28. Having emphasized the mythological aspects of Darwinism and Freudian theory (evident, *inter alia*, in the manner in which people cleave to, or are repelled by, these doctrines), having recalled his own demystification of infinity, and expressed his disgust with Jeans (*The Mysterious Universe*), W. continued: 'I am in a sense making propaganda for one style of thinking as opposed to another. I am honestly disgusted with the other.' He apparently concluded that lecture by emphasizing that much of what he was doing was changing, and persuading others to change, the style of thinking.

3   Spengler's book much impressed W. Other noteworthy mentions of it in the *Nachlass* are the following. (i) In MS. 154, 16, written in 1931, W. avows that Spengler (together with Boltzmann, Hertz, Schopenhauer, Frege, Russell, Kraus, Loos, Weininger, and Sraffa) was a primary inspiration. (ii) EBT 72 suggests that Spengler could have been better

---

[27] Spengler ackowledges a debt to Goethe and Nietzsche. Of Nietzsche's 'outlook' (*Ausblick*) Spengler made an 'overlook' (*Uberblick*) (ibid., p. xiv).

understood if he had said—I *compare* different cultural periods to the life
of a family—in that in a family there is a family resemblance. (iii) Spengler
is again invoked in discussion of family resemblance in PG 299: proof,
W. suggests, is a family resemblance concept 'Like words such as
"people", "being", "religion", etc., cf. Spengler.' (iv) In MS. 157(b), 16 f.,
W. compares his own type of investigations with Spengler's, and
criticizes Spengler for failing to see that the ideal (presumably the
archetypal life-cycle of a culture)[28] is a principle of a form of approach
(*Prinzip der Betrachtungsform*). This remark follows a version of PI §131;
in PPI §107, before the last sentence of (the correlate of) PI §131 is the
parenthetical remark '(Ich denke an die Betrachtungsweise Spenglers)'—
('(I am thinking of Spengler's approach)'). (v) In MS. 125, 31, written as
late as 1942, W., in the course of remarks on the philosophy of
mathematics, jots down 'wie sehr ich doch bei meinem Denken von
Spengler beeinflusst bin'. ('How very much I am influenced by Spengler
in my thought.')

SECTION 123

1   Straightforward. Though added in pen to PPI(A) and (B) as §133, this
originates in Vol. VIII, 46.

SECTION 124

1   Cf. 'The nature of philosophy' (pp. 280 ff.).

1.1   (i) 'it cannot give it any foundation either': as TLP had tried to do.
Grammar is autonomous.

(ii) 'It leaves everything as it is': taken out of context this might be
taken to intimate the impotence of philosophy. In context, however, it is
clear that this is a further gloss on the first sentence of §124. 'Everything'
here refers to the use of language, i.e. grammar. It is not the task of
philosophy to change the grammar of our language, but only to describe
it, and thereby to curb our constant temptation to misconstrue it. It does
not, of course, follow that the clarity of an *Übersicht*, which it is the goal
of philosophy to achieve, will not have any effect on our non-
philosophical activities. Hence, to the extent that 'in psychology there
are experimental methods and *conceptual confusion*' (PI p. 232), philosophical investigation into psychological concepts will affect empirical

---

[28] E.g. Spengler's remark, 'beyond and above all, there stood out the fact that these great
groups of morphological relations, each one of which symbolically represents a particular sort
of mankind in the whole picture of world-history, are strictly symmetrical in structure'
(ibid., Vol. I, p. 47).

psychology, even though the investigation is *not* a psychological one. Similar considerations apply to mathematics.

(iii) 'It also leaves mathematics as it is': in mathematics there are 'conceptual confusion and methods of proof' (PI p. 232), and here too philosophical investigation is not irrelevant. An investigation into 'the foundations of mathematics' is as little a mathematical investigation as an examination of psychological concepts and theories is a psychological one. 'It will *not* contain calculations, so it is not for example logistic' (PI p. 232). It leaves mathematics unaltered in so far as its task is not to solve problems of mathematics. But clarification of conceptual confusion in mathematics will affect the activities of mathematicians, especially their theorizing about their inventions.

2.1   (i) LFM 103 comments on Hilbert's remark that no one is going to turn us out of the paradise which Cantor has created: 'I wouldn't dream of trying to drive anyone out of this paradise. I would try to do something quite different: I would try to show you that it is not a paradise—so that you'll leave of your own accord.'

(ii) PG 381 makes clear that W. thinks his philosophy of mathematics should affect mathematics.

What will distinguish the mathematicians of the future from those of today will really be a greater sensitivity, and *that* will—as it were—prune mathematics; since people will then be more intent on absolute clarity than on the discovery of new games.

Philosophical clarity will have the same effect on the growth of mathematics as sunlight has on the growth of potato shoots. (In a dark cellar they grow yards long.)

(ii) ' "a leading problem of mathematical logic" ': BT 417 f. (= Vol. VI, 189) and PPI §101 connect this phrase with Ramsey. Cf. PG 296: 'So there cannot be any "leading problems" of mathematical logic, if these are supposed to be problems whose solution would at long last give us a right to do arithmetic as we do.'

3   'it can in the end only describe it': cf. Boltzmann:

Thus from insights or experiences already gained one can indeed demonstrate new aspects of them, but the simplest preconditions of all experience and the laws of thought one can, I think, at best describe. Once admit this and all contradictions vanish that one previously met in the attempt to answer certain questions, for example whether complexes of unextended atoms make up extensions or whether they can even sense, whether we can come to know the sensations of others or the existence of inanimate beings, whether matter and spirit can interact, whether both run parallel courses without interacting or even whether only one or the other exists. One sees that one did not know what one was really asking.[29]

SECTION 125

1   This is linked directly to §124 and to §§122–3. Philosophical problems are resolved by producing a surview of a segment of grammar, for philosophical difficulties arise through not 'knowing one's way about'. So all philosophy does is describe the topography of the grammatical landscape, not *change* it. So too in philosophy of mathematics: a problem in metamathematics is just another problem in mathematics, not in philosophy. Consequently, a contradiction in mathematics (or metamathematics) is not something which philosophy must resolve. Rather, it is the task of philosophy to describe the entanglement of rules which produces the contradiction.

In mathematics we lay down rules and connections between them by means of proofs. What is the significance of the emergence of a contradiction (e.g. in set theory)? That the calculus of mathematics is not really a calculus, that it is useless, has no application? But a hidden contradiction is not like a malignant disease infecting the body mathematical (PR 319). If a contradiction between the rules of a game comes to light, that does not mean that the rules have hitherto been useless or that we have never really played the game, or any game at all.

The rules of a game, the axioms of a calculus, are in order until a case of their contradicting each other turns up (PG 303). Then a *decision* is called for—a clarification of the existing rules or the introduction of a further rule to resolve the contradiction. For we did not *mean* the rules to conflict, but to guide us in our transactions with them (in our various practices of applying them). To the extent that they conflict, they do not guide us and to that extent are not rules (PG 305). To claim that there *cannot* be a contradiction in mathematics, that rules *must* not conflict, is to project a metaphysical necessity from a requirement for rules that can be followed, i.e. of which it makes sense to say that we are following them.

The emergence of a contradiction can readily be sealed off (e.g. Russell's theory of types). *That* is not problematic (and that is why contradictions *per se* are not the catastrophes mathematicians think they are (PR 319, 325)). After all, contradictions *say* the same as tautologies, viz. nothing. It is the *civil* status of contradictions, i.e. their application, which is problematic. For conflicting rules do not guide us. What is necessary is to find the 'entanglement' in the rules and disentangle it in a satisfactory way. Disentangling is a mathematical matter, viz. finding a new gram-

[29] Boltzmann, On the Question of the Objective Existence of Processes in Inanimate Nature', in *Ludwig Boltzmann: Theoretical Physics and Philosophical Problems*, p. 75.

matical rule or convention that will eliminate the contradiction without generating further problems. But the description of the entanglement of the rules, of which the contradiction is a symptom, is the task of philosophy. We 'do not know our way about' the calculus (RFM 210 ff.), and here philosophy must survey the state of mathematics to show how and why we inadvertently produced a contradiction.

1.1   (i) 'The civil status of a contradiction . . .': the philosophical problem lies in our reactions (in 'civil life', not in mathematics) to the emergence of a contradiction (cf. LFM 209 ff.).

(ii) 'den Zustand der Mathematik . . . übersehbar zu machen': 'to render the state of mathematics . . . surveyable'. The point is not to focus on the details of the derivation of the contradiction, but to obtain an *Übersicht* of the system of rules.

SECTION 126

1   This is a further corollary of §124. Cf. 'The nature of philosophy' (pp. 280 ff.).

1.1   (i) 'What is hidden . . . is of no interest to us': cf. PG 75—the discovery of a hidden property common to the elements of the extension of a family resemblance concept does not imply that the concept applies to the items to which it does apply in virtue of the discovered feature. There are no discoveries in grammar. Cf. also PG 256: 'If a new sense were discovered and followed from . . . [a] proposition wouldn't that mean that that proposition had altered its sense?' (For discussion of 'hidden contradictions' in logic and mathematics, LFM 209–11, 224–6.)

(ii) 'everything lies open to view': cf. PI §89.

2   Cf. PI §§654 f. for further rejection of explanation and stress on description (and hence the autonomy of grammar).

2.1   Vol. V, 212 comments on TLP:

In meinem früheren Buch ist die Lösung der Probleme noch viel zu wenig hausbacken dargestellt. Es hat noch zu sehr den Anschein als wären Entdeckungen notwendig um unsere Probleme zu lösen und es ist alles noch zu wenig die Form von grammatischen Selbstverständlichkeiten in gewöhnlicher Sprache gebracht. Es schaut alles noch zu sehr nach Entdeckungen aus.

(In my earlier book the solution of the problems was presented in a manner insufficiently down to earth. There is too much of an impression that discoveries are necessary for the solution of our problems, and things have been insufficiently brought to the form of grammatical truisms in ordinary language. It all appears too much like discoveries.)

The first sentence of PI §126 follows on p. 217.

SECTION 127

1.1   'for a particular purpose': viz. the obtaining of a surview and the resolution of philosophical problems (cf. §89).

2   W. sometimes stressed more the notion of reminding: 'To study philosophy is really to recollect. We remind ourselves that we really use words in this way' (BT 419). Cf. PPI §104.

SECTION 128

1   Possibly originally directed against Waismann's *Thesen* (WWK 233 ff.).

2   Cf. PI §599.

SECTION 129

2.1   (i) BT 419 (= GB 33, editor's note): substantially the same remark, but after '. . . has at some time struck him', W. added '(Frazer, etc. etc.).' Frazer is, in general, accused of finding the mundane, and its sublimation into myth, insufficiently puzzling or wonderful. Where he sees terrible or awe-inspiring rituals and practices, he thinks to *explain* their character in terms of 'primitive science'. Where he sees depth in some folk-practice (Beltane fire-festivals), he thinks to *explain* the impressiveness by an historical hypothesis. In W.'s view both moves are mistaken. Ritual practices are to be viewed as *symbols*, e.g. of what is terrible or awe-inspiring. The impressiveness of a (possibly residual, degenerate) ritual lies not in its hypothetical past but in our recognition of its possible past and its relations to features of human history, human characteristics, one's knowledge of oneself. Either way, the significance is something to be seen and understood by an *Übersicht*, not to be explained, let alone explained away, by an hypothesis.

        (ii) PPI §106 (= BT 409) follows this remark with: 'Der Philosoph trachtet das erlösende Wort zu finden, das ist das Wort, das uns endlich erlaubt, das zu fassen, was bis dahin, ungreifbar, unser Bewusstsein belastet hat.' ('The philosopher strives to find the key word, that is the word that will at last permit us to seize what has hitherto been ungraspable, and has burdened our consciousness.')

        This in turn is followed by the analogy between this search for the key, liberating, word and trying to get rid of a hair on one's tongue. One can feel it, but can't get hold of it. The sequel throws light on W.'s insistence (cf. Exg. §100, MS. 157(b), 13) that one must ask, with respect to one's idea of the Ideal, whence one derived it, of what material did one form it (cf. also Exg. §131). W. emphasizes the importance of finding exactly the right way of expressing every false train of thought, the way which the philosophically perplexed person will immediately recognize as expressing what he meant (and here there is a similarity to psychoanalysis). What is then recognized and acknowledged is the analogy we present him as the source of his misguided thoughts. It is thus essential to trace the exact physiognomy of error in order to make room for the truth.

The conception of the 'erlösende Wort', the key word, redeeming, liberating, or magical, word was extremely important for W. It crops up very early in his work (cf. NB 3 June 1916, and the letter to von Ficker of 24 July 1915).[30] It is a recurrent theme in his later philosophical writings. Philosophical bewilderment and disquiet will only be laid to rest when the 'erlösende Wort' is found (Vol. VI, 17; Vol. XI, 30, 66; MS. 158, 42—'Ich suche nach dem Zauberwort'). The similar conception in Goethe's poem 'Die Metamorphose der Pflanzen' (cf. GB 34, 'Übersicht', p. 303)—'O könnt' ich dir, liebliche Freundin,/Überliefern sogleich glücklich das lösende Wort!'—must have appealed to him.

3   The sentiment of §129 is attractively expressed by Lessing:[31]

Chief miracle it is
That the true miracles become to us
So commonplace, so everyday. Without
This universal miracle could it be
That thinking men should use the word like children,
Who only gape and stare upon what's strange,
And think what's newest is most wonderful.

SECTION 130

1   Changes in the location of this section and an alteration to the earlier wording make the interpretation problematic. In its source (MS. 157(b), 33) it succeeds PI §131 by a couple of pages. In PPI §115, Z §440 and PI §130 are embedded between PI §133(a) and (b). Furthermore, in PPI the opening sentence reads: 'Auch sind unsere exakten Sprachspiele nicht Vorstudien . . .' ('Moreover, our exact language-games are not preparatory studies . . .'), and after 'air-resistence' there occurs an additional sentence: 'Diese Auffassung führt zu Ungerechtigkeiten (Nicod und Russell).' ('This conception leads to distortions (Nicod and Russell).)'

---

[30] *Briefe an Ludwig von Ficker*, ed. G. H. von Wright (Müller, Salzburg, 1969).
[31] Lessing, *Nathan the Wise*, tr. W. A. Steel (Dent, London, 1930), I, ii.

Read in the PPI context the point is as follows: it was the aim of, e.g., Russell, to refine and complete the system of rules of our language in unheard of ways (§133(a)). But there is no such conception of completeness, nor any absolute conception (i.e. conception independent of our actual needs and purposes) of such an ideal (Z §440). The 'exact' calculi which philosophers invent are not preparatory studies for the reform of our language (cf. PI §132). If one thinks they are, as Russell did, one misunderstands the nature of language, the task of philosophy, and the point of inventing calculi. (Cf. BB 28: Whenever we make up "ideal languages" it is not in order to replace our ordinary language by them; but just to remove some trouble caused in someone's mind by thinking that he has got hold of the exact use of a common word. That is also why our method is . . . to invent new [uses] . . . .) So-called 'ideal languages' are no more than objects of comparison for our ordinary language. By noting the ways in which our language resembles and differs from such invented languages we can bring into sharp relief significant features of it.

In PPI(A) and (B), PI §130 immediately succeeds PI §131 (which in PPI came much earlier, at §107, in a different context). It is here that W. crossed out 'exakten' and wrote in 'klaren, einfachen' (clear, simple), although the sentence alluding to Nicod and Russell remained until TS. 227. Given these progressive alterations, it is not clear whether the final version is still meant as a comment on 'exact language-games' i.e. 'ideal' calculi, or on W.'s invented 'clear and simple language-games' encountered earlier in PI. Presumably the remark is now directed at both types.

It is *possible* to take §130 as a gloss on §129, since one way of remedying our failure to notice the 'most striking' is to set up clear and simple language-games as objects of comparison which will highlight aspects of language that are hidden 'because of their simplicity and familiarity'.

2   RC §35:

he constructed an ideal use from the actual one. The way we construct a geometry. And 'ideal' does not mean something specially good, but only something carried to extremes.
    And of course such a construct can in turn teach us something about the actual use.

3   The conception of clear and simple language-games that §130 criticizes informs Nicod's methodology in *Geometry in the Sensible World* (to which PPI §115 alludes). Nicod's aim was to discover the formal structure of geometry 'in the book of nature'. Since this task is too great to be accomplished with a single effort, he recommends starting with the analysis of a simplified type of experience whose geometrical laws can be apprehended at a glance. This procedure mimics that of physical science.

The physicist does not launch into the ocean of reality without the support of a lifebelt of the most utopian fictions of simplicity, and as he progresses in skill he casts off these fictions one by one and so his analysis gradually comes to approximate to nature more and more closely. This scientific method, paradoxically, is necessary for systematic, rigorous thought, for schematization facilitates the thorough examination of the objective consequences of hypotheses. The invention of simplified sensible geometries is parallel to studying the mechanics of point-masses or the optics of light rays. Nicod is content to outline this method and to mark out the beginning of the road which descends from schematic abstractions towards reality.[32]

PLP 71 ff., after introducing the notion of a language-game as an object of comparison useful for obtaining an *Übersicht* of language, proceeds at once to give an example relating the shape of physical objects to plane projections of them from different angles (i.e. views of them). This indicates a close connection between the emergence of the language-game method of analysis and W.'s reflections on the sensible geometries of Russell (OK Ch. 3) and Nicod.

SECTION 131

1   The interpretation of this remark is problematic. What is the 'model' ('Vorbild')? Is it our language, our form of representation? Or is it an 'ideal calculus' conceived as a model of our language? Is 'reality' here the world, or is it our language (as in §101)?

The source is MS. 157(b), 16. The remark occurs there at the end of the long discussion of misunderstanding the role of the ideal in our form of expression, hence it concerns the same theme as §100.

In PPI, however, it is worked into a discussion derived from BT 258 ff. PPI §107 begins by stressing that we free ourselves of the spell of the ideal ('constraints of a logical ideal' in PPI(A) §141) by recognizing it as a picture, and giving its source. Out of what material did we form it (cf. Exg. §§100, 129)? Until we can answer this we will not shake ourselves free from its misleading aspect. It is of the utmost significance, PPI continues, that when we have a logical calculus we should think of cases to which it actually applies, rather than produce examples with the rider that these are not the ideal ones which the calculus would really fit. (It is not fully clear in PPI whether the examples are examples of fragments of language which the logical calculus fits, or examples of objects in reality to which it can be applied. A remark about the syllogism on BT 259 v. suggests that W. has the former in mind in this passage.) We might think

[32] His methodological remarks are concentrated in Nicod, *Foundations of Geometry and Induction*, pp. 90–94, 189–92,

that the ideal cases to which the calculus applies are yet to be found (e.g. when language has been fully analysed and 'real names' revealed). But this shows a misconception. If one can apply a calculus at all, then that is its ideal and actual application. To think otherwise, namely that the actual examples, which possess a diversity and complexity overlooked by the calculus, are not the 'ideal' ones, is the confusion under which W. and Russell laboured with respect to 'logical analysis'.

The following paragraph deals with the relation of the calculus to reality. One could imagine someone thinking that one cannot count bundles of twigs, since various twigs may break off and fall out of a bundle, and the pure numbers of arithmetic can surely not apply to anything as 'impure' as this. But at some point or other one must make the transition from the pure and clear to the impure—its application in counting objects. The 'pure' is merely the game with signs.

After this follows PI §131, except that the final parenthesis begins: '(Ich denke an die Betrachtungsweise Spenglers.) Hierin nämlich liegt der Dogmatismus . . .' ('(I am thinking of Spengler's approach.) For here lies the dogmatism into which . . .'). The concluding paragraph of PPI §107 points out that a unit of measurement is well chosen if its application to those lengths we wish to measure usually yields results expressed in whole numbers. But it is dogmatism to think that *every* length must be some whole multiple of our chosen unit of measurement (cf. Exg. §67).

In PPI(A) and (B) the sequel to PI §131 is PI §130, and then PI §132.

This suggests that §131 is concerned with the relation between a model of language (an 'ideal calculus') and language. (In PPI(A) the reference to distortions or ineptness ('Ungerechtigkeit') of §131 is picked up in the sequel (§130) by accusing Russell and Nicod of *Ungerechtigkeiten*.) This is one possible interpretation. Against it one may cite the following points: (i) it is unusual for W. to use the metaphor of the measuring rod for the relation between a calculus and language rather than for the relation between language and reality; (ii) it is strained to interpret the phrase 'to which reality *must* correspond' as alluding to language rather than the world (but cf. §101); (iii) the replacement of 'exakten' by 'klaren und einfachen' in §130, and deletion of the reference to Russell and Nicod, may be seen as directing §130 only at W.'s own invented language-games—in which case the continuity of §131 is destroyed.

The alternative reading is to take §131 as a warning not to project features of our form of representation on to reality. This is one of the themes of PPI §107; in particular, it is the subject of the concluding paragraph which succeeds PI §131. This is a perfectly plausible interpretation, but does nothing to show why PI §131 is located as it is in the final text.

We can conclude W.'s various discussions of the role of the 'ideal' in language by distinguishing three threads in the argument. The first concerns, as it were, the Idea of the Ideal, i.e. the elevation of certain concepts to the status of super-concepts and their consequent projection on to language (*qua* formal concepts) and on to reality (*qua* metaphysical order of reality). The second strand is the conception of an ideal notation, an improved language, as in the notion of an ideal *Begriffsschrift*, the application of which we cannot (or think we cannot) find. *This* is not to be found *hidden* in language as it is, nor is it an *improvement* over existing language (since its requirement rests on misunderstanding and any practical improvements we *need* we *can* make (Exg. §132)). The third strand is the ideal *qua* our actual method of representation. Its 'ideality' is generated when we forget that it is no more than a measuring rod by which to evaluate reality, not something to which reality *must* correspond. *That* is dogmatism (thus the Law of Excluded Middle (PI §352), or the related illusory requirement of determinate indeterminacy (Z §441) or, differently, Spengler's archetypal life-cycles of a culture),

2.1   'Vorbild': MS. 157(b) 16 has 'Ideal', PPI §107 has 'Vorbild'.

SECTION 132

1   In PPI this section (= PPI §113) succeeds PI §§120–1. It too belongs to the 'therapeutic' prescriptions of this chapter. The PPI version begins slightly differently: 'Da unser Ziel ist, den Bann zu brechen, in welchem uns gewisse Sprachformen halten, so wollen wir in unserm Wissen vom Gebrauch der Sprache eine Ordnung herstellen, die dies möglich macht.' ('Since our aim is to break the spell in which certain forms of language hold us, therefore we want to establish an order in our knowledge of the use of language which will make this possible.') This makes clear what one would conjecture: the order which philosophy seeks is an *Übersicht* which will dispel philosophical illusion. And this, of course, is one sharp difference between the philosopher's and grammarian's concern with language. The 'order' which the grammarian seeks is of a different kind, determined by different purposes.

Although new language-games invented to illuminate neglected distinctions may look like reforms of language, they are not. They are merely objects for comparison (cf. §130). Reform is possible (e.g. in the sciences) but this is not the task of philosophy. For philosophical problems characteristically arise not out of a vagueness or ambiguity in the standard use of language (which science might eliminate by a reformed terminology), but out of a distorted vision of how language fulfils its role and a consequent misuse of language.

By contemporary standards W. was chary, in his later work, of introducing technical terminology, let alone of suggesting 'reforms' for language. Nevertheless, terms such as 'language-game', 'private language', 'criterion', 'family resemblance' owe their currency to him.

1.1   (i) '. . . nicht *die* Ordnung': PPi reads '(Keine *Ueber*-Ordnung.)' ('(Not a *super*-order.)'), alluding presumably to the TLP conception of the philosophical order.

(ii) 'like an engine idling': cf. §271; this mechanical metaphor occurs in Hertz, *Die Prinzipien der Mechanik* p. 13.

2   BT 420: all his considerations can be represented in a much homelier manner than he had earlier envisaged. And that is why philosophy does not have to use new words; for the old, ordinary words of our language suffice.

SECTION 133

1   This concludes the discussion of philosophy. It repudiates the conception of philosophy as the quest for the ideal ordering of language, affirms the goal of obtaining a surview of various segments of language which generate philosophical problems, and stresses that philosophy provides methods for resolving those problems (cf. TLP 6.53).

In PPI this section is split up. (a), appropriately, follows §132, as here. Philosophy does not aim at a future regularization of language (cf. PI §130), at producing an ideal language which will be, in a chimerical sense, complete. This remark is followed by Z §440, linking the notion of 'completing' the rules for the use of a word with the previous discussions of vagueness. There is, W. stresses, no absolute notion of completeness, no absolute ideal of order. For any list of rules we can always construct doubtful cases. This is succeeded by PI §130, then §133(b) and (c), and finally Z §447.

(b) concedes to the philosopher who seeks for an ideal language that we are indeed aiming at *complete* clarity, but that is not to be achieved by inventing an ideal language, or by purporting to discover, by analysis, that it is already latent in our own. The complete clarity we seek is that in which particular philosophical problems completely disappear. It is the clarity of a perspicuous representation, an *Übersicht*.

The first sentence of (c) (cf. BT 431) is obscure. Given that the 'real discovery' is the one that will legitimize philosophy, i.e. enable us to cease calling it in question, it is unclear why this 'makes me capable of stopping doing philosophy when I want to'. (It is reported that W. repudiated this remark in conversation with R. Rhees.) Why is philosophy constantly called in question, and what discovery puts an end to these qualms? If the enterprise of philosophy is wrongly conceived, and if its product is misunderstood, then both the activity and its outcome will be under constant challenge. Thus, if the task of philosophy is thought to be the invention of an ideally complete and determinate language, the very project may be undermined by revealing the logical incoherence of this ideal of completeness and this conception of determinacy of sense. This can be generalized. Metaphysicians once conceived of their task as that of revealing the ultimate nature of reality. This enterprise was challenged in principle by Kant's critique of metaphysics. Epistemologists conceived of their subject as a search for the incorrigible foundations of empirical knowledge. This enterprise, too, is undermined by arguments which show that the contention that knowledge has incorrigible foundations is incoherent. The challenge may apply to the results of philosophy no less than to the general enterprise, if the results are conceived as uniquely philosophical propositions, e.g. proofs of the existence of God or the external world, or general metaphysical statements about the ultimate nature of reality. Philosophy, thus conceived, constantly torments itself by questioning its own legitimacy. It is given peace only by 'the real discovery' of grasping the true nature of the philosophical enterprise, viz. the resolution of philosophical problems by methods which will yield, not philosophical knowledge, but an *Übersicht*.

Z §447 (= PPI §116(b–c)) amplifies the idea of disquietude in philosophy. It arises from looking at philosophy wrongly, as if it has to grasp once and for all an infinite longitudinal strip (the structure of language which in advance is prepared for the description of all possible worlds, conceived as language-independent). But in fact its task is that of describing finite latitudinal strips, a task which has no end, but each part of which can be achieved, piecemeal. Thus, 'problems are solved (difficulties eliminated), not a single problem'.

1.1   (i) 'not a *single* problem': in contrast with the spirit of W.'s early work, e.g. 'My *whole* task consists in explaining the nature of the proposition. That is to say, in giving the nature of all facts, whose picture the proposition *is*' (NB 39).

(ii) 'There is not *a* philosophical method . . .': this stands in superficial contrast with the remark in the 1930–3 lectures that a 'new method' has been found (M 322). In TS. 227 this final sentence of §133 is a footnote slip.

CHAPTER 5

The general propositional form

(§§134–142)

INTRODUCTION

§§132–42 are not sharply separated from their antecedents and sequel. They both round off the discussion of the topics introduced in §§65 ff. and also introduce the examination of the nature of understanding, which is the theme of §§143 ff. §§134–6 are concerned with the subject of a general propositional form, which, in PPI, was more prominently interwoven with the remarks on philosophy than it is in PI. The concept of a general propositional form expressed by the sentence 'Es verhält sich so und so' was misguided, obscuring the real role of such sentences in language. There is no such thing as 'the general propositional form', since the concept of a proposition is a family resemblance concept. In particular, the concepts true and false cannot be used to determine what is and what is not a proposition.

§§137–42 discuss objections to this conclusion which turn on an underlying picture (characteristic of the Augustinian conception of meaning) according to which grammar is determined by the geometry of)? meaning-bodies. §138 introduces one reason for adopting this picture, namely the phenomenon of instantaneous understanding. This phenomenon seems to demand a mental representation of a meaning which can be grasped in a flash. This conflicts with the claim that the meaning of an expression is given by its use, for the complex use of an expression is not something that can be represented in a instantaneously surveyable representation.

§§139–42 develop this issue further, making the following points: (i) that no mental representation of a meaning is itself a meaning; (ii) that no mental representation of a meaning contains its own method of application; (iii) that a representation of a method of application can at most contain the lines of projection, and not the way these are applied; (iv) that the representation of a method of projection is at most psychologically compelling, but there is no such thing as 'logically compelling'; (v) that the working of a linguistic practice presupposes the existence of normality conditions. These points implicitly contain important criticisms of TLP. But they are presented here too briefly and obscurely to be readily understood. On the other hand, the salient issues are clearly presented in the course of §§143–242, in which new ground is broken. It is in the context of the discussion of understanding and of following rules that these issues become clear and their paramount significance stands forth.

Structure of §§134–42.

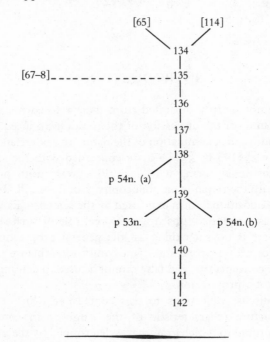

Correlations

Here PI n = PPI (n − 17), except PI §142, which drives from a handwritten addition at PPI(B) §158.

The general propositional form
1. '. . . a picture held us captive . . .' (PI §115)   2. 'We want to replace wild conjectures and explanations by quiet weighing of linguistic facts' (Z §447)   3. '. . . do we have a *single* concept of proposition?' (PG 112)
4. '. . . the use of the words "true" and "false" . . . *belongs* to our concept "proposition" but does not *"fit"* it . . .' (PI §136)

SECTION 134

1   'Things are thus-and-so' was, in TLP, thought to represent the general
propositional form. W.'s strategy here is to scrutinize the actual use of
this sentence in ordinary language, for it is from there that it was taken,
and it is there that it has its meaning (cf. PI §116). It is employed as a
propositional schema to allude to some other statement. It is itself an
English sentence, satisfying the syntactical rules of sentence-formation.
But its specific role as a propositional variable in discourse, a role which
could be fulfilled by a variable letter 'p', or an arbitrary sentence, e.g.
'The sky is blue', in no way justifies elevating it to the grandiose role of
representing the general propositional form. One important feature of
many expressions we call 'propositions' is agreement or disagreement
with reality, but *that* feature is conspicuously missing from 'Things are
thus-and-so'. This is called 'a proposition', *inter alia*, because it sounds
like one. Not everything that satisfies the syntactical rules of English
sentence-formation sounds like a proposition (e.g. 'This is the house that
the malt that the rat that the cat killed ate lay in'), but it is entirely natural
that we should employ, for the specific role in question, an expression
that also sounds like a proposition.

1.1   (i) 'So und so liegen die Sachen' is perhaps better rendered by 'Thus-
and-so is how things stand', just as 'Es verhält sich so und so' is better
translated as 'things are thus-and-so'. The more natural English translation, utilizing the simple indexical (e.g. 'This is how things are'), loses the
essential complexity (the 'concatenation of objects') intended to be
captured by the formula 'So und so liegen die Sachen' or 'Es verhält sich
so und so'.
    (ii) 'To say that this proposition agrees (or does not agree) with reality
would be obvious nonsense': the role of 'Things are thus-and-so' is not
to say something which agrees or disagrees with reality, but to allude
anaphorically or cataphorically to something of which it can be said that
it agrees or disagrees with reality.

2   (i) In PPI §117, this section is explicitly connected with the preceding
discussion of the general propositional form. One could readily imagine
a sentence with a perfectly ordinary sense, e.g. 'The sky is blue', being
used, in the appropriate contexts, as a propositional variable. Similarly,
someone brought up on the new logic might say 'He said "p, and

therefore I need an advance"'. But, W. concludes (as in PI), no one would call 'p' the general propositional form.

(ii) Z §448 was embedded in PPI §110 adjacent to PI §113 (cf. Exg. §§104 and 113 f.) and its argument belongs here. 'It is raining' does not have the form 'Such-and-such is the case', does not pick out 'objects in concatenation', since it has only a dummy subject term.

(iii) PLP 281 discusses the matter of the relation of being a sentence and sounding like a sentence. Although it does not discuss the question of whether there is an expression of the general form of a proposition, Waismann considers a close relative of that notion as presented in TLP, namely whether a proposition can be defined as the expression of a fact. This, he argues, is worthless since we cannot give an account of what a fact is which is independent of the notion of a proposition.

SECTION 135

1   This remark, identifying the concept of a proposition as a family resemblance concept, links the argument with §§65–8.

1.1   '(Compare the concept of a proposition with the concept of number)': in §68, W. has pointed out that 'number' is a family resemblance concept too. We could give both concepts rigid limits if we wished, but need not, and do not.

2.1   'Haven't we got a concept of what a proposition is?': BT 61 compares 'Do we have a general concept of a proposition?' with 'Do we have a general concept of reality?'

SECTION 136

1   §136(a) brushes aside the TLP conception of general propositional form. 'Such-and-such is true' (or 'Such-and-such is false') can fulfil the same role as 'Such-and-such is how things are'. So all the general propositional form amounts to is that a proposition can be defined in terms of its capacity for bearing truth-values. Given the redundancy account of truth (and the repudiation of the correspondence thesis of TLP), all that this boils down to is that we call something a proposition if it is an argument of a truth-function.

(b) exposes an apparent implication of the definition of a proposition as bearer of truth-values. This suggests that we can use the concepts true and false, taken as given, to determine whether something is a proposition.

This is repudiated in (c). One can no more use the concepts true and

false to determine whether something is a proposition than one can use
the concept of check to determine whether a piece is the king in chess. In
one sense of 'Satz', what a *Satz* is, is a matter of the syntax of language. In
another sense (i.e. where 'Satz' = 'sentence with a sense'), it is determined
by the use of the sign. 'True' and 'false' are parts of the 'game' we play
with propositions, but these words give us no independent determinant
of propositionhood. W. summarizes this conclusion by saying that 'true'
and 'false' *belong* to our concept of a proposition but do not *fit* it. A chess
analogy explains this metaphor. The concept check *belongs* to the king,
presumably because one could not know that *this* piece can be checked
without already knowing that it is the king. To say that check does not *fit*
our concept of a pawn is to take the concepts of pawn and of check as
independently characterizable and to claim that a game in which pawns
were checked would be uninteresting.

That 'true' and 'false' belong to our concept of a proposition could also
be expressed by saying that only formally are they *Merkmale* of propositionhood. Hence the definition of proposition as what can be true or
false differs from the norm of *Merkmal*-definition (e.g. 'human' =
'rational animal') in which the definientia can be grasped independently
of the definiendum.

1.1 'Denn, statt "Es verhält sich . . ."': better translated 'Instead of "It is the
case that . . ."'. W's point is that instead of 'It is the case that he is at
home', one could say 'Such-and-such is true', but equally, instead of 'It is
the case that he is not at home', one could say 'Such-and-such is false'.

2 (i) NB 112 shows that the conception of the general propositional form
was bound up with the correspondence theory of truth: 'In giving the
general form of a proposition you are explaining what kind of ways of
putting together the symbols of things and relations will correspond to
(be analogous to) the things having those relations in reality. In doing
thus you are saying what is meant by saying that a proposition is true;
and you must do it once and for all.'

(ii) PG 112: what do we want to distinguish a proposition from? From
parts of propositions (sentences) in its grammatical system (as an
equation from a sign of quality (cf. TS. 211, 115))? Or from everything
we do not call 'a proposition (sentence)'—this chair, my watch, etc.? TS.
211 continues: that there are written- and sound-pictures (*Schrift- oder
Lautbilder*) which are similar to sentences need not concern us. Must we
say that one can only talk about the concept of a proposition (or of a
proposition) within a grammatical system (or in the course of an
explanation of one)?

(iii) PG 123: to the standard equations of the redundancy account of
truth W. adds—'What he says is true = Things are as he says'. He had no
qualms over 'propositional quantification'.

(iv) PG 124 denies that one can combine words with '. . . is true (false)' by way of experiment to discover whether they constitute a proposition. One could only do that if 'true' and 'false' had definite meanings independently of these test contexts. But for these words to have definite meanings *is* for the possible contexts of their significant occurrence to be already determined. So there is no possibility of 'experiment'.

(v) BT 60: 'Sentence (proposition)' ('Satz') is like 'object' ('Gegenstand') in that it has a permissible application only within a restricted sphere. But when its natural range is extended so that the concept becomes a philosophical one, the meaning of the word evaporates, leaving only empty shadows. We must give it up in these new ranges, and use it only within its appropriate limits.

(vi) PLP 372 f. explores the analogy between chess and language. It is only incorrect (or misleading) to think that one gives the essence of the proposition by reference to its bearing truth-values if one thinks that the latter property *follows* from the nature of the proposition. The truth is that this is a *stipulation* which *determines* our concept of a proposition.

(vii) Waismann's essay 'Wahrheit' (preparatory for PLP) gives various answers to 'When is p true?': when p is the case, when the fact meant by p obtains, when the sentence p corresponds with reality, when things are as it says they are, when what is said by p is true, etc. These are explanations of 'true'. 'True', 'agreement with reality', etc., are expressions within a calculus, not expressions connecting the calculus with reality.

This strategy lies at the heart of W.'s resolution of the problem of pictoriality and repudiation of the picture theory of meaning. It is prominent in discussions of intentionality and agreement with reality (PG Ch VII); see also EBT 136:

'Das, was der Gedanke wahr macht, kann nicht vorausbestimmt sein, weil es eben sonst da wäre // der Fall wäre //.'—'Aber es ist vorausbestimmt, wie es ist // es sich verhält // wenn der Gedanke wahr ist.'—'Aber mehr brauchte es doch nicht, eben die Tatsache, die Verifikation, zu geben. Dieses "der Satz sagt (zeigt), was der Fall ist, wenn er wahr ist" sagt eben nichts, denn p zeigt eben, dass p der Fall ist, wenn etc . . . D.h. auf die Frage "was wäre (ist) denn der Fall, wenn . . .?" könnte nur p zur Antwort kommen. Das ist also eine blosse Tautologie.'—Die Schwierigkeit liegt im Begriff des Bestimmens.

Was der Satz eigentlich bestimmen müsste, wäre quasi, dass p oder non-p der Fall sein muss, aber das ist nur scheinbar eine Bestimmung, in Wirklichkeit bestimmt es aber gar nichts.

Und wenn ich sagte, dass er die Wahrheit auf Ja und Nein festlegt, so heisst das, dass er nichts festlegt, nichts was sich sagen lässt.

('That which makes the thought true cannot be determined in advance because then it would be so // would be the case //.'—'But it is determined in advance how it is. // things stand. // if the thought is true.'—'But there is no further need to specify the fact, the verification. This "the proposition says (shows) what is the case if it is true" says nothing, since p shows that p is the case, if, etc. That is, to the question "What would be (is) the case if. . .?" only p could be the answer. So this is merely a tautology." The difficulty lies in the concept of determination.

What the proposition would actually have to determine is, as it were, that either p or not p must be the case; but that is only apparently a determination, in reality it determines nothing at all.

And if I said that it fixes reality give or take 'Yes' or 'No' then that means that it fixes nothing—nothing which can be said.)

Section 137

1   This presents an objection to the conclusion that 'true' and 'false' do not *fit* but *belong* to the concept of a proposition, and the rebuttal of that objection. The previous section intimated (and PG 124 asserted) that one cannot combine words with '. . . is true' or '. . . is false' by way of experiment to see whether those words constitute (express) a proposition. The objection is that we teach children how to determine the subject of a sentence by asking 'Who or what?', exploiting the idea that the subject term *fits* the question. So surely we can determine whether a string of words expresses a proposition by asking ourselves whether we can say '. . . is true' after it, or '*This* is how things are . . .' before it.

The riposte is that in *this* sense of 'fit', the words 'true' and 'false' do fit propositions. But this is not the requisite sense. We 'find out' which letter of the alphabet succeeds 'K' by repeating the alphabet up to 'K' to ourselves, and we 'find ourselves' saying 'L' after 'K'. 'L' fits 'K' only in the sense that we have been trained to rehearse the alphabet in the order 'A, B, C . . . J, K, L . . .'. We don't *discover* the fit, as we discover that one cogwheel fits another (the metaphor of machinery and that of fitting belong together), we *remind* ourselves of the predetermined series. Determining the subject of a sentence by the question 'Who or what . . .?' is a move in syntax in which we remind ourselves of the form of the nominative case.

Section 138

1   This consists of a riposte to the argument of §§136–7. There *is*, W.'s interlocutor objects, a sense of 'fitting', distinct from that of §137, according to which meanings of words fit each other, and in terms of which 'is true' can be said to fit the sense of a sentence. We need this notion of fitting because we have the experience of instantaneous understanding. Of course, what we instantaneously understand cannot be the use of a word, for we cannot have the whole mode of application

of a word in our heads all at once (cf. PG 49). Rather, what we understand is the meaning, which must be something from which the use, the mode of application, flows. Hence our grasp of the use of an expression must be a consequence of our antecedent apprehension of its meaning.

This picture of meanings fitting each other in a geometry that is reflected in grammar is an important component of the Augustinian conception of meaning. If meanings are conceived of as entities, whether concrete, Platonic, or mental, accompanying the words we use, then we will be prone to think of the underlying meanings as fitting or failing to fit each other. Consequently the sentences we construct will make sense to the extent that the meanings of the constituent words fit each other. So 'The square is red' makes sense but 'The smell is red' does not. According to the Augustinian picture, the rules for the use of these words are derived from, and must faithfully reflect, the underlying meanings. This conception, W. noted, informs Frege's philosophy of language and mathematics (PG 40; BB 4; PLP 234). (In GA ii. §91, Frege, arguing against the formalists, writes: 'Whereas in meaningful arithmetic equations and inequations are sentences expressing thoughts, in formal arithmetic they are comparable with the positions of chess pieces, transformed in accordance with certain rules without consideration for any sense. For if they were viewed as having a sense, the rules could not be arbitrarily stipulated; they would have to be so chosen that from formulas expressing true propositions could be derived only formulas likewise expressing true propositions.') On this conception the sentence is a mechanism assembled from its parts, each of which has a particular shape which fits the rest of the mechanism.

It is as if each word had behind it a *'meaning-body'* (PI §559; PG 54; PLP 234 ff.). Imagine various geometrical solids, e.g. squares, prisms, pyramids, etc., made of glass and invisible, except for one painted surface. The visible forms that can be produced by their combination will be determined by the combinatorial possibilities of the invisible solids behind the visible surfaces. Analogously, the meaningful combinations of words are determined by the fit of the underlying meaning-bodies. The rules for the use of words describe the combinatorial laws of the meaning-bodies.

TLP was manifestly guilty of this misconception. The constituents of reality (objects) are the meanings of names. Accordingly, one expression fits another if the object which is its meaning fits the object which is the meaning of the other. The rules of logical syntax merely reflect the combinatorial possibilities of objects.

This conception of meaning also characterizes Frege's Platonism (although the imposition of the tier of sense upon the domain of reference complicates the picture). Thus, while it may be true that our only access to the logical structure of reality is via the logical syntax of language, nevertheless, according to Frege, that structure of language is not arbitrary or conventional as is ordinary grammar, but reflects the super-physics of objects and concepts.

An object, e.g. the number 2, cannot logically adhere to another object, e.g. Julius Caesar, without some means of connection. This, in turn, cannot be an object but rather must be unsaturated. A logical connection into a whole can come about only through this, that an unsaturated part is saturated or completed by one or more parts . . .

Now it follows from the fundamental difference of objects from concepts that an object can never occur predicatively or unsaturatedly; and that logically, a concept can never substitute for an object. (FG pp. 33 f.)

Consequently, the distinction between concept and object, and between first- and second-level concepts 'is founded deep in the nature of things' (FC 41; CO 50, 54).

W.'s reply to the challenge of §138 follows in §§139–41. Of course, if there is no such thing as a meaning-body from which the grammar of a word follows, then there can be no such thing as apprehending in a flash the fit or lack of fit between the meanings of one word and another. If the meaning is indeed the use of an expression, then a quite different account must be given of what it is to understand a word instantaneously. W.'s account is given in the course of the detailed examination of rule-following and understanding in the sequel.

2   (i) PI pp. 175 f., 181 make the following points. (a) The difficulty in understanding how one can grasp the meaning of a word in a flash is the dual reference to a point in time and to the way of using a word. The latter has, it seems, to be spelt out (as it were, over time). (b) If we can grasp a meaning in a flash, then it seems that what we grasp must be something which can occur, full-blown, in a moment, e.g. an image or picture. One reason why this is wrong has been examined, i.e. the multiple possibilities of application of such a representation. Other reasons are given here. (1) Instantaneous grasp of meaning cannot consist in having an image, since one can keep an image in mind over time (for five minutes, say), but not one's grasp of the meaning. Rather, once one has grasped the meaning, there is something one *can do*. (2) When one exclaims 'Now I have it', a picture may occur to one, and may remain in mind. But 'Now I have it' does not mean 'I have a picture in mind', and one's joyous exclamation may prove premature if it turns out that one cannot. . . (3) Grasping a meaning in a flash seems akin to experiencing a meaning, which in turn seems similar to experiencing a mental image. But the content of experiencing an image, of imagining (in this sense), is a picture or description. The 'experience of meaning' has no 'content'. (4) Even if someone were only able to do something when, and as long as,

he had a certain experience (image or picture), the ability he has is not the experience nor its content.

(ii) LFM 19–28 contains a lengthy discussion of understanding and application. One understands an expression when one knows how to use it. There is indeed such a thing as instantaneous understanding, but it does not involve having the whole use of the expression before one's mind. A picture or mental image may represent a rule, but not its application, or not its whole application, for the picture itself must be applied (cf. §141). Suppose one says 'This is the Greek letter sigma', pointing to the sign σ. Then one says 'Show me a Greek sigma in this book', and the learner cuts out the sign one initially showed and puts it in the book. Here, one might say, the learner got the right picture, but did not understand the application.

Page 53 Note

1   Cut from B i. §82, this passage originates in Vol. XII, 93, in the midst of a discussion of understanding and ability. Its immediate context is an early version of PI §181; however, this version is not concerned with sudden dawning of understanding, but simply with an assertion of ability, followed by failure to do what one said one could do. In what circumstances does it make sense to say 'When I said I could, I could, but now I can't' (cf. PI §182(a), example (5))?

The following section explores self-knowledge of abilities and degrees of understanding. To the questions 'Can you lift this weight?' and 'Can you still play chess?' it makes sense to reply 'I don't know; let's see'. But can one thus reply to 'Do you understand the word "tree"?'? One would respond 'You must surely *know* whether you understand it!' But this is too hasty. If one were asked 'Do you know how to move a pawn in chess?' and the reply were 'Let's see', then we would be inclined to respond 'You'll find out whether you know or not'. On the other hand, if one were asked whether one knew what 'pure' and 'impure' mean in Jewish dietary laws, one could well answer 'Let's see, such-and-such is called "pure", but whether *this* is called "pure". I do not know'.[1] Here, and also with a question like 'Do you understand the word "integral"?', one can say 'Up to a certain point I understand the word'. But now, can't one imagine circumstances in which one could say 'Up to a certain point I understand the word "tree", but just how far, well, let's see'?

Page 53 n. follows immediately upon this and is followed by Z

---

[1] It may be seen that one could reply here: 'Well, "pure" means that it is permissible to eat, "impure" that it is forbidden, but I don't know which specific items count as pure or impure'. So one could; just as one could specify the king in chess as the piece one checks (§136)! Does one then know how to apply the words?

§§193 f. (= B i. 83 and 194, cf. Vol. XII, 270 and 93). What is the central point? Understanding words, like abilities, is capable of degrees. There are various criteria of understanding, and satisfaction of some and non-satisfaction of others may justify ascription of partial understanding. It makes sense for a person to think he understands, but be wrong. There is, to be sure, the phenomenon of 'grasping the meaning of a word in a flash', but also that of thinking, wrongly, that one has done so. The moot question is what are the criteria for someone's having grasped the meaning of a word in a flash. They lie, of course, in his avowal, his subsequent applications, the explanations he gives of it. So the phenomenon of grasping the meaning in a flash does *not* show that the meaning grasped is something different from the use 'which is extended in time'; rather, to grasp the meaning is to have acquired the ability to use the word (not to have caught hold of an entity which 'fits' other similar entities).

To this extent p. 53 n. is a riposte to the final sentence of §138, or an elaboration on §139(a).

SECTION 139

1   This section elaborates the problematic relation between grasping a meaning in a flash and the idea that meaning is use. What is the relationship between the use of a word, which cannot be presented to the mind in a flash, and whatever does come before our mind when we understand the meaning of a word in a flash? Meaning is determined by use, but how can any object of instantaneous understanding either be, or accord with, a use? Suppose that what comes before one's mind when one understands the word 'cube' is a picture of a cube. How can the picture fit the use or fail to fit it? One is inclined to say that it fits if one applies the word to objects of which the mental picture is a picture, i.e. to cubes, and not to pyramids. But with a given method of projection a cube may well be the representation of a pyramid. To be sure, the picture *suggests* a use, but it does not *determine* one.

Consequently, instantaneous understanding, though it may be accompanied by mental representations, cannot consist in having (perceiving) mental representations, since any such representation would have to be applied and may be applied rightly or wrongly.

It is important to note that W. is not merely concerned with a mistake, i.e. when a person instantaneously understands the word 'cube' the picture of a cube comes to mind, but he goes on to apply the word to a triangular prism. First, the method of projection may not be the 'natural' one; a cube may indeed represent a pyramid, given a certain method of projection. Secondly, it may be that on understanding the word 'cube'

the picture of a pyramid comes to mind, but for all that, one applies the
word to cubes, not to pyramids, and one explains 'cube' by pointing at
cubes, not at pyramids. Does it now matter what comes before one's
mind? Is what comes before one's mind a criterion of understanding? It is
how one uses the word, and how one explains it that shows whether one
understands it (cf. Exg. §§140 f.).

Although nothing that comes before one's mind when one understands a word in a flash is a criterion of understanding, a picture of, e.g., a
cube can function as a rule for the application of a word ('cube'). Overt
presentation of such a picture in response to a request for explanation is a
criterion of understanding the word. Like all criteria it is defeasible, since
the rule may be misapplied. Nevertheless, neither mental nor overt
presentation of such a picture is what understanding a word in a flash
consists in.

2   Z §§297 f. (= B i. 48 and 15, cf. Vol. XII, 61 f. and 19) pursues matters
further. How do I manage always to use a word correctly? Not, indeed,
by consulting a grammar. Is it then by *meaning* something by what I say?
Of course, but that is not an explanation. My meaning something by the
words consists in my knowing that I can apply them (and doing so),
although I may believe that I can apply them and be wrong. Knowing
that I can apply a word is knowing that I understand it. But understanding is not an *inner activity* (event or process), nor is it the outer
manifestation of understanding (the criteria for understanding): it is
not an event, process or activity at all (cf. 'Understanding and ability',
pp. 331 ff.).

PAGE 54 NOTE (a)

1   This identifies another source of the error of thinking of meanings as
entities apprehended by the mind from which the use of a word *follows*,
viz. the fact that we sometimes choose between words, saying 'I believe
the right word in this case is . . .'.

This remark, from B i. §363, occurs there in the context of PI §624 f.
Similarly, its source (MS. 129, 198 f.) is concerned with kinaesthetic
sensations and knowing that one has moved.

Cf. PI §335.

PAGE 54 NOTE (b)

1   This is cut from B i. §335 (= MS. 129, 175), but that reveals nothing. Is
this remark meant to illustrate the notion of a picture *suggesting* a use,

even though it is possible to use it differently (§139(e))? Or the related thought in §140 that we are under a psychological but not a logical compulsion to take the picture thus and not otherwise?

Section 140

1   What was the mistake made (in §139) in thinking that a picture (a 'mental meaning') fits a use if it is a picture of the object to which the word is applied? The mistake lay in thinking that such a surrogate meaning carried with it its own application, that it forces an application on us. Consequently, if one has a picture of a cube in one's mind (when one 'thinks the sense of "cube"') and yet points at a triangular prism, saying 'That is a cube', one's mistake apparently consists in confusing the picture of a cube with that of a triangular prism.

The error involved in the conception of a mental surrogate of meaning as forcing an application on us can also be expressed by saying that we are at most under a psychological compulsion, that the picture forcefully suggests a use to us, but it does not logically compel us to apply it in the way it suggests. But this too is misleading (LFM 184 f.), for it suggests that we can and do distinguish two kinds of case, that of psychological, and that of logical, compulsion. In the sequel, and elsewhere (see esp. RFM), W. argues extensively against the intelligibility of 'logical compulsion', for there is no such thing as 'logically compelling', and the inexorability of logic is our inexorability in applying it as we do.

§139 showed that different uses of an expression could all, with justice, be called 'applying the picture of a so-and-so'. The illusion that a picture forces an application on us merely reflects the fact that by habit and training only one application is naturally suggested to us. If, however, the same mental representation occurs to us in relation to different applications, we will not claim that the word has the same ⟩ ?
meaning despite its different applications. Consequently, the meaning of a word is not a picture in the mind, nor any other entity, and grasping the meaning of a word 'in a flash' does not consist in having a mental representation, even though it may be accompanied by such an 'experience of meaning'.

The complex issue of understanding and grasping the meaning of the word is, henceforth, a leitmotiv running through the whole book. The matters raised so briefly in this and the adjacent sections are explored exhaustively in the subsequent discussion of following a rule. For just as having a mental picture (a 'meaning') in mind does not guarantee its application, so too having a rule in mind (or even in print) does not guarantee applying it correctly. Likewise, just as a picture cannot logically compel, neither can a rule; just as some applications of a picture come naturally and seem inexorable, so too do rules. So §§138–41 are a prologue to the elaborate arguments that follow.

SECTION 141

1   The argument thus far establishes that a mental 'meaning-picture' does not carry its application with it, does not force an application on us, and can be applied in different ways. In reply to this one might argue that what comes before our mind when we grasp the meaning of, e.g., 'cube' in a flash is not only the picture of the cube, but also the method of projection. This can be imagined as a representation of two cubes connected by lines of projection.

To this the riposte is that it does not advance matters, for this complex schema still has to be applied, and one can imagine different applications of it, none of which are 'compelled' by the schema.

The response to this is the question: 'Can't an application come before one's mind?', to which the answer is: 'Of course' (anything that is thinkable can come before one's mind). But how do we apply the expression 'an application came before his mind'? We accept two different criteria for an application coming before someone's mind.[2] First, the picture that comes before his mind,[3] e.g. the two cubes connected by lines of projection. What grounds do we have for saying that *this* picture comes before his mind? Surely, what he says in response to our question 'How did you represent to yourself the application of this expression, or this picture?' And his answer may involve producing a description, a drawing, or a model. Consequently, for the person to have a method of projection before his mind, it is unnecessary that he imagine anything at all, he can look at a drawing or model we put before him.

The second criterion that we use is the application he makes of what he imagines (or of the pictorial or three-dimensional representation of the method of projection with which he is presented). If he goes on to use the expression correctly (as we do), then we will say that the correct method of application occurred to him.

[2] The passage is confusing in that we begin with the argument that a representation of a method of projection does not carry with it its own application, to which the response is: 'Can't an application come before one's mind?'. The answer is 'Yes', and the example examined is then of a *method of projection* coming before one's mind. The confusion dissolves once one realizes that *any representation* of an application is a representation, not an application. The most obvious representation of an application consists of delineating lines of projection. To be sure, this leaves room for erroneous application. But nothing, certainly no further schema, picture, or representation, can bridge the 'gap' between the representation of an application (of a method of projection) and an application itself. After all, there is not a *gap* but a categorial difference.

[3] This has misled some into thinking that an inner state can constitute a criterion for something.

The two criteria can conflict (although not *contradict* each other) but they normally do not. A person might picture cubes connected by lines of projection and go on to call a triangular prism 'cube'. We would then take this to defeat the claim that the *application* came before his mind, and contend that he misapplied *the picture of the application*. But we only allow the picture that occurs to him to constitute a criterion for an application occurring to him in so far as normally people who have such a picture go on to apply the relevant expression in such-and-such a way.

The case is exactly the same with the avowal 'Now I understand' or (with respect to rules) 'Now I know how to go on'. We take such an avowal to be a criterion of understanding, but only in so far as people who exclaim that they understand normally go on to manifest their understanding in behaviour. If the regular correlation between avowal and performance did not obtain, our use of 'understand' would lose its point.

2   (i) LFM 23 points out that the use of 'understand' is based on the fact that in an enormous number of cases when we apply certain tests (criteria), we are able to predict that a person will use a word (which he is said, by those tests, to understand) in a certain way. If this were not so, there would be no *point* in using the word 'understand' at all.

(ii) LFM 25 draws attention to similarities between 'understand' and 'intend'. People say 'I intend to play chess' (like 'Now I understand'). Since chess is a complex game defined by its rules, one might wonder how they know that it is chess that they are going to play. Do they have all the rules in mind when they declare their intention? Can they be uncertain about what it is that they intend to play? Could one say 'I believe that I intend to play chess, but I don't know. Let's see'? It is intelligible that exceptionally people might say 'I intend to play chess' and then do something quite different. But this could not be the norm. If people commonly avowed 'I intend to Φ' and never went on to Φ then their use of 'intend' would differ fundamentally from ours, and the word would have a different sense. That the utterance 'I intend to Φ' is a criterion of people's intention depends on normal coincidence of that avowal of the intention to Φ and subsequent Φing.

(iii) W. once remarked that what was wrong with his conception of elementary propositions in TLP was the confusion of method of projection with lines of projection.[4] it is noteworthy that TLP 2.1513–2.1515 explicitly includes the 'pictorial relationship', conceived as 'the correlations of the picture's elements with things', as part of the picture. It is surely *à propos* this that W. remarks 'The lines of projection might be called "the connection between the picture and what it

---

[4] See P. Winch, 'The unity of Wittgenstein's Philosophy', in *Studies in the Philosophy of Wittgenstein*, ed. Winch (Routledge and Kegan Paul, London, 1969), p. 12.

depicts"; but so too might the technique of projection' (Z §291). In PI,
W.'s adversary conceives of grasping a meaning as having a picture
which includes its lines of projection, to which the response is that such a
picture could still be misapplied.

PG 213 f. remarks that a picture (proposition, blueprint, mental image)
together with its lines of projection leaves room for different applications
(as in the case of the cube above). So one may count the projection lines as
part of the picture. But what of the method of projection? One conceives
of it as a bridge between symbol and what it symbolizes. But if it is such
a bridge, it is not built until the application is made (the symbol is not
used until it is applied).[5] One hankers to incorporate the method of
projection, the way the symbol is applied, into the symbol (picture) itself.
But there is no such thing. One can only *describe* a method of application,
and although one can incorporate the description into the picture
(symbol), the description is still only a description, not itself an application, but something standing in need of an application.

SECTION 142

1   The realization that our linguistic practices, the rules which we apply
and the regularities to which our use of language conforms, rest upon
normality conditions is of paramount importance to philosophers who
strive for a surview of grammar. But the relation of grammar to
normality conditions is more problematic than is indicated in this brief
remark, and also more significant.

§§84 ff. have established that concepts are in no sense defective if the
rules and practices of application of words that express them do not
determine every conceivable case. We usually draw boundaries only
where we need them. Where we need them is in turn determined by
normality conditions. To the extent that these are overthrown, our
concepts become increasingly pointless. Two important areas are singled
out for comment here: the domain of psychological concepts, and that of
measurement.

The normality conditions emphasized in PI concern normal human
reactions and responses in standard conditions, particularly in learning
contexts, e.g. that we respond to ostension by looking in the direction
indicated (not at the hand), that there are, for human beings, standard
natural reactions to the requirements to 'go on and do the same', that
'once burnt, twice shy' is the expression of our natural behaviour, etc.

---

[5] Cf. MS. 165, 82: 'Nicht die *Deutung* schlägt die Brücke zwischen dem Zeichen und dem
Bezeichneten / / Gemeinten //. Nur die Praxis tut das.' ('It is not the *interpretation* which
builds the bridge between the sign and what is signified // what is meant //. Only a practice
does that.')

Such general facts are not the ground or justification of our practices, but if they were different, we would not use language as we do.

PAGE 56 NOTE

1   This belongs with §142, but only if further amplication is given. The point seems to be this: the significance, importance, a concept has for us, e.g. the concept of a metre or kilogram, depends upon the obtaining of very general pervasive facts of nature, e.g. that by and large objects do not change their weights at random, things do not suddenly shrink or expand unpredictably, rigid objects do not unexpectedly turn elastic every now and then, and such like. Were these facts different our concepts of measurement would be useless.

It is cut from B i. §357. W. added '(Hierher die Bemerkung von den "kuriosen Beiträgen")' ('(Here the remark about "curious contributions")'). The allusion is to PI §415 (cf. also RFM 92); B i. §357 is derived from MS. 129, 193, where it is preceded by the following:

Man kann uns Nominalisten nennen, wenn wir uns nicht bewusst sind, dass die Grenze, die eine Definition zieht um der Wichtigkeit dieser Grenze willen gezogen ist. Und Sätze die diese Wichtigkeit erklären sind nun nicht solche über die Sprache.

(It is possible to call us nominalists if we are not conscious that the boundary drawn by a definition is only drawn for the sake of the importance of this boundary. And the propositions which explain this importance are not propositions about language.)

Further light is shed on this by MS. 130, 136 f.:

Die *Fakten* der menschlichen Naturgeschichte, die auf unser Problem Licht werfen, sind uns [nur?] schwer zu sehen // finden //, denn unsre Sprache // Rede // *geht an ihnen vorbei*, sie ist mit andern Dingen beschäftig. (So sagen wir einem 'Geh ins Geschäft und kauf . . .'—nicht—'Setz den linken Fuss vor den rechten Fuss etc. etc., dann leg Geld auf den Schalter, etc.')

(The *facts* of human natural history which cast light upon our problem are difficult to see // find //, for our language // discourse //*passes them by*, being busy with other matters. (Thus we say to someone, 'Go to the shop and buy . . .'— not—'Put the left foot in front of the right foot, etc. etc., then put money on the counter, etc.').)

CHAPTER 6

Meaning and Understanding
(§§143–184)

INTRODUCTION

§§143–84 constitute a sustained argument which takes us to the heart of W.'s philosophy of language. We have already seen some of the baffling variety of links drawn between the concept of meaning and related concepts—baffling inasmuch as so many of the *apparent* equations seem non-equivalent (e.g. meaning is use, meaning is what is given by explanation of meaning, meaning is assertion-conditions, meaning is method of verification). Here at last W. begins to lay bare the core of his new philosophy. The pivotal concept is that of understanding (and to that extent W.'s conception could be summarized in the slogan 'A theory of meaning is a theory of understanding', *if understood correctly*, and if the term 'theory' is taken as thinly as possible). §§143–84 are an examination of the concept of understanding. §§185–242 (cf. Volume 2) will be an equally thorough examination of understanding rules, with the emphasis upon rules.

Meaning, W. has argued, is what is given by explanation of meaning (and explanation, like proof, must be surveyable, like truth, immanent). Explanation of meaning belongs to grammar, gives rules for the use of an expression. It is linked with understanding an expression inasmuch as giving a correct explanation is one criterion for knowing, understanding, its meaning (and using it correctly, in accord with the rules for its use, is another). Linguistic competence (understanding a language) is mastery of a rule-governed technique. Each of the connections is complex and has multiple ramifications. A proper grasp of them involves obtaining a surview which will enable us to see through the mists of confusion that envelop these internal relations.

The chapter divides into three parts: A §§143–55, B §§156–78, C §§179–84.

Part A(§§143–55) concerns the nature of understanding in general, understanding a rule in particular. The example which dominates the discussion is understanding the rule of an arithmetical series (which provides a model of understanding the meaning of an expression). If one knows the rule of a series, then one can apply the rule and produce a segment of the infinite series (just as, if one knows the meaning of 'x', one can apply it in the appropriate circumstances). The problem of the relation of rule and application is deferred. The indirect approach in strategy dictates that the standard misconceptions of understanding be assailed first.

Part A can be subdivided into three groups.

(a) §§143–6 introduce the problem. Conceptual abilities rest on brute, preconceptual abilities. Inasmuch as conceptual abilities are, with us, acquired, they rest on training. Training is only possible given standard natural reactions of trainees. It is important to look at our complex conceptual abilities as resting upon brute preconceptual abilities and to see that the hierarchical structure of conceptual abilities is, in one sense, contingent; e.g., our ability to survey is such-and-such, but could be more or less. If it were different, the conceptual structures we would create (the language-games we would engage in) would be different (§144). Explanation itself presupposes possession of abilities which, with us, are acquired through training; but it too rests upon standard normal reactions and abilities (e.g. recognition of recurrent patterns, discriminatory abilities). Mastery of a technique, however, is, in general, a matter of degree and there is no sharp borderline between partial and complete mastery. Since understanding (like an ability) is identical with none of its behavioural manifestations, one is inclined to think of it as the *source* of its manifestations, to see understanding a rule as a *state* from which applications of the rule flow. This is a false picture.

§147 is a bridging remark. Although application is a criterion of understanding, one is inclined to say that one's own knowledge that one understands is not an inductive inference from one's past performance. Understanding, one thinks, is an inner state (or process) which, in one's own case, one recognizes introspectively.

(β) §§148–50 explore this false picture by contrasting understanding with genuine mental states and processes. The latter take time, can be interrupted and continued. But 'being able to do . . .' does not take time (unlike learning to be able to do . . .). Knowing, understanding, and being able to do something are closely related, and categorially different from inner states (whether of mind or of brain, whether conscious or unconscious).

(γ) §§151–5 examine the phenomenon of sudden understanding ('Now I know!'), which may incline one initially to think that understanding is an event or performance. So W. describes what happens when one suddenly understands, namely various accompanying processes. So now one might think that understanding is one of those, or some further hidden process. But none of these accompanying processes are either necessary or sufficient for understanding. Understanding is not a mental process at all, although it may be accompanied by mental processes, and its overt manifestations are (defeasible) criteria for its attribution. What makes a person's utterance 'Now I understand!' right are not inner on-goings, but the circumstances of the utterance. This theme is resumed at §179.

The structure of Part A:

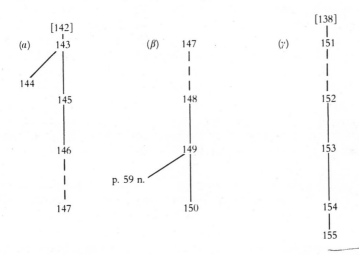

Part B (§§156–78) consists of a detailed examination of reading, conceived simply as mapping signs or sounds on to sounds or signs (irrespective of understanding what is read). The point of this lengthy interpolation is to destroy the numerous misleading pictures of rule-guided behaviour which we are inclined to adopt. The philosophical examination of reading is intended to illuminate the nature of understanding, conceived of as akin to an ability, in particular the nature of understanding a rule. It destroys false pictures of the 'subjective' aspect of rule-guidedness, i.e. of what it is to be following, applying, conforming, or intending to conform to a rule. It is complementary to PI §§185–242, which is concerned with the 'objective' aspect of rule-guidedness, i.e. with what it is for a certain consequence to be determined by, follow from, be derived from, a rule.

Five great misconceptions dominate the misleading pictures we make for ourselves in this area. (None of them are unique here, but are rather general, mutually supporting, illusions in the dialectic of reason.) First, our craving for the *essence* of an object or phenomenon drives us to look for a defining characteristic beneath the multiplicity of circumstances that justify the application of a term. Like Peer Gynt we strip the onion of its skins in search of its essence, discarding them successively, and when we fail to find its heart, we think we have come upon a singularly mysterious, elusive, phenomenon. Secondly, the inner/outer picture of the mind, rooted in the grammatical asymmetry between first- and third-person present-tense 'psychological' verbs, exercises a bewitching fascination. The 'inner' is hidden to all but its owner, whose access to it is privileged; others must make do with mere outward behaviour. I know whether I understand, am reading, can do thus-and-so; others can only conjecture. Thirdly, we are prone to construe verbs of ability as descriptions of states of the object which has the ability or power in question. In the special case of human 'psychological' abilities, we construe being able to read, speak, sing a tune, as special mental states, and the exercises of those abilities as special experiences (cf. Understanding and ability', pp. 322 ff.). Fourthly, we constantly tend, when philosophizing, to search for (and when we do not find, to postulate) intermediate, explanatory links. Since reading is not mere utterance of phonemes subsequent to seeing the appropriate words, we search for a special connecting experience or mechanism that will, we think, distinguish reading from pretending to read, and also explain the reading. So too in the case of understanding a rule, obeying a command, meaning something by what one says, acting voluntarily, and many other related phenomena. We are misled here by confusing philosophy with science, and by a consequent tendency to look for an *explanation*, a *theory*, instead of a description of the grounds of application or circumstances of correct use of an expression. We dimly apprehend categorial differences, e.g. between rule and application, ability and its exercise, psychological states or experiences and their behavioural manifestation, but, failing to apprehend the grammatical nature of a categorial distinction, we think we perceive a logical gap that must be bridged. So we look for, or postulate, a link. Finally, a wide range of misconceptions surround the notion of normativity. Following a rule is not merely acting in accord with it. It is being guided by it, acting because of it, deriving what is required from the rule. And here, under the impact of previous pressures, we search for the essence of guidance or derivation. We think that we can find it in a causal nexus or the feeling of one, in the experience of guidance or the feeling of motivating force, in a peculiar intimation given by a rule. And as the various attempts are seen to be unsatisfactory, we think that the 'experience of normativity' is quite particular, but indescribable, elusive and mysterious.

The examination of reading, conceived as mastery of (i.e. knowing or understanding) the 'rule of the alphabet', exemplifies the intermingling of these subtle poisons. In so doing it further clarifies the nature of understanding and ability. §§156–78 consist of fairly consecutive exposition (being immediately derived largely from Br.B. and its *Umarbeitung* EPB, which are among the most *continuous* of W.'s writings).

It can roughly be divided into three groups: (α) §§156–61; (β) §§162–4; (γ) §§165–78.

(a) §156 introduces the example of reading and lays bare the temptation to think that reading (like understanding in one of its aspects) is a special conscious activity of the mind. It also shows how, under pressure, alternative pictures are substituted, e.g. that reading is an *unconscious* activity of the mind or an activity of the brain. §§157–8 briefly dismiss the mechanical (neural) picture. §§159–61 return to the theme of §156, i.e. reading *qua* conscious activity; no matter what experiences accompany reading, they are neither necessary nor sufficient conditions for reading, nor are they criteria for reading.

The structure of Part B, group (α):

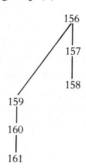

(β) In §§162 ff. a new departure is made. ((β) and (γ) could be treated as one continuous grouping. We have separated them because (β) does not emphasize the experiential component of normativity, which is prominent in (γ).) Thus far both a mechanistic connection and a mentalistic associationist one have been suggested to mediate between the operative facts (the letters) and the rule-guided action (reading), and both duly rejected. §162 attempts to introduce a normative component into the analysis of reading, i.e. one reads only when one *derives* the copy from the original. This is the first of many similar gambits. Deriving, it is argued in §§163–4, is no less a family resemblance concept than reading itself. It cannot help uncover the essence of reading in any conscious mental activity.

The structure of Part B, group (β):

(γ) §165 returns to the original suggestion of §156, i.e. to the thought that reading is a particular experience, elusive and slightly mysterious. The words I read (as opposed, say, to those I repeat from memory while pretending to read) *come* in a special way, 'of themselves' (for, to be sure, I don't make them up). But again, no *experiences* of the way they come are either individually necessary, not jointly or disjunctively sufficient for reading. The fiction of the special way the words come, and the idea that reading is a quite particular but elusive process, are examined in §§165–8.

§§169–78 attempt various related moves which might seem to illuminate the putative nexus which the idea of 'the special way the words come' failed to capture. Which way do they come? Do the signs cause the utterance, or constitute a reason for them, so that one feels the causation or justification (§169)? One is inclined to say that one *feels the influence* of the operative facts, or that one is *guided* by them, that the letters *intimate* the sounds to be uttered. The experience of guidance, influence, deliberation, 'experiencing the because', are severally examined up to §178. In each case the same general points hold: reading (following the rule of the alphabet) is a rule-guided activity, but its essence is not to be found in any accompanying experiences. Being able to read is an ability, not a mental state or reservoir, from which the overt performance flows. Reading is the exercise of that ability; it is not something defined by inner processes, but rather by the public criteria in the various circumstances that justify application of the term.

The structure of Part B, group (γ):

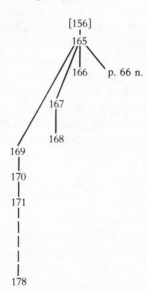

Part C returns to the theme of §151: the utterance 'Now I can go on (understand)', with its misleading suggestions of introspective inductive correlation of inner experience and outer performance. The utterance is akin to a signal (§180); it is an avowal, not a report upon an inner observation, nor a description of the circumstances of its correct employment. Indeed, the avowal may be correctly used even though the subsequent performance may not be forthcoming, for though the failure defeats the criterial support given by a sincere avowal, special circumstances (e.g. an interruption between avowal and performance) may defeat the defeating force of the failure (§181). §182 is a highly compressed discussion of ability and its defeasibility. §183 touches on different conditions of possibility, and §184 discusses again the reservoir picture associated with ability and its avowal.

The structure of Part C:

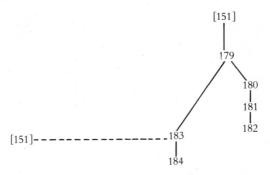

The illusions surrounding the concept of understanding that are so carefully dissected in §§143–84 (and its voluminous MS. sources) are not examined merely for their own sake. They are commonly correlates of fallacious conceptions of meaning. In particular, if meaning is conceived of on a calculus model, then a large variety of *distortions* of the concept of understanding must follow on pain of a total divorce of meaning from understanding. For the priority of meaning over understanding in the calculus model necessitates that the account of understanding be tailored to fit the shape of the theory of meaning. The theory of meaning, if truly 'scientific', will have the form of an axiomatic system from which all the meaningful sentences of a language flow. But if such a theory is to have any role in explaining linguistic behaviour, it must be systematically related to it. This is the task of the 'theory of understanding': it must provide principles in virtue of which we can correlate linguistic behaviour with understanding. Understanding is an implicit knowledge of the meaning-rules of the language. This implicit knowledge is something inferred from observable behaviour; understanding is an hypothesis about the *mechanism* that generates linguistic behaviour in accord with encoded meaning-rules. What the nature of the mechanism is is disputed. It may be conscious, or unconscious, accessible to introspection or inaccessible. It may be neural rather than mental. One day we shall discover. Understanding is the inner machinery, concealed in the 'black box' (mind or brain), the input of which is the circumstances and stimuli to which a language-user is exposed, and the output of which is speech. The rules of the mechanism are supplied by the 'theory of meaning'; the machinery which operates behind the overt linguistic behaviour is that with which a 'theory of understanding' concerns itself. It is W.'s aim in §§143–242 to undermine this picture completely.

Correlations

PI	PPI	PI	PPI
143	125	163 ⎫ 164 ⎬	141
144	126		
145	127	165	142
146	128	166	143
147	129	167	144
148	130	168	145
149 ⎫ 150 ⎬	131	169	146
		170	147
p. 59 n.	—	171	148
151	132	172	149
152 ⎫ 153 ⎬	133	173	150
154 (a) and (b) ⎫ 155 ⎬	134	174 ⎫ 175 ⎬	151
156	134, 135	176 ⎫ 177 ⎬	152
157 ⎫ 158 ⎬	136	178	153
159	137	179 ⎫ 180 ⎬	154
160	138	181	155
161	139	182	—
162	140	183	156
		184	157

Understanding and ability
1. Introduction   2. 'We regard understanding as the essential thing, and signs as something inessential' (PG 39)   3. Meaning and under-standing as mental phenomena   4. Understanding as a state, process, activity, or experience   5. Resultant philosophical confusions   6. Understanding and meaning are not processes, experiences, or mental states   7. Understanding and ability   8. Understanding as a family resemblance concept

SECTION 143

1   The opening move in an extended campaign to obtain a surview of understanding and hence of meaning is to examine the foundation of the ability to follow a rule. Using the example of an arithmetical rule, W. aims to establish general points about following rules. The ability to apply predicates, no less than the ability to expand a series according to a rule, is normative. (Why is the arithmetical example given pride of place? Partly because W. is waging a campaign on two fronts. It was no coincidence that the first continuation of PPI, which broke off at PI §189, was what is now RFM I (rearranged).)

W.'s first point is that the ability to understand the formation rule rests upon a brute reaction to training, namely repetition. The teaching, at this level, is not a matter of cognition and calculation, nor of explanation, but only of training. Secondly, the possibility of this training and subsequent training, teaching, and explanation rests on brute reaction which is *normal* (cf. §142). Thirdly, understanding, misunderstanding, and not under-standing are distinguished by the difference between reacting correctly to training, making systematic mistakes, and making random mistakes. Fourthly, the borderline between random and systematic error is fuzzy, and hence, by implication, the borderline between misunderstanding and not understanding. The close and complex connections between ability, performance, and understanding are already drawn here.

1.1   (i) '. . . die *Möglichkeit der Verständigung* . . .': 'the *possibility of communication*'. There are hierarchies of abilities. One can only learn the rule of a series (to apply the rule of a series) if one has learnt to repeat the figures, and so one can apply the rule only if one can repeat the figures.

(ii) 'And then communication stops at *that* point': i.e. random mistakes betoken lack of understanding, hence one cannot progress. If the pupil cannot copy out the series in anything but a random order, the teacher can do nothing with him. But a systematic mistake (§143(d)) may provide the basis for further development, although here too the capacity to learn may come to an end (cf. Exg. §144).

2   (i) PPI §125 begins 'Betrachten wir zur Klärung unsrer Begriffe diese Art von Sprachspiel' ('In order to clarify our concepts, let us examine this kind of language-game'), which makes it quite clear the point of the subsequent investigation is a perfectly general investigation into concept possession.

(ii) LFM 27 draws the same kind of distinction between misunderstanding and not understanding, and gives examples such as responding to '+2' correctly up to 100, and then adding threes, and beyond 1000 fours, etc. There W. moves directly on to the two central questions: (a) does it follow that we can never be sure that others understand? (b) *more importantly*, can we really know that we ourselves understand? (In PI these are deferred.)

(iii) Vol. XII, 35: 'Missverständnis—Unverständnis. Gegen das Missverständnis hilft Erklärung, gegen das Unverständnis—Abrichtung.—Wenn er sich abrichten läßt.' ('Misunderstanding—nonunderstanding. Explanation will help against misunderstanding, against non-understanding—training,—If he lets himself be trained.') Cf. Z §419 (MS. 136, 135): 'Any explanation has its foundation in training. (Educators ought to remember this.)'

SECTION 144

1   This discusses the last line of §143 (cf. PPI §126). The remark that the capacity to learn may come to an end is based neither on one's own experience (e.g., of finding that one just cannot master a certain branch of learning), nor simply on the fact that one can imagine a pupil's learning capacity ending here, there, or elsewhere. Rather the fact that one can imagine, i.e. that it is possible, that learning capacities should cease at a given point is of central importance in a general reorientation of one's over-all conception of language, meaning, and understanding. First, that abilities are hierarchically ordered is an important factor underlying our linguistic competence and a paramount factor in determining (but not justifying) the welter of language-games we do and can engage in. Secondly, that we do have certain elementary capacities (to imitate, react in standard ways, recognize shapes and colours, continue activities in a common pattern, etc.) is a general brute fact of human nature (cf. PI p. 56 n.) which is crucial for our having the kind of language we have. The *essential surveyability* of grammar (and of *proof* in arithmetic as part of grammar) depends for its limits upon our abilities (cf. RFM III).

1.1   (i) 'I wanted to put that picture . . .': this is a reply to the question 'Then what am I doing with that proposition?' With that proposition W. is sketching a possibility, not in order to draw attention to what can be imagined, but to effect a change in perspective. The picture of the new possibility invites novel ranges of comparisons, analogies, and similarities. The point of sketching out new possibilities is *not* to discover, or seek to persuade someone 'that, contrary to our preconceived ideas, it is possible to think such-and-such' (cf. Exg. §109), but to

bring about a new conception of the matter in view. Cf. Vol. XV, 106, 'Unsere Welt erscheint ganz anders, wenn man sie mit andern Möglichkeiten umgibt'. ('Our world appears quite different, if one surrounds it with different possibilities.')
Cf. also MS. 157(b), 14:

Die Lösung der Probleme besteht im Eliminieren des beunruhigenden Aspekts den gewisse Analogien in unserer Grammatik auslösen.
Die Philosophie verändert den Aspekt. Indem sie andere Analogien aufzeigt. Zwischenglieder einschiebt, etc.

(The solution of our problems consists in eliminating the disquieting aspects generated by certain analogies contained in our grammar.
Philosophy changes aspects—by bringing out different analogies—inserting connecting links, etc.)

(ii) '(Indian mathematicians: "Look at this.")': in PPI §126 (= Z §461) this was sufficiently long to be intelligible: 'I once read somewhere that a geometrical figure, with the words "Look at this!", serves as a proof for certain Indian mathematicians. This looking too effects an alteration in one's way of seeing (*Anschauungsweise*).' The text to which W. alludes may be von Hartmann's *Philosophy of the Unconscious*,[1] pp. 320 f.:

It is in ethno-psychological respects extremely characteristic that the treatment of geometry among the Greeks aims at a rigorous discursive mode of proof, and sedulously ignores the most obvious intuitive demonstrations; whereas that of the Hindoos, in spite of an endowment for arithmetic far surpassing the Greeks, is yet entirely based on direct intuition, and is usually confined to an artificial construction in support of intuition, to which the one word 'see!' is appended.

The general principle of intuitively perceptible proof is propounded by Schopenhauer (whom von Hartmann also discusses) in *The World as Will and Representation*, I, §15. Noteworthy in W.'s discussions of mathematics is the frequent appeal to stroke diagrams and the like as surveyable proofs (which look like, but are not, experiments, and seem to be, but are not, appeals to a common intuition).
Cf. also MS. 161, 6:

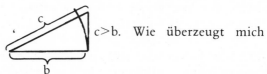

c>b. Wie überzeugt mich

dieser Beweis? It convinces my eyes.' ('. . . How does this proof convince me? . . .')

[1] Eduard von Hartmann, *Philosophy of the Unconscious, Speculative Results according to the Inductive Method of Physical Science*, with a preface by C. K. Ogden (Kegan Paul, Trench and Trubner, London, 1931). We owe this reference to Professor F. Cioffi.

SECTION 145

1   This continues §143. Four main points are made: first, if a person Φs it
does not follow that he has the ability to Φ, since we distinguish a fluke
(beginner's luck) from exercise of an ability. Secondly, the grounds for
ascription of an ability are, in a sense, partly indeterminate. Whether A
can Φ is determined by his usual success in Φing, but there is no sharp
ratio of success to failure, and no lower bound to the number of trials
necessary. Thirdly, the role which explanation can play in teaching
depends upon the pupil's reactions. Such things as using particular
emphases, underlining figures, writing them in columns to draw attention to regularities, all have a role in teaching and explaining. But if, e.g.,
the pupil suffers from various mental deficiencies, such as inability to
distinguish certain patterns of recurrences of written symbols, some such
explanations will be out of the question. The acquisition of the hierarchy
of abilities involved in a linguistic competence depends upon brute or
trained reactions. Moreover, this genetic point is mirrored analytically to
the extent that such reactions are, in the appropriate circumstances,
elements in the complex criteria for the possession of various abilities.
Fourthly, in §145(b) the central issue of the subsequent debate is raised
again. The criterion for having understood a rule with limitless application is not the successful completion of an infinite set of tasks. One
cannot state a limit to the number of times the pupil must apply the rule
'+1' before he can be said to be able to count, or to the number of things
he must identify as red before he can be said to know what 'red' means.
But it does not follow that we can never know whether he has
understood. Rather, understanding is determined by criteria, which are
in principle defeasible.

1.1   'this will only be the case when he is often successful': PPI §127 adds
'(Aber wie oft ist "*oft*")' ('(But how often is "*often*")').

2   (i) BB 89 f. elaborates the role of encouragement in training. Imagine
that one is training a pupil to use a table correlating words and pictures, with
the object of enabling him to use new tables or even to construct them
for himself. Acts of encouragement will play a central role in the training,
but they are only possible, only have a role, given certain responses. One
can train a dog to retrieve, and in the course of training use gestures or
sounds of encouragement. But they only have a point because of the way
the dog reacts to them. A cat does not respond to such encouragements,
and so such acts are pointless (cf. Z §187).
        (ii) LA 2 stresses the importance of exaggerated gestures and facial
grimaces in teaching a child (especially words like 'good'). The child

understands, reacts appropriately, to these gestures and grimaces. If he did not, he could understand *nothing*.

(iii) Vol. XII, 33 makes explicit the relation of explanation to a hierarchy of abilities. How can one ask for explanations of word-·meanings? Compare (1) What colour is called 'chrome-yellow'? (2) What is C'''?[2] (3) What does the (Latin) word 'nefas' mean? The first, and possibly the second, can be answered by pointing or showing. The third can be answered by a translation or by examples of its application. But what if someone who has not learnt mathematics asks 'What does "integral" mean?'? One can only answer: 'It is a mathematical expression which I cannot explain to you until you have learnt more mathematics.'

SECTION 146

1   This begins the examination of the false pictures of understanding which we are inclined to entertain. §145 argued that there is no specific lower bound to the numbers the pupil must write down if he is said to have grasped the rule of the series. So, confronted with the question 'Has he understood (grasped) the system if he continues up to the nth place?', one is inclined to distinguish understanding the system from applying one's understanding. (And this is right, for an ability is not identical with its exercise!) The infinite possible applications are then thought to be 'contained' in the understanding of the rule, and the actual applications to flow from one's understanding as water from a reservoir. So one thinks of understanding as a *state* which is the *source* of correct use.

The first move against this picture is to show the analogy between this (imagined) relation of understanding to use and the relation of the algebraic formula which expresses the rule of the series to its application (its infinite possible applications and any given segment of its actual application). But, W. remarks, this is where we were before: and this in two senses. First, we started out by trying to explain what is involved in B's understanding an order to expand a series according to a rule (§143). The suggested account of understanding a rule is simply a projection of a wholly misleading picture of the relationship of rule and application (formula and series), as if the series were contained in the rule like a string of pearls in a box, waiting to be pulled out (cf. 2). Secondly, as intimated in §141, one can think of different 'projection lines' for any rule, and any application can, with an appropriate interpretation, be brought into line with a given rule. So *what*, in this picture, constitutes understanding?

The fact of the matter is that the application is a *criterion* of understand-

----

[2] 'das dreigestrichene C': C three octaves above middle-C.

ing. And understanding is not a state but akin to an ability.

2   PG 44 gives further reasons for adopting this false picture of understanding, namely that understanding is something *inner*, spiritual
or mental, that we can only *manifest* it in its exercise, but cannot *exhibit*
it (just as one cannot exhibit one's pain). Here understanding is surrounded by the standard mythology of the mental. Cf. also PG 82 f.:
whether another understands is something he *knows*, but we can only
guess.

2.1   (i) 'The understanding itself is a state which is the *source* of the correct
use': PG 49 discusses the parallel moves with respect to knowledge and
ability. To conceive of knowledge as 'the hypothesized reservoir out of
which the visible water flows' is a false picture.

Tracing the metaphor back to BT 150 f. reveals the various ramifications of the model. When I use words, I do not know when or how I
learnt them. But if grammar, the rules for the use of these words, is
essential to their meaning, then must I not have these rules in my mind if
the words are to have any meaning for me? Or is it as in a piece of
machinery: the cogwheels do not know the laws that determine the
movements they can make when engaged. Do the rules of grammar
determine what I do with the words I use? (If the calculus model of
language is one of axioms, formation, and transformation rules, that will
'mechanically' generate all meaningful sentences of the language, is the
speaker of the language a biological mechanism, a sentence-generating
machine?) For, to be sure, I do not have the whole use (all the rules of
use) of a word before my mind when I use it. So how can I know what I
mean by 'x' when I use it (cf. Vol. XII, 98)?

Similarly, one can say that when I play chess I know the rules ('Have
them in my head'). But is not this 'having them in my head' just an
hypothesis, since I only 'have them' in so far as I apply them in playing?
So this 'knowing' is merely an hypothesized reservoir out of which the
visible water flows (cf. Exg. p. 59 n. (b)).

BB 143 calls the 'reservoir' model a 'general disease of thinking', and
gives as a further example 'The fashion changes because the taste of
people changes': here the taste is pictured as the mental reservoir from
which changes of style and fashion flow.

(ii) 'Isn't one thinking of the derivation of a series from its algebraic
formula?': the reason is clear (above). Cf. PG 55:

Here it can easily seem as if the sign [in this case the formula] contained the
whole of the grammar; as if the grammar were contained in the sign like a string
of pearls in a box and he had only to pull it out. (But this kind of picture is just
what is misleading us.) As if understanding were an instantaneous grasping of
something from which later we only draw consequences which already exist in
an ideal sense before they are drawn.

One here treats *understanding* as an inner state from which its manifestations flow in a way analogous or parallel to the classical conception of meaning as transcendently *determining* application and correct use.

It is fascinating to note here how different 'pictures' interlock, or succeed each other kaleidoscopically, each dragging in its wake a host of misconceptions. If, in the fundamental correlation between meaning and understanding, the two are not taken as equipollent, but the notion of meaning is taken as primary, the resultant conceptions of understanding are *forced* into the form of a 'theory' of mental (or neural) states (conscious or unconscious). It is from these that the manifestations of understanding flow, constituting evidence for *hypothesized* inner mechanisms.

Section 147

1   This picks up the last sentence of §146, and presents a classical objection resting on first-person/third-person asymmetry in respect of psychological verbs. When I say understand, I do not say so on the basis of my past applications! I know that I *mean* such-and-such a series (since I understand the rule) no matter how far I have developed it previously!

(b) ironically strengthens this objection: my knowledge of the rule (how to apply it) must surely be independent of my remembered applications, since the later are finite and the series infinite!

These two issues will be hounded mercilessly in the sequel. Saying 'I understand' is commonly an avowal, not a description; ascribing understanding to others rests on criteria. Possible applications of a rule may be infinite, but ascription of understanding is fully justified by a finite number of applications.

Section 148

1   This questions the categorial classification of knowledge and understanding as states of mind, processes, or events. The first line of attack concerns temporality: states and processes are continuous, having reasonably determinate beginnings and endings, can be clocked, interrupted, and then resumed. So when does one know (understand) the application of a rule—continuously, or only when one is thinking of it? One is inclined to answer 'Always', for one's understanding does not lapse when one falls asleep, but if continuously, not in the way that a headache, which is a 'mental state', is continuous (cf. 'Understanding and ability', pp. 335 f.). One's knowledge is like knowledge of the alphabet or

multiplication tables. But one is still inclined to think of one's understanding as a state of consciousness, process, or event. Why, and what is
wrong with this is examined subsequently.

2   (i) PPI §130 adds a paragraph: if you now know various tunes by heart
how is it that they do not together make a frightful cacophony? If you
know the alphabet now, it does not mean that you are running through it
in your mind, or that you are in a state of mind that is somehow
equivalent to reciting it.

(ii) Vol. XII, 101 discusses Mozart's remark in a letter[3] that when
composing he sometimes could behold the whole composition simultaneously in advance of writing it down. Does this not provide empirical
confirmation of the reservoir 'picture'? But Mozart cannot have meant
that he 'heard' the whole composition in a moment, as if all the notes
were being struck together, or as if the piece were being played at a great
speed. The question is: what does the combination of words ('I saw
(heard) the whole piece in a moment') mean? Under what circumstances
is it correctly used, and when incorrectly? Cf. MS. 180(a), 7.

SECTION 149

1   This is important, and extensively elaborated elsewhere in W.'s writings.
(Cf. 'Understanding and ability', pp. 326 ff.) One is inclined, for reasons
already explained, to think of knowing, e.g., the alphabet, as a state
underlying the application of the knowledge. The state is then conceived
as something which will explain the manifestation (application) of the
knowledge, hence the temptation to think that it is an occult mental
mechanism or an (as yet) unknown neurological mechanism. But the
'state' of knowing the ABC, multiplication tables, etc., is a disposition (and
a disposition is not a causal mechanism which explains its exercise).
Moreover, it is objectionable to talk of a state here at all. For if
understanding or knowing were a state of something (mind or brain),
then there would have to be two different criteria (a priori grounds) for its
attribution: the construction of the apparatus and its exercise. But it is the
latter, not the former, that is a criterion for knowing and understanding.
Of the former we know next to nothing, and what little we know is
neurological discovery, not grammatical convention. Our feeling that
there must be a neurological (or mental) apparatus underlying the exercise
of an ability results from the pressure of a false picture. There may or
may not be; and if there is, that structure is not the ability, but its causal

---

[3] This notorious letter is quoted in various writings on Mozart. e.g., Edward Holmes,
The Life of Mozart, reprinted in Everyman's Library (J. M. Dent and Sons, London, 1921),
pp. 254 ff. It is almost certainly a forgery (cf. Emily Anderson, *The Letters of Mozart*,
(Macmillan, London, 1966) vol. I, p. xvii), but this does not affect W.'s point.

foundation. 'Understanding' does not *mean* a certain unknown but conjectured neurological or mental structure.

Nor would it help to cover up the categorial distinctions between states of consciousness, like pain, and phenomena like understanding or knowing by means of the contrast between conscious and unconscious states. It is easy to see why one might try: for one might think that when one 'exercises' one's knowledge or understanding, then this is a conscious state, but when one does not, it 'lapses', as it were, into the unconscious. But the distinction between conscious and unconscious mental states (as used, e.g., by psychoanalysts) is not the distinction between conscious mental states and dispositions.

1.1   *ll.*1–2: after 'Zustand der Seele' (state of mind) PPI §131 continues: 'so kann (könnte) das nur den Zustand eines hypothetischen Seelenapparates bedeuten, etwa einen Zustand unsres Gehirns . . .' ('then it could only mean a state of a hypothetical mental apparatus, perhaps a state of the brain').

2   (i) PG 48 f.: if knowledge is called a 'state' it can only be in the sense in which we talk of states of the body or of a physical model. So to talk of unconscious states invokes the idea of a mind–model in psychology (or physiology). W. does not here dwell on the psychoanalytic sense of 'unconscious state', but on the implications of introducing talk of, e.g., unconscious toothache. The point he stresses is that this is a grammatical move to which sense has to be assigned, not an empirical discovery. I could talk of 'unconscious toothache' if I stipulated that this is to mean, e.g., having an infected tooth that does not hurt. 'Conscious state' (in the 'old' sense) does not stand to 'unconscious state' (in the 'new' sense) as 'a chair which I see' stands to 'a chair which I don't see' (because it is behind me).

(ii) PG 80: since we *do* distinguish understanding from its manifestation, how can we avoid postulating an inner state underlying and causing these manifestations (their *source*; cf. PI §146)? Is not W. saying that there is no such thing as understanding, but only manifestations of it (no such thing as pain, only pain behaviour)? Here he replies correctly, but misleadingly, that the question is as senseless as the question whether there is a number three. 'I can only describe piecemeal the grammar of the word "understand" and point out that it differs from what one is inclined to portray without looking closely', i.e. that it is not the grammar of a *state*.

2.1   'there ought to be two different criteria for such a state': cf. PG 82 where two moves are made: (a) we are inclined to call understanding a mental state or process, and this allocates the concept to the wrong grammatical category, namely an hypothesized (inductively inferred) state or process.

(b) This is exacerbated since there *are* similarities between mental states or processes (even though understanding is *not* a state or process) and, say, brain-processes which are (often) hypothesized processes (in a way in which genuine mental states are *not*). *But* it makes sense to conduct a direct check on a brain-process by, e.g., opening the skull, yet there is no such thing (it is senseless) in the case of mental processes.

PAGE 59 NOTE (a)

1   Cut from B i. §79, this further elaborates §§148–9. It reinforces that argument by comparing understanding with genuine mental states like depression, excitement, pain. The continuity of mental states is not paralleled by continuity of understanding, for although I may say that I have understood such-and-such since yesterday, it makes no sense to add 'continuously'. One can say 'I have understood the meaning of "x" since yesterday's lesson', but not 'I have understood it all day' (or 'continuously'). Mental states can be interrupted (e.g. pain, by an analgesic), but 'interruption' of understanding consists in no longer being able to do something, and normally would not have any sharp temporal location (when did you 'stop' understanding French?). To forget, temporarily, how to do something (e.g. to integrate) is not an interruption of a state, but a temporary loss of an ability.

1.1   Curiously, this begins by apparently asserting that understanding is a state, only not a mental one, a position W. clearly repudiates (cf. 'Understanding and ability', pp. 609 f., and 2 below). The MS. source (Vol. XII, 88) begins, less misleadingly, 'Ist "ein Wort verstehen" ein seelischer Zustand?' ('Is "understanding a word" a mental state?'). Possibly the rephrasing is merely ironic.

The MS. inserts after 'We also say "Since yesterday I have understood this word."' :

. . . wenn es mir etwa gestern erklärt wurde;—aber verstand ich es ununter-brochen?—Ja man könnte von einer Unterbrechung des Verstehens reden wenn ich es einmal vergessen und dann wieder gelernt hätte; aber hat es Sinn zu fragen: 'Um wieviel Uhr has Du aufgehört es zu verstehen?' wie man fragen kann: 'Um wieviel Uhr haben deine Schmerzen nachgelassen?'?

(If, perhaps, it was explained to me yesterday;—but have I understood it uninterruptedly? Yes, one could talk of an interruption of understanding if I had at some time forgotten it and had then learnt it again;[4] but does it make sense to ask: 'At what time did you cease understanding it?' as one can ask: 'At what time did your pains get less?'?)

---

[4] But cf. Z §85.

It continues:

'Ich verstehe das Wort "Ventil" seit gestern'—hast Du das Verstehen die ganze Zeit gespürt? Du konntest das Wort seit gestern anwenden; wie Du auch tausend andere Wörter anwenden kannst—und schon seit langer Zeit. Wenn man das Verstehen des Wortes einen Zustand der Seele nennen will, dann in dem Sinne wie gewisse *Fähigkeiten*. Z. B. die Fähigkeit zu Rechnen, eine Sprache zu sprechen, Schach zu spielen, ein Gedicht aufzusagen.

('I have understood the word "valve" since yesterday.'—did you sense the understanding the whole time? You have been able to use the word since yesterday; as you can also use thousands of other words—since long ago. If one wants to call understanding words a mental state, then in the sense of certain *abilities*, e.g. the ability to calculate, to speak a language, to play chess, to recite a poem.)

A certain ambiguity, however, remained at this stage, for W. was willing to call such abilities 'hypothetical states of mind' (Vol. XII, 90) or states of a hypothetical mind-model, brain or nervous system.

2   (i) BT 149 'Das Können und Verstehen wird von der Sprache scheinbar als Zustand dargestellt, wie der Zahnschmerz, und das ist die falsche Analogie, unter der ich laboriere.' ('Language represents being able to, and understanding, as if they were states, like toothache, and that is the false analogy under which I labour.') This 'state' conception of abilities, characteristic of BT and Vols. X–XII, is decisively repudiated in BB 117 f.

(ii) Z §§71 ff. (cf. B i. §80; TS 232, §57; Vol. XII, 89, and MS 135, 92) stresses the temporality distinction between abilities and states of consciousness such as pain, grief, anger. 'I can attend to the course of my pains, but not in the same way to that of my belief, or my translation, or my knowledge' (Z §75 = TS 229, §1639 = MS 134, 59).

Page 59 Note (b)

1   This strikes at a related target: if I know a system of rules (e.g. chess or arithmetical rules, or grammar), then that knowledge (i.e. ability) is possessed whether exercised or not (as my ability to run does not terminate when I sit down). The question 'When can you . . .?' is misleading in suggesting that being able to (knowing how) . . . is a process, event, or state. Since it bears a *kinship* to each, one is inclined to say both that one knows 'all the time', and that one knows at any given time when exercising the ability. *Then* it *does* seem odd that being able to play takes so little time and playing so long. But 'being able to do something' does not take time; it is not a process, state, or event, although acquiring the ability may take time, the sudden dawning of a

method of doing something may be an instantaneous event, and one may
have an ability for a time (between certain ages).

This snippet comes from B i. §86. Its MS. source (Vol. XII, 97) belongs
to a discussion of understanding and ability. Shortly before it is a section
(cf. Z §672) which points out that the fact that the conditions
(extraneous circumstances) for exercising an ability may be clockable
exacerbates our inclination to think that an ability is a state or process,
especially if we conflate ability with opportunity. Thus, if it is true that
so long as the temperature of the rod does not fall below . . . then it can
be forged, it would make sense to say, e.g., that I can forge it from 5.00 to
6.00. Or—so long as my pulse doesn't fall below . . . I can do the
calculation—which takes two minutes. One can rid oneself of the grip of
the wrong picture not by asking, misleadingly, 'When can you . . .?',
which is normally a question about *opportunity*, but slides readily into
'When do you know?'—but by asking 'How long does being able to . . .
take?', which is obviously nonsense.

In B i. §86, W. wrote '(Und nun überlege Dir den *alltäglichen* Gebrauch
von "Wann kannst Du Schach spielen?"!)'). ('(And now consider the
everyday use of "When can you play chess?"!)'). Consequently, 'Wann
kannst du Schach spielen?' would be better translated 'When *can* you play
chess?', and '. . . dass Schachspielenkönnen so kurze Zeit braucht' 'that
being able to play chess requires such a short time'. For the *everyday use* of
'When can you play chess?' is to make an appointment for a game (but
'When do you know how to play chess' has no everyday use! It is
philosophers' nonsense).

2   PG 50 illuminatingly compares the confusion about 'When can you . . .?'
with Augustine's confusion about '*When* do I measure a period of
time?'

SECTION 150

1.1   '"Mastery"': it is unclear why this is in scare-quotes. There are none in
parallel passages, cf. EBT 114 (= Vol. VII, 183), MS. 130, 47. The point
is that the grammar of 'Know' and 'understand' is related to that of
'mastering a technique' (cf. PI §199).

2   PLP 346: 'The grammar of "know" and of "can" runs for a stretch over
parallel tracks.'

SECTION 151

1   Hitherto the illusion of subsuming understanding under the category of
state has been examined. Now that the analogies between 'know', 'can',

and 'understand' have been brought out, we switch to the puzzles of 'instantaneous' understanding. Here is another analogy between the three terms: with all three one can *exclaim* 'Now I know (can do it; understand)!' This makes it look as if understanding is an event, 'something that makes its appearance in a moment'.

What is it that thus suddenly happens? W. describes various *very different* things that *might* happen. The theme is resumed at PI §§179 ff. and §§321 ff.

SECTION 152

1   Two curious phenomena have already surfaced. First, although we started in § 151 from the presumption that understanding is an event, when trying to describe it we immediately describe various mental processes. Secondly, none of the described processes are themselves understanding, i.e. none is either necessary or sufficient for understanding. Whether overt or 'inner', they are accompaniments or expressions of understanding, but not the thing itself!

1.1   '*Begleitvorgänge* oder *Äusserungen*': W. holds the cards close to his chest here. Ultimately he argues that the accompaniments are indeed mere accompaniments, and the manifestations of understanding are *critera* of understanding. Our original intuition that neither *are* understanding was, in a sense, correct. Our error is to think that they are symptoms of something that underlies them.

2   BB 113 elaborates the point: first, it is irrelevant whether the accompanying processes described are overt or covert, e.g. whether the formula of the series appears before my mind's eye, or whether I select it out of a list of formulae written on a blackboard before me. Secondly, understanding the principle of the series does not mean that such-and-such formula occurred to a person: if a parrot uttered the right formula we would not say that it understood!

SECTION 153

1   The visible accompaniments of understanding appear to be the crude manifestation of a subtle mental process (a typically Jamesian conception). So it looks as if we are trying, inductively or introspectively, to get hold of the real underlying process of understanding. But it is not a real attempt, for if we discovered any such thing (e.g. a certain electro-encephalographic wave), what would make *that* constant factor understanding, rather than a constant correlation of sudden understanding?

(The move is analogous to one with respect to family resemblance concepts.) Since it has to be *discovered* and *correlated* with understanding, it cannot itself be a ground for our ascribing understanding to a person. Finally, I can only look for something if I know what will count as finding it. If *real* understanding is 'hidden', what will count as finding *it*, as opposed to some accompaniment of it? The theme is picked up at PI §322: the question 'What happens when one suddenly understands?' is misleading, and the descriptions of the accompaniments of sudden understanding do not give us the meaning of 'understanding'. The question misleads us because it pushes us to the position of thinking that understanding is an indefinable experience. There *are* experiences of understanding, but the question to ask is *not* which of them *is* the understanding, but how do we compare these experiences, i.e. what criteria of identity *we fix* in virtue of which we denominate them 'experiences of understanding'. *That* will show us what we mean by 'understanding'!

One reason W.'s antagonist searches for *real understanding* beneath its apparent accompaniments is because he wishes to explain the avowal 'Now I understand' as an assertion made *because* I understood. (The idea is that certain phenomena must have something in common which makes us use the same word (cf. §65).) But this precludes the idea that the real process of understanding is *hidden*, for then I could never say 'Now I understand', since the evidence for it would be hidden from me.

1.1   'when I said "Now I understand" *because* I understood?!': a common move against which W. wars in his account of avowals (it is parallel to 'I said "I am in pain" *because* I was in pain'). The classical conception takes the avowal as a description of, or asserted on the grounds of, an identified inner state (cf. Exg. §180).

2   BB 113: we see that 'understanding' does not mean the same as the description of any of its accompaniments (since understanding is an ability, or akin to an ability, and its accompaniments are events, processes, or activities). We err when we jump to the conclusion that all the accompaniments are mere *symptoms*, inductively established correlates of a hidden mental process, activity, or state which is called 'being able to go on' and lies behind its exterior (or interior) manifestations.

Section 154

1   It is true that 'Now I understand the principle of the series' does not mean the same as 'The formula . . . occurs to me' (etc.). But it does *not* follow that the avowal of understanding describes a process behind or beside the

manifestation of understanding in uttering the formula, as if the latter were a symptom of understanding.

The idea of a hinterland ('behind') misleads us here. It is not a 'hidden' process which justifies my saying that I can go on. But W. now suggests that *if* there has to be anything 'behind the utterance of the formula' it is the circumstances which justify my utterance. This is unclear. The circumstances, together with the fact that the formula has occurred to me, do not constitute justifying grounds for my utterance (cf. PI §§179 f., 323 ff.). On the other hand, it is the circumstances, e.g. sitting in a classroom, being asked 'Who can continue?', together with the fact that the formula has occurred to me, which makes it *appropriate* to utter 'I can go on'. It is such circumstances which make it appropriate to *signal* one's comprehension (cf. PI §§179 ff.).

It is the idea that understanding is a mental process of *any* kind that misleads one here. One should rather look at the 'language-game' in which these expressions are used, how one is taught to use them (cf. § 179). There are characteristic processes, including mental ones, that accompany understanding (being able to go on), but understanding is not such a mental process. It is categorially distinct from mental processes.

2   PPI §134 does not contain PI §154 (d)–(e), but has instead what is now Z §446(b) (Z §446(a) = PI §154(c)). The point made is that our means of representation (grammar) produces an illusion. 'To understand' is a *verb*, so we think it must 'stand for' an *activity* of the mind. (Cf. BB 117: our inclination to think that abilities are *states* stems, *inter alia*, from the fact that we use the present-tense static verbs 'is capable of', 'is able to', 'can' when talking of abilities, thus suggesting that the phrases describe occurrent states.)

BB 113: 'B can continue . . .' does not mean the same as 'B says the formula . . .', but it does not follow that the former expression refers to an activity in the way the latter does. The error is analogous to this: we tell someone that the word 'chair' does not mean this particular chair, so he looks around the room for some other object which is its meaning; or worse, he tries to look *inside* the chair in order to find the *real* meaning of 'chair'.

SECTION 155

1.1   'justify': there is some tension throughout PI in respect of justification. On the one hand, criteria constitute justifying grounds for applying a term. On the other hand, many terms are used correctly but not on the basis of criterial grounds. Certainly there are, for them, criteria of understanding, distinctions between correct and incorrect use, etc. But the circumstances under which it is appropriate to utter an avowal, to apply a word like 'red' to an observed object, etc., are not justifying *grounds* for their use[5] (cf. §§377 ff.). PI §§89 (cf.RFM 406) marks this distinction by saying 'To use a word without a justification does not mean to use it without right.' Here, however, W. has resorted to the opaque formulation 'was ihn für uns berechtigt'.

Indeed it might be more perspicuous to claim that for us it is the circumstances under which he exclaims 'Now I can go on!' that constitute one criterion for saying that he understands that sentence. It is his utterance of that sentence, in those circumstances, that is a criterion for ascribing to him the ability to go on. In the language of §289, the circumstances do not justify him, but they do mean that he utters the avowal with right.

SECTION 156

1   This begins the lengthy interpolation of an examination of reading, the purpose of which is to illuminate the nature of understanding and ultimately of rule-following. It introduces various themes that are later considered in detail. (i) 'Reading' here is deliberately *detached* from understanding (cf. 2), since this example is to be used to illuminate understanding, and hence must not invoke understanding of what is read (but only understanding, mastery of the technique, of 'mapping' written words on to spoken or copied words, or spoken words on to written ones in dictation). Reading, therefore, is intended as an analogue of the rule-following involved in expanding a series. (ii) The variety of 'inner' and 'outer' accompaniments of reading is stressed. This too parallels the preceding discussion of understanding the principle of a series (§151). (iii) The inevitable inclination to think that reading is a 'special conscious activity of the mind' (just as understanding is conceived as a special state of mind) is argued to be derived particularly from distorted reflection upon the reading of a beginner (where phenomenological accompaniments and awareness of them is more pronounced). (iv) The temptation to think that only the pupil 'really knows' whether he is reading is mentioned, parallel to the suggestion that an agent has privileged access to his own understanding (§147). (v) The alternative 'classical' move to (iii) is raised, i.e. that reading is an hypothesis based on behaviour since it really is an 'inner mechanism' of the 'unconscious mind' or a neurological mechanism of the brain.

1.1   (i) 'Dies wird klarer werden . . .': PPI §134 explicitly introduces the

---

[5] There are important differences between groundless application of a predicate, e.g. 'red', and avowing.

examination of reading to throw light on understanding and knowing. BB 119 (EPB 172): the discussion of reading is introduced as a means of studying the idea of being guided by signs.

(ii) 'We have yet to discuss these propositions "He alone knows . . ."': a promise redeemed later on in the private language argument and doctrine of avowals.

(iii) 'And what goes on in them must distinguish reading from not reading.—But these mechanisms are only hypotheses': a methodological point. Any scientific hypothesis, if substantiated, may give a scientific explanation of a phenomenon designated by a concept. But it will not explain the meaning of the concept-word, which indeed it presupposes. Cf. Z §223 and 'The nature of philosophy', pp. 277 ff.

2   (i) PG 72 discusses reading *with* understanding in the context of a discussion of understanding. Reading with understanding is contrasted with reading without understanding, compared with following a melody, seeing the pattern of decorative ornament, etc. (The latter discussions (BB, EPB, PPI) separate reading from understanding.)

(ii) BB 119 f. is parallel but located *after* the discussion of the 'mechanism' conception of being guided, which, in PI, is deferred (§§158, 170, 172 ff.).

2.1   (i) 'But the part the word plays in our life, and therewith the language-game in which we employ it . . .': cf. BB 119, '(it would be extremely difficult to describe these circumstances even roughly)'.

(ii) 'we shall be inclined to say: it is a special conscious activity . . .': PG 99f. repudiates the move immediately, 'what is of interest to us can't be essentially something internal'; a derivation may be a perfectly overt performance. The 'inner'/'outer' distinction is of no interest in this context. (The strategy looks like a crude behaviourism—but it is neither crude, nor behaviourism. Cf. EBT 310: 'Ich fasse das Verstehen also, in irgend einem Sinne, behaviouristisch auf . . . Das Behaviouristische an meiner Auffassung besteht nur darin, dass ich keinen Unterschied zwischen "aussen" und "innen" mache. Weil mich die Psychologie nichts angeht.' ('I conceive of understanding, in a sense, behaviouristically . . . What is behaviouristic in my conception consists only in that I do not distinguish between "outer" and 'inner". Because psychology does not concern me.') What is not behaviouristic, of course, is W.'s refusal to equate understanding with the behaviour that is a criterion for it.)

(iii) 'The word "to read" is applied *differently* . . .': what in the one case we call an instance of reading, in the other we do not (BB 120). One is inclined to say that a beginner *can* read the numerals on the dial of a watch, whereas, in a sense, the practised reader cannot (PI §161(b)). Or, where a beginner, glancing at a sentence on an advertisement and producing the right utterance (e.g. 'Persil washes whiter'), will be said to be guessing or recognizing from the picture what slogan goes with it, the practised reader can rightly be said to read the slogan (cf. PI §164).

(iv) '. . . must distinguish reading from not reading': cf. BB 120—we imagine two different mechanisms (in reader and beginner) and that it is the internal working of the hypostatized mechanism that is the *real criterion* for a person's reading or not reading.

SECTION 157

1   The point is analogous to §145(b) and §146.

1.1   (i) 'This concept was therefore . . .' (§157 (d)): the *concept* of reading is independent of any reference to an internal mechanism. Whether reading involves a neural mechanism, and what it is, is another matter altogether, and of no direct philosophical concern (see Exg. §156).

(ii) 'Nor can the teacher here say . . . "Perhaps he was . . ."': it would only make sense to conjecture that *perhaps* he read a particular word if reading were an inner mechanism hypothesized on the basis of behaviour. But in the case of the 'living reading-machine', 'reading' means reacting to signs thus-and-so. It is not a matter of *our* not being able to *tell* which is the first word he read, but rather it makes no sense to speak of 'a first word in his new state' (of being able to read); cf. 2.1 (iv).

2.1   (i) 'Unless, indeed, we give a definition . . .': BB 120 reads 'unless I give an "artificial" explanation . . .' (cf. EPB 174).

(ii) '. . . a certain experience of transition. . .': BB 120 f. reads '. . . when a particular conscious process of spelling out the words takes place in a person's mind . . .'

(iii) 'a reading machine . . . pianola . . .': BB 121 makes the same point but links it with the illusory notion of the *mechanism* of being guided, a concrete paradigm of which is the pianola. In PI the discussion of being guided is deferred until §§172 ff. and the 'mechanical' model invoked only in the discussion of 'being influenced' in §170.

(iv) '. . . a change in his *behaviour* . . .': BB 121 argues that there is no sense in asking at what point did the pupil change from not being able to read to being able to read. (It is somewhat misleading to say that *this* is a change in behaviour; it is a change, an acquisition of an ability, the criterion for which is change in behaviour.) The case is compared with the following: a row of dots with large intervals succeeds a row of dots with small ones, but one cannot say which is the last dot of the first sequence and the first of the second (or, in the case of a siren, when the low pitch ceases and the high pitch begins). The change in behaviour when a pupil begins to read is analogous: '. . . we have in this case not given a meaning to the expression "the first word in the new era".'

SECTION 158

1   This contains the 'mechanist's' riposte to the preceding argument, and W.'s parry. That it makes no sense to speak of 'a first word in his new state' does not stem from our ignorance of neurophysiology. It 'stems from' the concept of reading, the way we use the verb 'to read' and the conditions of its application. Neither the ability to read nor its exercise are states of the brain. Whether there is or is not a specific neural state which can give a scientific explanation of the ability is an empirical, not a conceptual question, and has no bearing upon the concept of reading. Moreover, it is a scientific question the answer to which we do not know—and be it what it may, it is not part of the conditions of application of the verb. Indeed, the latter are presupposed by any scientific investigation into the neurological correlates of reading. If, on the other hand, we feel that there *must be* a neural 'reading connection' this merely shows that this is a form of representation (*Darstellungsform*) which appeals to us. This appeal rests on our inclination, following surface grammar, to assimilate abilities to states; our disposition to confuse philosophical questions with scientific ones; our hankering, in philosophy, for explanation (on the model of science), rather than realizing that our questions are only resolved by a surview of grammar; the charms of reductivism and the superstitions attractions of psychophysical parallelism.

1.1   'einleuchtende Darstellungsform': better translated 'clear form of re-presentation'. W. translated a similar phrase 'a form of presentation which attracts, satisfies, us' (PPI(R) §113 = Z §444).

2.1   Vol. XV, 21 ff. contains an interesting parallel discussion of the bewitching attraction of a form of representation. W. considers two quite different kinds of plants the seeds of which, after exhaustive examination, cannot be found to differ. But the seeds of the one type produce only plants of that type, and those of the other only plants of that other type. If we say that there *must* be a difference in the seeds, otherwise they *could not* produce different plants, that their previous history *could not* cause their subsequent development without leaving traces in the seeds, this merely means that we refuse to call this a 'causal connection'. So our insistence that there *must* be a difference only shows how firmly we cleave to the picture or schema of cause and effect. (Graphology, too, insists that character *must* express itself in handwriting.) It would by no means be pointless to say, W. concludes, that philosophy is the study of the grammar of 'must' and 'can', for it shows what is *a priori*, what *a posteriori*.

This lengthy discussion of the strength of our commitment to the schema of causality, and our particular interpretation of it, surfaces in Z §608 side by side with W.'s repudiation of the view that thought-processes *must be* mirrored by, correlated with, brain-processes. 'The prejudice in favour of psychophysical parallelism is a fruit of primitive interpretation of our concepts.'

The great attractions and bewitchment of misleading forms of representation ('This is *merely*, or *really*, that') is extensively discussed in LA. The attraction may lie in the apparent unifying force of the picture (e.g. Darwinism or Goethe's Primal Plant), which is so powerful as to induce us to brush aside the weakness of the evidence for it. Or, the attraction may, paradoxically, lie in the ugliness of the form of explanation (e.g. Freudian theory). Or, the spell may lie in the fine thread of overlapping similarities spun out by the picture with such finesse as to lead us to overlook and disregard deep dissimilarities.

SECTION 159

1   This picks up the thread from §156(e). The 'mechanical model' having been, for the moment, disposed of, we return to the 'mentalist model'. The mentalist is tempted to say that the *real* criterion of reading is private and mental (hence that only the reader *really* knows whether he is reading or merely pretending to read). Clearly, W. replies, there are sensations characteristic of reading, and different sensations or experiences characteristically accompanying pretence or cheating. But suppose that A wants to make B believe he can read Cyrillic and tells us so. We teach him to pronounce a Russian sentence. He then says it in front of B while looking at the printed words. Here we may certainly say that A knows that he is not reading, and we know it too. But our criteria for saying that he is not reading are quite independent of his alleged 'conscious act of reading'. We may also be in a position to say that A had characteristic experiences of pretence, but these are not criteria for reading or not reading either (cf. §160).

1.1   (i) '. . . the one real criterion . . .': of course, this 'conscious act of reading' is not even a *possible* criterion of reading. If there is such a thing as a conscious act or experience of reading, the concept thereof presupposes the concept of reading, the criteria for which must therefore be independent of experiences of reading. Furthermore, criteria must be public and capable of being embodied in explanations of meaning.

(ii) 'und er wird etwa eine Reihe von Empfindungen haben . . .': since nine lines earlier W. has asserted 'und er empfinde, während er zu lesen vorgibt, eben dies', this would be better translated 'and will for instance have a number of experiences'.

Section 160

1   The accompanying experiences of reading (or of merely pretending to read) are neither necessary nor sufficient for reading (or for pretending to read). Nor are they criteria for reading (or not reading).

Section 161

1   Perspicuous.

Section 162

1   §§159–61 have established that reading (i.e. following the rules connecting signs with phonemes) is not a matter of accompanying experiences or sensations. Here a new line is explored, which tries to introduce a normative component into the mentalist picture, hitherto merely an associationist mentalism. The new suggestion is that one reads if and only if one *derives* the 'reproduction' from the 'original' (the 'copy' from the 'model' (BB 122)). A parallel move with respect to expanding a series is to say that A is expanding a given series if and only if every number he writes down is *derived* from the formula for the series.

But what do we mean by 'deriving'? What is the nature of the normative guidance of a rule? In the primary case we teach the pupil the 'rule of the Cyrillic alphabet', i.e. tell him how each letter is to be pronounced. Then he goes on to read. Here we are inclined to say that he *derived* the spoken words from the script by means of the 'rule of the alphabet'. But what does the 'deriving' consist in? How did the rule 'enter into' the activity of reading? We taught him, and then he read correctly. What shows that he used the rule?

A case which would meet our requirement that the use of the rule be *manifest*, and hence that we know of a process of derivation mediating between teaching and execution, would be one in which the pupil has to copy from print into cursive script by using a correlating table. Here the 'deriving' manifests itself in his consulting the table or trying to visualize it from time to time. (Note the similarity here between the table and a chart of colour samples.)

2   PG 99f. (cf. PI §156) repudiates the view that no outward observation
can distinguish reading from mere reproduction of noises when viewing
a text. On the contrary, deriving a reproduction from an original may be
a visible process, like what takes place on paper in carrying out a
particular calculation. Here in PI §162(b), derivation from a table is
perfectly overt. However, derivation that is *not* overt, as in PI §162(a), is
not *covert* either.

PG 101 clarifies this point: every case of following a rule, 'deriving' an
action from a command, is the same kind of thing as writing down the
steps that lead to the answer of a sum or pointing to a table correlating
signs. The implication is that we can say that the pupil 'derives' his act
from the rule if he *justifies* it by reference to the rule.

SECTION 163

1   This rocks the boat. The example §162(a) seemed clearly one of
deriving, but one in which the deriving *appeared* to be concealed, unclear.
In the example (§162(b)) deriving was manifest, in that the rule 'entered
into' the activty. But if this seemed to be *real* deriving, our illusions are
rapidly swept away by reflection on further cases. The pupil might use
the table according to the second schema of PI §86, or in a highly
irregular way, or in a way that itself changes regularly. Can anything he
does *definitely* be classified as a random procedure? We could *impose* an
interpretation on his transcription *no matter what he wrote* (parallel to
expanding the series). What then remains of 'deriving', in so far as it is
invoked to *explain* reading?

2   PG 93 f. explores the theme of interpretation according to a chart, i.e. the
insertion of an intermediary rule between rule and application. The
conclusion is that one can insert as many intermediary rules as one
wishes, but none will bridge the categorial gap (the illusory gap) between
rule and application. (Just as postulating a creator does not resolve the
puzzle about the beginning of the world.)

BB 123 ff. adds these points: (i) in the case of deriving according to the
second schema of PI §86, the pupil, when actually looking up the table,
nevertheless passes his eyes (or finger) horizontally from left to right.
The gap between the intermediary overt derivation and the product still
remains. (ii) In the case of interpretation according to the second schema
of §86, one might say 'he understood the table differently, not in the
normal way. To this objection W. responds, 'What do we call "understanding the table in a particular way"?' Whatever process one imagines
understanding to be, it is only another link interposed between deriving
(as described, whether outward or inner) and transcription. In any

particular case, we could say that the pupil looked up the table thus: ≡⇉ , understood it thus: ≡⇉ and transcribed it thus: ⋊⇉

What, here, is the value of the intermediate step that is meant to represent understanding? And what, here, is the deriving? Does *anything* he does with the table count as deriving? Does *anything* he does count as understanding 'in a particular way'? Cf. EBT 514:

> Man kann nun fragen: ist es denn aber auch noch ein Spiel, wenn Einer die Buchstaben a b b c sieht und *irgend etwas* macht? Und wo hört das Spiel auf, und wo fängt es an?
> Die Antwort ist natürlich: Spiel ist es, wenn es nach einer Regel vor sich geht. Aber was ist noch eine Regel und was keine mehr?

> (One can now ask: but is it still a game, when someone sees the letters a b b c and does *something or other*? And where does the game cease, and where does it begin?
> The answer, naturally, is: it is a game if it is in accord with a rule. But what is still a rule and what no longer one?)

This crucial question is the central theme of PI §§185–243.

SECTION 164

1   §162(b) produced a 'manifest' case of deriving (following a table by horizontal interpretation), but nevertheless a special case (for not all deriving need be thus). But as more examples were examined the 'essence' of deriving dissolved, for 'deriving' is applied to a family of cases, linked by overlapping similarities.

In the same way 'reading' applies to a family of cases, in different circumstances different criteria justify its application. Hence invoking 'deriving' to capture the essence of reading is doubly futile: reading is not defined by *Merkmale* and neither is deriving. Neverthless, the *description of examples* is not a hint at an explanation, which could be better done in some other way. It *is* a grammatical explanation (cf. BB 125).

1.1   Last sentence of (b): cf. Exg. §156.

2   BB 125 elaborates the family resemblance point. It makes clear that the reference to §162 is to paragraph (b) not (a); and that the family resemblance explanation of deriving applies in general to 'being guided by symbols' (and hence to expansion of a series too).

Section 165

1   Invoking 'deriving' proved futile, so another mentalist strategy is explored, a variant on the theme examined in §§159–61. The line of attack chosen is that when I read, there is a special process or experience of the words 'coming in a particular way'. This will be examined (with occasional deviations) until §178.

The first counter-move consists in pointing out that the 'coming in a special way' is not the same as 'the sounds occur to me', since they can occur to me even though I am *not* reading. Secondly, it is phenomenologically false that the written word *reminds* me of the spoken one. The written sign 'nothing' does not *remind* me of the sound 'nothing', the sound 'comes' irresistibly. So both arbitrary occasionalism and mnemonic association are rejected; but 'coming in a special way' needs further probing.

2   C8, 5, introducing a version of PI §165, comments:

Man könnte sagen, wenn Du sehen willst worin lesen besteht, lies und gieb acht was geschieht. Nun was geschieht? Ich sehe Wörter und spreche sie aus. Aber es ist schwer zu sagen was eigentlich geschieht, es geht so schnell. Besser sehe ich es wenn ich Cyrillica lese denn das geht langsamer.

(One could say, if you want to see what reading consists in, read, and attend to what happens. Well, what happens? I see words and say them aloud. But it is difficult to say what really happens, it is all so quick. I should see it better if I read Cyrillic, for then it is slower.)

An attractive exemplification of this confusion occurs in W. James:

Reading exemplifies this kind of cohesion even more beautifully. It is an uninterrupted and protracted recall of sounds by sights which have always been coupled with them in the past. I find that I can name six hundred letters in two minutes on a printed page. Five distinct acts of association between sight and sound . . . must then have occurred in each second in my mind. In reading entire words the speed is much more rapid. Valentin relates in his *Physiology* that the reading of a single page of the proof, containing 2629 letters, took him 1 minute and 32 seconds. In this experiment each letter was *understood* in 1/28 of a second . . .[6]

Clearly Cyrillic should slow things down!!

Page 66 Note

1   This note, misleadingly made into one paragraph in translation, is

[6] W. James, *The Principles of Psychology*, Vol. I, p. 557.

cryptic. Paragraph (b) is a slip cut from B i. §395 (= Vol. XI, 10 = PG 169). The remark is clearly associated with the first sentence of § 165, for when we delve rather than survey we are frequently driven to the point of thinking that we are trying to capture, in the 'crude' net of language, something too delicate to be expressible (cf. PI §§106, 120, 608–10). So, in the case of reading, we are inclined to think that it is a 'quite particular' process, but are hard pushed to describe it. It has to be experienced, we think, it cannot be described. (The theme is picked up at §167 and §§173 f.: to say that the experience of deliberation 'just is a *particular* inner experience' is to add nothing. The *concept* of deliberation is obscured, not clarified, by this empty gesture.)

1.1   (i) '(atmosphere)': cf. PI §§608 ff.

(ii) *'particular* expression': cf. PI §606.

2   (i) In Vol. XI, 10, paragraph (b) is immediately followed by what is now PI §436 (but without the Latin quotation), which coheres with C 8, 5 (cf. Exg. §165). To believe that the difficulty of philosophy is the description of the ineffable or the perception of 'an indescribably rapid succession of inner experience' (as James so often insists) is a dead-end.

(ii) PI §435 (= PG 104, B i. 369) also brings out the same absurdity (reading Cyrillic will enable us to observe the 'quite particular' experience, because it is so much slower). We ask 'How do sentences manage to represent?', and W.'s ironic response is 'Don't you know? You certainly see it, when you use them (for nothing is concealed).' To this we are inclined to respond 'Yes, but it all goes by so quickly, and I should like to see it as it were laid open to view.'

SECTION 166

1   This dispels the fiction that in reading words come 'in a special way'. The difference between the way the words come in reading, as opposed to random association, does not lie in 'a quite peculiar experience', but in the difference of situation (circumstances).

1.1   The final parenthesis: this idea is a favourite empiricist gambit (e.g. Hume, Russell, James). W. discusses it in BB 182 ff., PI pp. 185, 231.

2   (i) EPB 181: after 'ein umgekehrtes Sigma' ('a reversed sigma') continues:

Und wenn Du sagst, der Buchstabe A *'erinnere'* Dich nicht an den Laut, wie etwa der Anblick eines Krokodils an das Wort 'fressen' so gibt es da Übergänge; Du könntest zum Beispiel die Form **A** an einem Holzbock oder an einem Dachstuhl sehen und der Laut 'a' fiele Dir nicht ein; oder aber der Anblick könnte Dich an ein A erinnern und Du sprichst den Laut aus.

(And if you say, the letter A does not 'remind' you of the sound, in the way the sight of a crocodile does of the word 'devour', nevertheless there are transitions; you could, for example, see an **A**-shaped trestle or roof-truss, without the sound 'a' occurring to you; or else the sight could remind you of an A and you then utter the sound.)

(ii) PI p. 219 contains a further move. How am I to see how a word 'comes'? By attending carefully? But that is no use, for what am I to attend to? I ought to have to wait until a word occurs to me again, but it is distinctive that it seems that I do not have to do so; I can, it seems, exhibit to myself how it comes, even when it is not happening. I *act* it! Namely, I produce certain characteristic accompaniments, gestures, faces, tones of voice. That shows something about the 'field of force' of a word—which is important—but nothing about the myth of the words 'coming in a special way'.

Section 167

1   Having disposed of 'the special way' words allegedly come, W. returns to the formula 'reading is a "quite particular process"'. What lies behind it? On the one hand the mental processes may differ greatly (as between, e.g., reading print and transcribing into Morse code (bearing in mind that for present purposes transcribing in Morse, writing from dictation, or copying, all count as reading (PI §156(a)). So to this extent it is wrong to think that, when one reads, one particular, introspectively identifiable process occurs. On the other hand, the experience of reading draws a certain uniformity from the more or less uniform process of reading (the overt production of sounds or signs). Moreover, the experience of arbitrary association at the sight of doodles, or the reaction to misspelling *is* distinctive—and different from normal reading.

By implication, our error is this: we infer from the distinctive and unusual experiences of association with arbitrary marks or reactions to misspellings that ordinary reading is accompanied by normal familiar and uniform experiences which constitute the truth-grounds or criteria for reading. One might say that the feeling of familiarity consists largely in the absence of feelings of unfamiliarity. But this 'familiarity' of the look of a word is not what reading it consists in, nor is it necessary, sufficient, or a criterion for reading.

2.1   Z §184 (cf. TS 232, §571; MS 137, 44) discusses the import of our sensitivity to orthography and correlates it with 'meaning-blindness' (and by implication 'aspect-blindness'); cf. Exg. §171.

Section 168

1   A perspicuous coda to the examination of the 'quite particular' process of reading.

Section 169

1   This section, though linked with §168 (in EPB the counterpart of *l*.4 is a row of arbitrary pothooks and flourishes as in its version of §168), branches out in a new direction. The nature of reading has been variously probed. We have explored the idea that reading, in the preferred sense of simply producing sounds or signs from sounds or signs according to a set of rules, is a matter of neural mechanisms or of mental experiences. The latter alternative has been explored from various angles: (i) accompanying experiences; (ii) deriving the reproduction from the original; (iii) that the words 'come in a particular way'; (iv) that the inner process of reading is special and peculiar. All these proved futile.

The new line to be pursued is causal, in the spirit of Russell's causal theory of meaning.[7] Why should we not argue that reading (as opposed to pretending to read) is a process that occurs when the signs cause the corresponding utterance, and that knowing that one is reading (as opposed to knowing that one is cheating) is a matter of *feeling* the causal connection between seeing the signs and uttering the words? One might even think that in inner experience one has a more direct access and insight into causal connectedness than by mere outer observation of concomitance.

W.'s response, here, is telescoped. To the extent that causation is something established by experiment, e.g. by observation of regular concomitance, one cannot say that one *feels* a causal connection. To the extent that a causal connection in a particular case implies a causal generalization it is unclear how any *feeling* could show that that particular case is an instance of a causal generalization. (And this point, if correct, holds even though observation of regular concomitance is not the only way to establish that a causal nexus obtains.) Finally, what feature of a *feeling* could indicate that α (seeing a sign) *caused* β (uttering a sound). Any *feeling* would merely be the interposition of a further element between α and β.

One might better say that the letters are the *reason* for my uttering such-and-such, since I would *justify* my utterance by reference to the letters ('justify', not 'causally explain'). But this, though correct, will not

---

[7] Cf. AM Ch. X, with which W. was familiar; also *An Inquiry into Meaning and Truth*. For a more thorough criticism see PLP Ch. VI.

salvage the appeal to a *feeling* of connectedness, whether causal or justificatory. For while there is such a thing as feeling justified, there is no such thing as feeling a justification; my justification is something I say or think, something I appeal to, not something I feel.

W. pays out still more rope; one wants to say that one feels a kind of influence when one reads, but not when one scans a doodle. (Note that here again, as in the parallel cases of deriving and guidance, we have an attempt to smuggle in a normative component within the neoclassical empiricist framework.) W.'s first move is to admit a phenomenological difference, *when one engages in such experiments*, between saying the sound 'i' aloud or silently, in response to seeing the letter, as opposed to a doodle.

Section 170

1   This is W.'s riposte. We do notice a difference between reading and associating sounds with doodles. In the context of our endeavour to fathom the essence of rule-following, e.g. of reading according to the rule of the alphabet, we misguidedly identify *this* difference with the difference between being influenced and not being influenced.

This 'phenomenological' interpretation (so attractive to James and other empiricists) is especially powerful when, under the spell of a *misconception* of our philosophical task, we read especially slowly (e.g. Cyrillic) in order better to observe what really happens when we read (fast!). It seems then that we let ourselves be *guided* by the letters. (Note again how the causal, phenomenological and normative are entangled.) But this amounts to no more than, say, looking carefully at the letters, and enunciating very deliberately.

§170(c) notes how the mechanistic model intertwines with the mentalist one. The hankering for a connection, material and causal, or spiritual and ephemeral, between letter and sound, rule of a series and the numeral written, meaning and application, understanding and use, is almost irresistible.

Section 171

1   Yet another variant to capture the illusory intermediate link is tried. The experience one has when reading is the experience of the written word *intimating* the sound. (The parallel move with respect to following rules is introduced at PI §§222 ff., and discussed at even greater length in RFM 414 ff.)

Again, one might strive to express this reaction by the idea of sound and letter forming a unity; to *feel* this unity is to *see or hear the sound in the written word*. This latter phrase connects the thought tacitly with the elaborate discussion of 'seeing aspects' in PI pp. 193 ff. (see 1.1).

The riposte to the endeavour to find 'the essence' of reading (following the 'rule of the alphabet') in the intimation, or the feeling of unity, etc., is to emphasize that these experiences characteristically occur when one is thinking about the concept of reading, not when one is reading; and if they do occur when one reads *while thinking about the concept of reading*, then to describe these feelings is not to describe what occurs when one normally reads, i.e. without simultaneously reflecting upon the nature of reading.

In view of the discussion of seeing aspects, the argument could well be much stronger. For it is arguable that the 'feeling of unity' presupposes the mastery of the technique of reading the nature of which is under scrutiny. Hence that feeling cannot be invoked in a *Merkmal*-definition to explain the essence of the normative nature of the technique.

1.1   (i) 'the written word *intimates* the sound': in the parallel direct discussion of following rules and necessity (PI §§222 ff.), five counter-moves are made. (a) If there were an experience of intimation, what that feeling intimated could conflict with what the rule 'requires', i.e. what we take to be compliance with it. (b) When one grasps a rule one does not await its intimations; one knows what to do next (namely the same), knows how to go on. (c) The notion of the rule 'intimating' what to do is a psychologistic representation or picture of the fact that the rule is my last arbiter, my final court of appeal, in justifying what I do. (d) If the rule's intimating is a kind of inspiration (an 'inner voice'), then, first, I would have to 'await direction', instead of acting in accord with the technique I had mastered ('blindly'), and, secondly, I could not teach another the particular technique of acting thus-and-so according to a given rule, but only train him in 'inner receptivity', which is not training him to follow the rule as I do. (e) If following a rule were essentially a kind of intimating, we could not distinguish seeming to intimate from intimating (following a rule from seeming to follow a rule). But then the whole structure of meaning and understanding collapses.

(ii) 'I see or hear the sound in the written word': this phenomenon is akin to 'aspect-seeing' and 'experiencing the meaning of a word'. What is this queer experience? It is not stranger than others, but rather differs in kind from some which we regard as fundamental, e.g. sense impressions (PI p. 215). Thus what we describe as 'I feel hot' or 'I hear a noise' are different in kind from what we describe as 'I feel as if I knew the city lay over there' or 'I feel as if the name "Schubert" fitted Schubert's works and Schubert's face'. The latter experiences presuppose the mastery of a technique (cf. p. 208); we are dealing here with a different, though related, concept of experience. For having such experience, unlike having toothache, presupposes conceptual abilities, presupposes mastery of techniques of rule-following. W. goes so far as to say that the concept of seeing (in such cases) is modified: the 'experience' is infused with a concept, soaked with a rule.[8] 'It is only if someone *can do*, has learnt, is master of, such-and-such, that it makes sense to say that he has had *this* experience' (PI p. 209).

Seeing or hearing the sound *in* the word exemplifies the normative irradiation of an experience characteristic of one kind of aspect-seeing. Various considerations support this conclusion. First, the Schubert example is pertinent here ('in the same way, e.g. the faces of famous men and the sound of their names are fused together'; cf. 2). Secondly, the peculiar phrase 'seeing the x *in* the y' is prominent in the various discussions of seeing aspects (e.g. PI pp. 194, 197, 202, etc.). Thirdly, the unity of letter and sound is an analogue of 'experiencing the meaning of a word' (cf. PI p. 218: 'The familiar physiognomy of a word, the feeling that it has taken up its meaning into itself, that it is an actual likeness of its meaning . . .'). Finally, Z §184 correlates orthography and seeing aspects. Sensitivity to orthographical change is not a kind of piety; if one treats spelling as merely a practical matter, 'the feeling you are lacking in is not unlike the one that a "meaning-blind" man would lack.'

If this is correct, then the attempt to pin down the essence of the experience of reading by reference to this feeling of unity of sound and letter can be rejected not only on the grounds given (which are, perhaps, excessively empirical) but also on the ground that the experience appealed to presupposes what it is meant to explain. For only someone who can read can have that peculiar experience at all.

2   (i) EPB 184 continues after '. . . dem Klang ihrer Namen' ('. . . fused together'):

Wenn Du Dir zum Beispiel Namen wie Schubert, Haydn, Mozart sagst und Dir dabei die Gesichter dieser Männer vorstellst, so kann es Dir so vorkommen, als ob jene Namen der richtige Ausdruck für diese Gesichtszüge wären; dass etwa mit dem Namen Schubert dieses Gesicht richtig beschrieben sei. Es ist mir, wenn ich das Erlebnis dieser Einheit habe, als könne ich zum Beispiel beim Lesen des Wortes 'ja' zwischen dem geschriebenen Wort und dem ausgesprochenen nicht unterscheiden; ich könnte sagen, das Aussprechen sei ein Teil der Wahrnehmung des Zeichens selbst.

(When you, for example, say to yourself names like Schubert, Haydn, Mozart, and simultaneously image the faces of these men, it can appear to you as if those names were the correct expression of these faces; that this face, for instance, is correctly described by the name Schubert. When I have this experience of unity, it is as if I could not, for example, while reading the word 'yes' distinguish the

---

[8] Cf. P. Strawson, 'Imagination and Perception', in *Freedom and Resentment and Other Essays* (Methuen, London, 1974), p. 57.

written and spoken word. I could say that the utterance is a part of the perception of the sign itself.)

This revealing remark was presumably dropped because this *is* 'experiencing the *meaning* of the word' ('the familiar physiognomy of a word . . .' (PI p. 218)), but the discussion of reading deliberately excluded considerations of meaning.

(ii) EPB 185 strengthens the argument of PI §171:

Ich kann zwar sagen, wer liest, werde von den Buchstaben geführt; und wer einen Satz sagt und dabei jener Reihe von Schnörkeln entlang schaut, werde nicht geführt. Dies ist eine Erklärung für den, der den Ausdruck 'von Buchstaben geführt werden' versteht, ehe er das Wort 'lesen' versteht. Aber es wäre falsch zu sagen: 'Wer liest, hat das Gefühl, Erlebnis, des Geführtwerdens'. (Es sei denn, dass damit bloss jedem Erlebnis beim Lesen der Name 'Erlebnis des Geführtwerdens' gegeben werden soll.)

(I could, to be sure, say that whoever reads is guided by the letters; and that someone who utters a sentence while looking along a row of flourishes is not guided. This is an explanation for someone who understands the expression 'being guided by letters' before he understands the word 'read'. But it would be wrong to say 'whoever reads has the feeling, the experience, of being guided'. (Unless we are simply to give the name 'experience of being guided' to any experience had while reading.))

2.1　'letter and sound form a *unity*': cf. EPB 184.

3　'the faces of famous men and the sound of their names are fused together': the thought is related to a passage in *Dichtung und Wahrheit* which impressed W. In response to a rude letter from Herder which punned on Goethe's name, Goethe wrote:

It was not polite, indeed, that he should have permitted himself this jest on my name; for a man's name is not like a mantle, which merely hangs about him, and which, perchance may be safely twitched and pulled, but is a perfectly fitting garment which has grown over and over him like his very skin, at which one cannot scratch and scrape without wounding the man himself.[9]

W. frequently referred to this passage in connection with proper names (e.g. MS. 131, 141; Z §184).

Section 172

1　This examines the idea that the normativity of the rule of the alphabet is, as it were, 'expressed' when a competent reader reads, for then he is guided by the letters to utter the appropriate sounds. So what distinguishes

[9] Goethe, *The Autobiography of Johann Wolfgang von Goethe*, tr. S. Oxenford (Sidgwick and Jackson, London, 1971), Vol. II, p. 14.

reading from haphazard utterances which accompany looking at arbitrary doodles or at words which one is not reading or cannot read is the peculiar experience of being guided. The counter-strategy here resembles the previous one: cast around for additional, different, cases! Then you will see that although there are similarities between various cases of being guided (in §172, cases of being guided in one's movements), there is no common core of a particular experience.

2   (i) EPB 185 (cf. Exg. §171) clarifies the link between PI §171 and §172.

(ii) BB 99 discusses being guided in the context of discussing following a rule which correlates signs (dots and dashes) with hops and steps. What does being guided by an order, say '— . . .', consist in? There are various possibilities: a person is guided by the signs if he 'reads' the order sign by sign (perhaps pointing at each sign, and then hopping or stepping as is appropriate); or he is guided if he goes through a conscious process connecting the pointing at the sign and the corresponding action (which process might be an overt consulting of the table correlating the signs with pictures of hopping and stepping, or consulting a memory image of it); or he is guided if he experiences a peculiar strain of 'trying to remember what the sign means' and a relaxation when the meaning comes to mind.

These alternatives seem unsatisfactory, and we are taken into a long digression which examines the concept of an ability (see 'Understanding and ability', pp. 336 ff.). Once the illusions surrounding the idea of being able to do something are dispelled, W. returns to the problem of being guided (BB 118). For it becomes clear that the first attempts to answer the question of what being guided consists in were tacitly dominated by a picture of a mechanism (in the mind or brain) *connecting* seeing the signs with acting according to them (akin to the mechanism of a pianola). But no such mechanisms are involved in the grounds for saying of a person that he is guided by signs (following a rule). The mechanical picture of being guided, in the sense in which the hammers of the pianola are guided by the perforated pianola roll, is only one kind of guidance, one kind within a family of kinds of guidance.

SECTION 173

1   This runs roughly parallel to the earlier examination of deriving (§164), i.e. we can think of many experiences that seem to characterize being guided (and do characterize the examples of being guided that come to mind). But none of them, on closer scrutiny, are the experience of being guided, and so we look for the 'real' artichoke (the real 'being guided') inside its 'mere outward' leaves.

1.1 'a particular experience': cf. Exg. p. 66 n. on pp. 298f.

2 EPB 185 f. stresses the irrelevance of any experiences to whether one is being guided by a rule.

SECTION 174

1.1 Final parenthesis: what is the connection? First, there is a similarity, in that when reflecting on the nature of intending and willing (or meaning and understanding (cf. EPB 187; C 8, 9)) we are strongly inclined to think that the answers to our questions are to be found in introspectively accessible acts or experiences. But the problems are not empirical and psychological, they are logical and grammatical; hence they are not answered by facts of experience (Z §590). Secondly, an intention (which we are inclined to think of as a peculiar experience) seems to contain a model of its execution. So too with willing, doing something with deliberation (which may nevertheless misfire) and meaning something— they apparently 'reach up to the paradigm and contain a general rule' (cf. 2 below).

2 This discussion is related to PG 98 f., where the connection with willing and intending is explicit. Various normative phenomena are examined: (i) copying a figure on a 1:10 scale, where one is guided by the pattern according to the rule of mapping; (ii) deciding to walk down the street until one meets N, and acting accordingly; (iii) intending to comply with an order to draw a line from a given point parallel to another line, but misfiring, and drawing it parallel to a further line with a different direction; (iv) intending to play the piano from written music. In each case the question arises what makes what one does accord (or fail to accord) with a given (intended) rule? How can the intention 'contain a general rule'? In the cases where the execution fails, is what happens when one acts the same as if one had intended to do what one actually does and succeeded in executing the intention? In all these cases the error is to search *in the alleged experience* for the picture or model of the act intended, meant, or required by the rule one means to comply with. Rather it is *the expression* or *the description of* the intention that contains the general rule, the paradigm, or model to be copied.

SECTION 175

1 The strategy resembles §171.

2.1 EPB 188 notes a connection with voluntary action and alludes to W.

James's account[10] of the role of the will in geting out of bed on a freezing morning: 'Now how do we *ever* get up under such circumstances? If I may generalize from my own experience, we more often than not get up without any struggle or decision at all. We suddenly find that we *have* got up . . .' (cf. BB 151, EPB 234, PI §§611 ff.).

What is the connection noted between misconceptions of being guided and the problem of voluntary action? In considering being guided, thinking, meaning, reading, etc., we are inclined to pick as a paradigm case a rather abnormal instance and try to force all other instances into the form of the misleading paradigm. So too in the case of voluntary action we are inclined to take as a paradigm a case of action preceded by deliberation, decision, and muscular exertion. This, we think, is a 'fully fledged' case of voluntary action. In the case of reading we are prone to take the case of first spelling out the words, while running one's finger over the text, as 'fully fledged' reading. Thoughtful speech, we are inclined to say, is speech preceded by acts of thought, and so on. In every case we try to interpose an intervening mechanism. Many factors contribute to our errors: the Cartesian or empiricist 'mind-model', the tendency to assimilate abilities to states that underlie and cause their exercise, the tendency to think of normative behaviour as an ethereal mechanical guidance by the operative facts, etc. (James's analysis is a mistaken reaction to this mistaken picture.)

Section 176

1   The guiding thought behind these numerous attempts to pin down the nature of rule-following (by means of 'deriving', 'causation', 'guidance', 'influence', 'intimation', etc., and an alleged array of corresponding 'particular' experiences) is that there *must* be a *connection*, not a mere simultaneity, between the 'operative facts' (the written letters, the formula of a series, the musical notation, etc.) and the acts of rule-following that correspond to them. That connectedness one is inclined to dub 'the experience of being influenced'. For this experience (e.g. a feeling of causation or of the motivating power of a reason) would satisfy our hankering for a psychological intermediary in the pictured mechanism. *But*, most curiously, we cannot find (although we often hypothesize) an experience which we would willingly call 'the experience of being influenced'. For an experience is a phenomenon, while an act of will—following a rule, doing thus-and-so for the reasons that such-and-such—is something we *do*, not something we observe. One wants to say that one 'experiences the because', inasmuch as one is also inclined to say

[10] W. James, *The Principles of Psychology*, Vol. II, p. 524.

that one knows that one did thus-and-so because such-and-such, and how should one know other than by noting the experience? On the other hand, no phenomenological candidate will fit the bill. (Since, *inter alia*, any experience will be a phenomenon, and the *link* between it and the antecedent phenomenon (e.g. of seeing the letters) and the subsequent act (e.g. reading) will be just as problematic. It will still appear a matter of arbitrary simultaneity, rather than normativity.)

1.1   '. . . the germ of the idea that the will is not a *phenomenon*': a Schopenhauerian preoccupation dating back to NB 89.

2   EPB 188 and PPI §152(b)–(c) (= Z §602) compare the inclination to assert that one 'experiences the because' with the inclination to describe what one feels when one has a weight resting on one's flat hand as not merely a pressure and muscular tension, but also 'a pull, a drive downwards on the part of the weight' (cf. the ancient Aristotelian picture of every object 'tending towards' its 'natural' place). Does one have a sensation of such a 'drive'? Yes, W. replies, when one thinks of the word 'drive', adopts this picture, and looks at the phenomena through the medium of the concept 'drive'.

SECTION 177

1.1   'even though this is not in general essential to being guided': failing to draw the line parallel to the model does *not* mean that one was not being guided (cf. PG 98, Exg. §178).

SECTION 178

1   This elaborates §177. A single form or picture of guidance, a symbol of guidance (for such-and-such a hand-movement *is* a symbol of guidance), imposes itself on us, and we view guidance through the medium of this form, searching for the essence of guidance in the form. What we should do is scout around and describe the environs of guidance.

2   EPB 189 strengthens the argument against conceiving of guidance as an experience.

Es kann aber auch das das Geführtwerden ausmachen, was ich über den Vorgang sage, wenn es schon geschehen ist; zum Beispiel, dass ich sage 'Ich bin geführt worden'.—Dies klingt befremdlich, denn wie kann etwas dadurch nachträglich wahr werden, dass ich sage, es habe sich so verhalten?—Die Verwendung der Vergangenheitsform ist aber hier ähnlich der des Verbums *'meinen'* in Sätzen wie 'Als ich von Heinrich IV sprach, meinte ich den König von

Frankreich'. (Hiervon muss später die Rede sein.) Wir werden *unter Umständen* auch darum sagen, jemand sei geführt worden, weil er nachträglich seine Handlung unter dem Begriff des Geführtwerdens sieht. (Das hängt auch damit zusammen, dass wir sagen, jemand könne mit Sicherheit das Motiv seiner Handlung wissen; nicht aber ihre Ursache.)

(But it can also be what I say about the event after it has happened that makes this being guided; for example, that I say 'I was guided'.—This sounds strange, for how can comething be made true subsequently by the fact that I say things were thus-and-so.—The use of the past tense here is however similar to that of the verb *'to mean'* in sentences like 'When I spoke of Henry IV, I meant the King of France'. (This must be discussed later.) We will, in certain circumstances also say that someone was guided because he subsequently viewed his action as falling under the concept of being guided. (This is also connected with the fact that we say that someone can know the motive of his action with certainty but not its cause.))

W. stresses the deceptiveness of the past tense of 'to mean' in PI §187, LFM 28, BB 39, 142.

SECTION 179

1   Having closed the long digression into the rule-guided phenomenon of reading, W. returns to the theme of §§151–5. The problem introduced at §151 was that of the sudden dawning of understanding, expressed by the exclamation 'Now I know (understand, can do it)!' For this phenomenon is yet another force that causes us to gravitate towards false conceptions of understanding—as an inner experience or process, as a quasi-mechanical interlocking of gears in the medium of the mind or in the mechanisms of the brain.

§179 summarizes and expands the conclusions previously reached. (a) makes two points. (i) B's right to say 'Now I know!' depends upon the context of the language-game, the context in which B learns to use such locutions, and the point of using them. Thus the mere thought of the formula does not justify B's saying 'Now I can go on!' (Eccentric decorators who used formulae of arithmetical series to decorate the wall might have the experience of a particular formula occurring to them, but that would not mean that they knew what to do with them—other than decorate the wall!) Clearly, in the appropriate context there is a connection between thinking of, writing down, or pointing at a formula, and knowing how to go on; namely, that normally, if B has been appropriately trained, and the formula occurs to him when faced with a segment of a series, then he can, and usually does, go on to expand it correctly. (ii) Nevertheless, 'I can go on' is not a report by B on an internal on-going which he has inductively correlated with his subsequent continuing of a given series. This is not what B means by his utterance (any more than the school-child who raises his hand to ask a question *means*, by his gesture, that he has had an experience which he inductively correlates with subsequent asking).

§179(b) elaborates these points: the exclamation is correctly used in this complex context, but is not a description of it.

§179(c) repeats §151, namely that B might utter 'Now I know' without anything at all crossing his mind and, in certain contexts, still have used the expression quite correctly.

1.1   'that does not mean that his statement is only short for a description. . . .': cf. PI §321 f.—the question 'What happens when one suddenly understands?' is misleading. If it asks for the meaning of 'sudden understanding', it misleads us into thinking that it is answered by a description of (possible) concurrent mental processes. It might mean 'What are the tokens of sudden understanding?' One's face lighting up, change in breathing, etc., are such tokens, but the agent is not commonly aware of these, and they are not the grounds of his exclamation. It might mean 'What are the characteristic psychical accompaniments of sudden understanding?' But these too are not grounds for the use of 'Now I know!'

The moot question we forget when we describe these various experiences is what is the criterion of identity *for them*, i.e. on what grounds do we say that these experiences are experiences (accompaniments) of sudden understanding.

2   (i) BB 114:

To say the phrase 'B can continue. . .' is correctly used when prompted by such occurrences . . . but that these occurrences justify its use only under certain circumstances (e.g. when experience has shown certain connections) is not to say that the sentence 'B can continue . . .' is short for the sentence which describes all these circumstances, i.e. the whole situation which is the background of our game.

The difficulty is obvious—for while the game may well be learnt in the context of (inner or outer) 'promptings', it continues irrespective of them.

(ii) Z §136 links the thought of §179 and §180:

Think of putting your hand up in school. Need you have rehearsed the answer silently to yourself, in order to have the right to put your hand up? And *what* must have gone on inside you?—Nothing need have. But it is important that you usually know an answer when you put your hand up; and that is the criterion for one's *understanding* of putting one's hand up.

Nothing need have gone on in you; and yet you would be remarkable if on such occasions you never had anything to report about what went on in you.

The question what is the criterion for someone's understanding the meaning of raising one's hand (in this context) reorients the viewpoint. (Cf. Exg. §§180–1.)

1   The *coup de grâce* is delivered abruptly and with little flourish. It is best to view 'Now I can go on!' as a signal (like raising one's hand at school), and we judge whether it was correctly used (as we judge the school-child) by what happens subsequently (with the qualifications of §181).

2   PI §323 ' "Now I know how to go on!" is an exclamation; it corresponds to an instinctive sound, a glad start.'
PI p. 218:

> 'Now I know!' What went on here?—So did I *not* know, when I declared that now I knew?
> You are looking at it wrong.
> (What is the signal for?)
> And could the 'knowing' be called an accompaniment of the exclamation?

If *nothing* went on, it does not, of course, mean that I did not know. The contrary view results from thinking that the utterance is a report, rather than viewing it as akin to a signal and asking what it is for. In what contexts does one learn to use it, what are the criteria for knowing its correct use—these are the pertinent questions. One raises one's hand in class, exclaims 'Now I know' when one knows. But knowing is not an accompaniment of the gesture or exclamation. It is an ability, not an inner state, process, or experience (though it may be accompanied by such).

This strategy will push one back on to the question: 'How do you *suddenly know* that you can do it, answer the question, etc.?' To this the answer is—not *any* how! (How do I know that this colour is green? When I am drowning and shout 'Help!', how do I know what 'Help' means? Cf. RFM 337.)

1   We use phrases like 'I can!', 'Now I know', etc., and gestures such as raising one's hand, like signals. We judge the correctness of their use by subsequent behaviour. But it may happen that someone who indicates his ability and readiness is unable to go on and carry out the task in question. This does not always mean that he misuses the 'signal'. Failure defeats the criterion constituted by the utterance or gesture, but *it is itself defeasible*.

1.1   '(Consider both kinds of case.)': the point is elaborated by rhetorical
question in §182. Cf. PI §323: it does not follow from my feeling
(conviction) that I know how to go on that I shall not find myself unable
to when I try. In some cases, as when an unforseen interruption occurs (a
distraction of attention, etc.), I might be justified in claiming that when I
avowed that I could go on, I could, but now I cannot. On the other hand,
what is unforeseen must not be simply the fact that I get stuck and cannot
go on. My getting stuck *simpliciter* is a criterion for my not being able to
go on. But it does not follow that my getting stuck after an unforeseen
interruption is such a criterion.

2.1   'different things in different cases': BB 115 f. gives a rich range of
examples. Suppose that when B says 'I can continue the series' (and is
then unable to), (i) he visualizes the formula, but when asked to continue
the series, he has forgotten it; (ii) he says to himself the next five terms of
the series, but when asked they do not come to mind; (iii) he still
remembers the next five terms as in (ii), but has forgotten how he had
calculated them; (iv) he says 'I felt I could, now I can't'. The various
examples demonstrate subtle variations between different kinds of cases.
In some instances we will firmly assert that when he said he knew, he
knew. In others we will equally firmly deny it. In yet others we will
hesitate; we may say (of a pupil) that he 'almost got it' (but was
interrupted), or that he thought he could do it and if not for the
interruption, he probably would have done it, etc.
    An early version of this remark (Vol. XII, 92) belongs to a general
discussion of abilities (cf. Exg. p. 53 n., see pp. 258 f.). So it was not specifically concerned with the expression of sudden dawning of understanding
('Now I understand!'), but with assertions of ability ('I can play chess, lift
this weight, integrate'). The text runs thus:

Jemand behauptet, er könne etwas Bestimmtes tun; er versucht es nun und es
gelingt ihm nicht. Stelle Dir Umstände vor, unter welchen es Sinn hat zu sagen:
'Als ich sagte, ich könne es, da konnte ich's wirklich, nur jetzt kann ich's nicht'—
und Umstände, unter welchen dies keinen Sinn hat.

(Someone states that he can do a certain thing; he tries and does not succeed.
Imagine circumstances in which it makes sense to say 'When I said I could do it,
I really could, only now I can't'—and circumstances under which this makes no
sense.)

    §181 has been modified to fit the context of sudden understanding.
(But §182 has not.) Arguably, there should be an overt consideration
of the differences between statements of ability ('I can lift a 200 lb.
weight; I did so this morning') and avowals of sudden understanding,
and a separate consideration of the consequences of a failed attempt to

perform the act in question upon the justifiability of the respective utterances. For it is not obvious that they are to be treated alike.

Section 182

1   This seems to elaborate §181, yet it is not concerned with dawning of understanding and its avowal, but with more general features of abilities and inaminate powers. Early versions (Vol. XV, 49 ff., Vol. XVII, 58 ff.) occur in a different context, and §182 does not obviously fit well here. It links up tenuously with the brief §150, but the thorough examinations of ability in Br.B. and various MSS, are omitted (cf. 'Understanding and ability', pp. 337 ff.).

The exercises: (i) When is a cylinder C said to fit into a hollow cylinder H? Only when C is stuck into H? That would involve an illegitimate Humean reduction of power to its exercise (BB 116 f.; Vol. XV, 49 ff.). (ii) What criteria are used for saying that C ceased to fit into H at t? Various—e.g. H contracted, or was damaged by a blow, at t; C expanded, or was likewise distorted at t. (iii) What are the criteria for a body changing weight at t (although not on scales at t)? Various—e.g. loss or accession of some constitutive matter at t. These in turn may be determined by various criteria, some by ordinary non-theoretic observation, others by theory-laden scientific observation.

(i)–(iii) are cases of inanimate powers. All are directed at Humean reductionism, and the moral is given in §182(b). W. then switches to human abilities. (iv) When does it make sense to assign a time to the loss of an ability? Primarily when one can associate the loss of ability with a temporally identifiable cause (a blow on the head, a sudden shock, etc.). Note that 'to forget' is *not* generally used to designate instantaneous loss of abilities by causal interference. (We would not say 'I was hit in the head by a bullet, and at that moment forgot how to speak French', nor even '. . . and that made me forget French', but more likely '. . . and I was not able to speak French thereafter' or '. . . and that deprived me of the ability to . . .'.) (v) The weight-lifting example is the nearest we get to the issue of §181, but it is still different. BB 116 gives one answer: when I said I could lift it my arm did not hurt, now it does! Many variants can be imagined.

2   Vol. XV, 49–59 is a significant source. It is preceded (26–44) by a version of PI §§193–7, followed (44–9) by a version of PI §§215 f. This discussion of identity, of the idea of 'everything fits into its own shape', leads on to the discussion of powers, abilities, and the determination of the time of their loss or change. Three examples are discussed: (i) the fit of cylinders; (ii) a medicine which will prolong by a month the life of

whoever takes it; (iii) determination of the time of change of weight of an object not on scales. Various possibilities are considered, reductionism is repudiated, a variety of possible conventions (in the spirit of the language-games of Br.B.) are suggested. The conclusion is a version of PI §182(b).

SECTION 183

1   This resumes the theme of §179. It is slightly curious inasmuch as W. has already argued at length that the two sentences do not have the same meaning. The point is perhaps this: the previous arguments have shown that 'B understands, can go on, etc.' does not mean 'The formula of the series has occurred to B' (§152), and equally that 'Now I understand' and 'The formula has occurred to me' differ in meaning (for I may use the former in circumstances in which it would be incorrect to use the latter (§154)). The argument of §183 is that in certain circumstances both sentences can legitimately be used to the same purpose. For when, in the appropriate circumstances, the formula occurs to me, it is indifferent whether I say 'I can go on!' or 'The formula has occurred to me!' Both exclamations achieve the same purpose—and to that extent W. is willing to say that *in these circumstances*, they have the same meaning. But they do not uniformly have the same use.

'We do say: "Now I can go on, I mean I know the formula" . . .' introduces an analogous point. Different kinds of conditions are relevant to whether someone can do something. The question 'Can A Φ?' may, in different contexts, be an inquiry into the logical possibility of A's Φing, the physical possibility, the legal or moral possibility, into A's *ability* to Φ, into the circumstantial possibility or opportunity for A's Φing, and many other conditions. Normally the context of the question will make clear its purpose. *Pari passu*, a speaker declaring that he can Φ (e.g. continue a series) may make explicit what type of possibility or condition for Φing he is alluding to. He may say 'Now I can go on, I mean . . .' and add such qualifiers as 'the formula has occurred to me', 'I have sharpened my pencil', 'the pain has passed', etc. Thus we can introduce 'the formula has occurred to me' in this sentence as *a condition* for being able to go on, *in contrast* with other conditions. To this extent, we would, *in certain contexts*, be willing to replace the question 'Can he go on?' by 'Has the formula occurred to him?' But it does not follow that the two interrogative sentences have the same meaning.

What is the warning given in the last sentence? Certainly there is no set of conditions of the type in question such that if they are satisfied a person cannot but walk; the most that a totality of such conditions will give is an 'all-in' *possibility* of walking. Even if all circumstantial conditions and agential powers obtain, it is still up to the agent whether he will take advantage of the opportunity and exercise his ability. But the analogue with 'Now I can go on' is not whether given the satisfaction of various conditions, the agent cannot but walk, but whether the satisfaction of certain conditions entails that he *can* walk.

1.1   (i) 'the two sentences have the same sense, achieve the same thing. But also that *in general* . . .': cf. PI §61.

(ii) 'We do say: "Now I can go on, I mean I know the formula"': what is in question is whether the formula has occurred to me, whether I can recite it. My success in applying it remains to be seen.

2   The section is derived from BB 114 f. (EPB 166). The question of identity of meaning of 'He can continue . . .' and 'He knows the formula' (i.e. can point it out, write it down, etc.) can, W. argues, be answered in different ways. He compares this case to a notional language in which two different sentences are used to say that a person's legs are in working order, the one being used only when a person is about to go on an expedition, walking tour, etc., the other when this is not so. We will be undecided whether the sentences do or do not have the same meaning. In general such questions can only be decided by examination of details of usage. But it is clear that if we decide to say that the expressions differ in meaning we cannot do so on the grounds that the fact that makes the first true differs from the fact that makes the second true, i.e. the difference in meaning is not determined by truth-conditions. *Pari passu*, W. argues, we are justified in saying that our pair of sentences differ in meaning, but *not* because 'He can continue . . .' refers to a particular state of affairs on a different level from the events that take place overtly or mentally (knowing or realizing the formula, imagining further terms, etc.). The difference lies in use.

SECTION 184

1   Yet another example, of a Jamesian type, that erroneously pushes us in the direction of the reservoir model of the mind. Whatever feelings, including the feeling that the tune was 'there' in my mind or being certain that I know it, may accompany my exclamation 'Now I know it!', they do not show what it *means* for it to be there. One sense that we might give to the sentence would be that we are justified in asserting it if someone sings the tune; or if he 'heard' it, mentally, from beginning to end (and told us). Or we might give it a quite different sense, e.g. that one has it written down on a piece of paper.

But this, of course, is not what one meant. One is inclined to say that the person says 'I know it!' or 'I'm certain I can sing it' *because*, in some other sense, it is 'there' in his mind, even though he has not hummed it through mentally, nor, of course, has it occurred to him, momentarily, in its entirety. W.'s response is to take the argument one stage back: of course one may be certain, but what does this certainty consist in? He does not answer the question here (but cf. PI §§323 ff.) but merely points out that a person's avowed certainty does not show that the tune (or the knowledge) is instantaneously present to him in its entirety since we have not yet explained what sense that expression is to have. Of course, we could stipulatively define the expression by reference to the avowal of certainty as a criterion of its application. But this is not what the Jamesian psychologist wants, since he wanted the 'presence of the tune to the mind' to be the *ground of*, and *explanation of*, the certainty. (Note connection with §§138–9.)

2.1   BB 130 compares 'He must know the tune before he can sing it' with 'He must understand an order before he can obey it' and 'He must know where his pain is before he can point to it'. In all these cases we are driven, by a variety of grammatical features in a certain philosophico-phenomenological context, *to demand an intermediate step* (between wanting to remember the tune and being able to sing it, between having a pain and pointing at it, between hearing the order and obeying it). This in turn is related to our demand to interpose between perception and utterance (e.g. 'that's red') an hypostatized recognition of similarity between cases, which experience *explains* why we use the same word. The innumerable knots in the web of the dialectic of reason are linked by similar threads.

Meaning and understanding
1. Introduction   2. Plato   3. Frege   4. Russell   5. The *Tractatus*
6. *Umblick*   7. *Überblick*

INDEX

(Since this is a volume of textual exegesis, this index should be used in conjunction with the original text and its index)